From *Misa* to *Mise en Scène*

Medieval and Renaissance
Texts and Studies

Volume 566

From *Misa* to *Mise en Scène*

Fra Francesc Moner's Prototype of the
Spanish Sacramental Theater
of the Fifteenth Century

by
Peter Cocozzella

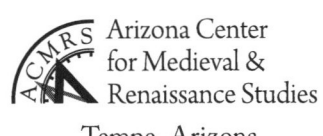 Arizona Center
for Medieval &
Renaissance Studies
Tempe, Arizona
2020

Arizona Center
for Medieval &
Renaissance Studies

Published by ACMRS (Arizona Center for Medieval and Renaissance Studies)
Tempe, Arizona

∞
This book is made to last. It is set in Adobe Caslon Pro,
smyth-sewn and printed on acid-free paper to library specifications.
Printed in the United States of America

To Edward Sarmiento

Contents

LIST OF ILLUSTRATIONS

ACKNOWLEDGMENTS

Words cannot express my appreciation to the National Endowment for the Humanities, the Research Foundation of the State University of New York, the University of Missouri and, in particular, the Comisión de Intercambio Cultural entre España y Estados Unidos and the Council for International Exchange of Scholars, for sponsoring my research with financial support and making it possible for me to spend extended periods of time in Madrid and Barcelona. With a thankful heart I salute the prominent fellow members of the North American Catalan Society: Robert Archer, Antoni Badia i Margarit, Patricia Boehne, Kenneth Brown, Manuel Duran, Jaume Ferran, Roberto González-Casanovas, Josep Gulsoy, Arseni Pacheco, Albert Porqueras Mayo, Josep Roca Pons, Donna Rogers, Josep Miquel Sobrer, Josep M. SolàSolé, David Viera, Curt Wittlin. I regret the failing memory that makes the list far from complete. I can never repay the benefits I have derived from my association and collaboration throughout the years with these fine scholars. A person of whom I cherish pleasant memories is Ricard Salvat, the renowned stage director, who appointed me to serve as member of the jury at the "XVII Festival Internacional de Teatre de Sitges" in the spring of 1985. At this unforgettable event I had the opportunity to rub elbows with personalities of the highest rank: the playwrights Joan Brossa, José Triana, Alfonso Sastre, and the Hispanist Joseph Silverman, among others. I shall be forever indebted to Salvat for this firsthand experience in the world of the theater.

My project on Moner's *misa* has taken many years to mature, and during that time my debt of gratitude has increased exponentially. Foremost in the list of names to be acknowledged is Edward Sarmiento, director of my dissertation, which turned out to be the first step in a long journey of exploration. The journey began at the Pius XII Memorial Library (Saint Louis University), where I discovered the only known manuscript of Moner's works, and continued at crucial stages of my research in the Biblioteca Nacional de Madrid, the Biblioteca de Catalunya, the Arxiu de la Corona d'Aragó, the Real Academia de Buenas Letras, and, last but not least, the Glenn G. Bartle Library at Binghamton University. I am grateful for the assistance I have received from the personnel of these institutions.

Among my revered mentors now departed, Josep Maria de Casacuberta, Martí de Riquer, Josep Romeu i Figueras, and Jordi Rubió Balaguer deserve special mention. My heartfelt thanks go to the colleagues that have listened to my presentations at professional conferences and have provided criticism and suggestions, challenging questions, and indispensable bibliographic data. I have found particularly rewarding my attendance at various triennial colloquia of the Société Internationale pour l'étude du Théâtre Médiéval (SITM). I thank Vicki L. Hamblin, Max Harris, Alexandra Johnston, Gordon Kipling, Lenke Kovács, Francesc Massip, Tiziano Pacchiarotti, Eckehard Simon, Ronald Surtz, among other participants at the colloquia, for their memorable presentations and for their interest in my work on the *misa* and kindred "Monerian" topics. I should like to give thanks to Philip Crispin, Cora Dietl, Garret Epp, Óscar Armando García, Jolanta Juszkievicz, Sharon King, Roberta Mullini, Josep Lluís Sirera, Curt S. Steindler. Either with their actual performances integrated into the SITM programs or with their suggestive reports on the creative use of medieval theater in their teaching, they have been a source of inspiration for my own quest for innovative approaches to medieval theatricality. I am indebted, also, to Véronique Dominguez-Guillaume, Jelle Koopmans, Josep Lluís Sirera for including my essays in their respective editions of sundry publications sponsored by SITM.

I am pleased to credit Ronald Surtz for including in his anthology of medieval Spanish theater the text of Moner's *Momería* as it appears in my edition of 1991. Consequently, in her surveys of said theater, Charlotte Stern has further publicized the significance of Moner's playlet, which appears, also, in two anthologies, both entitled *Teatro medieval*. They are edited by, respectively, Ana Mª Álvarez Pellitero (1990) and Miguel Ángel Pérez Priego (2009). Credit is due, also, to Linda Hutcheon and Pedro Manuel Cátedra, whose respective landmark studies have regaled me with rich food for thought.

I am indebted to the staff of The Arizona Center for Medieval and Renaissance Studies, especially to Roy Rukkila for his guidance through an e-mail conversation of long standing and to the editor for the invaluable assistance in the painstaking revision of my text. It is fair to accord recognition to the three anonymous readers of my monograph. I have benefitted greatly especially from the patient review that one of them undertook above and beyond the call of duty. I would be remiss, should I not add a note of commendation for my dear friends: Joe Marckx, who has devised for Moner's stage a diagram (figure 5) that Moner himself, doubtless, would have appreciated; and Ellen and Arthur Fawthrop, who never fail to bolster my confidence with solicitous queries about the progress of my writing, while helping out with the proofreading of the manuscript and dispensing sagacious advice. The list of benefactors includes fellow members of the faculty at Binghamton University: Marilynn R. Desmond, Salvador J. Fajardo, Thomas A. O'Connor, Antonio Sobejano Morán, to name a few. I must not forget three colleagues of beloved memory: Marilyn Gaddis Rose, Giovanni Gullace, and George Wellwarth. The list culminates in Carol Ann, my wife, whose inspiration and encouragement lighten even the heaviest burdens of my scholarly endeavors.

PREFACE

The present monograph is the result of an exploration in uncharted territory, which proves to be a field of considerable interest within the vast realm of Spanish literature of the late Middle Ages or early Renaissance. The field extends to the headwaters of a special kind of theatrical tradition that to this day has escaped the attention of the most authoritative critics. A steadfast probing into the origins of that tradition yields evidence that attests to the all-important role of Spanish lyric poetry of the fifteenth century. Just as the chrysalis mutates into a full-blown butterfly, so does the *canción*, quintessential expression of that poetry, evolve into a literary icon abounding in dramatic potential.

Of paramount significance in the esthetic of mutation adumbrated here is the gestation and early evolution of the protracted monologue of the auctorial persona, portrayed, more often than not, as the exemplary woebegone lover. This egocentric, highly subjectivistic monologue constitutes the core subject of the book-length study that follows. The focus of the study is the *Sepultura d'amor*, an ingenious poem by Francesc Moner, a Catalan writer who flourished in Barcelona in the 1480s. In his tour de force Moner showcases one of the most complex manifestations of the lover's introspective meditation. An index of complexity of the highest order may well be the ambitious construction and overall stage-worthy quality of Moner's composition. *Sepultura* encapsulates a *misa de amores* (Mass of love), a parodic version of the sacrosanct ritual of the Christian liturgy. It bears pointing out that the *misa* in question happens to be an integral component of a solemn ceremony that the author envisages as the unfolding of his own funeral. At the same time, in a noteworthy coup of ingeniousness, Moner's piece demonstrates a deft adaptation of a *mise en scène* that harks back to the principles set forth by none other than Isidore of Seville in some notable passages of his influential *Etymologies*.

There are numerous issues that enter into the full discussion broached by these prefatory remarks. For a start, we may delve into the psychic strains that said *canción* inherits from the lyricism of the troubadours. Concurrently, we may take into account the religious sentiment that comes to bear upon the monologue inherent in the *canción* and kindred love-centered poems and prose works. What segues from a painstaking analysis of the symbiosis that Moner intuits between passionate love and pious fervor is close attention to the nature of authentic parody, which, in accordance with the principles set forth in Linda Hutcheon's landmark study, does not transgress the reverence due to an age-old form of worship. Of course this is precisely the style of worship exemplified by the Mass.

Demonstrably, Moner's *misa de amores* is the ideal embodiment of Hutcheon's notion of a literary modality that may be called "reverential parody." In fact, on the basis of that modality, Moner elaborates a veritable esthetic of desacralization, by which he radically modifies the Eucharistic service, while taking extra care not to incur the excesses that would be tantamount to sacrilege and desecration. Moner's artistic enterprise may be summed up in the byword, "desacralization without desecration." Moner creates, all along, a paraliturgical Mass by scaling down the awesome Eucharistic service to a manageable human level.

True to the tenor of his creativity, Moner comes up with the implementation of an ersatz transubstantiation. In the course of the celebration of Moner's unusual Mass, at the crucial moment of the Offertory, two acolytes bring forth a transcript of a *canción* of the auctorial persona's own vintage. At this moment the significance of the substitution implicit in this surprising offering begins to dawn on us. What is being laid on the altar is not the regular oblation of bread and wine, the species of the consecration about to take place, but, rather, an iconic poem, the existential correlative, in artistic substance, of the author's selfhood. We realize that the transubstantiation we have just referred to has to do with a unique phenomenon of a scriptural nature. Thanks to the ministrations of the celebrant of Moner's *misa*, the écriture of the *canción* is sublimed into a preternatural order of textuality. By an unexpected twist of *imitatio Christi*, the *canción* is suffused by the aura of holiness that emanates from the Gospel itself. It becomes, in effect, a shining specimen of synecdoche: a miniature of sorts of the Gospel incarnated in the individual lover. Consequently, though far removed from the sphere of spirituality that pertains to the ritual of the Mass, the analogue of the transubstantiation fashioned by Moner holds in store its own sacramental efficacy.

In sum, the present monograph is an attempt to highlight Moner's pioneering inventiveness, which combines a paradigmatic staging derived from Isidore of Seville with the mechanics of desacralization brought to light by an up-to-date theory of parody. Evidently, Moner confronts us with a theater rich in allegorical representations and metaphysical functions. This type of theater exhibits a sacramentality that, in the light of available evidence, Moner devises for the first time. Doubtless, Moner's creation begs for appropriate contextualization in the history of early Spanish theater.

INTRODUCTION

A Noteworthy Poem

The parody of the Mass occupies a place of prominence in a number of recent monographs and essays that explore the interface between the sacred and the profane in Spanish love-centered literature of the fifteenth century.[1] An eminent specimen of these publications is Folke Gernert's magnum opus, *Parodia y "contrafacta,"* which stands out as a paragon of rigorous analysis, astute commentary, and abundant documentation.[2] Strange as it may seem, neither Gernert's work

---

[1] For an overview of the continuum between carnal and spiritual love, see Alexander Parker, *La filosofía del amor en la literatura española 1480–1680* (Madrid: Cátedra, 1986).

[2] See Folke Gernert, *Parodia y "contrafacta" en la literatura románica medieval y renacentista: historia, teoría y textos. I: Estudio. II: Textos.* 2 vols. (San Millán de la Cogolla: Cilengua, 2009), 1:289–327, for a well-documented history of the parody of the Mass in Latin (thirteenth and fourteenth centuries), French and Spanish (fourteenth and fifteenth centuries). Frank A. Domínguez, Carajicomedia: *Parody and Satire in Early Modern Spain* (Woodbridge, UK: Tamesis Books, 2015), 20–28, delves into the definition of "parody" and "contrafactum" in light of pertinent developments in Spanish literature of the fifteenth century and the early 1500s. In the process, he presents a succinct overview of the age-old tradition that comes to a head in the salient poetic elaborations on well-established literary models, such as Juan de Mena's *Las Trezientas* and Garcilaso de la Vega's sonnets. Of great interest is, also, this critic's survey of the recent scholarship on the burlesque modes, evinced in the various literatures of the Hispanic domain during the Middle Ages and the early Renaissance. Frank A. Domínguez, "The Burlesque, the Parodic and the Satiric," *La corónica* 38, no. 1 (Fall 2009): 43–53. Ryan D. Giles, *The Laughter of Saints: Parodies of Holiness in Late Medieval and Renaissance Spain* (Toronto: University of Toronto Press, 2009), finds examples of multifarious parodic modes in his book, which deals with various masterpieces of Spanish literature. These range from Pero López de Ayala's *Rimado de palacio* (late fourteenth century) to Miguel de Cervantes's *Don Quijote* (1605, 1615). As it will soon become apparent, it would be beyond the scope of my study to deal with any of these modes, other than the one illustrated by Fra Francesc Moner, who does not translate the liturgy of the Mass into a burlesque performance. Moner transforms the liturgical into the theatrical with the intention of enacting the canonization of the lover in a nonreligious ceremony, patterned after the most sacred of the religious ones (the Mass).

nor any of the kindred studies by other authors includes the slightest mention of the poem that is the focus of the present monograph.[3] The poem consists of a *misa de amores* (mass of love), a parody of the Eucharistic ritual. Its author is Francesc Moner, a talented, though little-known Catalan author, who flourished in Barcelona in the decade of the 1480s.[4] Moner distinguished himself for his bilin-

---

[3] The kindred studies I refer to make up an abundant bibliography. The following select list shows a good sample of the recent and current scholarship on Spanish literature of the fifteenth century regarding the "religion of love" in general and the parody of the Mass in particular: E. Michael Gerli, "La 'religión del amor' y el antifeminismo en las letras castellanas del siglo XV," *Hispanic Review* 49, no. 1 (1981): 65–86; Valentín Núñez Rivera, "Glosa y parodia de los *Salmos Penitenciales* en la poesía del cancioneros," *EPOS* 17 (2001): 107–39; Estela Pérez-Bosch, "La religión del amor a través del *Cancionero general*: Jaume Gassull y su versión profana del salmo *De profundis*, in *Líneas actuales de investigación literaria: Estudios de literatura hispánica*, ed. Verònica Arenas Lozano, et al. (Valencia: Universitat de València, 2004), 93–104;" Olga Perotti, "La poesía religiosa en el *Cancionero general* de 1511," in *I canzonieri di Lucrezia. Los cancioneros de Lucrecia. Atti del convegno internazionale sulle raccolte poetiche iberiche dei secoli XV-XVII*, ed. Andrea Baldissera and Giuseppe Mazzocchi (Padua: Unipress, 2005), 247–62; Dorothy Sherman Severin, "The *Misa de amor* in the Spanish *Cancioneros* and the Sentimental Romance," in *Medieval Hispanic Studies in Memory of Alan Deyermond*, ed. Andrew M. Beresford, Louise M. Haywood, and Julian Weiss (Woodbridge, UK: Tamesis, 2013), 174–88, and *Religious Parody and the Spanish Sentimental Romance* (Newark, DE: Juan de la Cuesta, 2005); Jane Yvonne Tillier, "Religious Elements in Fifteenth-Century Spanish 'Cancioneros'" (PhD diss., University of Cambridge, 1985). It is fair to say that there are some notable exceptions to the trend of silence that reigns within a select group of critics —Gernert, among others—regarding Moner's masterpiece. Pedro Manuel Cátedra, for example, devotes an important commentary to a core passage in Moner's *Sepultura* (*Amor y pedagogía en la Edad Media: estudios de doctrina amorosa y práctica literaria.* (Salamanca: Universidad de Salamanca, 1989, 173–75). For a testimony to the attention that Moner is beginning to garner from scholars and critics of our day see: Montserrat Ganges Garriga, "Poetes bilingües català castellà del segle XV," *Boletín Bibliográfico de la Asociación Hispánica de Literatura Medieval* 6, no. 1 (1992): 166–87; Vicent Martines Peres, "El codex *Vaticanus Latinus 4802*: Els textos literaris de Moner a cavall de diverses edicions," *Studi e Testi* 396 (2000): 215–41; Estrella Ruiz-Gálvez Priego, "La *Noche de Moner*, más propiamente llamada *Vida humana*," *Cahiers de linguistique hispanique medievale* 30 (2007): 167–82. Worthy of special note are Cátedra's critique of Moner's *Momería* ("Teatro fuera del Teatro," in *Teatro y espectáculo en la edad media: Actas del Festival d'Elx 1990*, ed. Luis Quirante Santacruz [Elche (Elx): Instituto de Cultura 'Juan Gil Albert', Diputación de Alicante y Ajuntament d'Elx, 1992], 39–42); and Sol Miguel-Prendes's comments on Moner' *La noche* ("Otra frontera de la ficción sentimental," *eHumanista* 28 (2014): 524–25).

[4] For a biographical sketch of Moner see Peter Cocozzella, Introducció, *Obres catalanes* [*Oc*]. By Francesc Moner. Edited by Peter Cocozzella. Els Nostres Clàssics 100 (Barcelona: Barcino, 1970), 9–28, and Introducción. Poemas menores. Vol. 1 of *Obras castellanas*. By Francisco Moner. Edited by Peter Cocozzella. Hispanic Literature 2.

gual production at a time when Castilian was gaining ascendancy over his native Catalan. As I hope to demonstrate, Moner's *misa*, despite its scanty recognition, may well turn out to be the most ingenious and accomplished composition of its kind.[5] For the sake of clarity I hasten to point out that the author incorporates the *misa* in question into his poem entitled *Sepultura d'amor* (Burial of Love).

The Author, the Count, and the Marquesa

The purpose of my study is to bring to light the complexity and dramatic qualities of Moner's *Sepultura*. Before delving into a close analysis of the poem, it is appropriate to begin with what we know about Moner's life and works. The essential data are provided by a certain Miguel Berenguer de Barutell, who identifies himself as Moner's cousin ("primo hermano que fue mío"). Barutell prepared and commissioned the printing of the *editio princeps*, published in Barcelona in 1528, which includes practically Moner's entire extant production.[6] Needless to say, the editor's groundwork is of great significance. His meritorious labor is enhanced by a foreword, which, short as it is, includes the only available account of Moner's career in addition to some comments on his achievements.[7] These the cousin-editor avowedly intends to memorialize:

> que la honra de un ingenio que en la vida tanto floresció, no era razón que en la muerte, donde havía creçer, se perdiesse (Barutell, 229; it would hardly be reasonable that the renown of such an ingenious writer, who flourished so much during his lifetime, should come to naught after his death, a time when it should increase).

Barutell's testimonial allows for a bare-bone sketch of his beloved cousin's biography. Moner was born in late December 1462 or early January 1463 in Perpignan, the capital of Roussillon, the Pyrenean region of Catalonia. From 1472 to

---

Lewiston, NY: Edwin Mellen Press, 1991), 3–38. Hereafter referred to as: Introducció; *Oc*; and *1 Introducción*, respectively.

[5] For a preliminary discussion of the central issues at play in Moner's *misa*, see the following essays: Peter Cocozzella, "Parody and Intrinsic Theatricality in a *Misa de Amores* by a Catalan Writer of the Fifteenth Century," *European Medieval Drama* 15 (2011): 199–232, and "The Dramatics of the *Misa de Amores*: Parody and Desacralized Ritual in the Gestation of Spanish Religious Theater of the Early Renaissance," *Anuario de Estudios Medievales* 46.2 (2016): 689–723.

[6] For the essential data on the *editio princeps* see the entry designated as *A* in the bibliography: *Obras nueuamete imprimidas assi en prosa como en metro* (Barcelona: Carlos Amorós, 1528).

[7] The text of this foreword is reproduced in my edition of *Obres catalanes* (*Oc*), 229–32.

1479 he resided at the court of John II of Aragon, father of Ferdinand the Catholic. After the king's death, he spent two years in the household of an unidentified French nobleman. From around 1481 to about 1485 he enlisted first in the army and then in the navy at the service of Joan Ramon Folch III, Count of Prades, head of the illustrious family of Cardona.[8] Under the Count's command, the young author participated in the last phase of the war against the Islamic kingdom of Granada. To underscore Moner's wholehearted commitment to the crusade, Barutell states: "fuese allá porque vio quán buena obra era servir en tal necesidad a Dios y a su príncipe" (he went because he saw how good a deed it was to serve God and king in that hour of need) (230). From 1485 to 1491 Moner became a permanent member of the entourage of the Cardonas in Barcelona. This was for the budding writer a period of intense literary activity. At this time Joan Ramon distinguished himself as sponsor of the cultural life of the Catalan metropolis. Thus, Moner had ample opportunity to frequent the intellectual circles that thrived thanks to the generous support of his Maecenas.[9]

Then, around 1491, in a sudden turn of events that cannot but strike us as surprising, Moner joined the Franciscan order. After a short residence within this religious community in the city of Lleida, he returned to the monastery of the same order in Barcelona. Barutell delivers with poignant precision the last detail of his biographic narrative:

---

[8] Vicenç Beltrán, *Poesía, escriptura i societat: els camins de March* (Castelló–Barcelona: Publicacions de l'Abadia de Montserrat, 2006), provides the essential data about the history of the counts of Prades from the institution of the title in 1324 by Jaume II of Aragon to the brilliant administration of the office by Joan Ramon Folch III (1418–1486). Beltrán describes in vivid terms the Count's personality:

> [F]ou un dels grans personatges polítics del seu temps, potser arrossegat per un temperament fogós o ambiciós: als divuit anys ja va proagonitzar un incident amb una nau de la seva propietat, i va jugar sempre un paper destacat en la vida parlamentària (33; He was one of the great political personalities of his time, driven, perhaps, by an impulsive, ambitious temperament. At the age of eighteen he took the lead in an event, in which he made use of a ship he owned. Time and again he played an outstanding role in parliamentary proceedings).

During his distinguished career the Count held the high posts of ambassador to France and viceroy of Sicily. Beltrán underscores Joan Ramon's remarkable role as literary maecenas and promoter of Catalan culture. (9, 33, 36–37)

[9] In reference to the court of the Cardonas during Moner's lifetime, Óscar Perea Rodríguez uses glowing language—"brillante espacio lúdico, cortesano y literario" (a brilliant space of courtly entertainment and literary activities) (*Estudio biográfico sobre los poetas del Cancionero general* [Madrid: Consejo Superior de Investigaciones Científicas, 2007]). See also, Jordi Rubió Balaguer, *Els Cardona i les lletres, discurso leído el día 7 de abril de 1957 en la recepción pública de D. Jorge Rubió y Balaguer en la Real Academia de Buenas Letres de Barcelona, contestación del académico numerario D. Agustín Durán Sanpere* (Barcelona: Imp. Hispano-Americana, 1957).

> Murió en esta casa de Barçelona de la misma orden, a do vino por serle
> más natural, y paresce que no sin misterio, porque al cabo del año o poco
> más, el día mismo que le hizieron professo, en tiempo que el hervor de su
> devoción se mostraba en major grado y le tenía más ocupado su juicio, a fin
> que no supiesse Moner de la religión sino el mejor d'ella (231; He [Moner]
> died in this house of Barcelona of the same Franciscan order. He moved to
> that monastery because he felt more at home there. Apparently, his death
> was not without some mystery because it occurred on the very day that he
> became professed at a time when the fervor of his piety had reached a high
> peak and held his mind completely absorbed. We may say that Moner came
> to know nothing but what is best in religion).

We are left wondering what this allusion (the *misterio* that envelops Moner's
death) is all about. Barutell dispatches in one vague sentence a significant issue
that, with some additional evidence, might shed some light on the mystery. He
has the following to declare in reference to the years his cousin lived with the
Cardonas:

> En este tiempo amó a una señora de su tierra, con tanta verdad, que basta
> para descargo de las liviendades que suelen traher los amores (231; During
> this period Moner loved a lady from his native land with such true love
> that is enough to exonerate him from the frivolities that often accompany
> amorous affairs).

Moner's relationship with the ladylove would make for a complete study of its
own. Perea Rodríguez suggests that the lady in question may well be Leonor
Centelles, Marquesa de Cotró, described by one chronicler as "dama de extraor-
dinaria belleza" (a lady of extraordinary beauty).[10] Perea underscores two details
of special significance: 1) Doña Leonor and Moner spent the same three years
(1487–90) at the court of the Cardonas; 2) Moner dedicated to the Marquesa a
short treatise in prose (*Estudio biográfico*, 105).[11] With good reason Perea inserts a
pointed question: "¿Podría tratarse de la misma marquesa de Crotone la dama por
la que penaba Moner y cuyo desengaño amoroso le indujo a entrar en religión"
(105; Could the Marquesa de Crotone be the very lady that caused the suffer-
ing and disenchantment in love that induced Moner to embrace religious life?).
Nevertheless, Perea's suggestion or hypothesis does not seem to jibe with "señora
de su tierra," the elusive label Barutell uses to identify Moner's *femme fatale*. As

---

[10] See quotation from Ferrán y Salvador in Perea Rodríguez, *Estudio biográfico*, 103.

[11] For the text and translation of the "Tratado sobre la paciencia" see Peter Cocoz-
zella, *Fra Francesc Moner's Bilingual Poetics of Love and Reason: The "Wisdom Text" by a
Catalan Writer of the Early Renaissance*, Currents in Comparative Romance Languages
and Literatures 173. (New York: Peter Lang, 2010), 179–84; a commentary on Moner's
piece is provided on 27–34.

a likely reference to the Pyrenean origins of Moner's family, that label would hardly be applicable to the Marquesa, born in Valencia and clearly of Valencian stock.[12]

Truth as Leitmotif

Barutell's casual observation about the virtues of Moner's love turns out to be, paradoxically enough, a resounding understatement. The contrast that Barutell envisions between *verdad* (truth) and *liviendades* (lightheartedness) closely parallels the antithesis between *veritat* (truth) and *escalf* (specious language) that none other than Ausiàs March, the widely acclaimed Valencian bard of the first half of the fifteenth century, postulates as the byword of his own artistic enterprise.[13]

---

[12] From Perea Rodríguez (*Estudio biográfico*, 97–108) we learn that Leonor Centelles (née Boil) was born in Valencia circa 1430 and died in Italy circa 1502. After her first husband (Lluís Cornell) died in 1448, she married, some twenty-five years later, Antonio de Centelles, from whom she obtained her nobiliary title. In October 1487, she was involved in an ugly incident, in which two courtiers—Felipe de Aragón, grand master of the Order of Montesa, and Joan de Vallterra, son of the Viceroy of Majorca—were in contention for her favors. In the course of the sordid affair, Montesa plotted and perpetrated the murder of Vallterra. Perea Rodríguez deduces that, in order to distance herself from the scandalous event, Leonor moved to Barcelona and took up residence with the Cardonas.

[13] The recent landmark publication *Història de la literatura catalana* (see bibliography below), provides an update on the scholarship on Ausiàs March. In vol. 2, we find the enlightening contribution of the following scholars: Lluís Cabré, "Ausiàs March: Vida, obra, transmisió i cultura" (pp. 353–71); Lluís Cabré and Marcel Ortín, "Lectura de la poesía d'Ausiàs March" (pp. 371–97); Jaume Torró and Francisco Rodríguez Risquete, "La poesia després d'Ausiàs March" (pp. 398–435); Albert Lloret, "La posteritat d'Ausiàs March i la transmisió impresa" (pp. 435–41). Martí de Riquer, *Història de la literatura catalana*. 3 vols. (Barcelona: Ariel, 1964) provides the essential details on March's life and works (2: 471–568). For a sketch of the poet's life, especially in terms of his career and far-reaching influence, see Robert Archer, *The Pervasive Image: The Role of Analogy in the Poetry of Ausiàs March*. Purdue University Monographs in Romance Languages 17. (Philadelphia: John Benjamins, 1985), 1–22, and Peter Cocozzella, "Salient Trends in Ausiàs March Criticism: Toward a Holistic Approach," in *Proceedings of the First Catalan Symposium* (Volume in Memory of Paulí Bellet), ed. Josep M. Solà-Solé. (New York, NY: Peter Lang, 1992), 29–56. Representative of the expanding bibliography on Ausiàs March in recent times are the following books: Rafael Alemany Ferrer, ed., *Ausiàs March i el món cultural del segle XV* (Alacant: Universitat d'Alacant, 1999); Lourdes Sánchez Rodríguez and Enrique J. Nogueras Valdivieso, eds., *Ausiàs March y las literaturas de su época* (Granada: Editorial Universidad de Granada, 2000); and Georges Martin and Marie-Claire Zimmermann, eds., *Ausiàs March (1400–1459): premier poète en langue catalane* (Paris: Klincksieck, 2000). Without doubt, the most authoritative biog-

Barutell evokes the first two verses of March's Poem 23: "Lleixant a part l'estil dels trobadors / qui, per escalf, trespassen veritat" (discarding the style of the troubadours, who are so inflamed that they cannot speak without exaggeration [Robert Archer's translation, 41]).[14] Here March employs the essential positive/ negative pattern that Barutell detects in Moner's works. No doubt Barutell recognizes the parallelism and appreciates the *gravedad* in March's extolling truth to the disparagement of what, in down-to-earth language, March identifies as escalf." In March's case, then, the formula becomes *veritat* without *escalf.* In the final analysis, Barutell's insight validates a hypothesis that may be phrased as follows: Moner assimilates thoroughly March's pronouncement and transforms it into a guiding principle for his own creative spirit.[15]

The hypothesis may be readily contextualized within the framework of Moner's extant production. This consists of seventy-four pieces, a miscellaneous collection of poems and prose works of varying length, written some in Catalan, some in Castilian.[16] Actually, Moner surpasses Ausiàs March in subscribing to

---

raphy of Ausiàs March is found in Jaume J. Chiner Gimeno, *Ausiàs March i la València del segle XV (1400–1459)* (València: Generalitat Valenciana. Consell Valencià de Cultura, 1997). See also, Ferran Garcia Oliver, *En la vida d'Ausiàs March* (Barcelona: Edicions 62, 1998). Very handy is the updated overview of March's biography provided by Costanzo Di Girolamo, "March, Ausiàs. Nota informativa / noticia biográfica," in Ausiàs March, *Páginas del cancionero*, ed. Costanzo Di Girolamo, trans. José Maria Micó (Madrid: Pretextos, 2004), 61–67. On the basis of recently discovered evidence, Chiner Gimeno convincingly proposes the year 1400 and the city of Valencia for March's date and place of birth. Chiner Gimeno lays to rest the previous widely accepted notion that March was born in Gandia (a town in the vicinity of Valencia) in 1397 ("1997, any March? Noves dades sobre el naixement d'Ausiàs" in *Ausiàs March i el món cultural del segle XV*, ed. Rafael Alemany Ferrer (Alacant: Universitat d'Alacant, 1999), 14. For a selection of essays on the Valencian bard, see the recently published "Ausiàs March," in *Poetry Criticism: Criticism of the Works of the Most Significant and Widely Studied Poets of World Literature* (listed under Trudeau, ed. in the bibliography below).

[14] Unless otherwise indicated, the references to March's poems throughout this study are to Archer's edition: Ausiàs March, *Obra completa*, ed. Robert Archer (Barcelona: Barcanova, 1997). For the text of Poem 23, see pp. 117–20 of that edition. See Archer's editorial comments on pp. 115–16.

[15] For further comments on this axiomatic contrast in both March and Moner, see Cocozzella, *Fra Francesc Moner's Bilingual Poetics of Love and Reason*, 4–7.

[16] For a synopsis showing the classification of Moner's works and their distribution as to language, see Cocozzella, *Fra Francesc Moner's Bilingual Poetics of Love and Reason*, 24. For additional details on that distribution, see Peter Cocozzella, "Fray Francisco Moner: Bilingualism, Love, and Experience in Spanish Pre-Renaissance Literature," in *Estudis de llengua, literatura i cultura catalanes. Actes del Primer Col·loqui d'Estudis Catalans a NordAmèrica (Urbana, 30 de març1 d'abril de 1978)*, ed. Albert PorquerasMayo, Spurgeon Baldwin, and Jaume MartíOlivella (Montserrat: Publicacions de l'Abadia de Montserrat, 1979), 209–39.

the intensive and persistent exploration of the nature of truth and in rejecting any aspect of falsehood, such as pretentious or deceitful behavior, specious speech, and downright slander. Indeed, in three of Moner's five major works, truth is represented as either a personage of godlike eminence and authority or an avatar of the Divinity (God-the-Truth). To be specific, allegorized Truth embodies supreme authority as the Catalan *Veritat* in *Bendir de dones* and becomes an epiphany of the Divinity as the Castilian *Verdad* in both *La noche* (Nighttime) and in the aforementioned *Sepultura d'amor*.

Truth does not appear at all in either *Obra en metro* (Poem in *Arte Mayor* [Long Verse])[17] or *L'ànima d'Oliver* (The Ghost of Oliver), the remaining two of said five pieces. The absence of any personification of "truth" in *Obra* is, in itself, significant. It signals a disturbing vacuum of an authoritative or controlling agent in the chaotic condition of the lover's psyche. The chaos is reflected in the emotional turmoil that brings about the protagonist's drawn-out monologue. The first-person speaker (the auctorial persona) voices his utter frustration as he decries the inefficacy of three personages: Razón (Reason), Voluntad (Will), Fortuna (Fortune). He proceeds to reproach them in short order, one by one. There is, of course, a moral hidden in the mini-drama encased in the monologue: without the intervention of God-the-Truth, the three ladies the protagonist confronts with such pathetic urgency cannot be of any avail, even though they prove to be formidable in their own right.

In *L'ànima*, the absence of God-the-Truth is compensated by the spectral presence of Oliver, with whom the auctorial persona strikes an engaging dialogue. The Ghost replaces Truth Deified. We may observe that the substitution represents a radical shift with respect to the mood and perspective that characterize *Obra en metro*. The Ghost, presented as an envoy from the Creator, bestows a measure of serenity upon the inner turmoil dramatized so forcefully in the monologue that makes up *Obra*. Thus, Oliver performs a role not unlike the one exhibited by Lady Philosophy in Boethius's classic *De Consolatione*.

Nuanced Writing

The contrast between *L'ànima* and *Obra* bears further discussion insofar as it brings to light an interplay of two perspectives, each of which determines its own field of vision or contemplation. This perspectivism is at play in Moner's overall approach to love and reason. Each work exhibits its own general orientation:

---

[17] Tomás Navarro Tomás, *Métrica española: reseña histórica y descriptiva* (New York: Las Américas Publishing Company, 1966). A well-demarcated caesura divides the verse of *arte mayor*, which, generally consists of hemistichs of six syllables each. It is not unusual, however, for this verse to fluctuate from ten to fourteen syllables (91–92). For a full discussion of *arte mayor* see 91–100.

L'ànima toward the abode of God-the-Truth, *Obra* toward the spatiality of the psychic conflict. Moner himself helps us define this dualistic outlook by calling attention to the concept of "letras matizadas del sentido" (written words nuanced with sense and sentiment).[18] The phrase encapsulates the sententious tenor of a poetic manifesto. Moner's incisive dictum hinges on the ambiguity of the term *sentido*, which encompasses two semantic fields. As my translation indicates, one of these is related to "sense;" the other, to "sentiment." The two terms differ in their respective denotations: sense indicates the intellective faculties (understanding, awareness, judgment, perspicacity, among others), whereas sentiment refers to the multifarious emotional makeup (feeling, sensation, susceptibility, and so on).[19]

The articulation of these denotations may be seen as a gauge of sorts by which to define Moner's textuality. In *L'ànima*, for instance, the reasoned and methodic argumentation adduced by God's emissary prevails over the querulous inquisitiveness and plaintive tone of his interlocutor (the auctorial persona) and unmistakably points the way, in true Boethian fashion, to the attainment of the Summum Bonum. Here reasoned argumentation clearly gains the upper hand over emotional expression. In *La noche*, by contrast, the scale does not tip on either side of the sense/sentiment polarity. Lady Reason's impeccable disquisition, based on Thomistic principles and doctrine, countervails the lover's spirited dialogue with the eleven passions identified by Aquinas. To put it differently, Reason's intellectual discourse interfaces with the vivid depiction of the personified passions and the dramatized altercation of the auctorial persona with each of them.

Lady Reason plays a prominent role in *Bendir de dones* as well. There are, to be sure, important distinctions to be made. The text of *La noche* exposes the Lady's utter frustration caused by her inability to put the lover in communion with the Supreme Being. After a long night spent in the exploration of the dark castle, Reason turns to Moner's persona, whom she has been guiding all along, and points to the castle's keep (torre de homenaje), still to be visited. Reason promptly recognizes that, at the sight of the tower, where *Verdad* is enthroned, the visitor is overtaken with awe. In a characteristic show of sympathy, she tries to put her companion's mind at ease:

> Pero no t'espantes, que dentro está la Sabiduría contemplando secretos, tan piadosa y tan buena, que endreçará tus passos a que la Verdad contemples. Es allí la teologal Esperança, que es muy segura amiga. Allí está la Caridad

---

[18] See *Sepultura d'amor*, vv. 5–6 (p. 173 below).

[19] The double-pronged semantic function of the term is well attested in the numerous instances *sentido* is used in *Cancionero general*: see Joaquín González Cuenca, ed., "Glosario," *Cancionero general [de Hernando del Castillo].* 5 vols. (Madrid: Castalia, 2004), 5: 369.

que, si te preparas, aliviará tus trabajos. Pero guarda que es menester que
seas no tal como estavas quando yo te hallé primero (ll. 1679–86; *TMPW*
200–201; Do not be alarmed. Inside resides Lady Wisdom, who is con-
templating profound mysteries. So compassionate and good-natured is she
that she will guide your steps toward the contemplation of God-the-Truth.
Close by stands Theological Hope, who is a very trustworthy friend. In the
same place dwells Charity, who will lighten your toils, provided that you
are well prepared. Bear in mind, all the while, that you must not be in the
same state you were in when I first met you).

At the same time, Reason cannot but acknowledge some feelings of awe of her
own and does not hesitate to admit to her limitations:

Esta torre es muy segura. Aquí podrás ver mucha gente si te abren la puerta.
Aquí tengo yo muchos amigos, y más la Verdad a quien sirven todos. Pero
hay una portera, Fe, cuyo gesto resplandece tanto que me ciega la vista.
Assí que si entrar quieres, havrásme de perdonar porque ende yo no sabría
guiarte (ll. 1672–78; *TMPW* 200; This tower is very securily guarded. Here
you will see many people, provided that they open the door for you. Here
I have friends, including Truth, whom they all serve. There is, I must add,
Faith, the doorkeeper, whose face is so bright that my eyes are blinded.
Well, if you want to go in, you will have to excuse me. Once inside, I would
not know how to guide you).

A major differentiating factor in *Bendir de dones* is the mind-set of Rahó, Catalan
counterpart of Razón. While recognizing her limitations, Rahó does not own
up to any frustration. Her poise is reflected in her self-assurance and dignified
deference to Veritat, the Catalanized Truth, whom she regards as a venerable
colleague of the highest rank. Rahó shows no signs of awe or self-effacement.
Rather, she delivers directly to the lover a prognosis of his ailment (*aegritudo
amoris*) (vv. 261–320) and, then, tactfully introduces him to Veritat. The latter,
in turn, enlightens him with a precise diagnosis of his affliction (vv. 348–460).
Immediately after Veritat's speech, a woman carrying a lamp and a trumpet
made of iron, complements with a prescription of sorts the clinical intervention
of Rahó and Veritat. This curious character, a misogynist curmudgeon named
Cautela (Caution), dispenses lavish advice as to how to forestall or counteract the
purported viciousness and abusive behavior of women in general (vv. 491–560).[20]

In *Bendir*, as in *La noche*, the equilibrium between sense and sentiment is
not impaired. The same may not be said, however, of *Obra en metro*, in which the
speaker of the monologue is beset by the constant surge of emotions despite his
repeated attempts to bring calm to his psychological conflict. In *Obra*, *sentido* as

---

[20] For further discussion on the collaborative efforts of Rahó and Veritat, see Cocoz-
zella, *Fra Francesc Moner's Bilingual Poetics*, 62–64.

a two-pronged signifier becomes index of the dysfunctional relationship between Razón (Reason) and Voluntad (Will). The speaker levels his bitter complaints at these semi-allegorized characters of commanding presence. He reproaches Voluntad for not asserting her authority and Razón for failing to carry out her natural function as a competent guide. In the full-fledged monologue of the disgruntled lover, Moner recaptures the dramatic verve of March's lyricism and the palpable gloom of the genre commonly known as *infierno de los enamorados* (hell of lovers).[21] He explores inner space and arrives at his own definition of the theater of the lover's psyche.

Moner faithfully documents how the tension between Reason and Will plays out in a dark world, which may be described as the realm of immanence. At the same time, he envisions a way of transcending the gloom of the *infierno* by a bold experimentation with the format of the sermon. Enter Experiencia (Lady Experience), who, as one of the three female celebrants of the *misa de amores*, delivers a homily of dubious coherence. She pays due tribute to the intellectual dimension of *sentido* by devoting the first of the three parts of her sermon (vv. 317–442) to a cursory explication of some axiomatic pronouncements on the nature of love. Her pontificating posture, matched by less than airtight argumentation, turns her handling of "letras matizadas del sentido" into an exemplum of the crisis of reason. In the second part of her specious disquisition (vv. 443–638), Experiencia gives up any pretense of dispassionate exposition and, instead, gives in to the furor of a misogynistic tirade, not unlike that of Cautela, already described. The following is a good sample of Experiencia's impassioned oratory:

> Son estrago de las vidas
> que por ellas syn mercedes
>   se despyenden.
> Do no temen ser vencidas,
> por offender con sus redes
>   se destyenden,
> pues saben que son queridas.
> A quyen el mal sobresana
> no l'aprovecha destresa
>   la más alta.
> Danlos cesto por mansana,
> y si no dexan la empresa,
>   nunca falta
> en fin la muerte temprana.
> (Vv. 499–512; *2 OC*, 149. For the translation see p. 204 below.)

At first blush, this unbridled emotionalism may surprise us; but soon we realize that only Razón can bring such an unseemly outburst under control by virtue of

---

[21] For a full discussion of this genre, see pp. 6–13 below.

her powers and special charisma. Razón, however, is not present to counteract Experiencia's intervention. Experiencia, for her part, attempts in vain to compensate for Razón's absence by appropriating her role.

There is a lesson to be learned from Experiencia's performance as an intellectual manqué. Her sermon provides an eloquent illustration of a subtle twist in Moner's ingenious artistry. In the complex orchestration of the *misa*, the impetus of Experiencia's antifeminist animosity does not function, as one might expect, as proof positive of skewed *sentido*, in which sentiment prevails over sense. Rather, it evolves as the primary thrust of a process of liberation from the melancholic condition in which the lover is wont to wallow in morbid contentment. It may be said that Experiencia's fits of ranting and raving rehearse the implementation of a therapy of catharsis. They rehearse for the lover an effective way of venting the pent-up resentment and other noxious feelings generated by the pathology of a relationship gone terribly sour. There is an important correlation between Experiencia's cathartic ministrations and the operation of transcendence carried out by Mancilla (Lady Compassion), who holds the office of chief celebrant.[22] By virtue of her ministry as primary priest, it is up to Mancilla to release the auctorial persona from the fetters of passionate love and to guide him along the path toward the blissful communion with the Divinity.

The *Cancionero* Phase

What we have seen so far is the multifarious recurrence of the *veritat*-vs-*escalf* principle that accounts for the overall cohesiveness and overarching design of Moner's production. That cohesiveness and design bear witness to the radical affinity between Moner's and March's truth-oriented esthetic. This strong bond of affinity does not, however, obfuscate the significance of a number of compositions that reflect a predominantly Castilian phase in Moner's bilingual poetics. I am referring to Moner's *canciones*, *glosas de motes*, and a few other introspective pieces that constitute the type of poetry collected in the numerous *cancioneros*, the anthologies compiled throughout the fifteenth century and the early years of the sixteenth.[23]

---

[22] The definition of *mancilla* as "compassion" or "pity" is warranted by the extensive documentation in the *Cancionero general*: see "manzilla" in González Cuenca, "Glosario," 5: 291. For the complicated etymology of the term, see Joan Corominas, Juan Antonio Pascual, *Diccionario crítico etimológico castellano e hispánico*. 6 vols. (Madrid: Gredos, 1980–1991), 3: 796–97. Hereafter referred to as *DCECH*.

[23] A modern edition of Moner's *cancionero* proper is found in *1 OC*, 165–208. See, also, my commentary in *1 OC* 107–20. For the essential scholarship on the *cancioneros*, see below, pp. 1–3, n. 2.

We may say that Moner produced a *cancionero* of his own, the contents of which would not be out of place in the monumental *Cancionero general* compiled by Hernando del Castillo and published in Valencia in 1511.[24] In fact, Moner's mini-*cancionero* bears evidence of a direct connection with such a leading exponent of Castillo's *magnum opus* as Pedro de Cartagena, at whose request our bilingual poet wrote a poem, entitled, plainly enough, "Coplas hechas a ruegos de Cartagena" (Stanzas Written at Cartagena's Request).[25] Cartagena enjoyed a privileged position among Castillo's favorite poets.[26] Incontrovertible evidence leads us to deduce that Moner's relationship with Cartagena began and became established during the Granada campaign, in which they both participated. Cartagena died in 1486 at the age of thirty during the siege of the city of Loja (Avalle-Arce, "Cartagena, poeta del Cancionero General," 292; Cocozzella, *1 Introducción*, 12; Perea Rodríguez, *Estudio biográfico*, 174). A scrutiny of the events in Moner's biography would indicate that the author composed most, if not all, his *cancionero* in his early twenties, shortly before or after 1486. With the death of Cartagena Moner lost a powerful sponsor, who maintained direct contact with Castillo himself. Castillo simply did not know about Moner's lyrics. Regardless of their unquestionable merit, these never made it into the *Cancionero general*.

The Bilingualism of an Introvert

There can be little doubt that Moner's taking up residence at the court of Joan Ramon Folch III marks an all-important turning point in the author's career. Even as the storm of the military service gave way to the mental turbulence occasioned by his problematic relationship with the ladylove, Moner found the leisure, if not the tranquility, to pursue his creative activities. Starting in his early twenties, he made considerable strides in asserting his particular brand of eclecticism. In *Sepultura d'amor*, for instance, he embarks upon a remarkable elaboration on motifs derived from the Castilian tradition. Putting his *cancionero* proper

---

[24] Arguably Castillo's is foremost in the trio formed in conjunction with two other famous *cancioneros*: that of Juan Alfonso de Baena, and the one by Lope de Estúñiga (see below, pp. 1–3, n. 2).

[25] In due time we will discuss the specifics of the relationship between Moner and this author (see below, pp. 38, n. 8; 101–2).

[26] Castillo entrusted Cartagena with the judging of the poetic compositions—the so-called *invenciones* and *letras*—featured in the festivities held at Valladolid in April 1475. See Perea Rodríguez, *Estudio biográfico*, 77. See pp. 173–74 for the names of the courtiers that participated in the festivities and contributed those compositions. One of the participants and contributors was none other than the young king Ferdinand the Catholic.

behind him, Moner achieves in *Sepultura* a veritable tour de force: he adapts the gloomy *infierno* to the complex structuralism inherent in the parody of the Mass. By contrast, in *Obra en metro* the vein of eclecticism draws from bilingual sources. *Obra* turns out to be an ingenious blending of two poetic modes: first, Cartagena's emotional surge and subtle conceit; and, second, March's sententiousness and rationalistic introspection.[27]

A digression into the aspects of Moner's bilingualism would take us far afield from the present discussion. Here we only need to concentrate on one point: Moner employs Catalan or Castilian in accordance with the suitability he perceives in each language to the issues at hand.[28] We notice that he finds Castilian particularly apt as a vehicle for the creative imagination. Witness the highly imaginative composition exhibited in such pieces as *Sepultura*, *La noche*, and *Obra*. By the same token, textual evidence indicates that Moner considers his native Catalan distinctively suited to a direct analysis of lived experience (mainly the rocky relationship with his ladylove). Moner's Catalan conveys the auctorial persona's immediate confrontation of that experience either dispassionately, as in *Comiat*, *Resposta a Jaume Ribes*, *L'ànima d'Oliver*, or with impassionate involvement, as in *Cartes a l'amada*, *Bendir de dones*, and *Retrets a l'amada*.[29]

---

[27] Gerli plumbs the depths of Cartagena's conceit in E. Michael Gerli, "Reading Cartagena: Blindness, Insight and Modernity in a *Cancionero* Poet," in *Poetry at Court in Trastamaran Spain: from the "Cancionero de Baena" to the "Cancionero General,"* MRTS 181, ed. E. Michael Gerli and Julian Weiss (Tempe, AZ: ACMRS, 1998), 171–83. For a specific analysis of "Coplas hechas a ruegos de Cartagena," see *1 OC* 139–44. A similar study focused on *Obra en metro* is found in *2 OC* 3–23.

[28] The point is extrapolated from the extensive argumentation I present in "Pere Torroella i Francesc Moner: aspectes del bilingüisme literari (catalano-castellà) a la segona meitat del segle XV," *Llengua & Literatura: Revista anual de la Societat Catalana de Llengua i Literatura* 2 (1987): 154–72.

[29] As a useful complement to these comments I would adduce the following excerpt from my study on the subject of Moner's bilingualism:
[Moner] destria, o, millor dit, intueix en les dues llengües . . . trets distintius que es presten a determinades funcions també ben diferenciades. Per una banda, els gèneres transmesos per mitjà del castellà exhibeixen una natural orientació cap al tòpic (la vindicació de l'amant ideal que Moner transforma en la projecció de la propia «persona» poètica). Per l'altra, els gèneres que mostren com a vehicle natural el català tenen el seu centre de gravitació en la *vivencia* personal. Aleshores, en l'àmbit del bilingüisme monerià, el català s'ajusta més a reflectir l'experiència viscuda, mentre que el castellà es presta a l'expressió de l'experiència sublimada en el tòpic ("Pere Torroella i Francesc Moner," 167; Moner makes out, or, more accurately, intuits in the two languages traits that lend themselves to specific functions, which, also, are clearly differentiated. The genres written in Castilian exhibit the author's natural inclination toward the literary topic: mainly the vindication of the ideal lover, whom Moner transforms into a projection of his own poetic persona. By contrast, the genres for which Catalan is the natural vehicle, have their center

The comparison between Moner's bilingualism and that of Pere Torroella (circa 1420–circa 1492), the other fifteenth-century master of Catalan as well as Castilian, is highly instructive as it points to notable similarities and differences.[30] The comparison may be posited in terms of the most recognizable features that Lluís Cabré identifies in Torroella's production. Cabré focuses on the essential points, which strike us as analogous to Moner's functional use of the two languages:

> Torroella's work cannot be divided on the basis of the language of composition alone. He chose the vernacular proper to each addressee and followed in all likelihood the dominant language in a given court—therefore Spanish (to use an all-embracing term) in Navarre, Aragon, and Naples. But there was no divide in terms of literary taste within the fluid milieu of the Trastámara circles he moved in. Languages were channels rather than barriers, which explains the consistency of Torroella's work ("From Ausiàs March to Petrarch: Torroella, Urrea, and Other Ausimarchides," 60).

The consistency underscored in Cabré's discussion stems from a protracted meditation on the ideology about love, inherited from Ausiàs March. Torroella engages in that meditation in collaboration with a number of literary personali-

---

of gravity in the personal *vivencia*. Thus, in the realm of Moner's bilingualism, Catalan is more suited to reflect lived experience, while Castilian lends itself to the expression of experience sublimated into a topic).

[30] For a comprehensive overview of Torroella's career, Rodríguez Risquete's extensive biographic study with all its ample documentation is indispensable (Francisco J. Rodríguez Risquete, Introducció, 1–54). Besides "Torroella," Riquer registers three other variants of the author's surname—Torrella, Torrellas, and Torrelles—in sundry combinations with three forms of his first name: Pere, Pero, Pedro (Riquer, *Història*, 3: 161). An essential biography of Torroella may be found in Charles V. Aubrun, "Introduction," *Le chansonnier espagnol d'Herberay des Essarts (XVe siècle)*, Bibliothèque de l'Ècole des Hautes Ètudes. (Bordeaux: Feret et Fils, 1951), xlv–li; Pedro Bach y Rita, "Introduction," in *The Works of Pere Torroella, a Catalan Writer of the Fifteenth Century*, ed. Pedro Bach y Rita (New York: Instituto de las Españas en los Estados Unidos, 1930), 12–27; Cocozzella, "Pere Torroella: Pan-Hispanic Poet of the Catalan Pre-Renaissance," *Hispanófila* 86 (1986): 4–6; Riquer, *Història*, 3: 174–86; Jordi Rubió Balaguer, "Literatura catalana," in *Historia general de las literaturas hispánicas*, ed. Guillermo Díaz-Plaja (Barcelona: Barna, 1953), 3: 871–73. As for the impact of Torroella's presence in the limelight of history, suffice it to point out the author's brilliant career as a high-ranking member of the military, a diplomat, and, of course, a man of letters. No less fascinating, albeit of dubious distinction, is the reputation that Torroella attained as woman-hater par excellence. Torroella's popularity and notoriety stem, no doubt, from his "Maldezir de mugeres," demonstrably one of the most widely read, discussed, and disputed Spanish poems of the fifteenth century (Robert Archer, *The Problem of Woman in Late-Medieval Hispanic Literature* [Woodbridge, UK: Tamesis-Boydell & Brewer, 2005], 170).

ties: Francesc Alegre, Francesc Ferrer, Lluís de Vilarrasa, Romeu Llull, Bernat Huc de Rocabertí, Pedro de Urrea, Hugo de Urríes, to list the names mentioned by Cabré as representative members of the literary establishment in Aragón and Catalonia during Moner's lifetime.[31]

In the final analysis, Cabré raises a crucial issue, in view of which we may draw a sharp contrast between Torroella's and Moner's respective outlooks on life and literary creativity. Elsewhere I point out that Moner reacted in his own separate way to the very circumstances that shape the lives of Torroella and cohorts ("Pere Torroella i Francesc Moner: aspectes del bilingüisme literari [catalanocastellà] a la segona meitat del segle XV," 165). We find in Moner's production little or no evidence of his interaction with a group of like-minded writers and intellectuals. After an early period, characterized, as we have seen, by his contact with Pedro de Cartagena, Moner becomes exceedingly self-absorbed to the point of being completely wrapped up in the emotional crisis precipitated by unrequited love. Needless to say, Moner's shut-in condition does not lend itself to easy communication with other writers or with his potential readers. Psychological plight goes hand in hand with the personal tenor of Moner's poetic, which is very much at odds with the in-group quality evident in the texts of the *cancioneros*.

---

[31] Riquer's provides the indispensable data on the careers of these authors. From Riquer we learn that they are March's younger contemporaries, who came of age in the course of the first two decades immediately after the poet's death. Following are the page references for each author in Riquer's *Història de la literatura catalana* 3: Alegre (249–52), Ferrer (35–43), Vilarrasa (43–47), Llull (195–204), Rocabertí (148–60), Torroella (161–86), Urrea (165, 171–72). For Urríes, see Aubrun, Introduction, xl–xli; and Barbara Matulka, *The Novels of Juan de Flores and Their European Diffusion* (New York: Institute of French Studies, 1931), 128. H. C. Heath's edition of Rocabertí's *La glòria d'amor* and concomitant study still hold great interest. Worthy of particular note are Antonio Cortijo Ocaña, "The Complications of the Narrative Techniques in 15th Century Prose Literature on Love: The *Somni de Francesc Alegre recitant lo procés d'una qüestió enamorada*" *Catalan Review* 11, no. 1–2 (1997): 49–64, on Alegre's *Somni*, and the pages that Cátedra devotes to that author's *Sermó de amor* (Pedro Manuel Cátedra, *Amor y pedagogía en la Edad Media: estudios de doctrina amorosa y práctica literaria*. Acta Salmaticensia, Estudios Filológicos 212 [Salamanca: Universidad de Salamanca, Secretariado de Publicaciones, 1989], 161–72). About Alegre's *Sermó* see, also, Cocozzella, *Fra Francesc Moner's Bilingual Poetics*, 35–37. We would be remiss if we should not mention here the admirable editions that Auferil, Torró i Torrent, and Rodríguez Risquete have prepared, respectively, for the works of Ferrer, Llull, and Torroella. These editions map out a vast field for research in textual analysis and literary criticism. Rodríguez Risquete complements Cabré's study with an enlightening essay of his own (Francisco J. Rodríguez Risquete, "El mestratge de Pere Torroella," *Actes AILLC* 13 (Girona 2003), Barcelona-Girona, PAM-ILCC, 2007, vol. 3, 337–62). Rodríguez Risquete traces through Torroella's works March's influence on known authors, such as Antoni Vallmanya and Narcís Vinyoles, and on others of obscure identity: Ramon Boter, mossèn Navarro, Lluís d'Avinnyó, and a certain Ramis.

Scholars have defined *cancionero* poetry, quite appropriately, in terms of the social conventions of the upper class. Take, for instance, the following description by Enrique Galé Casajús: "[L]os poemas recogidos en los cancioneros del siglo XV y la primera mitad del siglo XVI no nacen de una necesidad íntima de la expresión poética personal sino que son respuesta a una convención social" (The poems collected in the *cancioneros* of the fifteenth century and the first half of the sixteenth are not born of a deep-seated need for a personal poetic expression. Rather, they reflect a social convention [143].)[32] Moner definitely marches to the beat of his own drum. That is to say, he works against the powerful current of conventionality that, as Galé and others cogently argue, proved to be irresistible to most if not all of Moner's contemporaries.

Let us say that, as Rodríguez Risquete demonstrates, Torroella's glorious achievement resides in a spectacular work of synthesis, by virtue of which Torroella adapts the esthetic legacy of the post-troubadour tradition, especially as manifested in the *cancionero* convention, to the conflation of the specific strains that emanate from both Francesco Petrarca and Ausiàs March. In a synthetic statement of his own, Rodríguez Risquete describes Torroella's indelible contribution to world literature as follows:

[E]l camino desbrozado por Pere Torroella, la fórmula que conjugaba a March y Petrarca, la que él declinó por primera vez y mostró en la corte aragonesa, fue la que se impuso en la península: es la fórmula que, muy mejorada pero en esencia idéntica, cristaliza en Romeu Llull, pasa por las manos de Juan Boscán y madura en Garcilaso de la Vega, Gutierre de Cetina, Fernando de Herrera y Francisco de Quevedo. Todos estos poetas comprendieron, cómo por vez primera había enseñado Torroella allá en el siglo xv, un principio que muchos especialistas en poesía hispánica ignoran:

---

[32] Galé Casajús echoes the following statement by Vicenç Beltran:
Si para nosotros la poesía es, ante todo, expresión de la subjetividad, en la sociedad medieval, desde los orígenes de la lírica trovadoresca y de la novela, se trata, ante todo, de una experiencia colectiva: el público es siempre inmediato—los miembros del círculo donde el autor se desenvuelve—y la comunicación entre autor y receptor es, por tanto, personal y directa, lo que condiciona decisivamente la creación literaria (Vicenç Beltrán, "Prólogo," in J. Manrique, *Poesía* [Barcelona: Crítica, 1993], 3), quoted in Enrique Galé Casajús, "La creación literaria en el seno de un clan familiar: la obra de Pedro Manuel de Urrea," in *El Condado de Aranda y la nobleza española en el Antiguo Régimen*, ed. José Casaus Ballester (Zaragoza: Institucion «Fernando el Catolico» (C.S.I.C.), 2009) 143; For us poetry is, above all, an expression of subjectivity; but, for Medieval society, in the period that starts with origins of both the lyrics of the troubadours and the novel, poetry consists of, in the main, a collective experience: the public, that is, the members of the social circle in which the poet operates, is always an immediate presence, and the communication between the author and the receptive entity is, consequently, direct and personal, and this communication conditions decisively the act of literary creation.)

que la renovación bien entendida pasaba por la conjunción de un modelo
foráneo (Petrarca) y un modelo autóctono (March), y que esta semilla,
antes de fructificar y ramificarse con vigor, fue cosechada en la Corona de
Aragón por unos poetas a los que no leemos pero que, lo queramos o no,
acabaron triunfando silenciosamente (*Obra completa de Pere Torroella al cui-
dado de Francisco Rodríguez Risquete: Discurso de presentación*, 10–11; (The
trail blazed by Torroella led to the linkage [the manner, that is, of con-
joining March and Petrarch] that Torroella worked out for the first time
and made manifest in the court of Aragon. This manner eventually came
to prevail throughout the Iberian Peninsula. While remaining essentially
the same, it took shape, considerably improved, in Romeu Llull; was culti-
vated by Boscán; and brought to maturity by Garcilaso de la Vega, Gutie-
rre de Cetina, Fernando de Herrera, and Francisco de Quevedo. All these
poets understood that, back in the fifteenth century, Torroella highlighted
a criterion that many specialists in Spanish poetry have neglected. By that
criterion, the process of renewal, in the true sense of the term, would go
through the conflation of a foreign model (Petrarch) and an indigenous
one (March). The early crop of this renewal was harvested in the domain of
Aragon by a number of poets. Later that crop would would branch out vig-
orously and bear fruit abundantly. We are not accustomed to reading these
poets, but, whether we duly acknowledge them or not, there is no denying
that they, in the long run, triumphed in silence).

Rodríguez Risquete vindicates for Torroella the role of precursor of the most
important figures in the literary history of the Spanish Renaissance.[33] We may
conclude that Torroella produces a compendium of the Spanish love-centered
poetry of his time.

Moner, by contrast, withdraws from the social milieu. His creative imagi-
nation operates in the private space where the *circunstancia* in Ortega y Gasset's
sense of the term is condensed to the unique moment of intense lived experience.
Moner, in other words, devotes his best efforts in elaborating complex literary
forms that take shape in such compositions as *Bendir de dones, La noche, Obra
en metro, Sepultura d'amor*. Metaphorically speaking, Torroella synthesized the
various strains of the literary tradition he inherits especially from Ausiàs March;
Moner distills those strains. The metaphor of distillation illustrates the ways in
which he assimilates in his major works the poetic vein that issues from Ausiàs
March. One may see the process at play in the works just listed.

From March's poems Moner extracts the genetic makeup integrated into the
multifarious manifestations of the dramatic monologue. Let us take, for instance,
the monologue that makes up the entire frame of *Obra en metro*. Here the author,
while voicing the hard-to-restrain emotionality of the auctorial persona, effec-

---

[33] For the significance of the role of precursor assigned directly to Ausiàs March,
see Kathleen McNerney, *The Influence of Ausiàs March on Early Golden Age Castilian
Poetry* (Amsterdam: Rodopi, 1982).

tively recaptures March's emblematic introspection into the here-and-now of the lover's condition. Thus, the expanded monologue evolves into Moner's rendition of March's use of allegory. This allegory is connatural to the full gamut of March's ideology about love, encompassing both spiritual and erotic strains.

Throughout the present study I intend to pursue a close analysis of the points concerning the trends of *ausiasmarquismo* wedded to bilingualism. Now I shall advance a summary review of those points in order to highlight two contrasting purviews: the social championed by Torroella and the individualistic espoused by Moner. By those trends the nexus *ausiasmarquismo* and bilingualism finds in Catalan literature of the fifteenth century a striking manifestation, memorable for generations to come.

Moner excels in his private persona as does Torroella in his public one. We may anticipate some insights yielded by the very prospect of the analysis we are about to undertake. The traces of Italianate (mainly Petrarchan) influence that play such an important role in Torroella and the other members of his literary circle virtually vanish in Moner's works. Also, it is possible to perceive Moner's worthy counterpart of the compendium that critics like Rodríguez Risquete and Lluís Cabré rightfully acclaim as mainstay of Torroella's artistry. As a detailed study will bear out, Moner's art of the compendium is the ultimate epitome of deft assimilation. Moner carries out the process of assimilation to the point of effacing all vestiges of his sources, such vestiges as are exemplified by the direct quotations that crop up in Torroella's brand of *ausiasmarquismo* and bilingualism.[34]

At the same time, we cannot but observe that Moner's introversion, accompanied by the pessimistic mood that pervades his writings, is hardly conducive to easy contact with and response from the members of the cultured class. These members, it bears reminding ourselves, constituted the staunch devotees of the *cancioneros*. The posture of aloofness maintained by Moner's poetic persona does not invite, at first reading, a reaction of sympathy and strong interest. On occasion, that persona adopts a standoffish attitude that may actually keep a prospective reader at bay. Such is the case of the very last stanza of *Sepultura d'amor*, an unsavory passage, in which the first-person speaker, the alter ego of the author himself, deems appropriate to vent some rather sullen sentiments. These are addressed to anyone inclined to come too close. Here are the harsh words that a reader may well find hard to take:

> Con esta missa acabada
> son accabadas las bodas
> de my vida.

---

[34] For a close look at Moner's compendium see Cocozzella, *Fra Francesc Moner's Bilingual Poetics*, 137–38, 168.

De muchos fue p̈edada,
mas Manzilla sobre todas   755
    la ha plañida.
Si os paresçe qu'es pagada . . .
no me doy que no's deys nada!
Y, en fin, d'aquý enmudesco
    para syempre.   760
Mi muerte es bien empleada:
yo tengo lo que meresco.
    Vuestro tempre
puede tirar do hos agrada.
(For the translation see p. 208 below.)

Evidently, Moner, for reasons of his own, is not moved by the spirit of *captatio benevolentiae*, and, he is, definitively, not inclined to curry anyone's favors.

Another factor that could hardly ingratiate Moner to the readers of his time, members of the high society, is the "forma cetrina" (sour style) (*Sepultura*, v. 35), an expression Moner uses to designate what he himself considers the salient characteristic of his poetic diction. Moner's unapologetic acknowledgment of his less-than-mellifluous style may be linked directly to March's matter-of-fact attitude toward what March himself recognizes as lack of "bella eloquença" (beautiful eloquence) in his own poetry. Implicit in Moner's unabashed coming to terms with the "forma cetrina" is the effect that March ascribes broadly to his own style: "l'orella d'hom afalac no pot rebre" (the human ear will hardly get any flattering sound) (see Poem 62, vv. 35–36).[35] Evidently, neither March nor Moner can boast of the elegant and refined turn of phrase that popularized poets like El Comendador Escrivá, Guevara, Garci Sánchez de Badajoz, Nicolás Núñez, Suero de Ribera, and Pere Torroella himself, among others, and won for them a special niche in the *Cancionero general*. What saves the day for Moner is precisely the "forma cetrina," which, inadequate as it was for the rarefied ambiance of the *cancioneros*, may well prove to be quite attractive to the denizens of the everyday world and especially to the reader of our own day and age. The "forma cetrina" turns out to be the perfect vehicle for the special dramatic verve with which Moner endows a masterpiece like *Sepultura d'amor*.

The Editor, the Publisher, and the Sponsor

A word is in order about the significance of Barutell's editorial work. The following statement, which consists of the opening sentence in Barutell's foreword already mentioned, attests to his invaluable contribution:

---

[35] For a full discussion of Moner's "forma centrina" and March's counterpart, see pp. 37–41 below.

Las obras de Moner, primo hermano que fue mío, como yo mejor las he podido haver a mis manos, he acordado, my illustre señor, de poner por orden, y enmendallas, y hazer que se imprimiessen (Barutell, 229; Most illustrious Lord, I have taken measures to put in order, emend, and make ready for publication the works of Moner, who was a cousin of mine, the best way I could manage to get a hold of them).

Here Barutell gives us a glimpse of his crucial undertaking: the careful preparation of a manuscript, which would be printed as the *editio princeps* of 1528. The manuscript would contain as complete a compilation as possible of Moner's extant works, collected from disparate sources. Barutell's avowed zeal in gathering his cousin's works pays off in the preservation of such pieces as *Obra en metro* and *Coplas hechas a ruego de Cartagena*. These and some shorter compositions in Castilian, besides all the short prose works in Catalan, do not figure in Vaticanus Latinus 4802, the fifteenth-century codex, oldest extant primary source of Moner's production.[36]

Even without going into a minute textual analysis, which would be out of place within the limits of the present discussion, we can appreciate the solid textual evidence that only Barutell, thanks to his devoted efforts, can provide regarding Moner's "forma cetrina." We may consider, for instance, the love letters and the reproaches addressed to the ladylove, which in my edition of *Obres catalanes* bear the respective titles of *Cartes* and *Retrets a l'amada*.[37] In their unmitigated impassioned expressionism, both the *Cartes* and the *Retrets* reflect the dark side of Moner's introversion. Their *cetrina* mode (or "lemon-like tartness"), could not commend them to the refined taste of the *cancionero* readers in their author's lifetime.

Beyond the labor of love entailed in the preparation of the manuscript for the *editio princeps*, Barutell took special care to find an appropriate sponsor for that publication. He could not have come up with a better choice than the individual, whose name is inscribed in the dedication of the *editio princeps*. This beautiful book eventually saw the light of day in the prestigious establishment of Carlos Amorós (Barcelona 1528).[38] The dedication appears as a rubric at the heading of Barutell's foreword:

Carta de Miguel Berenguer de Barutell dirigida y endreçada al muy illustre señor don Hernando Folch, duque de Cardona y marqués de Pallás, etc. para el fin que en ella se contiene (A1–A2; Letter by Miguel Berenguer de Barutell, addressed to the most illustrious Lord, Don Hernando

---

[36] For a complete list of the works missing in Vaticanus Latinus 4802 see Cocozzella, *1 Introducción*, 73.

[37] See *Oc*, 99–111, and 113–19, respectively.

[38] For a full description of this all-important publication see Cocozzella, Introducció, 86–90, and *1 Introducción*, 65–69.

Folch, Duke of Cardona and Marquis de Pallars, etc. for the purpose stated therein).

The Castilianized "Hernando" belongs to Ferran de Cardona i Enríquez, second Duke of Cardona, who must have been very young when Moner got to know him, if Moner knew him at all. Ferran was the grandson of Count Joan Ramon Folch III and son of Joan Ramon Folch IV, the first Duke of Cardona. Moner, of course, was well acquainted with the two renowned noblemen, having joined the military forces led by the Count and having lived in the household of the Duke. As for Hernando or Ferran, it is reasonable to believe that he subsidized, at least in part, the handsome publication of 1528.

Of particular interest is the collaboration between the Duke and Barutell insofar as it foreshadows the collaboration in the early 1540s between another prominent Cardona (Ferran Folch de Cardona i d'Anglasola)[39] and a certain Pere Vilasaló, expert collector of manuscripts. At the behest and with the full sponsorship of this Ferran Folch, Vilasaló put together the two collections of poems that in 1543 were printed by the aforementioned Carles Amorós as, respectively, the first and second edition of the complete works of none other than Ausiàs March (Martos, "La restauración de las obras de Ausiàs March," 416–17).

In short, it is instructive to focus on two different manifestations of the triad: compiler of manuscripts, publisher, and sponsor. They both occurred in Barcelona in the establishment of Carles Amorós. The two events consisted of Moner's *editio princeps* of 1528 and the first two editions of March's poems in 1543. The parallelism highlights in each case the significance of the compiler's remarkable efforts to preserve, to the largest extent possible, the completeness and integrity of the literary production of each of the two writers in question. We may count on Barutell's resounding success in providing us sufficient documentation of his cousin's bilingualism. By the same token, Vilasaló's expertise allows us to reflect on the affinity between Moner's "forma cetrina" and March's lack of "bella eloqüença."

In the pages that follow we will explore the implications of that affinity especially in terms of the modes of parody and theatricality.

Of Mass and *Misa*:
Parodic Mutations / Conversion into a Spectacle

Before attending to the specific issues of parody and theatricality, a word is in order about the role that the Mass in particular and the liturgy in general played in the birth of Spanish theater. For a start, O. B. Hardison (*Christian Rite and*

---

[39] This member of a different branch of the Duke's family held the high post of Admiral and Viceroy of Naples.

Christian Drama in the Middle Ages) provides a solid theory concerning the centrality of the Eucharistic service during the embryonic phase of the European medieval theater. Hardison posits the theatricality of the Mass on the basis of the allegorized interpretation of the ritual as spelled out in the influential treatises of Amalarius, the distinguished German bishop of the Carolingian era.[40] Current scholarship reveals significant developments beyond the strict Amalarian purview on the dramatics of the Eucharistic ceremonies. Two notable cases in point are the landmark publications by Max Harris (*Sacred Folly*) and Pedro Manuel Cátedra (*Liturgia, poesía y teatro en la edad media*). Harris and Cátedra demonstrate that the developments in question are the fruits of, to use a colloquialism, an "inside job." What this means is that, in view of the abundant evidence adduced by these two scholars, we need look no further than inside the ecclesiastic community, made up of clergymen and parishioners alike, for the conditions that, at least in regard to France and Spain, fostered, throughout the Middle Ages, the gestation and growth of a full-fledged theater outside the Graeco-Roman tradition. Harris scrutinizes a daunting number of documents that attest to the festive celebrations — commonly known as the Feast of Fools — in vogue in various French cathedrals during the long period stretching from the twelfth to the sixteenth century. Harris would not have us forget that, though including what he calls "sporting or jocular entertainment" (115) and "popular recreation" (188), the Feast of Fools, inextricably linked to the Christmas season, invariably carried out to full effect a meticulously planned spectacle and a well-executed intention to enhance rather than disgrace in any way the Christmas liturgy.[41] In much the same vein, Cátedra calls attention to paraliturgical practices in vogue in the Castilian domain during the fifteenth century. Among the evidence he adduces, of special interest are some lyrical religious poems he has recently discovered. These compositions, imbued with unimpeachable devotional fervor, deal with the central motifs of the Christmas cycle. Cátedra is no less emphatic than is Harris in arguing that the lyrics he analyzes bear witness to an edifying

---

[40] O. B. Hardison, Jr., *Christian Rite and Christian Drama in the Middle Ages: Essays in the Origin and Early History of Modern Drama* (Baltimore: Johns Hopkins Press, 1965) provides the following sketch of the career of Amalarius, bishop of Metz (780?–850):

A prominent figure at the courts of Charlemagne and Louis the Pious, an ambassador to Constantinople, and a lifelong student of the liturgy, Amalarius wrote two, and perhaps three, interpretations of the Mass. The first is the *Eclogae de ordine Romano* (814), and the most influential is the *Liber officialis*, which Amalarius saw through three editions between 821 and 835 (37).

[41] Paraliturgical practices, analogous and roughly contemporary to the ones described by Harris, are reviewed in Alberto del Campo Tejedor's essay focused on various examples of dubious entertainment in vogue among the Spanish clergy ("Diversiones clericales burlescas en los siglos xiii a xvi: Las misas nuevas," *La corónica* 38, no. 1 [Fall 2009]: 55–95).

process: indeed, they prove to be adaptable to the best spectacular aspects of the Christmas liturgy and ultimately achieve the overall effect of accentuating rather than attenuating the reverential demeanor demanded by the circumstances and the very nature of the religious event.

In short, the findings adduced and the concomitant argumentation expounded by Hardison, Harris, and Cátedra, define the type of dramaturgy that conditions the birth of European theater in general and its Spanish manifestation in particular. At the heart of the contribution of these three scholars lies, as a well-established principle, the proposition that the liturgy served as a matrix for the European and Spanish theater in question. Interestingly enough, the three scholars coincide in echoing the theory of Manuel Cañete, the nineteenth-century Spanish critic, who asserted, categorically, "[el teatro] nació en el seno de la religión" (theater was born in the womb of religion) (quoted in López Morales, *Tradición y creación en los orígenes del teatro castellano*, 35).[42]

In the following pages I intend to refocus the discussion on the origins of Spanish medieval theater in order to deal squarely with the factors that determine the transition from ritual in Amalarius's sense of the term to a de-ritualized representation on stage. I embark on a trail of research blazed by a handful of scholars—Andrée Crabbé Rocha, Josep Lluís Sirera, Charlotte Stern, Ronald Surtz, among others—who have developed a keen sense of appreciation for the dramatic function illustrated in some representative texts of the ubiquitous *cancioneros*. The texts in question include four complete specimens and one fragment of the parody of the Mass, the so-called *misa de amores*, besides three kindred poems, which will be identified in the course of this study.

There is something to be said about the refocusing proposed here. In this operation the unconventional use of the *cancioneros* as a source of dramatic literature goes hand in hand with a sharp deviation from the traditional approach to that literature. The deviation consists of the radical shift from the liturgical cycle to the essential paradigm of the ritual—the Eucharistc ritual, to be precise. Contrary to the conventional contextualization of the nascent theater within the yearly celebrations of the main religious holidays, the shift betokens a concentration on the de-ritualization pertaining to a few parodic renditions of the Mass. The de-ritualization entails a withdrawal from the sacred realm of the religious ceremony, whereas the parody plays out its mimetic function that mirrors that ceremony but harbors no intention of mocking it. This noncomedic notion of

---

[42] It is fair to take into account the contrary viewpoint of Adolfo Bonilla y San Martín, another influential critic, who, in a notable study of his own published in 1921, defended, in López Morales's words, "fortalecida documentalmente la teoría del origen juglaresco" (35; the well documented theory of the origins from the jongleurs). Needless to say, Bonilla is partial to the proposition that the pagan theater, especially of the type created by Plautus and Terence, continued, uninterrupted, well into the Middle Ages.

parody stems essentially from Linda Hutcheon's landmark publication on the subject (*A Theory of Parody*).

There are, demonstrably, fresh insights in store in the reevaluation of the mechanics of a type of allegory that is a byproduct of Moner's esthetics of desacralization and parody. Also, there is the prospect of recovering some dramatic texts hitherto not recognized as such. As I hope to show, these texts are fully theatricalized by the creation of not only a plot through a monologue but also a stage through the spatiality of what I propose to call the dark chamber.

The monologue and the dark chamber constitute the constituents of a dramaturgy that Henry Ansgar Kelly, in his studies on medieval theater (*Ideas and Forms of Tragedy* and *Chaucerian Tragedy*, for example), traces back to Isidore of Seville and identifies as "dumbshow with voice-over" (*Chaucerian Tragedy*, 16). I submit that a compelling example of this Isidorian articulation of declamation and pantomime is found in Fra Francesc Moner's *Sepultura d'amor*, arguably the most complex composition of its kind, which displays an ingenious elaboration on the fundamental dynamics and core motifs of the Isidorian idea of a theater.

As we have indicated, the most intriguing aspect of this *Sepultura* resides in the assertion of the supremacy of Truth far above the universal hierarchy of created beings. In fact, the Supreme Being invoked in *Sepultura* is, as we have seen, God-the-Truth. It is the creative attribute of the Divinity of Truth that impels the unfolding of the poem's plot at two levels: one covert, the other overt. The former, which operates at the deepest layer of parody, illustrates the mystery of redemption through the sacramental display of the primordial transubstantiation — that of bread and wine. The latter level, which evinces the highly visible surface of the dramatic action, enacts the phenomenology of the vindication of the true lover. It illustrates, in other words, the virtual canonization of the auctorial persona, portrayed as the exemplary *mártir de amor* (martyr of love).

Inherent in the study of Moner's *Sepultura* is the challenge of recognizing the complementary interaction between the double-layered plot structured in accordance with the mechanics of parody and the distribution of dramatic action into a tripartite locus of performance. The three sections in this field of enactment may be identified as (1) the dark chamber, (2) the pulpit, and (3) the altar.

The nature of the dark chamber is consistent with the data provided by scholars like Mary Marshall, Joseph R. Jones, and the aforementioned Kelly in their research on the widespread influence of Isidore's observations on European theater of the Middle Ages. As Kelly points out, the visual details of the chamber are patterned after either the interpretation of some leading glossator of Isidore's text or the application of the interpretation to some venerable *auctoritas* like Plautus, Terence, and Seneca (Kelly, *Chaucerian Tragedy*, 11–25). On the basis of Kelly's and Jones's findings, I propose for Moner's *Sepultura* a dark chamber as a place in which the monologue originates and is played out. Inside or near that place, we hear steadily or watch intermittently the protagonist — that is, Moner's poetic persona — deliver in the voice-over the expression of a multifarious soliloquy, which encompasses complaints, reproaches, and, above all, a declaimed narrative.

The pulpit and the altar, the other two sections of the theatrical space in Moner's *Sepultura*, are the bailiwicks of, respectively, Experiencia (Lady Experience), the sermonizer, and Mancilla (Lady Compassion), the chief celebrant. Through the unfolding of the eponymous allegory (the impersonation, that is, of experience into Experiencia), what occurs on the pulpit is the preacher's attempt to display the principal strains of the phenomenology of love. In the final analysis, Experiencia, in her oratory, presents herself as the complementary "other" to Lady Reason, whose glaring absence she capitalizes upon, and whose supremacy she ultimately usurps. Not surprisingly, the a-rational or pseudo-rational sermon of Experiencia plays out the crisis of a rationalistic notion of human existence and ends up giving birth to a theatricalized cathartic purge of noxious emotions. She shows, perhaps unwittingly, how the lover can be relieved of the vehemence of his passions, especially the ones manifested in fits of misogynous rage.

At the altar, Mancilla picks up where Experiencia leaves off on the pulpit. But, rather than relying, as does Experiencia, on a rationalistic method *manqué*, Mancilla changes course completely. By overriding Experiencia's pseudoratiocination, Mancilla sets in operation an unusual but convincing consummation of a process that in Experiencia's sermon is beginning to show signs of going awry. Ipso facto, Mancilla reinvents the Eucharistic ritual by humanizing it considerably. Mancilla employs her sacerdotal powers, to effect a double mutation: (1) the conversion of the life of the true lover into what I propose to call a "life-text," and (2) the transubstantiation of that text into the existential correlative of the Gospel. In other words, Mancilla first objectifies a life experience into a literary icon, an emblematic *canción*, to be exact. Then, proceeding to a second momentous step in her hieratic ministrations, she ushers in an imaginative rendition of *imitatio Christi* and brings about the wondrous metamorphosis of that experience into a surrogate of Sacred Scripture.

Overview

It is now time to conduct a survey of the argumentation expounded in the present monograph. By calling attention to the nature of the dramatic monologue, I embark upon tracing the course of its evolution. The monologue's gestation occurs in the corpus of the *cancioneros* and kindred love-centered literature of the fifteenth century in the domain of both Castilian and Catalan. Such literature encompasses Ausiàs March's poetry and some passages derived from the *novela sentimental*. My study brings to light some notable specimens of the fullfledged prototypical monologue. These include Garci Sánchez's *Sueño*, Escrivá's *Querella*, Corella's *Tragèdia*, and four of Moner's compositions: *Obra en metro*, *Momería*, *Sepultura d'amor*, and *La noche*.

The works here listed provide ample evidence of the properties of the dramatic monologue. They exhibit, for instance, a remarkable flexibility of composition, which subsumes the functions of the dialogue and the narrative. The process of assimilation is at play especially in Moner's *Sepultura*, which conflates the *infierno de los enamorados* and the liturgical or paraliturgical components of the Mass. We have a great deal to learn from a study of the esthetics of two pieces: *Obra en metro* (an icon of introspection à la Ausiàs March) and *La noche* (a powerful testimony of the ultimate achievement of Moner's flair for the theater). I invite the reader to contemplate in the monologue not only the comprehensive design and assimilative capability we have already touched upon but also the modes of complexity and adaptability that remain to be analyzed. The exploration I propose extends to the phenomenology of the transition from ritual to theater. The subject remains uncharted territory in the history of Spanish theater of the Middle Ages. As I intend to demonstrate, a close reading of Moner's *Momería* yields some insights into the role of the monologue in the furtherance of that transition. Demonstrably, Moner's *Momería* falls in the mainstream of an age-old tradition that harks back to Isidore of Seville. It is the very tradition that thrived in the wide currency that Isidore's idea of a theater, described in some crucial passages of his *Etymologies*, attained throughout the Middle Ages. A switch in focus from *Momería* to Moner's handling of the *misa de amores* reveals how the "Isidorian model" is adapted to a process of desacralization. That process, in turn, illustrates Moner's creative meditation and elaboration on religious parody.

Next, I shall highlight the issues I am about to discuss in detail. The generic properties of Moner's *Sepultura* situate it clearly in the realm of the *cancioneros*. There is plenty of evidence of the poem's hybrid nature: one that shows traits stemming from two different genetic lines. These are the *infierno de los enamorados* and the *misa de amores*. Chapter 1 offers an extensive analysis of the atmosphere of gloom and the pervasive sense of alienation that betoken in Moner's composition a remarkable affinity with the main exponents of the two lines in question. Here I initiate a study that takes into account most of the extant texts of the *infierno* and all those of the *misa*.

In chapter 2, I intend to provide the guideposts for a well-informed reading of Moner's *Sepultura*. The basic distinction between *extra ecclesiam* and *intra ecclesiam* spatiality reflects the contrast between the nebulous region, the primary domain of the monologue, and the well-lit setting, the locus of the plot of the *misa* proper. Through the bare-bones exposition of that plot we may recognize three main phases of intense dramatic action. These phases are reviewed in detail. By the same token, we may detect the emergence of a leitmotif and the primary signs of the symbolic and allegorical infrastructure of the *sepultura-misa* composite.

In chapter 3, the general scope of the preceding discussion on the *infiernos, sepulturas, misas* and the like gives way to a narrow focus on the specific principles that have to do with the demarcation of the inner theater of the psyche. The indices of psychic space condition the lover's mournful expression, which, in turn, is the breeding ground for the all-important motifs of *psychomachia* (the inner conflict among the emotions), the "hall of mirrors" (the proliferation of passions), and the *ensimismamiento* (the withdrawal into the self). A review of these motifs is proffered as a way of profiling Moner's flair for drama, highlighted by contrasting his style with that of a group of distinguished writers. These include not only other representative figures of the *cancioneros*—Guevara, Pere Torroella, Pedro de Cartagena, for example—but also authors like Juan Rodríguez del Padrón and Diego de San Pedro, masters of the *novela sentimental*. The comparative analysis conducted in this chapter touches on the esthetic of nuanced writing (*letras matizadas*) and rough or plain language (*forma cetrina*). The esthetic is formulated as a vehicle of profound respect for truth: a reverential attitude that Moner ultimately turns into a veritable worship rendered to Verdad (God-the-Truth). What the analysis reveals is that said esthetic, which harks back to the troubadour Marcabru, is primarily an indicator of Moner's indebtedness to his predecessor and soul mate, Ausiàs March.

The next step in our attempt to come to grips with Moner's ideal of a theater is to envision a metaphysical perspective, from which we are able to perceive how the author's truth-oriented rhetoric resonates in unison with March's "mighty line" and does so within a "field of immanence." Still another step and we realize how the monologue conceived in the domain of immanence thrives in the potential of acoustic reverberation, ready to be projected onto a stage.

In chapter 4, I draw a connection between that perspective and the mind-set of the personage that Fernando de Rojas in his famous *Tragicomedia* identifies as "doctor varón." The dispassionate (stoic) position of Rojas's *docto varón* allows us to appreciate the full consequence of Moner's *forma cetrina*. We realize that the *forma* is the perfect vehicle for fathoming the depths of the monologue. With that realization, we gain an insight into the way Moner theatricalizes the phenomenology of the "split self" pertaining to the text of subjectivity.

Quite evident in *Sepultura d'amor* is the process of desacralization. This feature of Moner's artistry is the focus of chapter 5. Here we see how that process plays out in the way the author translates the ritual of the Mass into human terms. We contemplate the stellar performance of one of the celebrants: Experiencia (Lady Experience) takes center stage and carries out her duties as preacher by delivering her prolonged, tripartite sermon. She humanizes the sacred ceremony by expatiating upon two passages: those that constitute a reinvention of the Epistle (vv. 237–47) and the Gospel (vv. 251–89). She is less than successful in what one might consider the foremost pursuit of her oratory: the exposition of a comprehensive theory on the nature of love. In the long run, reasoned argumentation eludes the sermonizer, but she makes up for her shortcoming by a demonstration of great expertise in channeling her emotional energy to an effective cathartic outcome. In addition, her homily demonstrates an admirable skill in intuiting the climactic phase of "dead-man-talking." In that phase, Experiencia rewards us with a rare insight into desacralized or de-ritualized sacramentality.

Chapter 6 is focused on the unfolding of the transition from ritual to theater. The transition takes effect in the middle ground between unadulterated ritual and utter secularization. Here Moner's *Sepultura* is presented as an exemplary illustration of an intermediate status in the mutation of the sacred ceremony of the Mass. Hutcheon's theory on parody sheds light on that mutation by highlighting three main esthetic operations (a) the mechanics of superimposition, in which the sacred and the profane coexist at different levels of the text; (b) the fashioning of an allegory that reflects in the priestly office, embodied in the figure of the idealized ladylove, a symbiosis between human compassion and divine mercy; (c) a notion of sacramentality stemming from a surrogate transubstantiation, to wit, a conversion of an iconic *cancionero* poem into a scriptural substitute (an analogue of the Gospel).

Chapter 7 is taken up with the discussion of a certain type of courtly entertainment that involves choreographed performance and the use of curious costumes that display emblematic fixtures or devices, more often than not inscribed with epigrammatic statements in verse form. These versified aphorisms, which go by such names as *invención, mote, letra*, are genetically linked to the *canción*. In view of this kinship, Hispanists by and large regard the aforementioned shows of dance and curious accouterments as exemplars of a prototheatrical nature that stem directly from the *cancioneros*. Moner is no stranger to this embryonic theater. In fact, he contributes a rare specimen of a recitation-and-dance routine, entitled *Momería* (a mummery), a term which refers to a type of entertainment featuring mummers (*momos*). As one of very few extant texts of its kind, complete with stage directions and a description of special effects, this *Momería* is remarkable, indeed. Also, as it exhibits a full-fledged dramatization of the lover's monologue, *Momería* deserves special attention not only for its rarity but also because it represents a theatrical tradition, other than the one commonly included in the standard histories of Spanish literature of the Middle Ages and early Renaissance. I profile Moner's unconventional theater in reference to the thoroughly conventional counterpart, worthily championed by Juan del Encina, the widely acclaimed Spanish playwright of that period. In addition, chapter 7 shows how the data yielded by Cátedra's research complement Hutcheon's theory by contributing to an explanation as to the way Moner's *misa* develops into a representation on stage. According to Cátedra, that type of representation is an outgrowth of the ceremonial activities conducted within the confines of the temple (*intra ecclesiam*).

In chapter 8 the complexity of Moner's monologue (especially as manifested in *Momería*) is assessed in comparison with the French analogues studied by Jean-Claude Aubailly and with the few comparable samples found in Spanish balladry. In addition, a critique of Moner's achievement is supplemented with an excursion into the versions of the lover's monologue by three other Hispanic writers of the fifteenth century: Garci Sánchez de Badajoz, El Comendador Escrivá, and Joan Roís de Corella.

Chapter 9 segues with a step-by-step description of the evolution of the plot in an effort to not only take into account actions overtly represented but also recapture those details not explicitly mentioned in the text itself. In view of the type of spectacle evoked by Moner's *Sepultura*, the interpolation of musical and, for that matter, choreographic components is not hard to demonstrate. At issue is, also, the manner in which the dynamic interaction between Experiencia and Mancilla may be translated in terms of action dramatized on stage.

In chapter 10 we come to an unusual approach to the theatrical potential of a literary text such as Moner's *Sepultura*. The approach stems from the suggestive theories of Mary Carruthers concerning the manner in which the symbiosis between rhetorical and pictorial imagery comes to bear upon the creative imagination of European writers of the Middle Ages. We can rely on the insights of critics like Stephen G. Nichols, Jr., and Sol Miguel-Prendes, who, in the wake of Carruthers's landmark analysis, delve into the trope called ekphrasis and help us appreciate the primary significance of the visual arts in the gestation of a theatrical mode.

As shown in chapter 11, the visual dimension, which lies implicit in Moner's text, dovetails with the high point of Moner's innovative dramatics: the integration of the esthetic of the monologue derived from the *cancioneros* into the paradigmatic playacting that harks back to some crucial descriptions found in the *Etymologies* of Isidore of Seville. Arguably, Moner's *Momería*, an ingenious interplay between recitation or declamation in a small dark enclosure and silent pantomime on the open stage, constitutes a rare, if not unique, documentation of the adaptation of the monologue to the Isidorian stage.

Moner is quite capable of expanding that adaptation into the spectacular proportions of a full-blown allegory. In fact, as I expect to demonstrate, a close study of Moner's allegorized Mass holds in store the discovery of the kind of sacramentality inherent in the author's own experimentation with the desacralization and humanization of the Eucharistic ritual. How does Moner's notion of sacramentality make for an outstanding contribution to the early history of Spanish theater? This is the ultimate question I shall address in the closing section (chapter 12) of the present study.

Text and Translation

The text transcribed in the appendices (pp. 173–94 and 209–11 below) is that of *Sepultura d'amor* and *Momería* in my critical edition (see, respectively, *2 OC*, 131–94 and *1 OC*, 153–63). The reader may find helpful the abundant notes that complement that edition. On this occasion I keep the notes to the barest minimum. The primary aim of my translation is to capture the spirit of the down-to-earth manner that Moner himself calls "forma cetrina" (see pp. 39–41 below). Needless to say, in my search for the suitable English idiom, I have become keenly aware of the challenge posed by the interpretation of *cancionero* poetry in general and Moner's diction in particular. No need to belabor the arduousness of an interpretive task that has been lucidly described by Hispanists like Deyermond ("La micropoética de las invenciones"), Gerli,[43] Rico,[44] Surtz,[45] and Whinnom (*La poesía amatoria*, 47–62).[46] Downright daunting is that task in view of the impenetrable conceits embedded in some emblematic texts (primarily *letras*, *motes*, *invenciones* and, secondarily, entire *canciones*), such as the ones sampled

---

[43] Gerli discloses a wide range of connotations emanating from a very short and apparently simple poem by El Comendador Escrivá and concludes his lucid commentary with the following observation about *cancionero* poetry in general:

En la composición más mínima, se establecen redes de significación y se forjan vínculos de relaciones ingeniosas entre las cosas, muchas veces ocultas a la mentalidad moderna por su intencionada ambigüedad, los temas, y los asuntos más variados. "Lo mejor de la poesía de cancioneros está en las poesías breves," como observa Keith Whinnom [*La poesía amatoria de la época de los Reyes Católicos*, 84], y no conviene nunca rechazarla como trivial (*"Fue la caza d'este día:* De unicornios y otras especies," 114; In the most minuscule composition networks of signification are set up and ingenious links of relationships are created among a variety of things —relationships often hidden to the modern mentality because of their intentional ambiguity, their themes, and their varied subjects. *The best of* cancionero *poetry resides in the short poems*, observes Keith Whinnom, and should never be rejected as trivial).

[44] Francisco Rico, *Texto y contextos: estudios sobre la poesía española del siglo XV* (Barcelona: Editorial Crítica, 1990). In the chapter entitled "Un penacho de penas: de algunas invenciones y letras de caballeros" (189–227), Rico conducts a thorough review of the polysemic "pena" in various representative compositions of the *Cancionero general* and goes into a comparative analysis of analogous uses of the term in Portuguese, Italian, and French literature of the late Middle Ages or early Renaissance. In addition, Rico explores the cultural and social context that determined the persistence of said polysemy and the concomitant mode of the conceit in Spain well into the age of the baroque.

[45] In "Pus que demandat m'avets," a poem by the Valencian Jaume Escrivà, who flourished in the first half of the fifteenth century, Ronald Surtz discovers a consistent double-entendre stemming from the subtextual phallic symbolism of the word *ploma* (writing instrument) ("Jaume Escrivà and the Perils of Female Writing in Late Medieval Valencia," *Catalan Review* 26 (2012): 201–14). In the same essay Surtz transcribes the poem (211–12) and makes reference to the two manuscripts that contain respective variants of its primary text (213, n. 11).

[46] Whinnom provides a masterly explication of Diego de San Pedro's "El mayor bien de quereros," one of the most ingenious pieces in the *cancioneros*: see Whinnom, Introducción crítica 1979, 51–56. For the text of the poem, see San Pedro, *Poesías*, 258.

by Whinnom.[47] Those conceits are no different, of course, from the ones readily recognizable in *Sepultura*, *Momería*, and throughout Moner's production.[48]

Whinnom's cogent observations have served as guidelines and inspiration in my efforts to provide an accurate and readable English version of Moner's tour de force. As for Moner's counterparts of those "letras. . .casi indescifrables" (*letras* almost indecipherable) adduced by Whinnom (*La poesía amatoria*, 48), I would refer the reader to my explanatory notes.

---

[47] Following are the essential definitions that Whinnom provides for the technical terminology he uses:

La letra, invención o letra de invención—los términos son equivalentes—consta de dos o de tres versos, yo octosílabos simplemente, o bien octosílabos con un verso de pie quebrado. Tienen la particularidad de que la gran mayoría eran divisas que se llevaban bordadas o grabadas en la ropa o en las armas, por ejemplo en el casco o en la vaina de la espada, y muchas veces aludían al objeto o a su color. Aunque se puede sospechar que existe cierta confusión en la terminología, un mote que tiene tal referencia externa se califica de "letra" (47; The *letra*, *invención* or *letra de invención* —the terms are interchangeable—consists of two or three verses, either all octosyl-llables or octosyllables in combination with a tetrasyllable. The characteristic of these patterns is that, for the most part, they were designs worn either embroidered on clothes or etched into pieces of armor: for example, the headgear or the sheath of a sword. Often these designs represented an object and the color of that object. Although, as one may well expect, there is some confusion as to the meaning of these terms, a *mote* that refers to a particular object is considered a *letra*).

[48] In his comments on the genetics of the *canción* of the end of the fifteenth century, Whinnom alludes to the preponderance of the conceit in terms of the object of a veritable cult ("culto del concepto"). "Conceptismo" is quite common in the critical parlance relative to Spanish literature of the seventeenth century. In borrowing the term for his own purpose, Whinnom makes sure to draw the necessary distinctions:

Aunque no sea exactamente lo mismo que el conceptismo del XVII, no veo incon-veniente en hablar del conceptismo de la poesía de esta época, conceptismo que se basa, más en las relaciones ocultas entre las cosas—perlas, rocío, lágrimas, pelo, trigo—en la paradoja, en la ambigüedad y el doble sentido, en la referencia oblicua, en el decir callando y en el simple juego de palabras (*La poesía amatoria*, 4; Even though it is not exactly identical to the *conceptismo* of the seventeenth century, I do not consider it untoward to speak of the *conceptismo* of the poetry of this period [the end of the fifteenth century]. The latter is based not so much on the hidden relationship among various things—pearls, dew, tears, hair, gold, wheat—as in the paradox, ambiguous speech, double-entendre, or in the oblique reference, in the technique of speaking while remaining silent, or in word-play pure and simple).

I.
THE *CANCIONERO* BACKGROUND

A *Misa* in a *Sepultura*

Ours is a journey back in time that takes us to the love-centered poetry in vogue throughout the fifteenth century in the three linguistic domains (Castilian, Catalan, Galician-Portuguese) of the Iberian Peninsula. We are struck by the numerous specimens of the Castilian *canción*, the relatively short lyrical piece, descendant of the Provençal *canso*. The *canción* lends its name to the *cancionero*, the type of anthology that found widespread dissemination both in manuscript and printed form.[1] The numerous exemplars of the *cancionero* and its counterparts in the Catalan *cançoner* and Galician-Portuguese *cancioneiro* attest to the exuberant survival of the troubadour tradition in the Peninsula well beyond the heyday of troubadour poetry (Boase).[2] The *canción* is not the sole component of

---

[1] This is what Keith Whinnom has to say about the diffusion of the *cancioneros*: [Q]uisiera llamar la atención sobre la prodigiosa cantidad de poesía cancioneril que existe. Estamos ante una explosión creativa verdaderamente pasmosa (Whinnom, *Poesía amatoria*, 18; I should like to call attention to the prodigious amount of extant *cancionero* poetry. We are faced with a truly impressive explosion of creativity).
Later he adds:
Más concretamente, estamos ante la obra de más de setecientos poetas, cifra que supera, con mucha diferencia, a cualquiera que se podría aducir para las demás literaturas europeas de esta época (*Poesía amatoria*, 91, n. 20; Specifically, we are faced with the literary production of more than seven hundred poets, a total that surpasses by far any other amount that one may adduce apropos of the other European literatures of the same period).

[2] In the twenty-first century, students of Spanish poetry of the fifteenth century have at their disposal a rich menu of resources. Roger Boase, *The Troubadour Revival: A Study of Social Change and Traditionalism in Late Medieval Spain* (London: Routledge & Kegan Paul, 1978) and Keith Whinnom, *La poesía amatoria de la época de los Reyes Católicos* (Durham, UK: University of Durham, 1981) offer an informative introduction. There are magnificent editions of the monumental collections: J. M. Azáceta, ed., *Cancionero de Juan Alfonso de Baena*. 3 vols. (Madrid: Consejo Superior de Investigaciones

Científicas, 1966); Nicasio Salvador Miguel, ed., *Cancionero de Estúñiga* (Madrid: Editorial Alhambra, 1987); Brian Dutton, ed., *El cancionero del siglo XV: c. 1380–1520*. 7 vols. (Salamanca: Universidad de Salamanca, 1990–91); and Joaquín González Cuenca, ed., *Cancionero general [de Hernando del Castillo]*. 5 vols. (Madrid: Castalia, 2004). In *El cancionero del siglo XV: c. 1380–1520* and *Catálogo-índice de la poesía cancioneril del siglo XV*. 2 vols. (Madison, WI: Hispanic Seminary of Medieval Studies, 1982) Dutton and his team have devised indispensable tools of research for the budding and the seasoned scholar. Handy anthologies, such as José María Azáceta, ed., *Poesía cancioneril* (Barcelona: Plaza y Janés, 1984); Vicenç Beltrán, *Poesía, escriptura i societat: els camins de March* (Castelló–Barcelona: Publicacions de l'Abadia de Montserrat, 2006); E. Michael Gerli, *Poesía cancioneril castellana* (Madrid: Ediciones Alkal, 1994. 3–34); not to mention Brian Dutton and Victoriano Roncero López, eds., *La poesía cancioneril del siglo xv: Antología y estudio* (Madrid-Frankfurt: Iberoamericana-Vervuert, 2004); and Giovanni Caravaggi, Monika von Wunster, and Giovanni Mazzocchi, eds., *Poeti cancioneriles del sec. XV* (L'Aquila-Roma: Japadre, 1986) contain representative selections from numerous sources (in addition to the main *cancioneros* already mentioned). For a fruitful engagement with this bumper crop of *cancionero* poetry, we are indebted to such studies as Vicenç Beltrán, *La canción de amor en el otoño de la Edad Media* (Barcelona: PPU, 1988); and the respective monographs by Charles Fraker, *Studies on the Cancionero de Baena* (Chapel Hill: University of North Carolina Press, 1966); Pierre Le Gentil, *La poesie lyrique espagnole et portugaise a la fin du moyen age. Première partie: les thèmes et les genres. Deuxième partie: les formes*. 2 vols. (Rennes: Plihon Editeur, 1949, 1952); María Isabel Toro Pascua, *El arte de la poesía: el Cancionero (Teoría e ideas sobre la poesía en los siglos XV y XVI)* (Salamanca: SEMYR, 1999); and Julian Weiss, *The Poet's Art: Literary Theory in Castile c. 1400–60*, Medium Aevum Monographs 14 (Oxford: Society for the Study of Mediaeval Languages and Literatures, 1990), besides the various collections of essays, such as: E. Michael Gerli and Julian Weiss, eds. *Poetry at Court in Trastamaran Spain: from the "Cancionero de Baena" to the "Cancionero General,"* MRTS 181 (Tempe, AZ: ACMRS, 1998); Marta Haro Cortés, Rafael Beltrán, José Luis Canet, and Héctor H. Gassó, eds., *Estudios sobre el Cancionero General (Valencia, 1511): Poesía, manuscrito e imprenta*, 2 vols. (Universitat de València: Publicacions de la Universitat de València, 2012); Andrea Baldissera, and Giuseppe Mazzocchi, eds., *I canzonieri di Lucrezia. Los cancioneros de Lucrecia. Atti del convegno internazionale sulle raccolte poetiche iberiche dei secoli XV–XVII* (Padua: Unipress, 2005); and J. Casas Rigall and E. Ma Díaz Martínez, eds., *Iberia cantat Estudios sobre poesía hispánica medieval* (Santiago de Compostela, 2002). We would be remiss if we did not mention here the admirable scholarly production of Vincenç Beltran, who, in his pioneering work, is wont to open new paths of research on the *cancioneros*. For some key examples of the Catalan counterparts of the Castilian *cancioneros*, see: Mariano Baselga, ed., *El cancionero catalán de la Universidad de Zaragoza* (Zaragoza: Cecilio Gasca, 1896); and Ramon Aramon i Serra, ed., *Cançoner dels Masdovelles (Manuscrit n. 11 de la Biblioteca de Catalunya)* (Barcelona: Institut d'Estudis Catalans, 1938). Of special interest is Sergi Gascon, *Jardinet d'Orats: Barcelona, Biblioteca de la Universitat, ms. 151* (Bellaterra: Universitat Autònoma de Barcelona; Fundació "La Caixa," 1998). See, also, Jaume Torró i Torrent, "El ms. 151 de la Biblioteca Universitària de Barcelona (*Jardinet de orats*): descripció i estudi codicològic," *Boletín bibliográfico de la Asociación Hispánica de*

the extant eponymous anthologies.[3] In fact, more often than not, it is accompanied by longer poems, identified by such disparate rubrics as "infierno" (hell), "purgatorio" (purgatory), "sepultura" (burial), "misa" (the ritual of the Mass), "batalla" (battle), each usually joined to a general designation of their subject matter, dealing with love ("de amor," "de amores") or with lovers ("de los amadores," "de los enamorados").[4]

Of primary significance in our excursion into the realm of the *cancioneros* is a poem that turns out to be one of the most complex and accomplished exemplars of its kind. In one of its basic texts (MS. Vaticanus Latinus 4802, ff.33–38v) this composition bears the title of *Sepultura d'amor*, precisely one of the rubrics we have just mentioned (Figure 1).[5] This *Sepultura* was written in

---

Literatura Medieval 6 (1992): 1–55. The *Jardinet* is a miscellaneous collection of poems and prose works by various authors (including *Tragèdia de Caldesa* by Corella) (Sergi Gascon, ed., *Jardinet d'Orats: Barcelona, Biblioteca de la Universitat, ms. 151*. Bellaterra: Universitat Autònoma de Barcelona; Fundació "La Caixa," 1998). The following is a select list representative of the current study of the *cançoners*: Robert Archer, "L'obra poética de Pere Joan de Masdovelles." *Els Marges* 49 (1994): 63–78; Viçens Beltran, *El cançoner de Joan Berenguer de Masdovelles* (Barcelona: Publicacions de l'Abadia de Montserrat, 2006); Marion Coderch, *Ausiàs March, les dones i l'amor* (València: Institució Alfons el Magnànim—Diputació de València, 2009); Francisco J. Rodríguez Risquete, "El cancionero de Lleonard de Sos," in *Actas del IX Congreso Internacional de la Asociación Hispánica de la Literatura Medieval (A Coruña, 18–22 de septiembre de 2001)*. 3 vols., ed. Mercedes Pampín Barral and M. Carmen Parrilla García (A Coruña: Universidade da Coruña: Departamento de Filoloxia Española e Latina—Toxosoutos, 2005), 3: 455–63; Francisco J. Rodríguez Risquete, "El *Cançoner de l'Ateneu*," in *Translatar i Transferir: La transmissió dels textos i el saber (1200–1500)*, ed. Anna Alberni, Lola Badia, and Lluís Cabré (Santa Coloma de Queralt: Universitat Rovira i Virgili, 2010), 425–67; and Jaume Torró i Torrent, "El *cançoner de Saragossa*," in Alberni, Badia, and Cabré, *Translatar i Transferir*, 379–423.

 [3] In view of the diverse content of these anthologies, Dorothy Sherman Severin finds the term "cancionero" inappropriate ("*Cancionero*: un género mal nombrado," *Cultura Neolatina* 54 (1994): 95–105).

 [4] Le Gentil groups and discusses these miscellaneous compositions under the general heading of "le dit d'amour" (*La poesie lyrique espagnole et portugaise a la fin du moyen age*, 1: 237–93).

 [5] For the editions and primary texts of Moner's works, see the bibliography below. A full description of Vaticanus Latinus 4802 (manuscript from the end of the fifteenth century or the beginning of the sixteenth) may be found in Cocozzella, Introducció, 91–92, and *1 Introducción*, 69–75. Indispensable for a study of this manuscript is the excellent analysis and critique by Vicent Martines Peres ("El còdex *Vaticanus Latinus 4802*: Els textos literaris de Moner a cavall de diverses edicions." *Studi e Testi* 396 [2000]: 215–41). For the fully edited text of *Sepultura d'amor*, see *2 OC*, 131–58. The poem consists of 764 verses, arranged in 57 stanzas. With few exceptions, the stanzas of 14 verses are of the type commonly known as *cobla de pie quebrado*, a combination of eight- and four-syllable

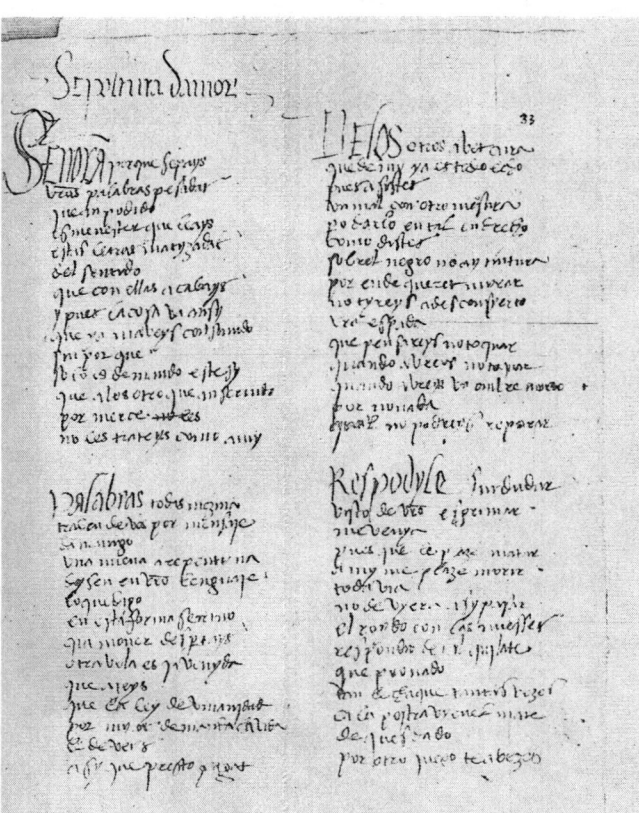

Figure 1. Title page of Moner's *Sepultura d'amor*, in MS. Vaticanus Latinus 4802, f. 33 (late fifteenth century).

Castilian, probably in the mid 1480s, by a Catalan author, a certain Fra Francesc Moner, who, as we have indicated, flourished in Barcelona during the two decades immediately following the marriage of Ferdinand of Aragon and Isabella of Castile in 1469.[6] In the context of Moner's extant *oeuvre*, consisting of seventy-four poems and prose works of varied lengths, *Sepultura* attests to the deft bilingualism of its author, who achieved a remarkable mastery of not only his native Catalan but also Castilian.[7] Here we cannot go into the vicissitudes of Moner's career and literary achievements in a period in which Castilian gained

verses (*octosílabos* and *tetrasílabos*). In *Sepultura*, the *cobla* in question has the following rhyme scheme: a(8) b(8) c(4) a(8) b(8) c(4) a(8) / d(8) e(8) f(4) d(8) e(8) f(4) d(8).

[6] For a biographical sketch of Moner, see pp. xvii–xx above.

[7] A broad critique of Moner's deft bilingualism may be found in Cocozzella, "Fray Francisco Moner: Bilingualism, Love, and Experience in Spanish PreRenaissance

ascendancy over the other national languages, Catalan included, within the new-born Spanish state. Instead, we will highlight his legacy precisely in terms of the stage-worthy textuality of *Sepultura*.

At this point a word is in order about a practical approach to the analysis of a text like *Sepultura*. It takes but a cursory reading to make us realize that a discussion of such a text in terms of a clear-cut definition of a genre is hardly feasible simply because, in view of the cultural circumstances in which Moner happened to live, the notion of "genre" is hard to pin down. There is, nevertheless, outside generic considerations, a firm ground from which to embark upon a fruitful exploration of said *Sepultura d'amor*. For a start, we may rely on the paradigm that emerges from comparing the poem to a number of analogous compositions well represented in those popular *cancioneros*.

A quick summary of the plot will help us adumbrate the paradigm in question. The plot of *Sepultura* reflects a surprising conceit that cannot fail to draw our attention. The protagonist, that is, the auctorial persona in the guise of a first-person narrator, portrays himself as a first-hand observer of his own funeral. He sees his inert body abandoned "en un campo de crueza" (in a field of cruelty) (v. 78). Two allegorical characters, Gentileza (Lady Gentility) and Mancilla (Lady Compassion) soon appear on the scene. Gentileza picks up the body, lays it on a shield, and carries it to a chapel, situated along the nave of a large church.[8] Mancilla, for her part, engages in an elaborate ceremony complete with a procession and a veritable dirge, full of praises for the deceased lover ("pues amaste a de veras" ['since you loved truly']) (v. 96) and reproaches for the ladylove ("o hermosura tan negra" ['o wretched beauty']) (v. 117). Soon afterwards, while Gentileza moves the body over to the space between the choir stalls and the main altar (vv. 135–36), Mancilla constructs, right next to the burial place of Amistad (Lady Friendship), an imposing sepulcher into which she enshrines the body of the lover in question (vv. 147–63). Thus, Mancilla concludes what turns out to be an introit of sorts for the main ceremony that is about to begin. What ensues is, as we will see immediately, the celebration of the funeral Mass.

Literature," and "Pere Torroella i Francesc Moner: aspectes del bilingüisme literari (cata-lano-castellà) a la segona meitat del segle XV" (see pp. xxvii–xxxiv above).

[8] Here is the passage in the original:

Vino por él Gentileza,
púsolo encima estendido
    d'un pavés
que l'enprestó la Simpleza.
Levólo en una capilla
que con fuego es consagrada
    d'afición.

(Vv. 81–87. For the translation, see p. 198 below.)

The Mass, which constitutes the bulk of Moner's poem, encompasses stanzas 15–56 (vv. 164–750), As for Moner's handling of the sacred liturgy, we are struck, first of all, by the prominence of the three female celebrants: Mancilla, joined by two other damsels, namely, Experiencia (Lady Experience) and Costumbre (Lady Custom) (see, especially, stanza 15 [vv. 164–70]). In addition, the author designates his version of the Eucharistic service as "misa seca" (a dry mass) (v. 220).[9] The author employs the precise, technical terminology to underscore his deliberate exclusion of the ritual that pertains to the transubstantiation of the bread and wine, the most solemn moment in the canon of the Mass. Yet another aspect of Moner's rendition is the disproportionate length of the homily delivered by Experiencia (stanzas 26–52 [vv. 317–694]). The sermon comprises 378 verses, that is, 63 percent of the Mass proper of 597 verses. Obviously, Moner invests the homily/sermon with a very special function.

Upon close analysis, the summary of the essential episodes in Moner's *Sepultura* reveals the convergence of two clusters of motifs: one, characterized by the extreme suffering of the unfortunate lover envisioned in a gloomy, otherworldly environment; the other, distinguished by an allegorical adaptation of a religious devotion or ritual to the condition of the aforementioned lover.[10] The components in each group find abundant representation in the *cancioneros*. The point to be made at the very outset of our exploratory journey is that the interaction between the two clusters generates a powerful dramatic impulse. What I will try to show in the course of my discussion is how this *vis dramatica* gives rise to the thrust of an evolution toward full-fledged theatrical expressivity.

Ambiance of Gloom

The motifs of the first cluster pertain to the "infierno," "purgatorio," "sepultura," and "batalla" already referred to. These compositions are the object of a detailed study by Chandler R. Post, who, in his landmark book *Medieval Spanish Allegory*, classifies them under the general heading of "erotic Hell" (75–102). Post

---

[9] Jungmann outlines the structure of the dry Mass in the following terms:
The term *missa sicca* was derived originally from a rite which was customary at the Communion of the sick; even here in the sick-room the Mass formulary was read, skipping however from the fore-Mass (this might even reach to the *Sanctus*) to the *Pater noster*, and then giving Communion in the usual way, but only under the form of bread (hence the *sicca*). (Joseph A. Jungmann, *The Mass of the Roman Rite: Its Origins and Development (Missarum Sollemnia)*, trans. Francis A. Brunner. 2 vols. [New York: Benziger, 1951–55], 1: 385, n. 46)

[10] Cocozzella proffers a general commentary on Moner's *Sepultura* (*2 Introducción*, 25–51); for specific considerations on the clusters mentioned here, see *2 Introducción*, 29–36.

avowedly derives the label from *Infierno de los enamorados*, the poem, so titled, by Íñigo López de Mendoza, better known as the Marqués de Santillana. Post offers a useful definition, precise and broad enough as to provide a convenient starting point for further discussion. He observes that the numerous specimens of the "erotic Hell"

> may be subdivided into two classes according to their allegorical attitude. To the first belong those in which, as in Santillana's *Infierno de Enamorados* itself, the author ideates a real abyss of retribution for ill-starred lovers; to the second those in which, as in the *Desert d'Amours* of Eustache Deschamps and the *Prison d'Amours* of Baudouin de Condé, he conceives more fancifully the torment of the visionary world simply as a crystallization of the lover's woes in the actual world (75).[11]

Post initiates and pursues a search of not only sources but also recurrent motifs and multifarious variations invested upon those motifs by talented authors, the likes of Santillana (1398–1458)[12] and many others: Juan Rodríguez del Padrón,[13] Juan

---

[11] Stephen G. Nichols, "Preface," *Eustache Deschamps, French Courtier Poet: His Work and His World*, ed. Deborah M. Sinnreich-Levi (New York: AMS Press, 1998), xiii–xix. Of particular interest is Deschamps, who, in the words of Nichols, "figures today as one of the true giants of fourteenth-century French culture" (xiii). After what Nichols describes as "all but complete effacement of Deschamps from the literary scene for almost four hundred years" (xvi), the author has been garnering due recognition in a number of recent publications, such as the volume of essays, edited by Sinnreich-Levi. Worthy of special mention is Curzon's and Fiskin's translation of selected poems in Ian Laurie and Deborah M. Sinnreich-Levi, eds., *Eustache Deschamps, Selected Poems* (New York: Routledge, 2003). The remarkable anthology undertaken under the direction of Boudet and Millet comprises a considerable number of poems, grouped into various thematic categories, each of which is complemented by a thorough analysis and commentary. For Deschamps's biography especially useful are Ernst Hoepffner, *Eustache Deschamps: Leben und Werke* (1904; repr. Genève: Slatkine Reprints, 1974), and Ian S. Laurie, "Eustache Deschamps: 1340(?)–1404," in Sinnreich-Levi, *Eustache Deschamps, French Courtier-Poet*, 1–72.

[12] For a concise overview of Santillana's career and an essential commentary on his literary production, see M. P. A. M. Kerkhof and A. Gómez Moreno, Introducción to *Poesías completas*, by Marqués de Santillana, edited by M. P. A. M. Kerkhof and A. Gómez Moreno. Clásicos Castalia 270. (Madrid: Castalia, 2003), 9–81.

[13] In my own study entitled "The Thematic Unity of Juan Rodríguez del Padrón's *Siervo libre de amor*," I rely on the authority of Antonio Paz y Melia, who "estimates that Juan Rodríguez was born in the late 1300s and died around the middle of the fifteenth century" (195, n. 2). Also, in my essay I provide the following essential data on the author:
> Juan Rodríguez was born and died in Galicia. He spent some time at the court of Juan II of Castile, where he fell in love with a lady of high rank. Due to the complications arising from this risky relationship, Juan Rodríguez was eventually exiled.

de Andújar,[14] Bachiller Ximénez,[15] Diego de San Pedro,[16] Nicolás Guevara,[17]

He resided in Italy in the entourage of Cardinal Cervantes, a relative of his. He attended the Council of Basel (1430) and around the year 1441 became professed in a Franciscan monastery in Jerusalem (195, n. 2).

[14] According to Salvador Miguel (*Poesía cancioneril*, 48–52), Juan de Andújar spent a considerable part of his life at the Neapolitan court of Alfonso V. In all probability, the poet returned to Spain after the King's death in 1458. On the basis of very scanty documentation, Salvador Miguel surmises that Andújar was still living in the period between 1461 and 1484.

[15] For Bachiller Ximénez, González Cuenca offers the following note: Los datos biográficos de este "Bachiller Ximénez" no son más que los que se desprenden de su participación en el *Cancionero general*. Probablemente se trata de un castellano afincado en Valencia, como el mismo Castillo, y también como él, vinculado al círculo literario del Conde de Oliva. Su *Purgatorio de Amor*, recogido en el *Cancionero* (871), en el que hace desfilar los integrantes de ese círculo, es prueba de tal vinculación (3: 426, n. 1; For this Bachiller, the only data available are those that come to light through his contribution to the *Cancionero general*. In all probability the Bachiller, not unlike Castillo himself [the compiler of the *Cancionero*], was a man from Castile established in Valencia and, like Castillo, became involved in the literary circle sponsored by the Conde de Oliva. A proof of this involvement is the Bachiller's *Purgatorio de Amor* included in the *Cancionero* (no. 871). In the *Purgatorio* the author parades the representative members of that circle).

[16] For an overview of San Pedro's life and works we may rely on Keith Whinnom's "Introducción biográfica y crítica" to his edition of that author's *Obras completas*. Despite his extensive research, Whinnom can only list as probable the following events in San Pedro's life: the beginning of his service in the entourage of Juan Téllez-Girón, Conde de Urueña, around 1472 (23); the participation in the war of Granada (specifically in the battle of Lucena of 1483) in the company of both the Conde and Diego Fernández de Córdoba, known as Alcaide de los Donceles, to whom San Pedro dedicated his *Cárcel de amor*, one of the main exponents of the sentimental romance (27). While refraining from conjecturing about San Pedro's date of birth, Whinnom states that the author died after 1498 (33). See, also, Whinnom, *Diego de San Pedro*, 13–34.

[17] On the basis of data derived from Vicenç Beltran's essay, "Guevara," Perea Rodríguez is able to make the following observation: "Nicolás Guevara (falleció ca. 1504) sirvió a Alfonso *el Inocente* y poco después, gracias a su Amistad con el mayordomo Gonzalo Chacón, entró a formar parte de la casa de Isabel la Católica, desarrollando casi toda su carrera cortesana en ese ámbito" (12, n. 30; Nicolás Guevara (died around 1504) served Alfonso *The Innocent* and not long afterwards, thanks to his friendship with the chamberlain Gonzalo Chacón, became a member of the retinue of Isabella the Catholic. He spent his entire career in that royal entourage.) (See, also, González Cuenca 2: 235, n.1.) Toro Pascua agrees with Cátedra in dating Guevara's *Sepultura de amor* around 1464 ("La *Sepultura de amor* de Guevara," 663). She adds that in the text of one of his poems Guevara himself specifies that the poem was written in the town of Ocaña (663, n. 3).

Garci Sánchez de Badajoz, Pedro Manuel Jiménez de Urrea.[18] The list is far from complete. These authors exhibit an admirable artistic flair while performing extraordinary feats of inventiveness.

There are scholars who have followed in Post's footsteps and yet have made significant contributions of their own. In his own noteworthy study of the *Infierno de amor* by Garci Sánchez de Badajoz, the aforementioned prominent *cancionerista* of the fifteenth century, Patrick Gallagher sheds light upon Post's definition by delineating a contrast between Santillana's prototype and Garci Sánchez's rendition of the "erotic Hell" (Gallagher, *The Life and Works of Garci Sánchez de Badajoz*, 188–233). According to Gallagher, the two *infiernos* exemplify, respectively, an "objective" and a "subjective" perspective. It is appropriate to quote directly from Gallagher. Referring to those particular *"cancionero* poets with their hells, purgatories and prisons of love" (188), he states:

> [T]he attempts of some were objective, while those of others were subjective: some dissociated themselves from, and others dentified themselves with, the torments of lovers whom they portrayed; some went to the places

---

Among Guevara's admirers we find none other than the legendary philologist and literary critic, Marcelino Menéndez y Pelayo. Comparing Guevara to the other poets of the *cancioneros*, he states:
> Cuento entre los mejores a un cierto Guevara. . ., de cuyas poesías pueden entresacarse cuatro o cinco muy lindas, de expresión mucho más natural y tierna que lo que suele encontrarse en los *Cancioneros*. (*Antología de poetas líricos castellanos* 3: 153; I regard a certain Guevara as one of the best of these *cancionero* poets. . ... Among his poems we may select four or five very fine specimens, which exhibit an expression much more fresh and natural than the one usually found in the *cancionero* poetry.)
Menéndez y Pelayo continues with this glowing commentary:
> [E]s sin duda uno de los más discretos poetas del *Cancionero* y es lástima que no quede mayor número de composiciones suyas. Comenzó a escribir en tiempo de Enrique IV (3: 155; Doubtless, he is one of the more perceptive poets of the *cancioneros*. What a pity that his compositions have not survived in greater number. He started writing in the era of Enrique IV).
Considering that Henry IV reigned from 1454 to 1474, we may deduce that Guevara flourished in the second half of the fifteenth century.

[18] For the sake of the broad context displayed in Post's comparative analysis, we may include here samples by Garci Sánchez and Urrea, authors much younger than Moner. Gallagher argues that Garci Sánchez was born around 1480 (3) and died around 1541 (22). For Garci Sánchez see, also, González Cuenca 2: 366, n. 1. Villar indicates that Urrea, another author, whose life extends well into the sixteenth century, was born in 1486, married in 1505, and died "por los años 1528 al 1530" (VIII). Galé Casajús, who provides the exact dates, 1485–1524, for Urrea's birth and death, embarks on an extensive discussion of the author's life and works (Enrique Galé Casajús, "La creación literaria en el seno de un clan familiar: la obra de Pedro Manuel de Urrea" (http://ifc.dpz.es/recursos/publicaciones/29/67/07gale.pdf).

of punishment to observe, others to experience; both went to record what they saw, but some as detached investigators, others as lovers. Santillana belongs to the former group and Garci Sánchez to the latter (188).

Among the scholars that follow in Post's footsteps, also worthy of mention are Antonio Cortijo Ocaña and Roxana C. Recio. They undertake a thorough analysis of the complex intertextuality of works by Catalan and Valencian authors. These texts escape Post's attention, even though they fall unmistakably within the purview of his study. Cortijo focusses on Francesc Alegre's *Somni* ("The Complications of the Narrative Techniques in 15th Century Prose Literature on Love"), whereas Recio delves into Bernat Hug de Rocabertí's *Glòria d'Amor* (*Petrarca en la Península Ibérica*, 1–40) and sundry pieces by various other writers, including Francesc Carrós's *Regoneixença i moral consideració contra les persuasions, vicis i forces d'amor* and a notable poem, also by Carrós, entitled *Consuelo de amor* ("Intertextuality in Carroç Pardo de la Casta").[19] In a more recent essay ("Los *Triunfos* de Petrarca en los cancioneros") Recio adds to Post's list representative samples hitherto unacknowledged and discovers in the generic *infierno* signs of Petrarchan influence through the widely read *Trionfi*.

Worthy of note are the fresh insights contributed by Pérez Priego in his "Los infiernos de amor." In the anonymous *Libro de Alexandre*, Gonzalo de Berceo's *Vida de Santo Domingo*, and Juan Ruiz's *Libro de buen amor*, among other works, Pérez Priego profiles a common background for all the *infiernos* of the fifteenth-century *cancioneros* (307); then proceeds to show traces of the influence of Virgil (*Aeneid*, book 6) and Dante (*Inferno*, canto 5) on Marqués de Santillana's *Bías contra Fortuna* and, of course, the *Infierno de los enamorados* (309–15). Pérez Priego does not exclude the possibility of other influences, not as demonstrable as Virgil's and Dante's: "La vision del infierno está construida . . . con elementos de diversa procedencia, aunque predomina con mucho la *Divina Commedia*" (314; The vision of Hell is made up of elements derived from a variety of sources, although what prevails by far is the *Divina Commedia*). Besides the respective *infierno* by Juan de Andújar, Nicolás Guevara, and Garci Sánchez de Badajoz (316–18), Pérez Priego takes into account a less known specimen by a certain García de Pedraza (315). The critic proposes a definition of the genre of the *infierno* in view of two factors: (1) "rasgos dominantes" (predominant traits), which consist of "la vision alegórica" (allegorical vision) and "el desfile de amantes

---

[19] For an overview of Rocabertí's and Carrós's life and works, see Riquer, *Història de la literatura catalana*, respectively 3: 148–60, and 3: 246–49. For recent studies on Carrós's *Regoneixença* see: Cocozzella, *Fra Francesc Moner's Bilingual Poetics*, 51–58; Miguel-Prendes, "Otra frontera," 522–25; and Rodríguez Risquete, "La regoneixença de Francesc Carrós Pardo de la Casta," in *Actes del X Congrés de l'Associació Hispànica de Literatura Medieval*, ed. Rafael Alemany Ferrer, Josep Lluís Martos, and Josep Miquel Manzanaro. 3 vols. (Alacant: Institut Interuniversitari de Filologia Valenciana, 2005).

ilustres" (the procession of illustrious lovers), and (2) the evolution from a serious, moralistic phase to a type of light courtly entertainment.[20]

In its overall atmosphere of gloom Moner's *Sepultura*, not unlike Garci Sánchez's composition, clearly belongs to the tradition of the "erotic Hell" that, according to both Post and Gallagher, stems, in the main, from Deschamps's and Condé's model texts rather than from Dante's *Inferno*.[21] Adhering to both

---

[20] Of special interest is the following description of the latter feature:
[E]s la variación lo que hace al género. Lo que parece más interesante en esa evolución es cómo el tema pierde su gravedad moral, su carácter reflexivo y aleccionador con que lo había tratado don Íñigo [Marqués de Santillana], y se convierte en un género galante, propio de la poesía áulica y de la fiesta cortesana (318; What distinguishes the *infierno* is its mutability. What turns out to be most important in the evolution of the genre is the process by which the thematic content loses its moral gravity, its reflexive and moralizing character—the way, that is, the Marqués had dealt with that content—and becomes an elegant literary mode, typical of aristocratic poetry and courtly celebrations).
For additional comments on the *infierno* see Deyermond, "Santillana's Love Allegories: Structure, Relation, and Message" and Rohland de Langbehn's "Problemas de texto y problemas constructivos en algunos poemas de Santillana." Of great interest is, also, Tocco's study of the Portuguese counterpart of the Castilian *infierno*.

[21] Even though direct word-for-word imitations are hard, if not impossible to come by, a reader can readily recognize how some memorable passages of Condé and Deschamps vintage found not slavish imitation but, rather, creative adaptation in the likes of Guevara, Garci Sánchez, and Moner. In *Prison d'Amours* we find, for instance, the following description of the place of suffering:
Dont est la prison d'amors teux,
Si dure ne si angoisseuse,
Ne fu com la prizons d'amors:
Tant que les plains et les clamors
Ne croit nus, que li amant font,
S'il n'a eüt d'amors parfont
Le cuer, comme jou, entamé;
Nus se sent les maus d'amours,
S'il n'aime ou s'il n'a amé.
(Vv. 21–29; Condé, 1: 268; No place is as harsh and as anguish-ridden a prison of love as is the prison of your love. Indeed, no man that has ever been in love would ever believe the lamentations and wailings that lovers utter unless his heart were subjugated, as mine is, by love. *No one will feel the ills of love unless he loves or has been in love.*)
These strains are echoed in the *Desert d'Amours*, specifically in the laments of the lover, who, in the following verses, depicts a definite setting for his desolation:
En ce lieu ou je suis ne pert,
Ne en obscur ne appert,
Que tempest et male aventure;
Pensers et plours y son appert

Post's and Gallagher's cogent argumentation, we may safely deduce that, in its unswerving focus on the protagonist's self-centered, not to say narcissistic, perspective, Moner's funeral of the self fits precisely within the subgroup that encompasses the kindred pieces by three admirable exponents of *cancionero* lyricism. Post and Gallagher clearly identify these poets as Guevara and Garci Sánchez with their respective *infierno*, and the Bachiller Ximénez with his *purgatorio*. To these exemplars we may add one that bears the same title as Moner's poem: the *Sepultura de amor* by Pedro Manuel Ximénez de Urrea.[22] Belonging to this list, also, is another poem by the aforementioned Garci Sánchez, which appears under the rubric "Otra suya, recontando a su amiga un sueño que soñó" (Another poem of his, recounting to his ladylove a dream he had). It begins with the verse "La mucha tristeza mía" (My great sadness). This supernal piece constitutes a veritable "sepultura de amor," a categorization admirable, if confirmation be needed, by the following commentary by Patrick Gallegher:

> [I]n Garci Sánchez's *Sueño*, addressed to his lady, it is the poet himself who dies. The idea is ingenious: the poet dreams that he dies of unrequited love

---

Et buissons d'espines couvert,
De ronsses et de grief pointure,
Le cahuant chante et murmure
Se chans de mort; la son ouvert,
La sont mi pensers a descouvert;
La est tristesce en pourtraiture;
La vient la mort en sa figure,
Noire et hydeuse a moy s'appert.
Je n'atten que ma sepulture;
Mais mon exil en gré endure
De pacience recouvert.

(Vv. 251–65; Deschamps, 2: 190–91; In the place in which I dwell nothing is visible, whether in the dark or in the open, but stormy weather and unfortunate events. Worries and tears are easy to see and bushes bristling with thorns—rose bushes with a nasty puncture. The screech owl hoots and gives out loud cries, the chants of death. There my painful thoughts are revealed: they are shown in the open. There Lady Sadness may be seen in her very portrait and Lady Death comes in her usual figure: all black and hideous she comes to me, and I expect nothing but a spot for my burial. All and all, I am willing to endure this exile of mine and endure it I will with a great deal of patience.)

Little wonder that the same afflicted personage should exclaim sooner or later: "Lieux tenebreus me son afin" (dark places are suited to me) (v. 276; Deschamps, 2: 291).

[22] There is, also, a *Sepultura de Macías* of doubtful authorship. It has been attributed to Diego de San Pedro, who may have expropriated the intriguing poem from a relative, a certain Juan de San Pedro. See Dorothy Sherman Severin, "The *Sepultura de Macías* by San Pedro—But Which San Pedro?" in *Medieval and Renaissance Spain and Portugal*, ed. Martha E. Schaffer and Antonio Cortijo Ocaña (Woodbridge, UK: Tamesis, 2006), 301.

in the presence of a nightingale; Love questions the nightingale and is told how Garci Sánchez died (the birds sing his funeral rites and now sing their love-songs on top of the laurel grove into which his body was converted); the poet then wakes up, and is disappointed to find he has not died after all:

recordé y halléme biuo
de la cual causa soy muerto
(276; I woke up and realized I was alive, and this causes me to die).[23]

This brief review of a few representative *cancionero* poets reveals in their signal treatments of the "erotic Hell" a tangible mood of darkness, the overall darkness of morbidity and despondency. These authors capitalize upon a lyrical strain in a poetics that may be labeled "funereal." This strain reverberates with special dramatic effect throughout Moner's production and relates to some memorable moments in not only the *Sepultura* but also his major prose works (*L'ànima d'Oliver* and *La noche*). In *La noche*, for instance, the first-person narrator describes the protagonist's walk through the dimly lit halls of a forbidding castle.[24] The remarkable episode, eerily suffused with a Miltonian "darkness visible" (*Paradise Lost,* 1.63), recaptures the frightening immediacy of any of the *infiernos de los enamorados*. It also triggers subliminal premonitions of a "tragic sense of life," to borrow Miguel de Unamuno's famous phrase. We will bear in mind the episode and others like it for the dramatic potential they hold in store and for their foreshadowing of an actual onstage representation.

---

[23] For the text of the *infiernos, purgatorios,* and *sepulturas* in question, see the bibliography below. There is, also, a *sepultura* by Guevara, about which we need not comment here because it shows substantial differences with respect to Moner's homonymous piece. Guevara focuses primarily on the death and condemnation of the allegorical personage representing love. While pointing out "the chastisement, not of Cupid's captives, but of Cupid himself" as a distinguishing feature of Guevara's presentation, Post adds the following sketch of Guevara's poem:

> After a long *débat* with Love upon his misdeeds, the author as judge condemns the god to death at the hands of the personified Sorrows that he has caused. He is to be buried in a tomb the details of which symbolize his various cruelties and upon the top of which are carved the names of those who died of affection. The latter part is plainly a reversal of the amorous interment which we shall soon see to be an offshoot of the Erotic Hell (91–92),

[24] For a commentary on this episode of *La noche*, see Cocozzella, *Fra Francesc Moner's Bilingual Poetics,* 105–7.

Self-Absorption and Estrangement

A significant point of coincidence between Moner's *Sepultura* and the specimens we have just attributed to the funereal poetics consists of what we may call the symbolism of desolation and alienation. Moner's recapturing of that symbolism in such verses as "En un campo de crueza / mi cuerpo muerto ha caýdo" (vv. 78–79) brings to mind, for instance, Garci Sánchez's haunting passage, "Yo los días no los vivo, / velo las noches, cativo, / y, si alguna noche duermo, / suéñome muerto en un yermo" (I am hardly alive during the day. Wretched that I am, I lie awake all night and, if some nights I manage to fall asleep, I dream I am dying in the desert) (*Sepultura*, vv. 6–9).[25] Moner's *campo* and Garci Sánchez's *yermo*, reiterated in the Bachiller Ximénez's "viendo el bien de mi dexado / quise dexar lo poblado / y perderme por los yermos" (considering the good things I was leaving behind, I decided to abandon the populated areas and lose myself in barren lands) (*Purgatorio*, vv. 3–5), become readily associated with typical expressions like "cuevas escuras" (dark caverns), "esto fosco" (this gloomy location), "aquellas cuevas" (those caves) found, also, in Ximénez's *Purgatorio* (see vv. 17, 67, 97), not to mention the "arboleda espesa y fragosa" (thick, rocky grove) and "la tierra tan llena de sierra" (the region full of mountainous territory), that we read in Ximénez de Urrea's *Sepultura* (205). These and many similar expressions that could be adduced create, in the final analysis, the effect of code words by which to diagnose the mental torment and overall malaise symptomatic of the lover's pitiful condition.

   Another factor to be taken into account within the context of that symbolism is the aforementioned "batalla de amor," one that includes a panoply of topical references to the fatal wound (vv. 57, 657–59, 667), the confrontation of a fierce warrior (vv. 44, 57–63, 653–80), of the aforementioned death in the barren field. The "batalla," which Moner develops into a telltale symptom of the lover's self-absorption, occurs shortly before (vv. 44–50) and after (vv. 653–80) the *misa* proper and, thus, creates a frame of sorts for his allegorical rendition of the sacred ritual.[26] Worth looking into is the parallelism between Moner's stanzas 50–51 (vv. 667–80), portraying the ladylove as a ferocious *ballestero* (archer), and stanza 19 (vv. 200–210) in Garci Sánchez's *Infierno*, where "una moça" (a young maiden), no less formidable than Moner's counterpart, is shown wielding

---

   [25] In one of Urrea's *villancicos*, closely related to the topics of the *Sepultura*, we read: "Amor perdone este muerto. . . .. / Baste aquel crudo dolor / Que tuuo en este desierto" (May Love forgive this dead man. . . .. Enough of the bitter pain that this man has endured in this desert!) [see Pedro Manuel Ximénez de Urrea, *Cancionero.* Edited by Martín Villar. Zaragoza: Imprenta del Hospiscio Provincial, 1878], 449).

   [26] Elsewhere, I have attempted to contextualize Moner's version of the topic of the "batalla" with analogous manifestations in Spanish literature of the fifteenth century: see Cocozzella, *2 Introducción*, 34.

a harpoon in her charge against her lover.[27] The similarities, considerable as they are, between the two texts should not distract our attention from the trademark egocentrism of Moner's presentation. Whereas Garci Sánchez makes reference to the "other"—that is, Diego de Mendoza, one of the denizens of the *infierno* —Moner clearly focuses on himself either directly in the first person (vv. 43–44: "Visto de vuestro esgremir / me venía" ['I came within the range of your fencing

---

[27] In a burlesque "justa" by Tristán de Estúñiga (see bibliography), we find a certain Ximón wounded by the arrow shot from a *ballesta* (crossbow) wielded by a lady (one of the nuns, mentioned in the epigraph of the poem):

> La dama luego soltara.
> Malherido fue Ximón,
> pero no le dio en la cara,
> que por las ingles le entrara,
> mas llególe al coraçón.
> (Vv. 91–95; The lady suddenly released the shaft. Ximón was badly wounded even though he was not hit in the face. The arrow pierced his groin and penetrated as far as his heart).

González Cuenca advises the reader about the equivocal connotation of the "batalla de amor" in this particular case: "Advertido por el epígrafe, el lector descubre enseguida la clave de la bisemia *justa/coito*" (Instructed by the rubric, the reader soon discovers the clue to the double entendre [joust/coitus]) (*Cancionero general [de Hernando del Castillo]* 3: 483, n. 2). Incidentally, in a side note added to the text of the poem, González Cuenca observes that Tristán de Estúñiga has not been identified. There is, also, a moralistic version of the allegorical "batalla." In his "Coplas. . .en vituperio de las malas hembras," Frey Íñigo de Mendoza imputes to those "wicked females"—to translate his vituperative sobriquet "—the devious techniques of the hunter, a *ballestero*, to be exact, who lures the prey by means of deceptive animal calls ("con voz fingida de cierva"). Here is the crucial passage (stanza 8):

> Son el grito con que llama,
> después que ya tiene armado,
> con voz fingida de cierva,
> el ballestero que brama
> para que venga el venado
> do le tire con la yerba,
> porque en la boca destas
> están dentro ascondidos
> los enemigos llamando,
> tienen las ballestas prestas
> para que siendo venidos
> nos puedan matar tirando.
> (Every one of them is the archer, who, after making his weapon ready, cries out feigning the call of a stag in order to entice his prey to a place where the animal may be targeted with a poisoned arrow. Thus, inside the mouths of these women hide our enemies that beckon us. Their crossbows are set so that, as we come by, they release the shaft and kill us.)

skills']), or through the mediacy of Lady Experience (see the aforementioned stanzas 50–51), the allegorical personage that turns out to be, after all, the existential and textual correlative of Moner's life itself.[28]

---

[28] For purposes of illustration, it is worthwhile to juxtapose Moner's passage with the corresponding one by Garci Sánchez. The following are, then, vv. 653–80 of Moner's *Sepultura*:

> Con todo, es cosa devida
> que diga quyén concertó
> que muriese:
> una tal, una escogida
> que nunqua hombre hirió
> que no fuesse
> peligrosa la herida.
> La d'éste no tuvo par,
> que la ballesta era gruesa
> y [l]e passa
> el braço; quyero callar
> porque no tengo cabeça,
> sino escasa,
> para poderl'alabar.
> Con la herida mostrada,
> fue dond'era el balestero
> que le dyo.
> Luego por él fue tentada
> con una prueva d'azero
> que tocó
> all alma temorizada.
> Quiso tornar do venía
> por no despertar la ira
> más sañuda;
> y al despedir que hazía,
> tiróle con una vira
> tan aguda
> que le mató en aquel dýa.

(For the translation, see pp. 206–7 below.)
And here are vv. 200–10 of Garci Sánchez's *Infierno*:

> Vi luego un gran harpón
> a don Diego de Mendoça
> le passava el coraçón,
> por la mano de una moça
> tirado con affectión,
> y diziendo: "Pues sin verte
> bive mi vida en la muerte,
> muera yo por que no pene."
> Y luego cantando viene:

Among the various works that we have reviewed within the mainstream of

"pues que no mejora mi suerte,
cedo morir me conviene.

(*Cancionero general,* ed. González Cuenca, 2: 393; Soon later I noticed that a large harpoon, launched vehemently by a young maiden, pierced through Diego de Mendoza's heart, just as he was saying: *If I don't set my eyes on you, my life is a living death. Let me die to avoid the agony!* He, then, chanted the following verses: *My life will not get any better. A sudden death is best for me.*)

For a discussion on Diego de Mendoza's problematic identification, see *Cancionero general,* 2: 434, n. 2. Another facet of the intricate web of intertextual affinities may be perceived in the quotation of Mendoza's verses. These belong to a *canción* (ID 0119), which González Cuenca reconstructs as follows:

Pues no mejora mi suerte,
cedo morir me conviene,
por ver si terná la muerte
lo que la vida no tiene.
Suspiros, lágrimas, fuego,
me aquexan sin ayudarme,
que una hora de sosiego
no tengo para apartarme;
hazen mi vida tan fuerte
que el morir más me conviene,
por ver si terná la muerte
lo que la vida no tiene.

(*Cancionero general,* 2: 393, n. 1; As my life is not getting any better, I'd rather die a sudden death. Let's see if death holds in store whatever is missing in my life. Sighs, tears, a burning flame, which bring me vexations without any comfort—not one moment of peace do I have away from this torment—make my life so stressful that it is better for me to die just to see if death holds in store whatever is missing in my life).

Mendoza's poem is echoed, in one of Moner's own *canciones,* which reads:

Pues no mejora mi suerte,
cedo morir me conviene.
¡Quiçá que terná la muerte
lo que la vida no tiene!
Sospiros, lágrimas, fuego
me matan a no dexarme.
sola una ora de assosyego,
para poder remediarme,
haze mi daño tan fuerte.

(Moner, *1 OC,* 180; Considering that my life is not getting any better, I had rather die a sudden death. I wonder if death holds in store what is missing in my life. Sighs, tears, a burning flame bring me death and never let up. The only hour of respite that should bring me relief makes my pain even harder to bear).

the funereal poetics, Guevara's *Infierno* calls for special consideration. This is because the affinities between Moner's *Sepultura* and Guevara's *Infierno* are of special significance as they hold in store the conditions for the gestation of the paradigm of self-absorption and estrangement. In other words, the nature of the paradigm is determined by the kinship between Moner's and Guevara's poem. Guevara, a poet of undisputed talent, provides a model version of what Gallagher, as we have just seen, designates the subjective type of "erotic Hell." Moner may well have found a propitious occasion and good reason to capitalize on Guevara's model in order to conceive the tenor of his own composition. With great efficacy Guevara, on his part, recaptures the mood of the protagonist in Deschamps's *Desert d'Amours*, who exclaims: "Lieux tenebreus me son afin" (gloomy places suit me) (v. 276; Deschamps, 2: 291). Guevara's minimalist plot has shed practically all traces of the narrative function. What remains is a highly imaginative evocation of a nightmarish setting. The poet paints a horrid picture in vivid brush strokes, faithfully recaptured in the following excerpt from Post's critique:

> Guevara's *Infierno de Amores* is cast completely in the more fanciful mould. Without the ordinary machinery of a vision, he describes his amorous woes directly under the image of hell. His lady's disfavour is equal to infernal agony. The customary physical torments of parts of the body are applied figuratively to his various faculties and emotions: his thoughts are consumed with fire, his hope is upset, his pleasures boil in cauldrons of grief, he is the prey of dogs, his well-being is rent to pieces, and he is blinded by his complaints. He encounters no other mortals in his *Infierno* and visualizes no realities; hell is merely the fictitious picture of his own sad plight (91).

Post's abstract adumbrates Guevara's prominent standing among the authors of the aforementioned *infiernos, purgatorios*, and *batallas* that make up the allegorical representations of the lover's condition. By highlighting Guevara's unique contribution to the funereal strain of *cancionero* lyricism, Post paves the way for an appreciation of Moner's own emulation of Guevara's achievements. What Guevara contributes and Moner emulates is the intuition of the lugubrious space of solitude. The vivid depiction of that space in incisive terms and compact expression attests to a sharp contrast between the conciseness of Guevara's *infierno* and the prolixity of the other exemplars of its kind.

One *Misa* among Others

In order to complete our survey of the *cancionero* background of Moner's *Sepultura*, it behooves us to take into account those *cancionero* pieces that exhibit special genetic affinities with Moner's *misa* proper. These affinities reside in the second cluster of motifs referred to above—the ones that, in order to dramatize the lover's plight, betoken elaborate adaptations of liturgical services, ritualistic performances, religious ceremonies, devotional practices, and scriptural readings.

Besides Moner's *misa*, which, to date, has received little attention from critics at large,[29] there are three other extant specimens, authored by, respectively, Juan de Dueñas,[30] Suero de Ribera,[31] and Nicolás Núñez.[32] Jane Y. Tillier, who provides a concise and informative commentary on the various *misas*, recognizes, also, a fragment by Juan de Tapia (Tillier 569).[33] It does not take a meticulous

---

[29] For the few recent studies about Moner's life and works, see above, p. xvi, n. 3.

[30] Marco Presotto, Introduzione to *La nao de amor. Misa de amores,* by Juan de Dueñas, ed. Marco Presotto. (Viareggio – Lucca: Mauro Baroni, 1997), 11–41. Presotto conjectures that Dueñas was born in the first decade of the fifteenth century in the village in the province of Palencia that bears his name (11). Presotto detects in Dueñas's life three successive periods, which correspond to the poet's residence in the courts of, respectively, Castile (Juan II), Navarre (Juan, *Infante* of Aragon and his wife Blanca, who inherited the throne), and Naples (Alfonso V) (11–17). Around 1440 Dueñas returned to Spain (18–19). For additional biographic information on Dueñas, see Nancy Marino, "Un exilio político en el siglo XV. El caso del poeta Juan de Dueñas," *Cuadernos Hispanoamericanos* 416 (1985): 139–51.

[31] Periñán summarizes Suero de Ribera's biography in the following terms:
En resumen, parece claro que Ribera vivió en pleno cuatrocientos, conoció la corte de Juan II en la primera parte de su vida, pasó después a la corte aragonesa y de allí a Italia donde vivió algún tiempo pero manteniendo contacto vivo con las cortes peninsulares, y es probable que muriera en la penúltima década del siglo (17; In sum, it appears that Ribera lived within the span of the 1400s. In his early life, he became well acquainted with the court of Juan II [of Castile]. He later transferred to the court of Aragon and, from there, moved to Italy, where he lived for some time while retaining an active connection with the courts of the Iberian Peninsula. In all probability, he died in the next-to-last decade of the fifteenth century).
In addition, this scholar contextualizes Ribera's *misa* within a broad, abundantly documented discussion of the religious parody stemming from love motifs, very much in vogue in Spain during Ribera's lifetime (24–32).

[32] Very little is known about Núñez. Deyermond describes him as follows:
[A]uthor of a brief sentimental romance and of a substantial group of *cancionero* poems, is biographically little more than a name.. . . He may have been a Valencian, or may have lived in Valencia for some time; his sequel to San Pedro's *Cárcel de Amor* was published in 1496, just four years after the original, and the first appearance of his poems—apart from those in his romance—is in the *Cancionero general* of 1511. ("The Poetry of Nicolás Núñez," 25).

[33] For each of these *misas*, see Dutton's *Catálogo-índice*, and the entry for the respective author in the bibliography. For useful biographic studies about Dueñas, Ribera, and Tapia see Gernert, 304–16. Gernert observes that the three, whom Vendrell de Millás describes as "poetas que brillaron especialmente en la corte d Aragón," "se podrían haber conocido ya antes de 1432 en Castilla, aunque lo más probable es que se encontrasen después de esta fecha en el séquito de Alfonso V" (poets who flourished especially in the court of Aragon, could have already been acquainted with one another before 1432 in

comparative analysis to support the initial impression that Moner's *misa* varies substantially from the homonymous poems by the other writers mentioned here. It would appear that Moner's *misa* constitutes a unique extant exemplar of a special type of religious theater. What strikes our attention immediately is Moner's inventive elaboration on the ritual of the Catholic Mass. As we shall see, the elaboration involves a radical change, not in the structure of the Mass *per se* but, rather, in the language of the liturgical text: Moner substitutes the original Latin with his own version in the vernacular, which, far from a verbatim translation, is in its entirety a product of the author's creative imagination.

In addition to the specific *misas* there are a number of compositions, like the "Salmos penitenciales" and the "Letanía de Amor," by Diego de Valera, or the "Liciones de Job," by Garci Sánchez de Badajoz,[34] which, together with the *misas*, provide a *prima facie* evidence of some rather fanciful renditions of very serious religious subjects.[35] One would readily associate Moner with the group of authors mentioned here, who traditionally have been identified as exponents of religious parody. This broad categorization cannot be justified, however, in terms of the harsh reaction — not to say wholesale condemnation — that the parodic vein documented in the *cancioneros* has provoked among many connoisseurs

---

Castile, although it is more probable that they coincided after that year in the entourage of Alfonso V) (1: 305). Of special interest is Gernert's edition of the *misa*, respectively, by Ribera and Dueñas (*Parodia y "contrafacta,"* 2: 155–64; for the Tapia fragment see 2: 165). Gernert edits Núñez's composition under the heading "El libro de las horas" (*Parodia y "contrafacta,"* 2: 25–30). In fact, Núñez integrates his *misa* into his parody of the book of hours. Of utmost interest is a "lover's mass," written in Middle English. Akin in its formal and thematic aspects to the *misas* under consideration here, the composition is of uncertain authorship, attributed by some to Geoffrey Chaucer, by others to John Lydgate (Kathleen Forni, "Literature of Courtly Love: Introduction," in *The Chaucerian Apochrypha: A Selection*, ed. Kathleen Forni [Kalamazoo, MI: Medieval Institute Publications, 2005], 1–6).

[34] Gernert goes into a full discussion as to how the Penitential Psalms came to be classified as a discrete group; then takes up the distinction between the straightforward rendition and the erotic parody of said Psalms, exemplified, respectively, by the composition of Pero Guillén de Segovia and that of Diego de Valera (Gernert, *Parodia y "contrafacta,"* 1: 218–38). Noteworthy is Gernert's edition of Garci Sánchez's "Liciones de Job" (2: 67–81) and Valera's "Salmos Penitenciales" (2: 115–22). Regarding Valera's compositions, see, also, the entry found in the bibliography below. We may add that they are found, also, in *El cancionero del siglo XV: c. 1380–1520,* 4: 197–200.

[35] Valentín Núñez Rivera, "Glosa y parodia de los Salmos Penitenciales en la poesía del cancionero," *EPOS* 17 (2001): 107–39, goes into an extensive discussion on those compositions by the *cancionero* poets that borrow a model or prototype from the Scriptures or the Christian liturgy — the Psalms, say, the Lord's Prayer, the Commandments, not to mention the *misas, purgatorios, infiernos,* and the like — and adapt it to the so-called religion of love (126–27). On 126–27, Rivera compiles a representative list of these poems.

of Hispanic letters.[36] The truth of the matter is that the entire notion of parody needs to be revised fundamentally in light of the theory set forth by Linda Hutcheon in her suggestive study.

---

[36] For notable samples of this adverse reaction, see p. 77 below.

II.
A SPECTACLE ON DISPLAY

Spatial Indicators

When reflecting upon the makeup of Moner's *Sepultura*, a musical analogy may easily come to mind: various motifs are integrated à la Wagner into a composition of considerable complexity. For a start we may take a look at the two sections, one at the beginning (vv. 1–70, 78–84) and the other toward the end (vv. 653–80), of the *Sepultura*. These passages dealing with the details of the *infierno* and the *batalla* already mentioned make up a frame of sorts for the *misa* proper. They demarcate a nebulous area located outside the church (*extra ecclesiam*, so to speak) and define, concurrently, the field of operation encompassed within the church itself (*intra ecclesiam*).

What we have learned so far is that the atmosphere of darkness concomitant to the *infierno* and the *batalla* is pervasive throughout the frame we have just referred to. That palpable gloom conditions the psychic theater of innerness and other modalities of Moner's dramatic monologue. For the sake of a complete overview of Moner's *Sepultura*, we need to undertake a journey *intra ecclesiam* beyond the dark precincts of the *infierno*.[1]

---

[1] Teresa Ferrer Valls engages in a broad discussion of space and theatricality especially as it pertains to the domains of Castilian and Catalan in the late Middle Ages ("El espectáculo profano en la Edad Media: espacio escénico y escenografía," in *Historias y ficciones: coloquio sobre la literatura del siglo XV (Actas del Coloquio Internacional organizado por el Departamento de Filologia Espanyola de la Universitat de València, celebrado en Valencia los días 29, 30 y 31 de octubre de 1990)*, ed. R. Beltrán, J. L. Canet, and J. L. Sirera (València: Universitat de València—Departament de Filologia Espanyola, 1992), 307–22. She reviews the evolution of spatiality from the communal super-spectacle staged in monumental urban structures (such as the palace, the plaza, and the city gate) to the private representation within a locality specifically built as a theatrical venue.

The Advancement of a Plot

In discussing the plot of the *misa de amores* proper, the larger segment of Moner's *Sepultura*, we may start our analysis with a self-evident declaration: the dramatic action stems from the ritual of the Mass.[2] The acknowledgment of Moner's ritualistic, Mass-oriented dramatics, automatically raises the issue of the influence that, as we have noted, Amalarius exercised over generations of dramatists from the high Middle Ages up to the Renaissance. How does Moner respond to that influence? What is clear is that Moner, while not contravening Amalarius's allegorical approach altogether, differs from it radically by the very nature of the *misa seca* structured into *Sepultura d'amor*. Moner's rendition of the "dry Mass" entails, true to form, the excision of the rite of transubstantiation proper, that is, the very core of the sacred liturgy that provides the raison d'être for Amalarius's interpretation.[3] Moner secularizes the ritual of the Mass but retains the overall dynamics and tempo of that ritual. Also, he abides by the traditional structure and normal sequence of the various phases, the names of which he scrupulously preserves: the Kyrie Eleison, the Epistle, the Gospel, the Offertory, the Preface (introduction to the canon), the preamble for the Lord's prayer (*Preceptis*), the *Agnus Dei*, the concluding prayer (*Requiescat in pace*).[4] Indeed, a tenuous adher-

---

[2] For a detailed outline of Moner's *Sepultura/Misa*, see figure 6 on p. 218 below.

[3] According to Gernert, the absence of the ritual of consecration in Dueñas's and Ribera's respective *misa* is due not to a sense of reverence for the Eucharist but, rather, to a lack of an appropriate model in the textual source the two poets were imitating. Following is Gernert's explanation:

> [L]a costumbre de omitir el *Canon Missae* en los formularios de la misa recogidos en los libros de horas, por tratarse de una sección reservada al sacerdote, explica por qué se pasa por alto el Canon en las misas de Suero de Ribera y Juan de Dueñas. Tal vez se prescinde de la hostia, que sí recogen tanto la *Messe des aiseaux* como la composición de Nicolás Núñez, porque el libro de horas no ponía a su disposición un modelo textual para la imitación, y no porque estuviera excluido de todo intento de adaptación erótica por tratarse de una sección especialmente sagrada y llena de significado teológico (Gernert, *Parodia y "contrafacta" en la literatura románica medieval y renacentista*, 1: 326–27; The canon was customarily omitted in the formularies of the Mass that were integrated into the Books of Hours because that section was reserved for the priest. That explains why Suero de Ribera skipped the canon in his *misa* as did Juan de Dueñas. Possibly, each of these two authors dispenses with the host, which, indeed, is very much in use in [Jean de Condé's] *Messe des aiseaux* and in Núñez's piece, because he does not find in his own Book of Hours a text that could serve as a model. It is not because the Book would exclude any intention of an erotic adaptation in view of the nature of such a specially sacred section [the canon], full of theological significance.)

[4] Antonio Alatorre, "Algunas notas sobre la Misa de amores," *Nueva Revista de Filología Hispánica* 14 (1960): 325–28. For comparative purposes one may study Alatorre's

ence to tradition allows Moner to refashion these phases of the liturgy in order to adapt them to his own allegorical agenda.

The *intra ecclesiam* plot follows a course of action, progressively intensified in an ascending trajectory at three levels. Each of these showcases its own intention, symbolism, and type of action. Each level may be interpreted as a scene in a theatrical performance. In scene 1 (vv. 78–163), which takes place in the chapel-mausoleum, Gentileza and Mancilla conspicuously act out their profound grief in a routine of chants and lamentations. Their expression in words and ceremonial sway is orchestrated as a veritable dirge, steeped in emotion, though quite free of ostentatious mannerism. The dirge comes to a head in a curious incident, which turns out to be emblematic of scene 1. Mancilla notices a piece of paper lumped up and lodged in the mouth of the dead lover, personified as Moner's alter ego. After she manages to extract the paper, the priestess notices a text of three inscribed verses, which she proceeds to read aloud:

> Con todo, Muerte, me pesas,
> que si tal vida durara,
> major culpa me matara.
> (Vv. 127–29) (For the translation, see p. 199 below.)

The epigrammatic passage resounds as an embryonic statement of one of the primary motifs of the entire composition. The motif signals an all-important phenomenon that may be called "dead man talking." The symbolism itself of the episode would oblige us to ponder in wonderment the efficacy of Mancilla's operation. By virtue of her sacerdotal office, Mancilla is able to revitalize the *logos* recovered from a dead man's lips.

Scene 2 (vv. 164–316) encapsulates a cluster of hieratic acts, officiated close to the main altar. The three celebrants in unison assert the divinity of Truth and declare the loyalty of their devotion. Mindful of the suffering endured by an entire community of faithful lovers, victims of deceit and abuse, Mancilla segues with some prayers of intercession on behalf of the individual for whom the Mass is being offered. The priestess shows no restraint in adding a curse on those who with their lies, slander, and all manner of foul play thwart the ways of Truth:

> Al que s'arma de mentira,
> tu justicia le condene
>   de manera
> que ayan temor de tu ira.
> (Vv. 188–91. For the translation, see p. 200 below.)

---

comments on Dueñas's *misa*. This scholar goes into the specifics concerning the fixed and variable sections of the *Ordo missae* parodied by the author.

Next, Costumbre and Experiencia take their turn, each intoning her own version of the Epistle and the Gospel. In an admonitory tone, Costumbre's chant alludes to the dire retribution attendant upon those women that employ their charms as bait to ensnare naïve young men, their unsuspecting victims. Experiencia, on her part, broaches a vein of skepticism, not to say cynicism. "Trust but verify" is her message. Experiencia's Gospel sounds very much like a soliloquy bristling with jaundiced comments about a man-woman relationship that shall remain dysfunctional as long as it does not abide by the inviolate bond between love and truth.

We may observe that, even while using the traditional nomenclature that designates the sections of the Mass, the Kyrie Eleison, the Epistle, the Gospel, and so forth, Moner radically deviates from age-old tradition by excluding from his *misa* the formulas of the liturgy and the Scriptural excerpts that make up the conventional sections of the Epistle and the Gospel. Moner strives for an adaptation of the ceremonial of the Mass to his own esthetic purpose. An eloquent case in point is his rendition of the Offertory, which makes for the climactic moment in scene 2. The role of Firmeza (Steadfastness) and Baldón (Insult), two extraneous personages, who, in their cameo appearance, join Mancilla in the ceremony, serves as a reminder of the participation of the congregation in the Mass in accordance to time-honored protocol. Moner may well have in mind a procedure that harks as far back as Amalarius's explication. Hardison aptly observes:

> The ninth-century Offertory, during which the people bring candles, obla-
> tion loaves, and wine to the deacon or celebrant, links them to the ceremony
> as participants rather than as passive witnesses (*Christian Rite and Christian
> Drama in the Middle Ages*, 1: 59).

Not to be missed, of course, is one glaring difference from the ritual prescribed by Amalarius: Moner does not include any of the items mentioned by Hardison. Instead, the one and only object of the offering in Moner's *misa* is, as has been indicated, the *canción* that epitomizes the lover's lifelong suffering. In its pivotal function, this *canción* holds in store an abundance of food for thought. For one thing, the poem expands the motif we have labeled "dead man talking." Once again, Mancilla plies her salvific services in revitalizing the dead letter set in written form.

The transition from the first to the second statement of the motif allows us to envisage a significant phase in the unfolding of the plot. From a broad perspective, it may be said that, in view of the shift of the *mise en scène* from the tomb to the altar, we witness an appreciable advancement in the evolution of the text of subjectivity. One index of the advancement consists of the symbolism residing in the very names of the personages involved in the bearing and receiving of the *canción*. Semantically, Firmeza and Baldón denote the much-too-human tension between the unswerving devotion of the lover and the injurious behavior of the ladylove. The onomastic symbolism tells the sad, tragic story of *fin'amors*. Mancilla, by contrast, stands for a signifier that resonates with an ambivalent conflation of human emotions (pity, compassion) and a divine attribute (mercy). The compassion of one human being toward another and the response of God's mercy and grace reflect the primordial impulse of charity culminating in the mystical union of the soul with the Creator.

The coming together of the two acolytes (Firmeza and Baldón) with the priestess (Mancilla) foreshadows the amalgamation of other symbols. These merge into the allegory of the movement from the tomb to the altar (scene 1 to scene 2 of Moner's stage). The movement symbolizes the crossing of the boundary between the natural and the supernatural realms. Central to the configuration of the supernatural realm is the altar, a symbol of the wondrous powers of Mancilla and the other priestesses. From the well-known protocol pertaining to the celebration of the Mass, we may infer that Firmeza and Baldón place the offering (the *canción*) on the altar. In accordance with the same protocol, it is up to Mancilla and her cohorts to enact a miraculous transformation of their own: a kind of subsidiary rite in substitution for the primary transubstantiation, which is missing in Moner's *misa seca*. Needless to say, the "species" for Moner's surrogate transubstantiation is not bread and wine but none other than the *canción* in question.

In order to envisage the extent of this sui generis metamorphosis of the text, whether in written or oral form, we must follow the transfer of the plot to scene 3 (vv. 317–694) of Moner's *Sepultura*. Now it is Experiencia's turn to take center stage. Because of its considerable extension and unique role, we shall reserve the analysis of Experiencia's sermon for a separate section of this study (see, below, p. 135–51).

After the sermon, the ritual resumes with Moner's version of the preface, the *preceptis*, the *Agnus Dei*, and the *Requiem* (vv. 695–750).

III.
The Gestation of Dramatic Modes

The "Topophilia" of Innerness

The "frame" of gloom calls for special attention because it manifests a distinctive mode of Moner's esthetic, the mode that, borrowing a phrase from Gaston Bachelard we may call a "poetics of space." In a thoughtful critique of Bachelard's landmark study that bears that very phrase as a title, John R. Stilgoe piques our interest by proposing an explication couched in a catchy neologism. Especially pertinent is the following observation:

> This book opens its readers to the titanic importance of setting in so much art from painting to poetry to fiction to autobiography. In *The Poetics of Space*, Bachelard reveals time after time that setting is more than scene in works of art, that it is often the armature around which the work revolves. He elevates setting to its rightful place alongside character and plot, and offers readers a new angle of vision that reshapes any understanding of great paintings and novels, and folktales too. His is a work of genuine topophilia ("Foreword," x).

Arguably, Moner provides a remarkable rendition of various manifestations of this topophilia à la Bachelard. In *Sepultura* and other works by Moner, which we will have occasion to examine, the semiotic function adumbrated in Stilgoe's definition of the neologism involves the full assimilation of the type of setting mentioned above into the field of the author's creativity. Moner, in other words, fashions a textual embodiment of his own concept of the environmental *campo de crueza* by obviating the common boundary between the notion of exterior and that of interior. The existential environment (the *campo*) thus conceived becomes a true poetic symbol of the self: it loses the natural accouterments of exteriority and, paradoxical as it may seem, acquires the function of the inner world, the psychic space that remains to be reckoned with. We may envisage Moner's topophilia as a trajectory of introspection, an inward journey to the type of space that Kenneth Burke identifies with the term "innerness" (*The Rhetoric of Religion*, 51–58). The locus of innerness, a notion that Burke derives from St. Augustine, implies, by extension, the depiction of the dark night of the psyche or, to put it differently, the description of the cavernous recesses of the conscious and unconscious regions of the self. The connotations of the mode of selfhood or self-consciousness crystallize into a written expression, which may be designated as a text of loneliness par excellence. By a meditation on this type of Augustinian *écriture* steeped in the psyche, Burke himself refers to some Latin terms borrowed from St. Augustine, who, in his *Confessions* observes that "there is no science of letters more inward (*interior*) than conscience put into writing (*conscientia scripta*)" (quoted in Burke, 57).[1]

Apropos of Moner's notion of innerness it is instructive to bear in mind the handling of spatial coordinates by Diego de San Pedro, Moner's renowned contemporary, author of the famous romance, *Cárcel de amor (Prison of Love)*.[2] Worthy of note is Barbara Kurtz's analysis of San Pedro's depiction of a formidable edifice: the bleak "torre" (tower or fortress), which represents the prison of the unfortunate lover (Leriano), the protagonist of San Pedro's somber narrative (San Pedro, 84–92). Kurtz brings to light an intense degree of co-penetration between the interior and the exterior of said prison of love. Take, for instance, the following quotation:

> To a certain extent, the interior scene duplicates parts of the allegorical exterior: the table of steadfastness is the equivalent of the foundation of faith, the three servants (*mal, pena, dolor*) recall the three images (*tristeza, congoja, trabajo*) of the allegorized edifice. This duplication, together with the profusion of scarcely distinguishable terms of grief (*congoja, trabajo, dolor, angustia, desesperación, mal, pena, dolor, cuidado*) leads to some confusion in the allegorical design. The synonymy of the terms pushes the allegory in the direction of verbal play instead of genuine analysis of emo-

---

[1] Francesc de la Via, *Obres*, ed. Arseni Pacheco (Barcelona: Quaderns Crema. 1997). A significant antecedent of Moner's handling of spatial indicators may be found in the works of Francesc de la Via, a Catalan writer, who flourished in the city of Girona in the first half of the fifteenth century. In his commentary on Via's long narrative poem, entitled *Procés de Corona d'Aur contra En Bertran Tudela* (159–288), Arseni Pacheco points to a phenomenon of "individualització" (individualization) evidenced in the existential correlation between *vivència personal* (personal existence) and *entorn vital* (life environment). Reminiscent of José Ortega y Gasset's principles of *yo* and *circunstancia* and Américo Castro's notion of *vivència*, Pacheco's terminology is pertinent to the symbiosis exteriority/interiority we have profiled in Moner's text of "innerness." For a comprehensive definition of *yo* and *circunstancia*, the mutually complementary principles in Ortega y Gasset's metaphysics, see Jean-Paul Borel, *Raison et vie chez Ortega y Gasset* (Neuchatel: A la Baconnière, 1959), 37–76. Díez Taboada discusses Ortega y Gasset's terminology together with Américo Castro's notion of *vivencia* (Juan María Díez Taboada, "Vivencia y género literario en Espronceda y Bécquer," *Homenajes: Estudios de Filología Española* vol. 1., ed. Juan María Díez Taboada. [Madrid: Talleres Gráficos Romarga, 1964], (17–18).

[2] San Pedro is the chief exponent of the so-called *novela sentimental*. For a definition of the genre, see Whinnom's discussion ("Introducción biográfica y crítica," 48–64).

tions to be portrayed; but the very confusion and monotony are a reasonably accurate transcription of the protagonist's tenebrous psychological world ("Diego de San Pedro's *Cárcel de amor* and the Tradition of the Allegorical Edifice," 128).

Kurtz's paragraph not only calls to mind Moner's topophilia, in terms of the interplay between interiority and exteriority, but also speaks eloquently of the type of duplication, confusion, and tenebrous aspects germane to Moner's rendition of the *infierno de los enamorados*. In the discussion that Kurtz broaches on the mutation of allegorical representation into an icon of a shadowy mindscape, we find suggestive implications as to the lover's turbulent psychological condition.

Lovelorn Expressionism

Saint Augustine, as we have just seen, raises our awareness of a text that consists of "conscience put into writing." For the poets of the *cancioneros* and for Moner in particular, we would do well to modify slightly the dictum to read "self-consciousness put into writing." Indeed, in the numerous *cancioneros* we would find abundant documentation of this psychic rather than ethical *conscientia scripta*. Moner's *Sepultura* is no exception. In fact, as we have indicated already, the poem reflects the overall mood of self-absorption and estrangement typical of the *cancioneros*. The aforementioned "frame" of *Sepultura*, in particular, strikes us as a veritable epiphany of the sense of complete isolation usually labeled with the expressive Spanish term, *ensimismamiento*. This notwithstanding, for practical reasons it is convenient to leave for the next stage of our discussion a full analysis of these shades of *ensimismamiento* that in Moner's *Sepultura* are bound to an intricate web of related issues. We will look elsewhere, then, for a sample of Moner's straightforward, psychological rendering of the Augustinian "conscientia scripta." Such a sample, in all likelihood the most important among many another of its kind in Moner's production, is found in the exordium of Moner's longest composition, a prose work entitled *La noche*.

A word is in order about the contextualization of what turns out to be a resounding outburst of emotions impelled by a powerful thrust of expression. Remarkably, as is the case of two other works of Moner—namely, the *Bendir de dones* and *L'ànima d'Oliver*, a poem and a prose work, respectively, both written in Catalan—the contextualization of *La noche* stems from a concrete topographical setting. By the magic of Moner's topophilia such a setting mutates into an imaginary counterpart fit for the allegorical world. Let us focus, then, on the workaday short narrative that ushers in the allegorical plot of *La noche*. Moner's auctorial persona recounts an episode that reads like an entry in a diary. The episode takes place in the countryside surrounding Torà, a village situated in the hinterlands, smack in the center of Catalonia.

The first-person narrator tells us that he is spending two days as a guest in the castle of the Count of Cardona, his patron. It is a late Tuesday evening. The protagonist feels the need to step out of the castle "poco antes que anochessiesse" (shortly before nightfall) in order to distract the melancholy that has overtaken him after the Count and the Countess have left on a trip to the nearby village of Tarroja. Recorded, painstakingly, in a minute-to-minute presentation, the walk he takes down to the river (the Llanera) proves to be downright frightening. During his somber sauntering, the protagonist suddenly finds himself in a precarious situation. As he comes to the end of the downhill stretch, he takes a fall to the bottom of a ravine. At this point, Moner's persona depicts, within the murky regions of the lover's psyche, a landscape of despair and desolation. The ambiance is, unmistakably, one of the *infierno de los enamorados*. Integrated into the narrative are the protagonist's lamentations, which emanate from a mind at war with itself. These are the complaints likely to be voiced by any of the denizens of the numerous *infiernos*. The author's artistic alter ego delves into a strange *psychomachia* being waged between, on the one hand, the natural inclination to vent one's passion in weeping spells and, on the other, a curious masochistic compulsion to repress any ostentation of sorrow. Illustrative of this unwholesome condition are the lover's self-conscious musings, such as those revealed in a confessionary tone straight out of the pit of despondency. Let us hear firsthand the woes of a star-crossed lover if there ever lived one:

Poco tardaron a moverse en mi alma los pensamientos tristes como enxambre en colmena. El coraçón rompía de apretado. Yo m'esforçava por no llorar, teniendo malicia que mi dolor como los otros comunes se quexasse, mas no pudo ser que las amargas lágrimas no sobreveniessen por su camino vezado. Quería la passión dar vozes, pues de justa querella tenía sobra; pero el callar para mý era más encaresser porque dava lugar al pensar y tanbién porque cualquiera razón era falta, por lastimera que fuesse. Es syerto que la palabra, liviana o de peso, me diera alyvio. Mas la pena del enmudesser se vengava de mí mesmo, my mayor enemigo, y esto me hazía querer bien a mi mal (*La noche*, ll. 39–53; *TMPW* 75–76; It was not long before sad thoughts began to stir within my mind as would a swarm in a beehive. My heart was about to break in such great distress. I made every effort not to weep, averse as I was to the idea that I should vent my grief through the usual complaints. I could not, however, refrain from shedding tears, as I often do. My passion needed a good loud cry: it had more than enough justification for that. In my case, however, silence would have been more appropriate, for it would have given me a chance to reflect. Besides, any lamentation on my part, no matter how pitiful, would do me no good. To be sure, any word, whether softly or loudly uttered, would soothe my pain. This notwithstanding, the strain from having to keep silent took its revenge on me and made me fall in love with my malady. I was, indeed, my own worst enemy.)

It stands to reason to acknowledge the prima facie evidence of the effects Moner is apt to produce by the mere vocalization of the kind exemplified in the passage just quoted. For another example of dramatic verve, we may contemplate the scene at the beginning of *L'ànima d'Oliver*, Moner's longest prose work in Catalan. The protagonist, the same first-person speaker of *La noche*, makes no bones about his disappointment and annoyance with his unnamed friend, unwilling to be or incapable of being of comfort in the hour of need. So, as the highly peeved speaker confesses,

> "digué'm tants annuygs que·l dexí, y ab fúria dresí los passos a la vall vesina de San Yerònim de Ebron, per hoyr aquel so nomenat èchon, de qui ere cert que, sixm respongués, diguera lo que yo, y, sens fer-me contrari, ensemps ab mi se dolguera." (*Oc* 138–39; he [my friend] responded with such an annoying talk that I upped and left. Full of anger, I headed for the nearby Vall d'Hebron, eager to hear that sound called echo, certain as I was that it would answer me, saying whatever I would say, and, without contradicting me, would be my companion in my grief.)

Demonstrably, then, the author's persona is searching for a stage and finds it, ready-made, well demarcated in a location that, to this day, is easily recognizable: the Vall d'Hebron, situated a few miles north of medieval Barcelona. And, needless to say, upon that stage the protagonist's lamentations attain—echo and all—full-fledged expression and pertinent resonance:

> ¿Per què no·m responeu, amiga mia tan enemiga? ¿Per què m'aveu condempnat sens culpa y sens hoyr-me? ¿He-us pogut fallir yo, que per vostra servey só fet, yo que nunca sabí ni volguí ofendre-us? Si ara que m'aveu fet pesses vos adora, ¿en quin temps vos he pogut errar? (*Oc* 139; Beloved, now turned enemy! Why don't you answer my call? Why do you condemn me without hearing me out? Am I to be blamed for anything? I was born to be at your service. Could I have done you any wrong? Never have I been willing or able to offend you in any way! You have shattered my life, and, still, I worship you! When could I have done you any harm?).[3]

---

[3] In *La noche*, we may find other statements that prove to be typical of Moner's emotionalism. Take, for instance, the following lamentation, uttered by the protagonist at the sight of Costumbre (Custom), a provocative young maiden, one of the allegorical personages he encounters:

> O mugeril hermosura, ¿por qué, siendo tan engañosa, puedes tanto? ¡O enemiga de quien más te quiere! Quien no te conosse te sigue. Húyete de quien detrás te mira, porque donde tú eres mandan soberbia, crueldad y desconocimiento. Salada d'antojos y mudanssas, a tu te siguen sin causa (*La noche*, ll. 153–59; *TMPW* 92–93, O womanly beauty! How can you be so deceiving and yet so powerful? O foe of those who desire you most intensely! The people that have a yearning for you do not know you very well. I wish you would stay away from those who gaze upon you

Some passages in Moner's two major prose works are emblematic of a text imbued with intense emotion. That text is ready to be exploited as a matrix of forceful dramatic expression through gesture and voice (verbal or otherwise). By the same token, the straight, dramatic impulse evinced at the inception of the narrative in both *La noche* and *L'ànima d'Oliver* acquires considerable complexity in *Sepultura d'amor.* [4] Let us make ready to explore that complexity in the next section.

Emotions in a "Hall of Mirrors"

The passages just quoted of Moner's prose works foreshadow the enhanced expressivity dominant in the *Sepultura d'amor.* Moner's versified strains of the funereal kind, mentioned above, evoke a sense of aggravated *ensimismamiento* and confinement in a very dark space. Thus, Moner capitalizes on a lyrical vein that generates a fundamental dramatic mode. It is not hard to perceive at the heart of Moner's dramatics the same conciseness, intensification, and synthesis that characterize Guevara's *Infierno.* [5]

---

with longing in their eyes. No matter where you are, pride, cruelty, and ingratitude reign with you. Seasoned you are with whims and fickleness. What reason is there for anyone to yearn for you?).

[4] For the purpose of comparison, we may adduce here the considerable psychological turmoil shown, also, in the opening verses of two poems written in Catalan: the afore-mentioned *Bendir de dones* and the shorter piece, entitled *Cobles de les tisores.* In contrast to the obsessive, slow self-analysis demonstrated in *La noche* and *L'ànima*, in the latter poems the self-examining is conducted in a summary fashion. In *Cobles*, for instance, the protagonist makes fleeting references to not only his perturbed state of mind — "tant fora de mi restí" (I was beside myself) (v. 4) and "vengut en extasís" (I felt I was out of my mind) (v. 19) — but also the telltale symptoms of that state ("descolorida la cara") (of wan complexion) (v. 20). In much the same fashion, both the lover's malaise and its symptoms are dispatched in three short verses of *Bendir*: "fatigat, pensant al clau / que m'à fet lo cor esclau / de congoxa, sens remey" (enfeebled as I was, I kept thinking of the spike that keeps my heart enslaved to a grief that knows no remedy) (vv. 18–20, *Oc,* 180). For additional comments on the mode of *ensimismamiento* in *La noche* and in the two other majors works by Moner — namely, *Bendir de dones* and *L'ànima d'Oliver* — see Cocozzella, *Fra Francesc Moner's Bilingual Poetics of Love and Reason*, 41–42, 83–85.

[5] The aspects I highlight here coincide with the ones identified by Whinnom in his approach to the "conceptismo cancioneril." Whinnom specifies "la concentración, la condensación y la brevedad" (concentration, condensation, and brevity) and considers the *mote*, "el poema reducido a un solo verso, a un solo octosílabo" (a poem reduced to only one verse, only one octosyllable) the exponent par excellence of the *conceptismo* in question (*La poesía amatoria*, 47).

A perusal of Guevara's poem brings to the fore unmistakable signs of a poetics of condensed expression. Consider, for instance, stanza 3 (vv. 17–24), in which a sense of intensity and economy of language is produced by the reiteration of the imagery of the fiery torments endured in the "encendida casa" (house ablaze), an unmistakable reference to the "erotic Hell:"

> Que en su encendida casa
> se queman mis pensamientos.
> Allí montan los tormentos,
> mis entrañas hacen brasa;
> allí sospiro los días
> que morir no pude luego;
> allí las lágrimas mías
> fortalescen más en fuego
>
> (*Cancionero general*, ed. González Cuenca 2: 261; In the house of Love, all ablaze, my thoughts burn away. There my torments increase and multiply and my innards turn to embers. There I have been sighing all these days that I have not met with immediate death. There, the hotter the flames, the more abundant my tears!)

It is quite evident that, here. the sensation of excruciating burning is bound by an enhanced sense of space, made palpable by the technique of anaphora: the "allí" (there) repeated throughout the poem.

Demonstrably, two characteristics stand out from the epitome of *cancionero* lyricism created by Guevara. First, we are struck by the agglomeration of terms, such as *pensamientos* (thoughts), *tormentos* (torments), *brasa* (embers), *sospiros* (sighs), *lágrimas* (tears), and *fuego* (fire) that appear in the stanza we have just quoted. Many other code words crop up at every turn throughout the poem: for instance, *esperanza perdida* (lost hope) (v. 26), *pasiones guerreras* (warring passions) (v. 29), *amargos aferes* (bitter relationship) (v. 30), *clamores* (wailings) (v. 34), *lloros y dolores* (weeping and suffering) (v. 35), *afanes* (anxieties) (v. 44), *bozes y gritos* (shouts and screams) (v. 47). The relentless repetition of the terminology of extreme suffering bears the stamp of the author's artistry and finds repercussions in Moner's *Sepultura*. The reiterative effect pertains to an ingenious interplay between two realms: one conscious, the other subconscious. Those realms constitute the overall mind-scape of the lover. The conscious, projected into the subconscious, becomes a reflection from a multiplicity of angles. The lover's inner world, then, may be described as a hall of mirrors. The general consciousness of a feeling of malaise multiplies itself in countless reflections of reflections produced by subconscious mirrors. As a result, the reflected images boomerang and assail the lover's mind.[6] The second characteristic we have foreshadowed in Guevara's iconic composition consists of the vivid depiction of the space of innerness.

For the sake of specificity, the criterion by which to compare Guevara's *Infierno* and Moner's *Sepultura* needs to be clarified. The two poets do not deal in the same manner with the aforementioned "hall of mirrors." Whereas Guevara crams his concise versification with a considerable flourish of interrelated terms, Moner concentrates on the display of contrastive phrases, delivered with the force of a paradox or an oxymoron. Typical of Moner's *Sepultura* is the poetics of synthesis, a suitable sample of which is incorporated into the text of the composition. In the course of the "misa seca," there is an opportune moment —that of the Offertory—in which two allegorical personages—namely, Firmeza (Steadfastness) and Baldón (Insult)—bring forth the sample in question as the object of that ceremony. The object consists of what the first-person narrator designates as "esta canción / qu'el muerto, quando bivía / sin plazer, / la hizo de su passion" (the following *canción* that the deceased fashioned out of his passion during his cheerless life) (vv. 300–03). What Firmeza and Baldón offer, then, is one of Moner's poems, treated as an integral component of the *misa*, even though it differs from the other stanzas in rhyme scheme and structure (i.e., the absence of the *pie quebrado*). Thus, the *canción* becomes stanza 25, which, because of its aberrant metrics and privileged function, may be considered, according to Moner's own definition, the author's *cancionero* piece par excellence. The text of stanza 25 reads as follows:

> ¡Ay del byen que mal me haze,
> mi grave dulce tristeza!
> Quanto la pena me plaze,
> el desconcyerto me pesa.
> ¡Amor, dolor comportar,
> haver por byen vuestro no,
> jamás nadye como yo . . . !
> ¡Mas nunca vos suppe amar,
> ny vos sabéys ultrajar!
> Vuestro tratar me deshaze
> porque passa de crueza:
> ser vos la causa me plaze,
> mas la manera me pesa.
> (Vv. 304–16; *2 OC,* 142. See the translation on p. 201 below.)

The synthesis just referred to is at play here in the conflation of various sets of opposites: *byen/mal, grave/dulce, dulce/tristeza, pena/plaze*. At issue is, also, the

---

[6] Similar to Guevara's "hall of mirrors" is the vicious circle that, apropos of the protagonist's plight in Diego de San Pedro's *Cárcel de amor,* Kurtz perceives in the proliferation of the symptoms of lovesickness (see pp. 30–31 above).

mind-boggling suggestiveness of one conceit juxtaposed to another. The protagonist, for instance, confesses that the extreme cruelty of the ladylove pains him to the point of distraction and, still, brings him pleasure all in one. Also, as he reproaches his *belle dame sans merci* in absentia, he ponders with dismay how he could ever have been brought to consider as beneficial the *amada*'s categorical rejection ("vuestro no").

At this juncture, we have come to grips with two samples of the iconic textuality of innerness. Through a comparison between Guevara's *Infierno* and Moner's *Sepultura* proper (to be distinguished from the strict rituality of the *misa de amores*), we have come face to face with the intense feeling, compressed lyricism, semantic overload, complex emotional reverberations of the quintessential *canción*. Here we are witnessing the gestational phase of a dramatics that holds in store the potential for a performance. As we will soon discover, Moner himself provides the coordinates and bearings to help us draw the road map for the journey that we are about to undertake.

Guideposts: "Letras matizadas" and "Forma cetrina"

We have shown, so far, that Moner's *Sepultura d'amor* encompasses two main literary modes well represented in the *cancioneros*—namely, the *sepultura* proper and the parodic *misa*. Each of these is made up of an organic assimilation of its own cluster of motifs. A focus on the primary object of our study—that is, the *Sepultura d'amor* as a complete dramatic text—brings to light the presence of an auctorial master plan. A close look at the function of such a plan is of great importance in determining the bond between the two modes we have been referring to. What stems from the *sepultura/misa* symbiosis and from the integration of the motifs pertaining to each of the two main components is the trajectory of the evolution from lyricism to drama, from drama to performance.

As we may have surmised all along, Moner manifests a profound intuition into that symbiosis. What may come as a surprise is that Moner himself provides the guideposts for anyone interested in tracing the course of that evolution. Let us address, then, the two guideposts that Moner himself strategically situates, respectively, in stanzas 1 (vv. 5–6) and 3 (vv. 33–35). In order to appreciate the powerful effect of vv. 5–6, it is appropriate to quote the entire first stanza, which constitutes the natural context of the two verses. The stanza reads as follows:

> Señora, por que sepáys
> vuestras palabras pesadas
> qué han podido,
> es menester que leáys
> estas letras matizadas
> del sentido;

que con ellas acabáys.
Y pues la cosa va ansí,
que ya m'avéys consumido
      sin porqué,
sól'os demando este sí:
que a los otros que an servido,
      por mercé,
no los tratéys como a mí.
(Vv. 1–14. See the translation on p. 197 below.)

There can be little doubt that Moner delves, quite consciously, into the esthetic of synthesis adumbrated in the Offertory *canción* already analyzed. Aside from the *canción*, what the first stanza of *Sepultura* provides is an emblematic phrase that may well serve as a label for the esthetic in question. When referring to the entire poem as "estas letras matizadas / del sentido" (this writing nuanced with sense and sentiment), the protagonist announces with the aphoristic power of a veritable motto the overarching synthesis between the intellective and emotive faculties of the lover portrayed as the typical denizen of the *infierno de los enamorados*. The synthetic property of the aphorism is enhanced by the ambivalence of the term "sentido," which signifies simultaneously both 'sense' and 'sentiment,' both 'meaning' (intellectual content) and 'feeling' (emotional charge).[7]

Elsewhere I have attempted to contextualize these "letras matizadas" in terms of the literary tradition with which Moner may claim affiliation in association with other Catalan and Valencian writers that flourished during his lifetime. I have proffered the following explication for Moner's special syncretic technique:

> Strictly speaking, the *letras* stand for the main strain in the author's artistic pedigree: the ultimate affiliation of his literary output to the troubadours through Catalan and Castilian branches, embodied, respectively, by Ausiàs March and by the most prominent *cancionero* poets or kindred writers such as Pedro de Cartagena, Pere Torroella, Juan Rodríguez del Padrón, Diego de San Pedro, Juan de Mena, the Comendador Escrivá.[8] At the same

---

[7] The double-pronged semantic function of the term is well attested in the numerous instances *sentido* is used in *Cancionero general*: see González Cuenca, "Glosario," 5: 369.

[8] In deference to the literary legacy these writers share with Moner, I have decided not to trim this rather long list of worthy representatives of that legacy. Cartagena, whose talent is duly acknowledged by Gerli ("Reading Cartagena"), played a significant role in Moner's career (see, also, above, pp. xxvi–xxvii). As we have pointed out (above, pp. xxvii–xxxiv), Torroella, a Catalan writer who belongs to the generation immediately preceding that of Moner, enjoys, as does Moner, renown as a distinguished exponent of the bilingual movement in the Catalan domain (see Cocozzella, "Pere Torroella i Francesc Moner: aspectes del bilingüisme literari [catalano-castellà] a la segona meitat del

time, the semantic value of the *sentido* component of Moner's emblematic expression is highly polysemous. The field of significance of that key term encompasses not only its primary, common acceptation—*sentido*, after all, means "meaning"—but also its reference to the emotive charge inherent in the poetic expression, a reference, that is, to *sentimiento*, also assumed by the term in the fifteenth-century Castilian discourse ("Fray Francisco Moner's Dramatic Text: The Evolution of the Spanish *Auto de Amores* of the Fifteenth Century," 25–26).

Here we cannot go into the contribution of each of the writers listed in the quotation. For the time being, we shall let their names stand in testimony to the wide spectrum of the aforementioned tradition. Nevertheless, we can hardly forgo due consideration of Ausiàs March, whose innovative poetics comes to bear on the "letras matizadas" and the other "guidepost" we are about to introduce.[9]

The second passage listed above affords a rewarding glimpse into the auctorial intention behind the master plan of Moner's *Sepultura*. In the crucial verses contained in stanza 3, we see how Moner weds his *letras matizadas* with a particular speech register for which he devises a special label. The auctorial persona addresses the *amada*'s as follows: "palabras, todas metzina. . .[d]izen en vuestro language, / lo que digo / en esta forma cetrina" (vv. 29, 33–35). I would paraphrase the passage as follows: "Your poisonous words. . .say in your language what I say in this sour style of mine." Here the label in question is "forma cetrina." The context indicates that Moner invests the adjective *cetrino/-a* with a special significance that calls for explanation. In strict accord with its etymology from the Latin *citrinus*, the term, seldom documented in the *cancionero*, generally denotes color: that of the lemon.[10] Moner, nevertheless, employs *cetrina* in a figurative sense related not to color but to taste. In fact, the allusion is to the tartness and other unsavory attributes of the lemon.[11]

---

segle XV"). Author of *Siervo libre de amor*, prototypical *novela sentimental*, Rodríguez del Padrón is a notable precursor of the aforementioned Diego de San Pedro (Cocozzella, "The Thematic Unity of Juan Rodríguez del Padrón's *Siervo libre de amor*"). Mena's and Escrivá's influence on Moner is addressed in two of Cocozzella's studies: see, respectively, *Fra Francesc Moner's Bilingual Poetics of Love and Reason*, 102–4, and "El Comendador Escrivá's Legacy: The Valencian *Auto de Amores* of the Fifteenth Century."

[9] For the essential data on March's life and works, see above, p. xx. n. 13.

[10] *Cetrino* is not registered in González Cuenca's "Glosario." For the etymology and semantics of the term see *DCECH*, 2: 58.

[11] Nicolás Núñez addresses the properties of the lemon in one of his poems collected in the *Cancionero General* ("Canción de Núñez, porque pidió a su amiga un limón" [a *canción* by Núñez, who asked his lady to give him a lemon] [ID 6208; ed. González Cuenca, 2: 416–17]). The poem mentions two beneficial effects produced by the lemon: its color cheers the heart of the lover ("por dar al coraçón / con su color alegría" [to cheer his heart with its color] [v. 5]); its sourness has medicinal effects in assuaging the lover's

The purport of Moner's use of *forma cetrina* resides in the subtextual reso-
nance of that expression and the attitude of self-recognition that it implies. It
may be said that Moner's *forma cetrina* betokens a legacy from none other than
the master himself, Ausiàs March, who avows tartness in his own verses. March
has no compunction in confessing: "nós freturans de bella eloqüença, / l'orella
d'hom afalac no pot rebre" (since we lack beautiful eloquence, the human ear will
hardly get any flattering sound from us) (Poem 42.35–36; my translation; see
Archer, ed. 293).[12] These aphoristic mighty lines inspire Martí de Riquer with
the following observation:

> [C]ontenen una confessió que Ausias March fa sense cap recança, i fins i
> tot podríem dir que amb un cert orgull: ell no posseeix bella eloqüença i
> les seves cançons manquen d'aquella harmonia o dolcesa que afalaga l'oïda
> dels homes. En el món literari culte medieval, i sobretot en el nostre món
> del XV, on els poetes seguien l'estreta retòrica trobadoresca tan detallada-
> ment codificada per l'escola de Tolosa i els preceptistes catalans, aquesta
> afirmació té molt de detonant i de revolucionària (*Història de la literatura
> catalana* 2: 541; They contain a confession that Ausias March proffers with-
> out any regret and, we may even add, with a good measure of pride: he is
> not endowed with polished eloquence; his poems lack that particular har-
> mony and sweet melody that flatter the human ear. In the cultural world
> of medieval literature, especially in the realm of our Middle Ages (a world
> in which the poets followed the strict rhetoric of the troubadours, meticu-
> lously codified by the School of Toulouse and by the rhetoricians of Cata-
> lonia), March's assertion bespeaks a good deal of dissonance and conveys a
> revolutionary thrust).[13]

In light of Riquer's observations, we can detect telltale signs of the poet's influ-
ence on Moner's attitude, "sense cap recança," and "amb un cert orgull" toward
precisely the overall stylistic rusticity of his *Sepultura d'amor*. It pays to round out
Riquer's commentary with some observations that he adds apropos of what he
calls "estil dur" (rough style), the Valencian bard's veritable trademark (*Història
de la literatura catalana* 2: 548). In addition, Riquer's critique concerning March's
"inhabilitat d'expressió" and "condensació del pensament" (*Història de la litera-*

---

pain ("El agro tomara yo / por más dulce que rosquillas / para sanar las manzillas. . ." [I
had rather take the sour one, which I consider sweeter than pastry and very good to heal
my afflictions] [vv. 6–8]).

[12] For the references to and quotations from March's poems I make use of Robert
Archer's edition.

[13] For an extensive list of publications concerning the *gay saber* and its *leys*, see Boase,
The Troubadour Revival, 53, n. 4. Boase provides a review of the literary tradition stem-
ming from the Academy of Toulouse—the Consistory dels Sept Troubadours, founded
in 1327—and spreading through the Catalan, Aragonese, and Castilian domains in the
fourteenth and fifteenth centuries (6–8).

tura catalana 2: 548) are tailor-made for the description of Moner's poetics of ompactness, conciseness, and synthesis.[14]

So Que Veritatz Autreia[15]

Since "letras matizadas" and "forma cetrina" constitute an inseparable twosome, being two sides of the same esthetic coin, Riquer's explication of March's "estil" is applicable, as well, to Moner's stylistic trademarks. Although it may not be apparent at first reading, the significance of the two "guideposts" is extraordinary. They rivet our attention straightaway on Moner's primary interest as he molds the deft articulation of *sepultura* and *misa*, with all their attendant motifs, into an engrossing dramatic modality. While pointing to the strong bond between March and Moner, "forma" and "letras" invite us to probe into the age-old tradition of troubadour lyricism and to explore the phenomenology of the love/truth symbiosis.

Let us bear in mind this threefold conflation of truth, love, and language, which Moner inherits form March and adapts to the working of an esthetic all his own. Evidently, neither March nor Moner indulges in the embellished and refined style championed by the aforementioned "escola de Tolosa," also known as the Consistori del Gai Saber. By the same token, both March and Moner do not have much use for the exquisite musicality attained by the exponents of the *dolce stil nuovo*. Moner's esthetic of "estil dur," to borrow Riquer's phrase, needs to be defined in view of two indicators: first, an affiliation with March and, second, an ultimate source that through March harks as far back as Marcabru, the renowned troubadour of the twelfth century. Crucial for the understanding of Moner's esthetic are two constant drives evidenced in March's poems: namely, the obsessive pursuit of truth and the repudiation of the abuses of rhetoric. These drives find their primary impulse in a poetic stemming from what Marcabru defines as "so que veritatz autreia" (whatever conveys truth) (Cocozzella, "Ausiàs March and the 'Truth' of the Troubadours," 114–15). Two modes, commonly called "trobar naturau" and "trobar braus," come to bear upon Marcabru's poetic.

---

[14] Marie-Claire Zimmermann, *Ausiàs March o l'emergència del jo* (València: Institut Interuniversitari de Filologia Valenciana / Barcelona: Publicacions de l'Abadia de Montserrat, 1998). Zimmermann, also, pinpoints in Ausiàs March's diction "un llenguatge oral, un *català quotidià* transcrit en termes d'escriptura poètica, una *paraula*, únic instrument adient per a la reconstrucció del Jo" (an oral language, a Catalan of every day, transcribed in terms of a poetic text, the only instrument suitable for the reconstruction of the self) (36). We may recognize a signal antecedent of Moner's "forma cetrina" in this rhetorical feature aptly identified by Zimmermann.

[15] This clause is taken from v. 10 of Marcabru's poem XXXVII. For the text of the poem see the bibliography below.

According to Linda M. Paterson, the *naturau* consists of "the art of composing according to 'so que veritatz autreia,' as opposed to 'artificially' or 'falsely' in not only a formal but also a moral sense" (*Trobadours and Eloquence*, 29). The *braus*, by contrast, bespeaks a rejection of "smooth language associated with deceiving flatterers" (*Trobadours and Eloquence*, 54). Incidentally, this is the smooth, sweet, flowery talk (an effective bait, so to speak, in the flatterer's trap), against which Andreas Capellanus warns his pupil Gualterius.[16]

We may perceive in Moner's memorable "letras" a reflection of not only Marcabru's truth-oriented manner but also the lexical deflation and revitalization of *sentido* that, apropos of March's style, Di Girolamo describes in the following manner: "A[usiàs] March deflates a vocabulary which the troubadours had overladen with 'sacred' literary meanings, and often restores the ordinary semantic value of most of the courtly terminology" ("Ausiàs March and the Troubadour Code," 236).[17] Arguably, Ausiàs March's dedication to rejuvenating the vocabulary he inherits from the troubadours contributes substantially toward the *letras matizadas del sentido*, fashioned by Moner. The issues that come to the fore have

---

[16] Andreas Capellanus, *Andreas Capellanus on Love*, ed. and trans. P. G. Walsh (London: Gerald Duckworth & Co., 1982). Before entering into details apropos of the harmful effects of adulation in the love relationship, Capellanus proffers the following advice to young Gualterius:

> Sermonis facundia multotiens ad amandum non amantium corda compellit. Ornatum etenim amantis eloquium amoris consuevit concitare aculeo et de loquentis facit probitate praesumi (44; Eloquence of speech frequently impels the hearts of indifferent persons to love. The adorned language of a lover usually unleashes love's darts; it creates a good impression about the speaker's moral worth, 45).

[17] Di Girolamo's conclusions deserve to be quoted at length. Following are some observations of particular interest:

> Apart from the new quantitative relations, the semantic value of a particular set of terms is in crisis here: any word used by A. March is precise and has few possible secondary meanings or overtones: this explains why terms, avoided by his predecessors, are present in his vocabulary. And this is one of the most important aspects of his language: it is semantically concrete, in contrast with the semantic hypertrophy of the troubadours; one might almost speak of "verbal realism," and this is the only sense in which "realism" can be used with reference to A. March. In contrast to his contemporaries or predecessors, he has attempted a reduction of the poetic word, bringing to it a less elevated level, and rendering its interpretation possible without the help of any medieval semantic or stylistic filters (236).

On the basis of his studies of March's lexicon, Di Girolamo argues that the poet makes a radical departure from the troubadour tradition. In my own investigation of this matter, I point out, nevertheless, that, by privileging, as does Marcabru, the values of *veritatz*, and in emulating some of the principles of the esthetic championed by Arnaut Daniel, Ausiàs March bears witness to his legacy from the lyricists of Provençe. (See Cocozzella, "Ausiàs March and the 'Truth' of the Troubadours").

to do with March's dialogue with the troubadours: that is, with March's radical response to the trans-Pyrenean legacy. This profound existential dialogue plays out in a phenomenology of rescued meaning and asserted authenticity of the lover's experience. Not in vain does the Valencian bard, at the start of one of his most quoted poems, proclaim a bold new esthetic agenda by means of two incisive verses: "Llexant a part l'estil dels trobadors / qui, per escalf, trespassen veritat" (Discarding the style of the troubadours, those that are so inflamed that they cannot speak without exaggeration).[18] An explication of these verses will open, no doubt, a new chapter in the history of post-troubadour love-centered literature.

These fragmentary clauses give us a glimpse of three dimensions of March's poetry: notion of language, sense of reality, and attitude toward the troubadours. It is not necessary at this time to go into the interpretive corpus that a number of scholars have devoted to these two verses.[19] Suffice it to say that here March is not casting aspersions on the troubadours in general. He is targeting only those that indulge in *escalf*: that is, the excessive flourish or histrionic manner that in verse 3 of Poem 23 is characterized as "voler afectat" (affected emotions). Of this blemish March does not consider himself completely immune. After all, in that same verse the poet expresses his firm purpose to purge his poem of his own false show of emotion ("mon voler afectat"). It follows, then, that in eschewing *escalf* and *voler afectat*, March privileges and extols truth, the revered entity that, in his judgment, a sect of hypocritical troubadours has egregiously profaned.

The Adoration of Truth

Let us dwell here a bit longer on the topic of truth in an effort to investigate how a concept that incubates in the author's imagination hatches out as a salient motif. We begin with an idea that haunts the author's mind. The idea gets to be obsessive as it becomes more and more evident as a determinant of the plot that Moner devises for *Sepultura*. The overall direction of the plot is charted in the epigraph affixed to *Sepultura* in the *editio princeps* (1528). The epigraph reads as follows: "Finge Moner en esta obra que se sigue ser muerto damor verdadero por lo qual le manda manzilla gentilesa y otras amigas y compañeras dellas hazerle obsequias en vn templo so inuocation de la verdad" (*A*, fol. C7ᵛ; *2 OC*, 159; In the following work Moner imagines that he has died because of his devotion to true

---

[18] These are vv. 1–2 of March's Poem 23 (see Archer, 115–20). I adopt Robert Archer's translation with an emendation, changing "the troubadours, who" to "the troubadours, those that."

[19] Examples of the leading trends of interpretation of these verses may be found in Archer, notes 115–16; Di Girolamo, "Ausiàs March and the Troubadour Poetic Code," 424–29; and Riquer, *Història* 2: 542–44.

love. In response, Lady Compassion bids Lady Gentility and other friends and companions of theirs to render homage to him in a temple dedicated to God-the-Truth). This heading is matched and complemented by the one that, in the same *editio princeps*, pertains to the poem entitled *Bendir de dones* and, in the guise of a veritable abstract of that piece, provides the following background information: "Obra de Moner en lengua catalana, feta per escusar-se de una culpa que un cert cavaller y unes senyores, absent Moner de la dama que servia, lo avien falçament inculpat" (*A*, fol. F7; *Oc*, 179; A work of Moner's, written in Catalan to refute the charges of a misdeed, of which a certain gentleman and some ladies had falsely accused him, while he was away from the lady he served). A conflation of the two rubrics, added, in all probability, by the editor of 1528, makes quite specific the sense of purpose and direction that shapes the plot of each corresponding poem: in *Bendir*, the vindication ("per escusar-se de una culpa") of the genuine love of the protagonist (the auctorial persona); in *Sepultura*, the proper homage ("obsequias") rendered to him.

At the time of its gestation, the plan of vindicating the lover's devotion to the principles of truth is conditioned by the spatial poetics we have touched upon already. Take, for instance, the transition from the realm of *extra ecclesiam* to that of *intra ecclesiam*. Concomitant to the transition is the shift from the mode of the *infierno* to that of the ritual (i.e., the celebration of the Mass). The shift, in turn, involves a substantial mutation in the nature of spatiality inherent in each of those modes. We witness a veritable evolution that may be envisaged from the nature of "space" to that of "place." We are confronted with a transformation from the space of the psyche to the place of the soul. The parameters of "space" and "place" adumbrate, at the heart of Moner's poetics of love, the charting of a journey of transcendence from the desolation of the psyche to the regeneration of the soul.[20]

Here Moner's tour de force reaches its high point. It defines the field of devotion and spirituality, in which Mancilla carries out her hieratic duties. The coordinates that demarcate that field are provided at the very beginning of the Mass (stanza 15), where we find a description of the physical setting, "ell altar de Verdad" (v. 172). At the same time, we discover the prmary orientation of the religious service: the form of worship comes to a full realization in the Mass. We witness three priestesses ("con gesto de manssedumbre") at the start of their collaborative demonstrations of homage and prayerful submission to the Divinity:

> La yglesia llena de lumbre,
> las campanas a gran pryssa,
>   son salidas

---

[20] For a full discussion of this journey, see Cocozzella, "Fra Francesc Moner's Psychic Space / Soulful Place."

Esperiencia y la Costumbre
y Manzilla, por la missa
    ya vestidas,
con gestos de manssedumbre.
Y todas tres a la par
en ell altar de Verdad
    pobrezico,
escomiençan confessar
a la Verdad l'amistad,
    y baxico,
en esta forma rezar.
(Vv. 164–77.) (For the translation see p. 199 below.)

In an explosion of light and sound, especially surprising as it emerges as a sudden contrast with the darkness of the *infierno*, stanza 15 introduces a two-pronged motif, echoed throughout Moner's *Sepultura*. First, there is the presentation of Verdad as an epiphany of the Divine. There is, to be sure, nothing heretical in designating Verdad as a name for God. For strong support of that designation, we need look no further than the Gospel of John, where the Messiah identifies Himself in the following terms: "Ego sum via, veritas, et vita" (I am the way, the truth, and the life) (John 14:6). This notwithstanding, one would readily agree that, though truth is an appropriate attribute of the Supreme Being, Verdad (God-the-Truth) is hardly a conventional appellative to be incorporated into the liturgy of the Mass. Evidently, Moner teases our imagination with a display of the unconventional. While according Verdad the highest privilege as a name, Moner does not tamper with the identity of God. Neither does he vitiate the mode of worship authorized by Holy Mother Church. Thus, even when introducing radical changes in the letter of the liturgy, Moner shows the highest respect for the spirit and the integrity of the traditional way of worship. The second dimension of the leitmotif announced above fuses the duly adapted ritual of the Mass with the radical conversion of the fictionalized Moner into a canonized personage. The *mártir de amor* becomes the saint of Truth. Moner's rendition of the solemn Mass, officiated by three female priests and dedicated to a female avatar of God—"A ti, Verdad, nuestro dýa" (v. 178); "O Verdad, nuestra abogada" (v. 195); "Verdad, aquel que te pecca" (v. 223)—turns out to be, all in one, the apotheosis of Truth and the sacralization of the lifetime experience of the true lover. It would hardly surprise anyone, then, that *Sepultura d'amor* should stand out as a powerful testimony of Moner's indebtedness to Ausiàs March's truth-oriented poetic.

IV.

The Dramatization of the Monologue

The Mode of Immanence

Ausiàs March brings into focus one issue: that of the tension between *veritat* and *escalf* or *voler afectat*. Moner capitalizes upon this tension, ultimately derived from Marcabru (see pp. xlii, 41–43 above), and sets it in full operation in *Sepultura d'amor*. In *Sepultura*, Moner develops a text that points to itself and, by its sheer power of conviction and straightforwardness of a latter-day *trobar naturau*, lays claim to being taken at face value. It also compels the reader or the hearer to be a listener. Like Marcabru, March, and company, Moner aims at a diaphanous writing that, without any distracting embellishment, attains and retains its full signification strictly within the limits of itself. What Moner achieves by means of *letras matizadas* is the effect of the immanence revealed by March in the here-and-now symptoms of the lover's passion.[1] As we come to terms with Moner's notion of immanence, we gain insight into the effectiveness of Moner's dramatics: the stage presence of a self-evident authenticity that, as such, requires no proof and makes no demands, except that it be witnessed firsthand.

Upon close study, we see how the leitmotif of truth becomes a primordial factor in the shaping of the plot. Let us turn our attention back to the text of solitude that mirrors the "topophilia of innerness." This meditation on solitude and innerness opens our eyes to the notion of immanence, yet another source of dramatics in Moner's *Sepultura*. Immanence may be defined in terms of the lover's direct confrontation with his passions. What prevails in the sphere of immanence is the mood and the ambiance of the *infierno de enamorados*. We find that the aspects of immanence featured in the text of solitude constitute the preliminary phase in the evolution of the *sepultura/misa* dyad.

One of Moner's major compositions reveals that those very aspects stem from the mechanics of expansion and enhancement. The composition in question is *Obra en metro*, a poem, written in Castilian, which consists of 700 verses of the type commonly called "arte mayor." The last word in the title refers to

---

[1] For a methodical analysis of these symptoms see Robert Archer, *Aproximació a Ausiàs March: estructura, tradició, metàfora* (Barcelona: Empúries, 1996).

this type of verse, nothing unusual in Castilian literature of the fifteenth century. The term "metro" indicates a pronounced caesura, and hemistichs, which, according to the Spanish system of scansion, count six syllables each.[2]

Obra en metro reflects a state of immanence, a condition that pertains to the psychological space of the erotic Hell. What is unusual about this poem is the paradoxical bond between the obvious emotionality of the lover's temperament and his no-less-evident penchant for the operations of reason. The paradox is born of the mutual dependency of these otherwise contentious entities. Each relies upon the other for its very subsistence. One does not obliterate but, rather, invigorates the other.

Thus, *Obra en metro* becomes a bold statement of ratiocination articulated within a context of emotions ebbing and flowing. This interplay of sedate discursiveness and impassioned remonstration may be divided into four main sections. The function of these is analogous to that of the movements in a Mozartian symphony. The first three sections, addressed respectively to Voluntad, Razón, and Fortuna, reiterate a tripartite pattern, which begins with a vehement venting of emotions, shifts into digressions of a reflective or speculative nature, and concludes with a reference to a state of resignation and relative tranquility. Each of these sections evokes the grand style that harks far back to Prudentius's *Psychomachia*, or echoes, closer to Moner's time, the epic decorum of Juan de Mena's *Laberinto de Fortuna*. What is really remarkable in *Obra en metro* is the manner in which Moner's poetic alter ego personalizes his plight and his relationship with the three redoubtable ladies (Voluntad, Razón, and Fortuna) he feels the urge to conjure up or call upon.[3]

A simple juxtaposition of a couple of passages will bring to light this process of personalization. Let us take, for instance, the following verses, in which Mena, in the second stanza of his *Laberinto* (vv. 9–12), summarizes the central theme of his poem:

Tus casos falaçes, Fortuna, cantamos,
estados de gentes que giras e trocas,
tus grandes discordias, tus firmezas pocas,
e los que en tu rueda quexosos fallamos.
(Of your works of deceit, Lady Fortune, we sing,
of the people, whose lives you turn and turn over:
so great is your turmoil, so little your constancy,
so mournful are those that ride on your wheel.)

---

[2] For a definition of the *verso de arte mayor*, see above, p. xxii, n. 17.

[3] The reader may find useful the summary, general outline, and explication of *Obra en metro* in Cocozzella, *2 Introducción*, 3–23.

It is easy to see how the foregoing declaration warrants a comparison with the analogous invective against Fortuna found in Moner's *Obra en metro*. Of particular interest is the following passage (vv. 321–25):

Contigo las he,   maldita Fortuna;
no quiero dexar   de inculparte de mí
porque m'as sido   adversa, syempre una.
Sé que muy poca   emyenda o ninguna,
por mutcho que diga,   s'espera de ty.

(Accursed Fortune, with you I take grievance.
For my ills I shall blame you and will not desist:
toward me you are hostile and will be the same!
My complaints may be many, but well do I know
that little or no help from you will I get.)

While retaining the majestic tonalily of a Juan de Mena, Moner evidently restricts the universal scope that usually accompanies an epic like Mena's *Laberinto*. Moner transforms the epic sway à la Juan de Mena into a lyric compass: he converts generalized pronouncements concerning the proverbial Everyman into the concerns of a single individual of flesh and blood.[4]

What *Obra en metro* contributes to our knowledge of Moner's art of allegory becomes apparent through a comparison with *Bendir de dones* and *La noche*. That simple comparative exercise reveals that *Obra en metro*, though throbbing at every moment with dramatic dynamism, lacks the theatrical projection characterizing the other two compositions also located in immanent psychic space. This means that Moner in *Obra* enhances the feel of immanence by delving deeper and deeper into the crevasse of stark interiority. *Obra en metro* illustrates how the descent into the recesses of conciousness sets into operation a pernicious downswing of frustration. That glimpse into the abyss of the self rebounds in the prevailing speech of alienation. Frustration and alienation come to the fore in such passages as the following, directed to Lady Reason:

Y por que sepáys   que más ensayé
por ver si pudiera   iamás olvidalla,
irm'en destyerro   determiné;
y con un dolor,   que dezirhos no sé,
dexé su presencia   sin nunca dexalla.
(Vv. 151–55; *2 OC*, 80–81;

---

[4] It bears pointing out that in vv. 151–210 there are specific autobiographical references that accentuate the personal nature of the poem. See the commentary in Cocozzella, *2 Introducción*, 5.

> I want you to know I made every effort,
> anxious to see: could I ever forget her?
> Thus, I decided to go into exile.
> Indeed, with a grief I cannot describe,
> her presence I left but then could not leave her).

More often than not, the expression of alienation undermines the vein of ratiocination. The philosophical disquisition and logical argumentation may be intended to produce the wholesome effect of purging away harmful passions. The effect, however, is far from realized. The very process of said purging shows symptoms of a perverse turnabout that thwarts the lover's deepseated desire for liberation from his psychological conflict. *Obra en metro* is conceived in the very matrix of a crisis. In diametric contrast to the verve of disputation that stirs in *L'ànima d'Oliver* and *La noche*, the strain of ratiocination that courses through *Obra en metro* does not find fulfillment in a well-rounded dialogue. Instead, it expresses itself as an instinctive venting of a soliloquy, at times compulsive, at times doleful, and, in any case, extremely agitated. The speeches that the author's persona addresses to the allegorical personages—Razón, Voluntad, Fortuna —become amalgamated into the soliloquy. Far from bringing about the serenity of conscience, that solipsistic exercise bespeaks the lover's anxiety vis-à-vis the existential paradox discernible at the heart of the malady of eros.

Demonstrably, the notion of the "monodiálogo," borrowed from Miguel de Unamuno, may be applied to the give-and-take manqué that Moner dramatizes between the lover and the aforementioned three formidable ladies. In foreshadowing Unamuno's insights, Moner shows that the lover's anxiety or perturbed state jeopardizes the external projection of the psychological conflict and thus obstructs the normal channel of the catharsis achievable through a dialogue in the unfolding of an allegory. Yet another Unamunian factor perceptible *avant la lettre* in *Obra en metro* is the disquieting crisis of reason and the intellect. The author implores the aid of Lady Reason, who, in her office as a guide, should but does not signal the way to sanity and salvation. The desperate tone of the lover's invocation is evident in speeches such as the following:

> Socorredme pues vos,   Razón, que soys guía
> y vía segura,   regla sin yerro.
> Sin vos no he poder   sobre quien me desvía.
> (Vv. 81–83; *2 OC,* 78;

> Then, o Reason, come to my aid,
> You are my guide, a norm without flaw!
> Without you I have no power over the woman that leads me astray).

This impassioned appeal finds little satisfaction in the awareness that, as Unamuno would point out many centuries after Moner's lifetime, Razón flounders in dejection from one defeat to another and, ultimately, proves to be an utter failure in the discharge of her main duty: helping human beings come to grips with destiny. Not surprisingly, in an aside imbued with feelings of resentment and disappointment, Moner's alter ego undercuts the dialogue with these bitter words:

> ¿Qué me fatigo   sin consolación
> a quyen no aprovecha   contar amarguras?
> Do no está consejo   ni ay election
> presumir de ajudarse   con la razón
> es querer hazer   con seso locuras.
> (Vv. 290–95; *2 OC,* 86;

> Why do I drive myself to exhaustion without consolation
> for the sake of one to whom I confess my sorrows to no avail?
> For a person bereft of discernment and free choice
> to presume to get help from reason
> is tantamount to turning sanity into madness.)

It is fair to conclude that in *Obra en metro* Moner does not deal with a concrete space, such as the one exemplified by a stage intended for an actual theatrical performance. Indeed, the kind of space evoked in *Obra* has an abstract quality to it. It is concomitant with the sense of drama that has to do with the wide resonance of the protagonist's voice. The resonance in itself situates the reader or listener in the realm of psycho-drama. In the "galerías del alma," to borrow Antonio Machado's happy phrase (quoted in Baker, "Antonio Machado y las galerías del alma," 647), or in the "dark world and wide," to use John Milton's expression (Sonnet 19, v. 2), tormented lovers come to grips with their tragic condition. Gradually they grow accustomed to wearing buskins, so to speak. So, as we listen closely to Moner's poetic voice utter, stentoriously, "Voluntad, ¿qué es de vos? ¿Qué es lo que sentís?" (v. 11), "Socorredme pues vos, Razón, que soys guía" (v. 81), and "Contigo las he, maldita Fortuna" (v. 321), we may recall the lamentations of the aggrieved Pleberio, who in act 21 of Fernando de Rojas's *Celestina,* deprecates the abuses perpetrated by the capricious goddess, dispenser of worldly goods. The dramatic outcome of Pleberio's woeful cries may be surmised even from a few of his mournful words:

> ¡O fortuna variable, ministra y mayordoma de los temporales bienes! ¿Por qué no executaste tu cruel yra, tus mudables ondas, en aquello que a ti es subjeto? (Rojas, 338; Oh, Fortune, stewardess of earthly goods, why lashed you not with fickle waves—why wreaked you not your wrath—on that which lay in your dominion? (Rojas, translated by Singleton, 247)

In sum, as we lean over in order to look into what Unamuno calls "el brocal sin fondo de la conciencia humana" (the bottomless pit of human consciousness),[5] we experience the effect of "De profundis clamavi ad te, Domine" (Psalm 130, v. 1; 'Out of the depths have I cried unto thee, Lord). The cry may come from Moner's persona or from any other denizen of the *infierno de enamorados*. We may hear, also, the protestations from the likes of Pleberio or, for that matter, from any tragic hero in the company of Shakespeare's Hamlet or Calderón's Segismundo. Moner, in *Obra en metro* recaptures the ambiance and mood, if not the actual staging, of the tragic.

Corollaries

We have seen how the esthetics of *Obra en metro* is rooted in a profound medita-tion on the mode of immanence pertaining to the lover's inner turmoil. By delv-ing into that mode Moner endows the text of solitude with a sense of expanded space and heightened emotional tension. Moreover, by the design of *Obra en metro*, Moner sets in operation a play of alterity between the presence of the lover bemoaning his plight and the shadowy figure of the beholder, enticed to witness the lover's struggle with an array of passions. We begin to realize that the delivery of the monologue or mono-dialogue, as the case may be, in *Obra en metro* conditions a determinate reaction on the part of the beholder. To be spe-cific, Moner engineers for the beholder a privileged position that presupposes a perspective of one who is serene, learned, and wise.

Let us see how Moner's esthetic of alterity plays out. In the fourth and last section of *Obra en metro* (vv. 531–690), the poetic ego desists from yet another emotional surge and withdraws into a serene discussion of considerable length on the momentous issues of free will and predestination. Even as he lays out his ideology in some one hundred and seventy verses, Moner's persona leaves no doubt as to his firm adherence to orthodox Christian doctrine. As for the car-dinal tenets of that doctrine regarding the issues mentioned above, the section shows complete agreement with such prominent thinkers of his day and age as Alfonso Martínez de Toledo, Alonso de Cartagena, Lope Barrientos, and Mar-tín de Córdoba.[6]

---

[5] The statement is taken from Unamuno's "autocrítica" which prefaces the text of his play *El otro*. (Quoted in Cocozzella, "Salvador Espriu's Idea of a Theater: The *Sotjador* vs. the Demiurge," 475).

[6] For a summary review of the ideology of these "doctos varones," see Juan de Dios Mendoza Negrillo, *Fortuna y providencia en la literatura castellana del siglo XV*, Anejos del Boletín de la Real Academia Española 27 (Madrid: Real Academia Española, 1973), 123–57. There is, as we may surmise, a vast background of ideologies that come to bear on Moner's meditation on Fortune. Whinnom presents a compendium of the theories

In light of the heightened ratiocination with which Moner brings his *Obra en metro* to a dispassionate conclusion, it is safe to observe that in it Moner strives to arrive at a perspective born of a withdrawal from the realm of the erotic Hell. Naturally, such a withdrawal engenders a locus of alterity: it implies a sense of being ensconced in a refuge, at a safe distance from that "other" place, the breeding ground of sorrows. Specifically, it may be argued that what Moner has in mind is the standpoint of one of those "doctos varones castellanos," to whom Fernando de Rojas accords pride of place in one of the two prefatory texts he added to *Celestina*.[7] At this point, we may mention a detail that Rojas adds in his expanded version of *Celestina*: a version that the author himself entitles *Tragicomedia*. The detail consists of the suggestion that the *docto varón*, for whom Rojas still refuses to provide a definitive identity, is someone no less talented than Juan de Mena and Rodrigo Cota.[8] The insight to be derived from a work like Moner's *Obra en metro*, will not solve, of course, the controversy that arose from Rojas's own statements. It does shed light, nevertheless, on the mind-set of that all-important *varón*. Indeed, the dispassionate detachment we have just witnessed in Moner's persona may well turn out to be one of the telling harbingers of the stoic aloofness of the personage typified, according to Rojas, by Mena and Cota. A writer like Moner would help us realize that the *docto varón* of Mena's and Cota's caliber is installed atop the watchtower of his wholesome impartiality, redolent of *senequismo* and blended with a healthy dose of unadulterated Christian doctrine.

A perusal of *Obra en metro* conjures up visions of the field of solitude in which the monologue of the grieving lover dramatically projects itself, inside out, in overtones of haunting lamentations. An excursion into the realm of *Obra*

---

about Fortuna that prevailed in classical antiquity and spread far and wide with sundry adaptations throughout the Middle Ages (Introducción crítica 1979, 59–77).

[7] See "El autor a un su amigo" (the author to a friend of his) (Rojas, 69–71).

[8] Rojas lavishes high praise on "los claros ingenios de doctos varones castellanos" (in the minds of sage and learned Castilians' [trans. Singleton, 4]) and goes so far as to attribute to one of the "doctos varones" the authorship of a manuscript he purports to have found and used as the first act of *Celestina* (70). Rojas chooses not to identify the alleged author. This has motivated much speculation. By the same token, there is a spirited debate as to how to interpret Rojas's reference to the manuscript. There are those who regard Rojas's account as factual and those who consider it a clever literary ruse, an antecedent of sorts to the fictive manuscript of *Don Quijote*, authored, according to Cervantes's narrator, by the Arabian author, Cide Hamete Benengeli. For a full discussion of the issues attendant upon the identity and authorship of the "docto varón," see Cocozzella, "From Lyricism to Drama: The Evolution of Fernando de Rojas' Egocentric Subtext." For an overview of Mena's and Cota's contribution to the Spanish literature of the late Middle Ages and early Renaissance, see, respectively, Elisa Aragone, introduction to *Diálogo entre el Amor y un Viejo*, by Rodrigo Cota, ed. Elisa Aragone (Firenze: Felice Le Monnier, 1961); and María Rosa Lida de Malkiel, *Juan de Mena, poeta del prerrenacimiento español.* (México: Fondo de Cultura Económica, 1950).

makes us aware that the *campo de crueza*, as Moner calls it, may attain considerable expanse, and the monologue is typically the result of a frustrated dialogue. Hence, the Unamunian connotations of the "mono-dialogue."

As we come to grips with the semiotic unfolding of *Obra en metro*, a theorem gradually takes shape in our minds. The theorem, which consists of the equation between the mode of immanence and the text of solitude, yields a number of corollaries of sorts. These become more and more evident as we investigate the crucial aspects in Moner's esthetic in general. Let us take, for instance, the aforementioned resonance of a monologue that turns out to be a frustrated dialogue. The overtones of that monologue automatically create a sense of spatiality. Here we witness the unusual phenomenology of a lonesome voice in search of a stage. We experience, at the same time, a palpable, complementary bond between, on the one hand, the exemplary sufferer (the *mártir de amor*), confined in the *cárcel de amor* or the *infierno* and *purgatorio de los enamorados*, and, on the other hand, the observer accommodated in the privileged position of the stoic *doctor varón*.

A Voice in Search of a Stage

For a reader of *Obra en metro* the resonance of the protracted soliloquy produces an indelible impression. The same strain of lamentation—the tone of a *vox clamantis*, so to speak—may be heard throughout Moner's *Sepultura*. In the spirit of affirming "so que veritatz autreia" in repudiation of the "escalf" of the troubadours, Moner fashions the "forma cetrina" as an instrument sine qua non for furthering March's grand project: the revitalization of the poetic language by plumbing the depths of "innerness" and highlighting the authenticity of the lover's experience. What Moner enhances in March's legacy is a special resonance of the auctorial voice: a voice that brings out fully the drama inherent in the poetic text. It is useful to compare the first stanza of Guevara's *Infierno* with the equivalent passage in Moner's *Sepultura*. In a conceit heaving with a host of morbid emotions, Guevara personifies his poem. Thus, it is the poem itself—the *otra obra suya, llamada Infierno de amores*, identified in the epigraph—that salutes and kisses the hands of the formidable lady. A short quotation will suffice to recapture the impassioned oratory of the embittered *amante*:

> La boz, amarga, llorosa,
> de mis afanes vfanos,
> con dolor besa las manos
> de Tu Merced engañosa:
> con la qual sin galardones
> te suplican mis tormentos
> que contemples las passiones
> de mis altos pensamientos.

(Vv. 1–8; Full of sorrow, the embittered, mournful voice of my persistent attempts, kisses your hand, o my deceitful lady. With this voice, my torments, though unrewarded, beseech you to show some regard for the passions that accompany my honorable sentiments).

For an illustrative example of how Moner's emblematic *amador* addresses his less-than-sympathetic *amada*, we may refer back to the first stanza of *Sepultura* quoted above (see p. 36)

At the very first reading of the two stanzas we perceive the contrast between the two kinds of rhetoric that the novelist, Pío Baroja, labels "de tono mayor" (in a major tone) and "de tono menor" (in a minor tone). While we would not inflict upon Guevara the rather negative connotation that Baroja ascribes to the "tono mayor,"[9] we need not hesitate in assigning to Moner's style the virtues of the "retórica de tono menor," which, to quote Baroja, "a primera vista parece pobre, luego resulta más atractiva, tiene un ritmo más vivo, más vital, menos ampuloso" (at first blush, looks impoverished, later turns out to be rather attractive, shows a livelier, more vital, less pretentious rhythm, 174–75). In the final analysis, both Guevara and Moner foreshadow, each in his own way, the symptoms of the so-called *culteranismo* or *gongorismo* and *conceptismo* that in Spanish literature of the seventeenth century are superbly exemplified by Luis de Góngora and Francisco de Quevedo.[10] Indeed, Guevara's refinement and slightly recherché elegance, evidenced in such phrases as "de mis afanes vfanos" and "passiones / de mis altos pensamientos," are not lost on Pierre Le Gentil, distinguished connoisseur of *cancionero* poetry. Apropos, precisely, of Guevara's *Infierno*, Le Gentil spots "certaines subtilités," which he interprets as symptoms of a *culteranismo avant la lettre* and associates, contrary to the opinion and expectation of many a critic, not with "les pétrarquistes italiens du XVe siècle" (the fifteenth-century Italian followers of Petrarch) but, rather, with Charles d'Orléans, the influential French poet of the fifteenth century (Le Gentil, *La poesie lyrique espagnole et portugaise a la fin du moyen age,* 1: 274).[11]

---

[9] This trait, observes Baroja, pertains to "la retórica heredada de los romanos, que intenta dar solemnidad a todo, a lo que ya lo tiene de por sí y a lo que no lo tiene" (the rhetoric inherited from the Romans, which intends to bestow solemnity on everything, on what has solemnity in its own right, and what does not, 174–75).

[10] For a full discussion of these literary fashions in conjunction with their pertinent terminology, see Dámaso Alonso, *Góngora y el "Polifemo."* 3 vols. (Madrid: Gredos, 1967) 1: 80–94.

[11] Le Gentil pinpoints in Guevara's style some "minutieuses correspondences entre. . .sentiment et la réalité" (minute correspondences between. . .feeling and reality) together with a special interest "plus à la valeur abstraite de la métaphore qu'à son élément concret" (1: 274; in the abstract value of the metaphor rather than in its concrete meaning) and adds the following observation:

At the risk of oversimplification, we would venture to say that Guevara, among other exponents of the *subtilités* highlighted by Le Gentil, represents in Spanish literature of the fifteenth century an embryonic *gongorismo* that comes into full bloom in the seventeenth. Moner, for his part, resorts to a latter-day poetics of *trobar naturau*, which, starting from the first stanza of *Sepultura* quoted above, reflects throughout *Sepultura* the rugged manners of everyday speech: "pues la cosa va ansí" (v. 8), "sol'os demando este sí" (v. 11). In other words, what Moner puts forth is a sneak preview of that *desgarrón afectivo*—that is, the sensational ripping or slashing effect à la Quevedo or à la Lope de Vega —that Dámaso Alonso diagnoses within the secluded "innerness" of subjectivity. In his own obsessive introspection into the lover's tormented mind and soul, Moner adumbrates the *desgarrón*, through which, according to Alonso, "entran en el mundo noble heredado del Renacimiento las voces ásperas o las vislumbres infrahumanas, como en tantas páginas de Quevedo, o todo el desenfreno vital y literario de Lope de Vega" (*Góngora y el "Polifemo,"* 1: 85; harsh words and infrahuman visions work their way into the lofty world inherited from the Renaissance as they do in so many of Quevedo's passages or in the vitality, utterly irrepressible, of Lope de Vega's literary creativity). Alonso's mention of *voces ásperas* is enough to remind us of Moner's indebtedness to Ausiàs March. After all, March, also, by virtue of his own *estil dur, forma cetrina*, and *voces ásperas*, bears witness to a *desgarrón afectivo* that Josep Miquel Sobrer describes as "to shout a kind of truth that needed to be chewed from its raw essence" ("Ausiàs March, the Myth of Language, and the Troubadour Tradition," 332).

By now, we realize that the insight into Moner's brand of *conceptismo* leads us to a self-evident proposition that has to do with the sheer vocality of *letras matizadas* and *forma cetrina*. The very resonance of that vigorous, raw utterance augurs a natural fulfillment in a theatrical performance.[12] In *Sepultura* the auctorial voice carries a stage effect and a theatrical resonance. The sheer directness of the auctorial speech generates, all along, the base of self-authenticating sincerity and trustworthiness, with which we can easily sympathize or even identify. Indeed, Moner enters boldly into the precincts of the dramatic monologue that finds analogs in the literary creations of a Robert Browning or a Miguel de Unamuno.

Enfin, il y a encore quelque chose de bien espagnol dans le poème de Guevara; cet enfer symbolique est en effet une manière de *parodie*, et nous avons souligné combien le procédé, appliqué à l'amour, avait eu de succès au Sud des Pyrénées (1: 274; In sum, there is something distinctly Spanish in Guevara's poem; this symbolic Hell is, in effect, a kind of parody. We have pointed out how, when applied to love, this literary process became very successful south of the Pyrenees).

[12] A memorable stage effect has been pointed out already in reference to a crucial passage in *L'ànima d'Oliver*: the lover's lament echoed in the Vall d'Hebron. (See p. 33 above.)

The evocation of these authors broaches the analysis of two manifestations of Moner's dramatics: (1) the dynamics of a projection mechanism that, as in Browning's case, culminates in the individuation of a lifelike characterization;[13] (2) the existential metaphysics of a soliloquy that, as in Unamuno's "monodiálogo," turns out to be the auctorial persona's dialogue with a split self.[14] Worthy of spe-

---

[13] Michael Mason, "Browning and the Dramatic Monologue," in *Robert Browning*, ed. Isobel Armstrong (Athens: Ohio University Press, 1975), 231–66. In his full discussion of Browning's dramatics, Mason calls attention to the speaker's instinctive and direct analysis of his own condition: "The speaker betrays important aspects of his state of mind rather than articulating them" (234). Mason points to Browning's effective use of colloquialism, a trait that reminds us of March's and Moner's brand of "retórica de tono menor." According to Mason, that colloquialism "is the most consistently distinguishing trait of Browning's dramatic monologues" (238).

[14] Paul Ilie engages in a discussion of how Unamuno's confrontation with the self may serve as a principle for a theatricalization as evidenced in Unamuno's play, *El otro*. See Paul Ilie, *Unamuno: An Existential View of Self and Society* (Madison: University of Wisconsin Press, 1967), 19–47, 91–116. I would argue that an analogous principle is at work in Moner's interaction with his own complex vision of the self. *La noche*, for instance, portrays the metaphysics of the split or splintered self. Moner relies heavily on Aquinas treatise on human passion (*Summa*, questions 25–48 of IaIIae). (For a summary of Moner's exposition on the passions, see Cocozzella, "The Theatrics of the *Auto de amores* in the *Tragicomedia* called *Celestina*," 83, n. 5, and *Fra Francesc Moner's Bilingual Poetics of Love and Reason*, 86–95.) Moner converts Thomistic ideology into a dramatized allegorization. As we follow, step-by-step, the altercation that the protagonist sustains with Costumbre (Lady Custom) and the twelve passions, dwelling in chambers located along the staircase of the castle, it becomes apparent that the auctorial persona envisages at the core of the self two complementary factors (A and B) linked reciprocally in a symbiosis of alterity: A is the "other" with respect to B, and vice versa. One could say that Moner foreshadows the dialectic of the "split self" that, as Paul Ilie cogently argues, distinguishes Miguel de Unamuno's existentialist perspective on the human psyche. There is, however, a marked difference. Whereas Unamuno sees no distinction between the two factors, Moner recognizes in each a discrete function: to A he attributes the primary level of consciousness; to B he ascribes the fragmentation of that consciousness into multiple manifestations. Therefore, in this episode of multifarious confrontations, A acts as an integral unit, a whole complete unto itself, oriented toward an "omega point," which, in Scholastic terminology, constitutes the final cause of Moner and, for that matter, of any other human being, qua lover. B, on the other hand, is exposed to the contingency (in the Scholastic sense of the term) of a limited outlook, typical of one who gropes in the darkness of the *infierno de los enamorados*. In its necessity to survive by remaining bound to the "other," A, by means of an existential dialectic, gradually reconciles itself with its own reflection and projection in B. In this fashion, A advances in the process of self-assertion, enhancing, all the while, its holistic presence, always directed toward that final cause. By looking closely into the process, we intuit that the final cause, as manifested in *La noche*, is none other than the idealized or canonized lover, enshrined in the topic of the "mártir de amor."

cial attention are the implications of Moner's foreshadowing of some memorable Unamunian concepts. Among these we recognize a process of disintegration in the interaction between the author's self-conscious subjectivity and the various manifestations of selfhood.[15] In *Sepultura*, to be specific, those manifestations are embodied in the three protagonists: the allegorical personages Mancilla, Costumbre, and Experiencia.

According to the proverb, the proof of the pudding is in the eating. The dramatic quality of Moner's monologue resides in the recitation or in the reading aloud. The same may be said, in particular, for the first stanza of the *Sepultura*, even though in that crucial passage there is no designation of a physical setting: that is, of the actual staging of the monologue. Such a staging, nevertheless, is implied by the assertive tone of Moner's idiom, which bespeaks a "local habitation," to borrow Shakespeare's happy phrase. We are referring, of course, to the "habitation" of "innerness," the inner theater of the mind or psyche.

To summarize: if we compare the aforementioned two stanzas, Guevara's and Moner's, we may deduce that the psychological or mental space adaptable to the stage, though unremarkable in the former, is an integral component of the latter. To confirm the significance of this theatrical factor, which we see operative in Moner's *Sepultura*, we may introduce, as yet another term of comparison, a third text excerpted from the play *Fuente Ovejuna* by none other than Lope de Vega. The excerpt in question is the sonnet that constitutes Laurencia's soliloquy and takes up an entire scene 13 of act 3 (vv. 2161–74; *Fuente Ovejuna*, 238–39).[16]

Thus, through the protagonist's spirited confrontation with each of his passions, the allegory dramatizes Moner's insight into the metaphysics of the lover's psyche. At the same time, it highlights the conflictive dialogue, the integration/disintegration interplay between two states of the "I," represented as *A* and *B*. We have discovered that *A* is the ontological correlative of the author of flesh and blood—the integrating persona, that is —that aspires to find reconciliation with *B*, its multifarious "other." *A* and *B*, thus perceived, are the existential codeterminants of the text of the self.

[15] Sobrer perceives a similar esthetic of the split self in some memorable poems of Ausiàs March (especially Poem 105). In his study of March's poetics, Sobrer refers to "divisió interna" (internal divisiveness), "ment en lluita constant amb ella mateixa" (a mind in a constant struggle with itself), the "fragments d'un jo" (fragments of the self), "la partició de la personalitat" (the partitioning of personhood) (*La doble soledat d'Ausias March*, respectively, 34, 39–40, 60, 65–66). Zimmermann, also, duly recognizes this phenomenon: see the mention of "l'escissió del Jo," "les escissions del Jo," and "l'escissió ontològica" (*Ausiàs March o l'emergència del jo*, respectively, 73, 84, 86).

[16] The text of the poem is as follows:

Amando, recelar daño en lo amado,
nueva pena de amor se considera,
que quien en lo que ama daño espera
aumenta en el temor nuevo cuidado.
El firme pensamiento desvelado,

It goes without saying that, when we juxtapose a composition like Moner's *Sepultura* to the creation of a playwright of Lope's caliber, we must allow for the most rigorous application of the *mutatis mutandis*. All in all, it is not hard to detect in Laurencia's sonnet the abundant terminology symptomatic of the disintegrating self as featured in the *cancioneros* in general and in the aforementioned *Sepultura* in particular. What we may call "standard *cancionero* fare" becomes evident in the proliferation of emotions or passions and the familiar effect of the "hall of mirrors" (see pp. 34–37 above).[17] Witness how the mind of the distraught Laurencia, a newlywed tormented by her apprehensions concerning the safety of her beloved spouse (Frondoso), spawns, at a relentless pace, undefined premonitions ("recelar daño"), sensations of unceasing pain ("nueva pena"), hints of impending harm ("daño espera"), fear and trepidations constantly reviving themselves ("aumenta en el temor nuevo cuidado"). More of the same may be easily documented in the second quartet. In the two tercets, Lope intensifies the effect of *conceptismo* by the use of the paradox: "si está presente, está cierta mi pena; / si está en ausencia, está cierta mi muerte" (vv. 13–14). At the same time, in an attitude that reminds us of Ausiàs March's rejection of the *escalf* of certain troubadours, Lope turns literary tradition on its head. What Lope rejects is the conventional narcissism of the male lover as portrayed in the *cancioneros*. Lope, in other words, focuses

---

si le aflige el temor, fácil se altera,
que no es, a firme fe, pena ligera
ver llevar el temor el bien robado.

    Mi esposo adoro; la ocasión que veo,
el temor de su daño, me condena,
si no le ayuda la felice suerte.

    Al bien suyo se inclina mi deseo:
si está presente, está cierta mi pena;
si está en ausencia, está cierta mi muerte.

(I have made some slight changes in the punctuation presented by López Estrada.)

(To be in love and fear the worst for a loved one may be considered a self-renewing pain: the lover that foresees the beloved in harm's way adds to apprehension a newly born anxiety.

When awakened, that constant preoccupation, beset by fear, is likely to be in turmoil: to see fear make off with the beloved that has been abducted is a pain not easy to bear.

I adore my husband. This is my plight, as I see it: I am cursed by the fear of his being harmed if he is not favored by a stroke of good fortune.

I am moved by my wishes for his welfare. If I envision him in my presence, my pain is for real; if he is away from me, what's for real is my dying.)

[17] Josep Miquel Sobrer, *La doble soledat d'Ausiàs March* (Barcelona: Quaderns Crema, 1987), 73. Interestingly enough, Sobrer uses the "cambra emmirallada" as an image of the inner world (the psychic space of torment), from which the afflicted lover longs to escape.

on the tormented psyche, not of the *amador* but of the *amada*. Thus, in a stroke
of genius the dramatist shifts from narcissism to altruism. In Laurencia's sonnet,
Lope brings to the fore the torments not of a self-absorbed consciousness but of
a mind definitely fixated upon the plight of the "other": "Mi esposo adoro." It is
clear that Lope borrows from the *cancioneros* and thoroughly assimilates the spe-
cial mode and implicit space of psychic theater. In Laurencia's sonnet-soliloquy,
the points of affinity confirm the significance of that very mode and those tech-
niques not so much in Guevara's verses as in Moner's counterpart, the first stanza
of *Sepultura d'amor*.

V.

The Sermon in Dramatic Effects

Homily as Compendium: The Phenomenology of Love

The sermon, which Experiencia divides into three parts, begins with a concise statement of the theme:

> Humanal inclinatión,
> por la discreta acordança
> de Natura
> en el gentil coraçón,
> o yrá Amor, con esperança
> de folgura,
> tras el byen de su intentión.
> (Vv. 324–30.) (Translation on p. 201 below.)

A précis of the first part, which the preacher describes as a declaration of the theme ("del tema declarativa"), follows two stanzas later:

> Natura, a ffin que recrezca
> las obras de quyen es syerva
> natural,
> no dexa el hombre peresca:
> en el fijo le conserva;
> por lo qual
> pedernal quyere la yesca.
> Encyende por el cañón
> del sentymyento al sensible,
> razonable,
> y dales inclinatión
> necessaria y convenible,
> deleytable,
> para su generación.
> (Vv. 345–58.) (Translation on p. 201 below.)

Cátedra, who has shown a particular interest in Experiencia's sermon, explains these two passages as follows:

> Al parecer, se trata de la misma transposición que veíamos en la psicología amorosa de Juan Ruiz y que se presta al juego y a la ironía, si es que se quiere extremar la funcionalidad del argumento naturalista del nacimiento y del desarrollo del amor. Aquí subyace también la falacia del estudiante del *Tratado de cómo al hombre es necesario amar*, reforzada por el salto imprevisto en la geometría aristotélica del alma. Todo lo cual está compendiado en el *tema* declarado por Moner (174;[1] Evidently, the verses deal with the same transposition we have noticed in Juan Ruiz's psychology of love, a subject that lends itself to word play and irony in line with the argument, carried out to a full extent, about the *naturalist* function evinced in the gestation and development of love. In addition, at the subsurface of the argument lies the fallacy of the student, author of the *Tratado de cómo al hombre es necesario amar* [*Treatise on how It Is Necessary for Man to Love*]. The fallacy is reinforced by an unexpected jump in the exposition of Aristotle's airtight theory on love. All this is epitomized in the theme stated by Moner).

A thorough review, which is out of the question on this occasion, would involve an extensive discussion of what Experiencia calls "humanal inclinatión"—that is, the instinct of the preservation of the human race. In fact, Experiencia's theme turns out to constitute the core motif, to which Cátedra in *Amor y pedagogía* applies various labels, such as "pensamiento naturalista universitario" (the naturalist thought in vogue in the universities) (41), "razonamiento filosófico naturalista" (the philosophical ratiocination of the naturalist brand) (162), "formulaciones teóricas del naturalismo amoroso" (the fashioning of theories concerning love-centered naturalism) (165), "fenemenología amorosa naturalista" (naturalist love-centered phenomenology) (168), not to mention the "argumento naturalista" (naturalist argument), referred to in the passage quoted above. Cátedra sketches out a background for Experiencia's pivotal topic in the *Libro de buen amor* by Juan Ruiz, alias Arcipreste de Hita, and in the anonymous *Tratado de cómo al hombre es necesario amar*.[2] Cátedra, of course, deals with other significant manifestations of that background in other signal works, such as the *Breviloquio de amor y amiçiçia* by Alfonso Fernández de Madrigal, better known as El Tostado; the *Repetición*

---

[1] Cátedra's quotes in this chapter are taken from *Amor y pedagogía*.

[2] For the relevance of the "naturalismo propuesto para Juan Ruiz" (naturalism proposed in reference to Juan Ruiz's position), see Cátedra, 41–46. As Cátedra indicates, the crucial passage is *Libro de buen amor*, coplas, 71–76 (ed. Gybbon-Monypenny, 123–24). On 113–25, Cátedra highlights the content and provides the essential data pertaining to the *Tratado de cómo al hombre es necesario amar*. He demurs at the attribution of the *Tratado* to El Tostado (114). As for the dating of the influential treatise, Cátedra only commits himself to the year 1496 as a *terminus ad quem* (125, n. 265).

de amores by Luis de Lucena; and, closer to home from Moner's standpoint, the *Sermón de amor* by Francesc Alegre.[3]

It goes without saying that Cátedra helps considerably in identifying the textual strains epitomized in Experiencia's bully pulpit eloquence. One textual strain that Cátedra calls attention to on more than one occasion stems from a tendency to meld a wide variety of sources with uneven success into a more or less unified theory of love. An example that easily comes to mind is chapter 5 of *Breviloquio*, in which, as Cátedra explains, El Tostado makes a valiant attempt at maintaining "la unidad de todos los sentimientos de *amor* (en términos dionisianos, reunión de *eros* y *agape*)" (the blending together of all the emotions of love [in Dionysian terms, the coming together of *eros* and *agape*], 32). Furthermore, he borrows ideological ingredients from Aristotle, Dionysius (the Areopagite), Séneca, Saint Augustine, Hugh of Saint Victor, Aquinas, and even Dante.[4] The author of the *Tratado de cómo al hombre es necesario amar* follows suit in striving for a holistic handling of matters of *eros* and *agape*. And so, we may add, do Lucena, Alegre, and, of course, Moner. Apropos of the *Tratado*, Cátedra points to "un mestizaje de procedimientos expresivos" (a type of hybridization of

---

[3] The pertinent texts excerpted from the anonymous *Tratado* and Madrigal's *Breviloquio* are found in Cátedra's edition of *El Tostado sobre el amor* (see bibliography). For a detailed description of the *Tratado*, see Gregory B. Kaplan, "Tratado que fizo el obispo: La contribución pre-renacentista de Alfonso Fernández de Madrigal a la evolución de la novela sentimental," *eHumanista* 4 (2004): 13–21. Cátedra undertakes a meticulous analysis of El Tostado's *Breviloquio*, which he dates between 1432 and 1437 (23). An example of El Tostado's eclecticism, kindred to Experiencia's ideological mind-set, is evidenced in the fifth chapter of *Breviloquio*: "la fusión de la delectación y la conveniencia en su ámbito de natura" (the conflation of delight and propriety in the natural realm) (31). For further explication of that chapter, se pp. 31–32. Analogous to Experiencia's notion of "humanal inclinación" is the crucial issue of the *vis generativa*, also addressed in *Breviloquio*. In exploring the probable link between *Libro de buen amor* and *Breviloquio*, Cátedra notes that "en el grado de superioridad de la *vis generativa* se comprenderá naturalmente que el varón quiera 'aver juntamiento con fembra plazentera' [*Libro de buen amor*, 71d], porque, como interpreta el Tostado, nos movemos animales y hombres espoleados por el 'aguijón de delectación'" (by the degree of the overwhelming *vis generativa* we, of course, will come, to an understanding that a male wishes to *have a conjoining with a pleasurable female* because, as El Tostado explains, we, men and beasts, are driven by the prodding of sensual pleasure) (52). Evidently, Cátedra's observation is applicable verbatim to Experiencia's exposition. Additional points of affinity that shed light on the makeup of Experiencia's homily are unveiled in Cátedra's astute critique of the text and context of both Lucena's *Repetición* and Alegre's *Sermó* (see Cátedra, 126–41 and 162–72, respectively). Cátedra estimates Alegre's piece to have been written between 1473 and 1479 (164). As for the date of composition of Lucena's treatise, Cátedra can only allude to a wide span from 1480 to 1497 (140, n. 307). For the essential bibliography on Lucena's misogyny, see 126, n. 267.

[4] For a full discussion of *Breviloquio*, chap. 5, see Cátedra, 31–32.

expression, 117). The *mestizaje*, that is, the hybrid nature of the *Tratado*, stems from the heterogeneous sources that Cátedra's erudition is able to bring to light, 122–25).

Lest we digress far afield from the analysis of Moner's *Sepultura*, we need not delve into many other interesting details that Cátedra puts forth. Suffice it to touch upon one characteristic, which Cátedra defines as the "intento de reclamar todos los tópicos de la fenomenología amorosa naturalista" (an attempt to reclaim the totality of topics pertaining to the naturalist phenomenology of love, 168). From Cátedra's broad argumentation, we may deduce that the valiant "intento," which he considers prevalent in Alegre's *Sermó*, is indicative of a trend that also finds commendable representation in Moner's exposition of Experiencia's homily. Experiencia strives to integrate, into a more or less coherent whole, topics derived from a variety of sources.

Fallacious Reasoning

Evidently, Experiencia's ingenious creativity coincides with the best efforts of the authors that Cátedra calls attention to: specifically, the exponents of the aforementioned "pensamiento naturalista universitario." Experiencia shares with those exponents not only a multifarious ideology but also a tendentious argumentation that adapts such an ideology to the justification of a parti pris. In the case of Alegre's *Sermó*, to name a typical example, Cátedra alerts us to the "caso tendencioso de formas serias mal empleadas" (tendentious case of serious formulations put to fallacious use) (168). Here the expression "mal empleadas" refers to the fallacious ratiocination expressly contrived for the attainment of a twofold objective: first, the assertion of the connatural goodness of love ("la bondad consustancial del amor" [32]);[5] second, the encomiastic portrait of the devoted lover that invariably turns out to be an exemplary, albeit naïve, sufferer: an ingenuous *mártir de amor*, in other words. With good reason, Cátedra explicates time and again examples of what he calls "la falacia dialéctica consciente" (intentional dialectic fallacy) (120), "la casuística del absoluto poder de amor" (the casuistry of the absolute power of love) (121), and the "falsas argucias argumentativas" (the fallacious sophistries of an argument) (169). These and similar labels designate the less-than-rational strategies marshaled by many a *tratadista* in order to arrive at the aforementioned two objectives.

Two symptoms of these strategies clearly stand out: on the one hand, the ambiguous use of key terms; on the other, the less than coherent formulation of the main argument. Witness, for instance, in the anonymous *Tratado de cómo*

---

[5] The assertion is reminiscent of one of Hugo of Saint Victor's famous *dicta*, which Cátedra paraphrases as "el mal está en amar mal, no en amar precisamente" (evil consists not in love itself but in loving in an evil way) (32).

al hombre es necesario amar, the indiscriminate notion of *cupiditas* that leads to a flawed conclusion. Cátedra explains that the author

> [e]stablece una proposición categórica universal, la primera conclusión, sobre "ser nesçesario a los hombres amar a las mujeres." Y justifica esta proposición con la natural *cobdiçia, cupiditas* de la naturaleza humana. (118, establishes a categorical proposition of universal acceptance: the upper-most deduction, that is, stemming from *it is necessary for men to love women.* Then the author justifies the proposition by making reference to *cobdiçia* — that is, the *cupiditas* inherent in human nature).

Cátedra proceeds to demonstrate how the author, in effect, glosses over a crucial distinction, propounded by none other than Thomas Aquinas (*Summa Theologiae,* 1a IIae 30.3), between the natural and unnatural kind of *cupiditas.*[6] There are, also, examples of dysfunctional argumentation, the second symptom mentioned above. In the *Tratado,* Cátedra cites "la secuencia inorgánica de yuxta-posición a base de fragmentos espigados indiscriminadamente" (the incoherent sequencing by way of stringing together bits and pieces gleaned indiscriminately) and "el planteamiento de *quaestiones* comprometidas y desarrolladas a la ligera" (the posing of *quaestiones* affected by a certain bias and argued in a lighthearted

---

[6] Instructive is Cátedra's commentary on Aquinas's distinction:
[S]orprenderemos aquí la primera ironía del anónimo, quien, al utilizar *cupiditas,* estaría manejando la acepción no natural de la concupiscencia, como podía saber entonces cualquier mediano filósofo ("delectabilis concupiscencia dicitur no natu-ralis, et solet magis dici *cupiditas*," como exponía santo Tomás [Ia IIae 30.3]) con lo que se recarga más la ironía en esta parte doctrinal, pues se achaca a la natu-raleza aquello que realmente no le compete, en clara formulación naturalista que interesadamente no establece ningún tipo de distingo (118; At this point we come upon the first example of the irony of the anonymous author, who, by using the term *cupiditas,* must be playing with the notion of *unnatural concupiscence*: a notion familiar at that time to any budding philosopher [according to Saint Thomas Ia IIae 30.3]. The irony is intensified on this point of doctrine because the anony-mous author imputes to Nature a flaw extraneous to Nature. The irony is well in line with standard naturalist formulation, which, because of its inherent bias, does not make distinctions of any kind).
In addition, Cátedra criticizes "lógica risible" (ludicrous logic) inherent in a false syl-logism:
[L]a materia de una proposición como la primera del *Tratado* debiera ser contin-gente y formularse con ciertos límites: 'necesariamente algunos hombres aman'. Sin embargo, aparece enunciada en sentido absoluto: 'necesariamente, todos los hombres aman' (121; The subject matter of a proposition, such as the first one adduced by El Tostado, should not be so categorical; it should be stated with some reservations: for example, *it is necessary for some men to love.* The proposition, how-ever, is posited in an absolute sense: *all men love by necessity*).

way) (132). By the same token, he detects in Alegre's *Sermó* the operation of erroneous reasoning that eventually turns the interpretation of the main theme on its head. In summation, the *Sermó* reveals, in Cátedra's words, "[una] subversión semántica del tema" (a semantic subversion of the main theme), a process, which he explains as follows:

> Pues el aristotélico principio de la apetencia humana de conservar su propia especie (*appetitus procreandi causa*, en palabras de Cicerón) es desplazado por Alegre con falsas argucias argumentativas y la consciente utilización ambigua del término *amor*, haciendo de paso a la mujer oscuro objeto del deseo, protagonista del mismo. (169; The Aristotelian principle of the human drive toward the preservation of the species [*appetitus procreandi causa*, in Cicero's words] is replaced by Alegre with the subtleties of fallacious argumentation and with the intentional ambiguous usage of the word *love*. In the process, Alegre converts woman from an object of desire to a protagonist of that desire).

In view of the notable predecessors, whose writings make up a veritable background for Moner's theorizing on love, we should not be surprised to discover signs of skewed ratiocination in Experiencia's disquisition, integrated into the plot of Moner's *Sepultura*. In line with those predecessors, Experiencia takes stock of the "inclinatión / necessaria y convenible" (vv. 355–56) emanating from "Natura" (v. 345) and, thus, sets up a premise for an argument a fortiori "de cómo al hombre es necesario amar." The premise is, to be sure, an axiomatic assertion of sound Scholastic doctrine. Referring to the soul's exercise of free choice, Experiencia states:

> La bondad y la maldad
> son los dos hytos en quyen
>   ell'atina,
> mas la noble voluntad,
> syempre so color de byen,
>   determina
> qu'es un tino de bondad.
> (Vv. 422–28.) (Translation on p. 202–3 below.)

Here we detect unmistakable echoes of Aquinas's concept of *appetitus intellectivus*: "objectum appetitus intellectivi, qui voluntas dicitur, est bonum secundum communem boni rationem. Nec potest esse aliquis appetitus, nisi boni" (*Summa Theologiae*, Ia, 59.4c) (the object of the intellectual appetite, which is called the will, is good according to the common notion of goodness; nor can there be any appetite except of what is good) (trans. Fathers of the English Dominican Province 1: 309). Not so sound, however, or clear, for that matter, is the congeries of fragmented thoughts Experiencia aggregates to her premise. In fact, Experiencia's oratorical construct readily brings to mind the aforementioned strains of sophistry and specious terminology: especially the "mestizaje de procedimientos expresivos" and the "falsas argucias argumentativas," diagnosed by Cátedra. Whether purposefully or not, Experiencia pays no attention to such elemental distinctions as the one between natural and unbridled *cupiditas*, handed down by age-old tradition. Despite its high rank and prestigious position, the *noble voluntad* is not immune to the devastating effects of pernicious habits. Tradition and common sense dictate that the vitiated will nurtures vitiated love.

To put it differently, Experiencia strives for a comprehensive approach to the phenomenology of eros. The approach is reflected in what Cátedra, apropos of Alegre's *Sermó*, calls "el andamiaje y las autoridades que [Alegre] maneja en el cuerpo de su 'doctrina'" (the ideological framework and authoritative sources Alegre skillfully manipulates within the body of his *doctrina*) (164). Not unlike Alegre, Lucena, and cohorts, Experiencia envisages the wide spectrum of that phenomenology from the perspective of the cause rather than the effect. The cause Experiencia capitalizes upon is the innate goodness of love: *buen amor*, to borrow El Arcipreste de Hita's terminology. Experiencia is aware that *mal amor* per se does not exist. This datum blurs her vision of a glaring reality: the deleterious effects that unfavorable circumstances bring to bear on *buen amor*. Here we have the transformation of *buen amor* (love good by nature) into *amor malo* (love gone bad on account of the influence of inordinate passion).

In short, Experiencia easily slips into the pitfall inherent in the position that abides by the overwhelming power of love. As she reaches the conclusion of part 1, the philosophical section of her sermon, she cavalierly skirts the moral issue altogether. Witness the following declaration:

Assí que aquel qu'enamora,
la razón por la qual ama
  le dispensa.
(Vv. 429–31.) (For the translation, see p. 203 below.)

These words attest to the clever twist of the "técnica de exculpación" (technique of exculpation) that Cátedra detects in the *Tratado de cómo al hombre es necesario amar* (117). Highly ironic and misleading is the term razón adduced in the passage. The truth of the matter is that the lovesick individual does not pay attention to the guidance of reason. Equally misleading is Experiencia's use of the term "dispensa." Obviously, reason cannot absolve anyone from the culpability incurred in exercising the faculty of free will. In addition, the good intention, also mentioned in Experiencia's conclusion[7] does not imply, as Experiencia claims, exonerating the lover from the responsibility of a ruinous choice prompted by eros run amuck.

---

[7] See "el byen de su intentión" (v. 436).

Let us reflect on a crucial juncture in the unfolding text of Moner's *Sepultura*. We have just witnessed Experiencia's frustration in touching on the weighty issues to be integrated into a theory on the nature of love. Also, we have become aware of Experiencia's loose-jointed argumentation, unconvincing conclusion, and unsuccessful plan of exculpation. What needs to be pointed out is that, with all its fallacies shared with the various treatises analyzed by Cátedra, Experiencia's sermon constitutes, warts and all, suitable grist for Moner's artistic mill. In the final analysis, precisely because of its dysfunctional ratiocination and flawed argumentation, said sermon reveals itself as a catalyst of dramatic action, fully functional in the unfolding of the plot.[8] Fully operational in the creative integration of Experiencia's sermon into the macrostructure of *Sepultura* is the role of Experiencia as the eponymous allegorization of the human entity it represents. In other words, the principle of the aforementioned onomastic symbolism is fully at play in that role. Experiencia, as the personage identified by a proper noun, can rely only on the workaday reality marked by the homonymous signifier: the common noun "experiencia."[9]

---

[8] In view of the overall semiotic framework of onomastic symbolism, there is a corollary of sorts to be derived from our meditation on Experiencia's role. What is quite clear is that Experiencia is not, nor should be expected to be, a champion of sound ratiocination. After all, Experiencia is not Razón (Lady Reason), also known as Rahó in her Catalan counterpart. Poignantly, Razón is notably absent in *Sepultura*, even though her presence is quite prominent in three other major works by Moner: namely, *Bendir de dones*, *La noche*, and *Obra en metro*. It is not less important in *L'ànima d'Oliver*, where her role is appropriated by the protagonist, the ghostly individual referred to in the title. Experiencia's performance validates an insight that confers to the plot of *Sepultura* a characteristically a-rational or pararational spin. The spin is worthy of special attention, as it may well constitute the high mark of Moner's innovating, not to say revolutionary approach to the shaping of a theatrical plot.

[9] Susanne K. Langer, *Philosophy in a New Key: A Study in the Symbolism of Reason, Rite, and Art* (New York: Mentor-The New American Library, 1959). The onomastic symbolism reviewed here apropos of Experiencia is consonant with the role that Langer envisages for experience in the dawning of a new age: that of the Renaissance. Apropos of the Renaissance, Langer envisages a vast ideological panorama:

This new epoch had a mighty and revolutionary generative idea: the dichotomy of all reality into *inner experience and outer world*. The very language of what is now traditional epistemology betrays this basic notion; when we speak of the "given," of "sense-data," "the phenomenon," or "other selves," we take for granted the immediacy of an internal experience and the continuity of the external world. (22)

After acknowledging the various systems of thought born of that revolutionary idea, Langer articulates the following observation:

The most complete and characteristic of all these doctrines are the earliest ones: empiricism and idealism. They are the full, unguarded, vigorous formulations of the new generative notion, *Experience*. . ... Not only the universities, but all the literary circles, felt the liberation from the time-worn, oppressive concepts, from

Cathartic Misogyny

Now, let us turn back to the crucial moment in Experiencia's sermon, in which part 1 ("del tema declarativa") draws to a close, and part 2 ("expositiva del evangelio") is about to begin. At this point, after a glaring exhibition of a less-than-cogent argument, Experiencia's oratory manifests a palpably emotive rather than intellective tenor. Throughout part 2, the homily expands upon the passage (vv. 251–89) that constitutes Moner's invention of the Gospel quotation for the day. The expansion confronts head-on a core motif fraught with thorny issues. As ingeniously foreshadowed in said "Gospel," the issues pertain to the problematic condition of the typical young man that unwisely lavishes his loyalty and affections on a woman. He has neglected to put her character to a rigorous test beforehand: "[q]uyen ama d'amor leal / a muger que no ha provado" (vv. 251–52). With the zeal of one who revisits a venerable urtext, Experiencia transfers the tone of embittered reproach she has already voiced in that chanted "Gospel" into a diatribe leveled against the foibles and capricious behavior she attributes ever so smugly to the *inmensa mayoría* of the daughters of Eve.

It is fair to observe that the fervor of Experiencia's invective is well in keeping with the plot taking shape before our very eyes. The impassioned, unreasoned, and irrational antifeminism reaches a high pitch of expression in a string of lamentations:

> ¡Ay, ayes y más ay ay!
> ¡Llaga que el seso se come!
> ¡Desventuras,
> querellas, agravyos assay!
> (Vv. 586–89.) (For the translation, see p. 205 below.)

Experiencia's emotional oratory, in its ebb and flow, points to the course of a twofold therapy of catharsis and redemption: the catharsis that brings into effect the purging of resentment and other obnoxious passions; the redemption that comes as a liberation from the moral degeneration brought about by lovesickness. Thus, the plot is being advanced by the different phases of Experiencia's speech. The latest phase (that is, part 2 of the sermon) may be adduced as evidence of Experiencia's adherence to a master plan, which includes the enactment of a purification ceremony (the catharsis and redemption we have just referred to). Moner would not have us forget that central in that master plan is the figure of the auctorial persona, singled out as the embodiment of the faithful lover, exemplary in his suffering (*mártir de amor*) and devotion to Truth. In the final analysis, Moner strives to impress upon the mind of a contemplator the image of

---

baffling limits of inquiry, and hailed the new world-picture with a hope of truer orientation in life, art, and action. (22)

a worthy lover, purified by his suffering and prepared for the consummation of a process that comes to a head in part 3 ("*historia prosecutiva*") of Experiencia's sermon.

Experience as Gospel of True Love

As we approach part 3 of Experiencia's sermon, we have the impression that a subtextual strain is emerging into the limelight of the allegorical stage. The strain consists of a climactic reprise of the motif we have already identified as "dead man talking" (see above p. 25), for which we find multiple manifestations. These are: (1) the epigram dislodged from the dead man's mouth (vv. 127–29); (2) the inscription on the protagonist's tomb (vv. 144–46); (3) the inscription on the neck of the sculptured ostrich (vv. 161–63); and, most important of all, (4) the author's *canción* as the object of the Offertory (vv. 304–16). In view of the aforementioned passages, Experiencia's reprise of a leading motif raises an issue full of profound metatextual resonances.

The issue has to do with a momentous shift in the plot, which reflects, in turn, a radical metamorphosis of the text. The powerful impact of this meta-textual phenomenology becomes manifest in stanza 49, which marks the beginning of part 3 of Experiencia's sermon. The stanza opens with a remarkable octosyllable: "L'ystoria de quien muryó" (v. 639). The verse is supercharged with signification, as it demarcates a high point of an evolution from lyrical intensity (the *canción* of the Offertory) to the substantiality of *historia*. *Canción* and *historia* may be taken respectively, then, as indices of the inception and completion of the momentous shift just alluded to. Thus, the plot of *Sepultura* is enriched by the fruition of poetic logos that oscillates according to the inception/completion polarity appreciated so far.

In the four stanzas (nos. 49–52) that make up the "historia prosecutiva," Moner would have us appreciate the breadth and depth of the radical textual metamorphosis adumbrated previously in our discussion. What comes into view here is a veritable tour de force that combines the operations of concretization and individuation at the service of an overall epiphany of subjectivity. Here subjectivity is gauged by the exemplarity ("amor y firmeza / y fe tanta" [647–48]) of a lover, who has suffered heroically and magnanimously endured abuse from the ladylove ("una tal, una escogida" [v. 655]) and utter persecution from slanderers.[10] In this iconic self-portrait of the auctorial persona as an exemplary sufferer, it will not be difficult to make out the embodiment of the existential correlative of an entire life. This correlative may be encapsulated into the notion of a

---

[10] These are, precisely, "un cert cavaller y unes senyores" referred to in the epigraph of the *Bendir*. See p. 44 above.

"life-text," the crowning achievement of Moner's artistry the author allows us to contemplate.

There is one further step on the complex operation involved in Experiencia's contribution to the shaping of the plot. Let us remember that the "life-text" here proposed is the "historia prosecutiva." Upon close inspection, we discover that the "historia" is presented not only as an expansion of the *canción* of the Offertory, but also as a form of the Gospel especially devised and adapted to the structure of the *misa* within *Sepultura*. It follows that the "historia prosecutiva" is conceived as the analogue (a human counterpart, so to speak) of Sacred Scripture. Now let us look even closer. The workings of a primordial mimesis are implicit, we discover, in the analogy that jumps to our attention. Moreover, the mimesis that Experiencia capitalizes upon is indicative of a quintessential *imitatio Christi*. Still, Moner does not cease to challenge our intuitive faculties. Inherent in this bold feat of mimesis or *imitatio* is a poetics of conflation, suggestively illustrated by the literary trope of *superposición* (superimposition) that the poet and critic Carlos Bousoño diagnoses under that very name in twentieth-century Spanish literature (*Teoría de la expresión poética*, 1: 388–431). We may deduce that the "Gospel" fashioned in Experiencia's "historia prosecutiva" is superimposed upon or conflated with the Gospel of the New Testament (the Christian Bible). To put it in metaphorical terms, we may think of a graft of the former onto the latter. The result is a parasacramental phenomenon: the human lover — Moner's persona — partakes of the life of his divine counterpart. We may surmise that the parasacramental quality of Experiencia's rendition of the Scripture stems from a Scriptural subtext consisting of such passages as

> I am the vine, ye are the branches: He that abideth in me, and I in him, the same bringeth much fruit (John 15:5).

and

> He that eateth my flesh, and drinketh my blood, dwelleth in me, and I in him (John 6:15).

It may be argued, then, that the Scriptural subtext accounts for the ersatz transubstantiation that, as we have indicated, takes place in Moner's *misa seca*. Against the backdrop of an awesome ritual (that of the traditional transubstantiation of bread and wine), Moner ideates an *imitatio Christi*, through which he allows us to envisage the wondrous metamorphosis of the faithful lover into a martyr. What we envisage is a de facto canonization, inherent in the contrast that, at the end of her sermon, Experiencia draws between *él*, the persona of the defunct poet ("[l]a muerte Moner nos priva" [v. 681]), and *ella* ("la dama" [v. 682]):

Ella, hermosa y esquiva,
él, de firme y transportado,
     no ternán
ygual ninguno que viva.
(Vv. 684–87.)[11] (For the translation, see p. 207 below.)

(For the translation, see p. 207 below.)

[11] For an extensive discussion of the motif of "canonization," see Cocozzella, "The Thematic Unity of Juan Rodríguez del Padrón's *Siervo Libre de amor*," and Martin Gilderman, "La apoteosis del amante cortés. Hacia una interpretación del *Siervo libre de amor*," *Boletín de Filología Española* 12 (1972): 37–50.

VI.
Parody as Desacralization

A Fresh Approach

At the end of our meditation on the monologue of the *cancioneros*, the formidable issue confronting us is made plain by those who, like Luis García Montero, argue against the very existence of a Spanish theater in the Middle Ages.[1] He insists on maintaining a sharp demarcation between liturgy and theater, and, according to García Montero, a neglect of such differentiation leads to a mirage ("espejismo"), which includes the appearance ("mera apariencia") of a continuum between liturgy ("práctica litúrgica") and theater ("escenificación teatral") in medieval Spanish literature (49). García Montero bears in mind the innocuous and even praiseworthy "inversiones carnavalescas" (inversions à la Mardi Gras) (68), such as the curious ceremony of the Boy Bishop (68–70). The critic also takes into account the perversions and abuses of clerics behaving as jesters, which became the targets of relentless condemnation from theologians, scholars, and jurists: the likes of Saint Augustine, Saint Isidore of Seville, and Alfonso el Sabio (79–84).[2] García Montero deduces that neither said "inversiones" nor

---

[1] Humberto López Morales is another leading exponent of the highly controversial position regarding the alleged inexistence of the medieval theater in the Castilian domain. See his *Tradición y creación en los orígenes del teatro castellano*, and "Problemas en el estudio del teatro medieval castellano: Hacia el examen de los testimonios."

[2] Max Harris provides an extensive survey of those who condemn the questionable practices that, throughout the Middle Ages, infiltrated the Christian liturgy in various European countries (Harris, *Feast of Fools*, 11–24). A case in point is that of Caesarius, bishop of Arles (470–542), who, according to William Klingshirn, indiscriminately inveighed against not only the "phenomenon of Gallo-Roman religion" but "all other ritual activity that evaded his control, much of which was arguably Christian or religiously neutral in intention, if not in appearance" (quoted in Harris, 19). Klingshirn observes that the performers

> were not rejecting Christianity in favor of paganism, as Caesarius charged, but were rather adapting Christian ceremonies to their own patterns of religious expression. (Quoted in Harris, 20)

Harris segues with the following reflection:

the unseemly histrionics, which he categorizes as "la cara diabólica de la sacralización cristiana" (the diabolical other countenance of Christian sacralization) (*El teatro medieval*, 82), may be regarded as manifestations of a genuine theater. He goes so far as to assert:

> No podemos. . .utilizar las actas conciliares, ni ninguna otra clase de documento oficial, para demostrar la existencia, en la Edad Media, del teatro, tal y como lo entendemos actualmente. Las críticas eclesiásticas medievales sólo demuestran la existencia de rituales en los que no se respeta el orden divino; rituales llevados a la práctica por fieles, sólo que pecadores, y no por unos actores y un público distanciado de lo que se representa. Por ello son también acciones litúrgicas (83; We may not adduce the proceedings of the various councils or any other kind of official documentation to demonstrate the existence in the Middle Ages of a theater such as we understand theater to be in our day and age. The adverse criticism voiced by the clergy during the Middle Ages only demonstrates the practice of rituals in which the sacred protocol is not respected: rituals performed by churchgoers, sinners though they are, and not by actors in the presence of spectators, who maintain the appropriate distance from the action being represented. Under the circumstances, that practice is still a liturgical activity).

Thus, from this point of view, the conclusion is inevitable. García Montero does not perceive the elements that constitute a sine qua non for a representation: performers, spectators, and, needless to say, a sufficient esthetic distance between the former and the latter. Therefore, for him there is no theater. There is only, at best, inverted and, at worst, perverted or vitiated liturgy.

In response to this line of argumentation, we are now ready to try a new approach that reflects the phenomenology of parody defined and analyzed within the purview of Linda Hutcheon's landmark study. Here I intend to demonstrate that Hutcheon's insights shed considerable light on the esthetics operative in Moner's rendition of the *misa de amores*. In addressing the suitability of Hutcheon's theory to the workings of parody in Moner's *Sepultura*, I shall attempt to demonstrate that the contribution of Moner's dramatics resides in a process that evolves in complete contrast to the one envisioned by García Montero. The dramatics of Moner's parody take effect, not in the corruption or vitiation but rather in the mutation of the liturgy: the mutation evinced, that is, in the transition from ritual to theater. This means that what Moner brings about is not the sacralization of pagan elements (the vestiges of Roman theater that

---

To appreciate his point, one need only think of the wide range of traditional dances, mimetic and otherwise, still performed in front of (or even inside) churches as an act of Christian devotion on patronal saints' days and other Christian festivals throughout the Spanish-speaking world. (20)

García Montero refers to) but rather the desacralization of the Christian ritual, especially as epitomized in the sacramentality of the Eucharistic services.

The Serious Slant of Parody

In her introduction (*A Theory of Parody*, 1–29), Linda Hutcheon touches upon various parodic modes, for which she devises such labels as "artistic recycling" (15), "extended refunctioning" (16), "very complex textual intentionality" (15), "complex forms of 'transcontextualization' and inversion" (15), and "transformative power in creating new syntheses" (20). By relying on a profusion of technical terms, she broaches a sophisticated discussion of the issues of intertextuality, which is relevant apropos of the complexity of form embodied in Moner's *misa*. Those issues are illustrated in the ritual, one that Moner transforms into a spectacular display.

Sketched out in the following passage is Hutcheon's definition that sheds light on the theatricality of Moner's *misa*:

> [W]hat I am calling parody here is not just that ridiculing imitation mentioned in standard dictionary definitions. The challenge to this limitation of its original meaning, as suggested. . .by the etymology and history of the term, is one of the lessons of modern art that must be heeded in any attempt to work out a theory of parody that is adequate to it. . . ..Parody, therefore, is a form of imitation, but imitation characterized by ironic inversion, not always at the expense of the parodied text (5–6).

The topic that commands top priority in our discussion is Hutcheon's notion of parody, purged of ridiculing or mocking mechanisms with which it has been associated traditionally.[3] For the purpose of our study, a perusal of Hutcheon's

---

[3] The conventional view of parody stresses a process of imitation by way of mockery with humorous effect, occasionally verging on caricature. The entry for parody in one of the standard dictionaries reads as follows:

> A literary or musical work imitating the characteristic style of some other work or of a writer or composer in a satirical or humorous way, usually by applying it to an inappropriate subject" (*Webster's New World Dictionary*, 3rd ed.).

In keeping with this acceptation, June Hall Martin, *Love's Fools: Aucassin, Troilus, Calisto and the Parody of the Courtly Lover* (London: Tamesis, 1972), perceives Calisto, a well-known personage in medieval Spanish literature, as an emblematic parody of the courtly lover. Martin's broad definition is encapsulated in the following passage:

> Perhaps the most fundamental characteristic of parody is that it must bear an essential similarity to the original, whether it be a specific work, a style, a convention, or a stylized character within that convention. Yet it is not simply imitative.

definition is well-suited for the noncomedic tenor of the *misas de amores* and kindred pieces, in general, and Moner's *misa*, in particular.

Now, we may resume our analysis by focusing on some salient passages culled from the parodic poems already referred to (see pp. 18–21 above). Let us take, for instance, the following stanza addressed to "Deus de amor," in which Dueñas blithely paganizes the most awesome of Christian mysteries:

> Gloria patri, linpio manto
> de amores, el qual cobijo
> válgame con el tu fijo,
> graçia del espíritu santo;
> Cupido, Venus y Apolo,
> tres personas y vn dios solo:
> esto creo y más de tanto.

(Piccus, "La *Misa de Amores* de Juan de Dueñas," 323[4]; Glory be to You, Father! May You and Your Son, grant me, I pray, the shelter of love's pure mantle and the grace of the Holy Spirit. Cupid, Venus, Apollo, three persons and one God: This is what I believe and much more!)

Not to be overcome, Suero de Ribera, on his part, regales us with a startling, if banal, rendition of such formulaic standbys as the Confiteor, the Gloria, the Credo, the Sanctus, and, as in the following passage, the Agnus Dei:

> "Cordero de Dios de Venus
> —dezían los desamados—,
> tú, que pones los cuidados,
> quita los que sean menos,
> pues tienes poder mundano,
> o señor tan soberano,
> *Miserere nobis.*"

(*Cancionero de Estúñiga,* ed. Salvador Miguel, 671; "O Lamb of God of Venus"—thus spoke the unloved lovers. "You are the cause of all our woes.

---

some basic element must be altered so that the resulting incongruity may reveal some weakness in the original. (15)
For a full discussion of the stylistic devices of parody at play in the characterization of Calisto, see Martin, 71–134.

[4] A passage of this nature is still likely to raise the eyebrow of a critic or two. Núñez Rivera considers these verses "el blasfemo gloria de la composición [Dueñas's *Misa*], uno de los textos más irrespetuosos de todo el corpus paródico" (the poem's blasphemous Gloria, one of the most disrespectful texts in the entire parodic corpus) ("Glosa y parodia de los Salmos Penitenciales en la poesía del cancionero," 135).

Take away the lesser sorrows, o Lord supreme, in your absolute sway the world over. *Miserere nobis.*")

It is easy to understand why the serious tone of these compositions, in itself, should offend, as it did, the religious sensitivity of many a critic. To the type of parody exemplified in these two passages reputable scholars have reacted, far and wide, on impulse and with no regard for even the slightest possibility of an innocuous intention behind what might pass as amusing versification. Emblematic is the reaction of the scrupulous, self-righteous reader—anonymous, to be sure—who was not at all amused and who felt no compunction in ripping out the text of Ribera's *misa* bodily from the manuscript in which it was included (Salvador Miguel, 22–23, 26–27).[5] Some venerable figures (the likes of José Amador de los Ríos and Marcelino Menéndez y Pelayo, two of the veritable founders of modern literary criticism in Spain) respond with harsh censure.[6] The same poems upon which Amador, Menéndez y Pelayo, and others unload their severe commentaries are proscribed en masse by Le Gentil in his all-important book, where they are relegated to a chapter titled "Rhétorique et mauvais goût" (Rhetoric in bad taste) (*La poesie lyrique espagnole et portugaise a la fin du moyen age*, 1: 185–204).[7]

This rapid review may leave the impression that seasoned students of Spanish literature are unanimous in their repudiation of what they consider mock religious poems of the *cancioneros*. Actually, this is not the case. There are scholars who keep an open mind toward that poetry and, in so doing, blaze a trail toward sound criticism and productive research.[8] Two such scholars, the aforementioned

---

[5] The codex containing the *Cancionero de Estúñiga* is housed in the Biblioteca Nacional de Madrid (Va 17-7). For a full bibliographic description, see Salvador Miguel, 15–45.

[6] See Amador de los Ríos's comments on Valera's parodies (*Historia crítica* 6: 179–80) and Menéndez y Pelayo's statements on Garci Sánchez's "Liciones" (*Antología* 3: 141–44).

[7] For additional data and discussion on this accursed lot of poetry, see Cocozzella, *2 Introducción*, 36–45; Blanca Periñán, Introducción, "Las poesías de Suero de Ribera. Estudio y edición crítica anotada de los textos," *Miscellanea di studi ispanici* 16 (1968), 24–32; Piccus, "La Misa de Amores de Juan de Dueñas," 322 n. 2; and Presotto, "Introduzione," 31–35.

[8] María Rosa Lida de Malkiel discusses the evidence of a sympathetic intermingling of the religious and the profane within the parody in question. Besides the "confiada intimidad entre lo humano y lo divino que sustentó tantos siglos de cristiandad" (the trustful intimacy between the human and the divine that sustained Christianity for so many centuries) ("La hipérbole sagrada en la poesía castellana del siglo XV," 130), this distinguished medievalist perceives the concomitant factor of the pessimism generated by the plight of the Jewish converts in fifteenth-century Spanish society: "el amargo desconcierto que desgarró oscuramente el alma de las últimas generaciones de conversos"

Tillier and Gallagher, point to a fruitful line of investigation by focusing, respectively, on Nicolás Núñez's "Misa" and Garci Sánchez's "Liciones." Both discover notable differences that call into question the pigeonholing of these poems in the catchall category of the numerous compositions they regard as parodies.

According to Tillier, what differentiates Núñez's "Misa" is, precisely, its questionable "parodic intention." On the basis of this distinguishing trait, Tillier adumbrates the notion of a reverse parody that, far from making light of heartfelt piety, ends up asserting the merits of an edifying devotional practice, such as the one associated with the Book of Hours. As Tillier puts it:

> [t]he poet [Nicolás Núñez] is ostensibly directing his lady in the devotional use of the Book of Hours. . ... Here the poet not only employs the structural form of his source but also appeals to its spiritual and moral content. (569)

In much the same vein, Gallagher is keen to Garci Sánchez's disregard of the "ludicrous effect" that the Oxford English Dictionary considers a sine qua non in the definition of parody. Not surprisingly, Gallagher perceives a less-than-parodic slant in Garci Sánchez's elaboration of a revered Biblical source. Following is Gallagher's cogent critique of the ingenious piece:

> No such burlesque spirit can be said to have prompted Garci Sánchez. On the contrary, it is because he wishes to invest his amatory plight with a special gravity and solemnity that he chooses to accommodate so grave and sonorous a sacred text as the lessons from the Book of Job in the Office of the Dead. The accommodation consists in Garci Sánchez's addressing his lady where Job addresses God. Otherwise the text is substantially unaltered. It appears sporadically in Latin, but most of it is paraphrased into Spanish (175).[9]

There are scholars who may be quoted in support of Tillier's and Gallagher's comments. Núñez Rivera, for instance, ascribes to the bond between the erotic and religious experience evinced in *cancionero* poetry the very "gravity and solemnity" underscored by Gallagher: "la imbricación erótico-divina de los cancioneros desconoce cualquier tipo de matiz risible" (the crossbreeding of the erotic and the

---

(the bitter turmoil that ripped, in some obscure manner, into the souls of the last generations of converted Jews) ("La hipérbole sagrada en la poesía castellana del siglo XV," 130).

[9] With respect to the theory that Hutcheon and others espouse regarding the nature of parody, a noteworthy voice of dissent is that of Dorothy Severin, who observes:

> [I]n the Spanish sentimental romance, the religion of love is always basically ludic and humorous, a concept developed in *cancionero* poetry and then transposed into prose. (*Religious Parody and the Spanish Sentimental Romance,* 175)

See, also, Severin, "The *Misa de amor* in the Spanish *Cancioneros* and the Sentimental Romance."

divine in the *cancioneros* does not make any allowance for comic nuance) (Núñez Rivera, "Glosa y parodia de los *Salmos Penitenciales* en la poesía del cancionero," 126). Gerli would do away with the categorization altogether. He observes the following:

> lo que encontramos en la lírica del siglo XV no se pueden considerar paro-
> dias. Aunque sí son intentos de lucir ingenio poético, estas composiciones
> eroticorreligiosas no demuestran ni la más mínima nota satírica o escar-
> necedora. El elemento clave que les falta. . .es el humor ("La 'religión del
> amor' y el antifeminismo en las letras castellanas del siglo XV," 67; what we
> find in fifteenth-century lyricism should not be considered parody. Granted
> they are intended to show off poetic ingenuity, these erotic-religious com-
> positions do not demonstrate the least indication of satire or derision. They
> lack a key ingredient: humor).

Needless to say, there are conflicting judgments regarding the type of poetry we have been sampling or referring to in our quick review. In any attempt to come to terms with a signficant contingent of the *cancioneros*, that is, these audacious renditions of Christian doctrine, liturgical ceremonies, and devotional practices, a number of fundamental questions still arise as to either the artistic intention behind the poems or their overall effect upon the readership. In concrete terms, those questions may be stated as follows: are the poems to be taken seriously at face value or are they the tongue in cheek expression of a mocking, ridiculing purpose reflecting a jocular agenda? Ultimately, the questions boil down to one unavoidable query: are the poems blasphemous and sacrilegious, let alone irrev-erent and indiscreet?

Reading through the Palimpsest

As we attempt to answer the questions just posed, we cannot but hypothesize about the motivation that lies behind the religious parodies of Dueñas, Núñez, Ribera, Sánchez, Tapia, and others. There is no reason to suspect perverse, not to say diabolic, intention in these fine poets. Their flair for parody stems not from an interest in some religious agenda but, rather, from a commitment to esthetic experimentation. Hutcheon meets us in support of our hypothesis by anatomiz-ing the parodic mode as one would a complex syndrome. To wit, that mode encompasses a wide variety of symptoms. Among these, two clearly stand out. Hutcheon identifies one as "superimposition" (*A Theory of Parody,* 33, 34), the other as "bitextual synthesis" (35) or "bitextual determination" (42). Following is Hutcheon's gloss on the notion of superimposition:

> Both irony and parody operate on two levels — a primary, surface, or fore-
> ground; and a secondary, implied, or backgrounded one. But the latter, in

both cases, derives its meaning from the context in which it is found. The final meaning of irony or parody rests on the recognition of the superimposition of these levels. (34)

As for the other symptom, we may borrow yet another statement from her:

Parody has a stronger bitextual determination than does simple quotation or even allusion: it partakes of both the code of a particular text parodied, and also the parodic generic code in general. (42)

In the two stanzas quoted earlier from the *misas* of Dueñas and Ribera respectively, we see illustrated the criteria of hermeneutics broached by Hutcheon. In both cases, we find the superimposition of the same semiotic levels: we are allowed a glimpse of not only the pagan myth, daringly presented on the surface of the text, but also the Christian Divinity in the textual substratum. Specifically, the two authors entice us with the perception of a palimpsest of sorts. What we take in at first reading is the representation of some emblematic figures of the pagan pantheon: the trio made up of Cupid, Venus, and Apollo, in one case; the image of the God of Love (Cupid), in the other. The jarring effect is produced, of course, by the semiotic conflation that Dueñas and Ribera bring about: the former between said trio and the Trinity, the latter between Cupid and the Agnus Dei.

The technique of superimposition is not, by any means, an exclusive characteristic of Dueñas and Ribera. Other examples may be found in fifteenth-century literature of both the Castilian and the Catalan domain. Diego de San Pedro's *Cárcel de amor*, the exemplary *novela sentimental*, exhibits the interfacing of the portrait of Leriano, the protagonist, with the icon of the Man of Sorrows (*Ecce Homo*): the former vividly depicted at the surface level of the narrative, the latter descried in the textual substratum (Miguel-Prendes, "Otra frontera de la ficcion sentimental, 19).[10] Before San Pedro, the Galician author Juan Rodríguez del Padrón, who flourished in the first half of the fifteenth century, developed the esthetic of superimposition into a veritable mutually complimentary bond between the sacred and the profane. In *Siervo libre de amor*, generally considered a prototype of the *novela sentimental*, Juan Rodríguez fashions the apotheosis of the lover (Ardanlier) into a leitmotif modeled after the cult of Saint James (Santiago de Compostela) (Menéndez y Pelayo, *Orígenes de la novella*, 2: 21–22; Cocozzella, "The Thematic Unity of Juan Rodríguez del Padrón's *Siervo Libre de amor*," 190; Gilderman, "La apoteosis del amante cortés," 45–50).[11] We may also

---

[10] For Leriano's portrait, see San Pedro, *Cárcel de amor*, 86–88. Deyermond sketches out a convincing definition of the *novela sentimental* (see *Tradiciones y puntos de vista en la ficción sentimental*).

[11] For additional information on Juan Rodríguez and Diego de San Pedro see, respectively, pp. 7, n. 13, and 8, n. 16 above.

consider stanzas 2 and 3 of Poem 5 by Ausiàs March. In that passage (vv. 9–24), we witness another conflation of two images: one in the foreground (the auctorial persona in the guise of the suffering lover), the other in the background (the Divine Lover envisaged as the persecuted Christ) (Cocozzella, "Ausiàs March's *Imitatio Christi*, 429–30).[12] An additional example to be adduced here includes a passage from *Libro de buen amor*, the fourteenth-century masterpiece by Juan Ruiz, who is better known as Arcipreste de Hita. In couplets 1225–1241 of the *Libro*, the description of the splendid pageantry of a parade in honor of the pagan God of Love (Don Amor) is highlighted against the backdrop of repeated references to Easter celebrations (Arcipreste de Hita, 363–67; Cocozzella, "The Journey of Transcendence," 125–27).[13]

It is useful to include in our rapid survey an example that may not prove to be a parody in the strict sense. Let us turn our attention to a text of the twentieth century: the poem, entitled "El alma" (The Soul) by the Spanish Nobel laureate Vicente Aleixandre. Carlos Bousoño, a critic and poet in his own right, regards "El alma" as an exemplary specimen of superimposition, which, as we have seen, figures prominently as a parodic symptom par excellence in Hutcheon's theory.[14] To be precise, Bousoño refines Hutcheon's classification a step further and categorizes Aleixandre's piece as "superposición significacional" (superimposition of signifiers) (*Teoría de la expresión poética*, 423–31).[15] Bousoño traces the full cycle of what we may consider the primordial parodic display. In other words, Bousoño

---

[12] For the text of Poem 5, see March, 52–55.

[13] Leading authorities on *Libro de buen amor* have long recognized a parodic element in Juan Ruiz's "Easter parade." After compiling a long list of sources, stretching as far back as Ovid's *Amores* (1.2.23–52), Félix Lecoy refines his judgment and adds:

> Le cortège que nous décrit Juan Ruiz n'est pas un cortège triomphal, c'est une parodie de procession liturgique, et probablement même de la procession la plus ancienne du rite chrétien, la procession des Rameaux. L'Amour rentrant dans ses États, s'est le Christ arrivant à Jérusalem, aux acclamations d'une foule enthousiaste (Félix Lecoy, *Recherches sur le "Libro de buen amor"*, 261; The parade that Juan Ruiz describes for us is not a triumphal parade. It is, rather, a parody of a liturgical ceremony, indeed, the oldest of its kind, the procession of Palm Sunday. Sir Love, who returns to his domain, is Christ, who enters into Jerusalem, amidst the acclaim of an enthusiastic crowd).

G. B. Gybbon-Monypenny, editor of the *Libro* concludes his erudite commentary on *copla* 1225 with the following observation: "En el fondo, como da a entender Juan Ruiz en 1225a, son las procesiones del Domingo de la Resurrección las que se parodian" (In the final analysis, as Juan Ruiz explains in copla 1225a, the object of the parody is the Easter Sunday processions) (Notes 364).

[14] Carlos Bousoño, *Teoría de la expresión poética*. 6th ed. 2 vols. (Madrid: Gredos, 1976), quotes Aleixandre's poem in its entirety (1: 424–25).

[15] Besides the "significacional," the other subcategories studied by Bousoño are the "temporal" (1: 389–411), "espacial" (1: 411–15), and "situacional" (1: 415–23).

privileges Aleixandre's complete effacement of the boundaries between two exis-
tential spheres—the spiritual and the material—pertaining, respectively, to the
soul (*el alma*) and the body (*el cuerpo*). The soul and the body are conventionally
regarded as two separate, if complementary, entities. The lesson we learn from
Aleixandre's poem and Bousoño's explication is the paradoxical effect of the
parodic function of superimposition. The critic epitomizes that function in an
emblematic phrase—"espiritualización de la materia" (spiritualization of matter)
(424)—the signification of which will reverberate at various junctures during
our discussion.

As we begin to attain a firm hold on this double-layered intertextuality, we
are struck by the distinction that Hutcheon posits between parody and satire.
She observes, at the heart of satire, an intention "to distort, to belittle, to wound"
(44).[16] Not so for parody. As Hutcheon is quick to point out,

> In modern parody. . .we have found that no such negative judgment is nec-
> essarily suggested in the ironic contrasting of texts. Parodic art both devi-
> ates from an aesthetic norm and includes that norm within itself and back-
> grounded material. Any real attack would be self-destructive (44).

The modern and not-so-modern works just listed clearly bear out the lesson
Hutcheon would have us learn. The shining examples of parodic superimposi-
tion, masterfully elaborated by Diego de San Pedro, Juan Rodríguez del Padrón,
Ausiàs March, Juan Ruiz, and Vicente Aleixandre evince no sign of a "negative
judgment" or perverse intention. All of them convey an overall sense of equilib-
rium that brings to mind, in turn, the pertinence of Ziva Ben-Porat's definition:

> The parodic representations expose the model's conventions and lay bare
> its devices through the coexistence of the two codes in the same message
> (quoted in Hutcheon, 49).

In Hutcheon's view, shared by Ben-Porat, the foreground/background perspec-
tivism hinges on a perfect balance as would a well-thought-out algebraic equa-
tion. Could this view apply as well to Dueñas's and Ribera's *misas*, which have
elicited, in some cases, puzzlement and, at times, provoked self-righteous indig-
nation and downright rebuke? Hutcheon's definition allows us to hypothesize
that neither Dueñas nor Ribera intends to fabricate a disparaging version of sac-
rosanct Christian doctrine. Hutcheon's theory invites us to consider the pos-
sibility that Dueñas, by installing the Trinitarian pattern in a pagan context,
actually asserts his belief—"esto creo y más de tanto"—in a Divinity that tran-
scends cultural boundaries. Similarly, it may be said that Ribera, by projecting
the Agnus icon onto the relationship between Venus and Cupid, does nothing

---

[16] The words are borrowed from Gilbert Highet's *The Anatomy of Satire*.

more than confirm his adherence to the universality of the faith he has imbibed with his mother's milk.[17] Thus, to the question we have posed above we may add another that stems from Bousoño's insight: Are Dueñas and Ribera, in effect, carrying out a process of Christianizing the pagan cult in a manner analogous to the "espiritualización de la materia" that Bousoño discerns in Aleixandre's poetry? At this point we may answer, I believe, with a cautious affirmative. We will have to wait and see if the analysis of further texts validates our hypothetical interpretation of a parodic intention in line with Hutcheon's principles of "trans-contextualization" and "bitextual determination."

Degrees of Desacralization

Dueñas's and Ribera's audacious attempts at a harmonious blend of Christian and pagan elements prove to be, at best, ingenuous and awkward. The severity of those formidable readers, who see in those attempts nothing but a reprehensible pollution of Christian liturgy with pagan notions of the divine, should not, however, cause us to lose sight of the equilibrium that both Hutcheon and Ben-Porat consider an inherent principle of parody. Bearing that principle in mind we are able to envision an overarching pattern of desacralization. The pattern illustrates a trajectory of transition at different stages from the sacred to the profane. Each stage reveals an example of alterity, which hinges on the mechanism of "super-imposition" and "bitextual determination" explained above.

The first stage is represented by Dueñas and Ribera, who raise the specter of an alarming substitution: the Christian Deity being replaced by a pagan counterpart. In the second stage, the risk of that allegedly egregious interchange is reduced appreciably. Such is the case of Núñez's *misa*, which secularizes the pious meditation on the Book of Hours. Typical is the following passage pertaining to the Hour of Prime:

A *Prima* quando amanesce,
rezá la *Salve Regina*,
aquella que os hizo digna
del valer que más meresce
y de mi mal diciplina.
Y, rezada, os retraé
a contemplar en mi fe,

---

[17] Another nonderogatory interpretation of the two *misas* may be stated as follows: Dueñas attempts to fathom the awe-inspiring presence of the Trinity by envisaging the sublime mystery at two different levels; Ribera proposes an enhanced meditation on the image of the Agnus Dei by transposing or—to use Hutcheon's terminology—transcon-textualizing its sphere of reference into the realm of pagan religion.

sin oír nuevas consejas,
que quien oye a malas viejas
nunca llora sin porqué

(vv. 41–50; *Cancionero general*, ed. González Cuenca, 3: 151–52; At the hour
of Prime, at the crack of dawn, recite the *Salve Regina*, to that Holy Queen,
who has allowed you to measure up to your highest merit and be a scourge
to my evil ways. After your prayers, retire a while to regard my faithful love,
and pay no attention to rash advice. Whoever listens to old wives' tales will
forever weep, and do so with very good reason).

At first reading, one may notice that here the *Salve Regina* is lifted out of the
original devotional milieu and transposed to the context of the cult of Eros. In
effect, by an uncanny maneuver on the part of the author, the sacred text becomes
a vehicle for the furtherance of the relationship between the lover (the poet him-
self) and the *amada*. With oblique subtlety, Núñez employs the mechanics of
transference, adaptation, and secularization.

At play, here, is what may well prove to be a primary aspect of Núñez's subtle
artistry. The poet works out an esthetic of alterity and, above all, impersonation.
In his wistful imagination, the auctorial persona envisages the lady in the role of
a channeling agent. He entreats her to meditate profoundly at every step of her
devotion: that is, the recitation of the *Salve*. She will do so to condition herself to
requite the lover's own devotion toward her. The beloved becomes, at least from
the lover's perspective, a mediatrix that ensures the efficacy of the devotional
practice. The lover faithfully expects the merits attained by the beloved's prayer-
ful and conscientious observance of her pious duties to redound, ultimately, to
his own benefit: the enhancement of his own spiritual life. In Núñez's ingenious
stanza the ladylove ends up mirroring the intermediary agency of the Virgin
Mary. To put it succinctly, Núñez skillfully adopts the classic paradigm of super-
imposing the profane upon the sacred: specifically, the image of the ladylove
upon that of the Holy Virgin. In so doing, the poet assigns to the *amada* one of
the functions of the *Mater Misericordiae* (Mother of Mercy), primarily embla-
zoned in the *Salve Regina*. Consequently, the *amada* is portrayed as an imperson-
ator of the Virgin; the impersonation hinges on a characterization modeled after
the office of the mediatrix in the world view of many members of the worldwide
Christian community.[18]

---

[18] By contrast, Garci Sánchez runs a much greater risk than does Núñez and leaves
himself wide open to the charge of sacrilege. For an apt example of this poet's blunt
address to the lady, we may peruse the stanza that heads the "Lición quarta," based on
Job 13:22–28:

> *Responde michi, quantas habeo. . .*
> *Responde michi*, señora:
> *quantas habeo iniquitates,*

Profiling the Primary Priest

At the third stage of desacralization we find the crowning achievement of Francesc Moner: the obviation of the risky Christian/pagan interface. A close reading of Moner's *Sepultura* makes us realize that the allegorical personage, Mancilla, takes pride of place among the three celebrants of the Mass and stands out as a fair match for Núñez's characterization of his ladylove. Comparative analysis brings to light the interplay of versions and counter-versions stemming from two age-old topoi: (1) *la belle dame sans merci*, and (2) *la donna angelicata*. Núñez's and Moner's poems hold in store, at the deepest textual stratum, a field that may be called "onomastic symbolism," which evinces multiple semiotic implications. Amidst the iridescence of signification lies ensconced the term "merci" in full regalia as poetic logos, integrated into the complete title of the famous poem by Alain Chartier: *La belle dame sans merci.*[19] Within the semiotic context evoked

---

> *peccata, scelera mea?*
> O ¿por qué es merescedora
> mi vida que assí la tractes,
> pues que servirte desea?
> *Cur faciem tuam abscondis?*
> ¿Piensas que só tu enemigo?
> *Contra folium quod vento*
> *rapitur nichil respondis*
> a las palabras que digo,
> que muestran el mal que siento. (Vv. 195–206; *Cancionero general*, ed.
González Cuenca, 2: 373;

> *Responde michi*, my Lady: *quantas habeo iniquitates, peccata, scelera mea?* Alas,
> why does my life deserve to be treated so? My only wish is to serve you. *Cur faciem
> tuam abscondis?* Do you think I am your enemy? *Contra folium quod vento rapitur
> nichil respondis* to the words I utter — the words that show you how ill I feel).

Gallagher's pithy comment goes right to the point of this passage in particular and the entire composition, in general:

> The nine lessons which Garci Sánchez adapts to his profane love are those of the
> common Office of the Dead at Matins, selected verses from the Book of Job. The
> analogy is simple: Job's position vis-à-vis God becomes Garci Sánchez's vis-à-vis
> his lady. Hence the fundamentally idolatrous nature of the poem. (*The Life and
> Works of Garci Sánchez de Badajoz*, 178)

   [19] For the text of Chartier's masterpiece and its translation into English, see the bibliography below. McRae estimates that the *La belle dame sans mercy* was written around 1424. See McRae, Introduction, 6. Moner, who lived in France for two years (around 1479–1481) (see *1 Introducción*, 9) in his late teens and learned the language of that country, may well have been familiar with Chartier's emblematic poem. A special connection between Moner and the celebrated piece of French medieval literature is indicated by the role of protagonist that a certain Fra Francesc Oliver plays in Moner's prose work bearing the title, precisely, of *L'ànima d'Oliver* (The Ghost of Oliver). According to Jordi Rubió

by Núñez's creative imagination, the denotation and connotation encapsulated in the logos of *merci* beckon the reader in their deafening silence. Núñez capitalizes on a tradition of long standing, which alerts the reader to the interaction between the *merci* notoriously denied by the French *belle dame* and the *misericordia* to be procured only if duly assimilated by the obdurate *amada* and implored by said reader in the recitation of the *Salve Regina*. Núñez arrives at an intuition of the ultimate analogy between divine *misericordia* and human *merci* as signified, respectively, by the Latin and the French term.

As if he were bent upon taking up the challenge posed by Núñez and the likes of Núñez, Moner develops the analogy to a particularly deep insight. First, he completely disengages the *amada* from the office of mediatrix, reflected in the conventional rendition of parody. The disengagement involves, on the one hand, divesting the ladylove of the powers appertaining to that office and, on the other, vesting those powers in an allegorical personage, Mancilla herself. Secondly, Moner sets in operation the development of the *merci/misericordia* analogy by capitalizing upon the principles of onomastic semiotics. Mancilla embodies the "lástima" (pity) and "compasión" (compassion) that her very name signifies.[20] Evidently, Moner allegorizes in Mancilla that disposition that the afflicted lover in Núñez's *misa* finds sorely lacking in the *amada* and, thus, yearns to elicit from her. Thirdly, Moner takes full advantage of the method of superimposition and elaborates upon a poetics of interaction between the fully visualized presence of Mancilla and the nebulous figure of the *donna angelicata*, the ideal woman of the *dolce stil nuovo*, barely discernible in the substratum of the literary palimpsest: the text, that is, of *Sepultura*.[21]

Now we begin to comprehend the wide scope of Moner's analogy. There is an equation of sorts between the notion of personified *merci/mancilla* and the office of a priest. The wondrous powers of the metaphor meld the two terms of the equation: *Merci/Mancilla* = Priest. What Moner demonstrates in his representation of Mancilla is the expansion of the metaphor into an allegory in accordance to Quintilian's principle of "continua metaphora" (expanded metaphor)

Balaguer ("Literatura catalana," 874) and Martí de Riquer (*Història de la literatura catalana*, 3: 112–14), this Oliver is, in all probability, the translator of *La belle dame sans merci* into Catalan. It is worth noting that Oliver acquired a dubious distinction after committing suicide on account of unrequited love of his own *belle dame sans merci*, the Comtessa de Luna (Violant Lluïsa de Mur), a noble lady of the highest rank (Riquer, *Història de la literatura catalana*, 3: 109–16).

[20] The dominance of these two meanings in the *Cancionero general* is abundantly documented. See above, p. 29, n. 22.

[21] As for the portrayal of the idealized woman, one may think of Dante's Beatrice and Petrarch's Laura.

(Quintilian 11.2.46).[22] This means that in his allegory Moner exploits to a full extent the sacerdotal stature attained by Mancilla. In her priestly ministrations, Mancilla soars to the highest level in the Great Chain of Being: precisely the level of the Divine. By virtue of the principles of onomastic symbolism, Mancilla gets in touch with Divine Mercy, kindred, *mutatis mutandis*, to the attributes of pity and compassion that provide the priestess with her allegorical raison d'être in the first place. Within the spiritual ecology of Moner's *misa*, Mancilla is, indeed, the chief purveyor of God's mercy.

We may deduce, then, that Mancilla borrows from the Virgin Mary the privileged position of intermediary and intercessor. Moner's representation allows us to envisage the Mancilla-Priest compound as a "pontifex" in the etymological and radical sense of "bridge-maker." Mancilla makes of herself a bridge between God—or, to be exact, God-the-Truth—and humankind. In addition, Mancilla's hieratic functions assume the powers of the *donna angelicata* in the journey of transcendence from the woes of passionate love to the blissful state of the Beatific Vision.

To sum up: Moner's *Sepultura* attests to a bold advancement in the journey from hieratic ritual to secularized performance. Specifically, Moner's *misa* comes at the culmination of an evolutionary development that originates in the awkward experimentation conducted by Dueñas and Ribera. Dueñas's and Ribera's heavy-handed intermingling of the sacred and the profane gives way to Núñez's suggestive interplay of juxtaposition and conversion: the juxtaposition of the figure of the Virgin Mary and that of the ladylove, the conversion of the ladylove from *belle dame sans merci* to *donna angelicata*. By projecting the iconic presence of the *donna* into the role of the super-priest, Moner not only creates a memorable allegorical personification of the idealized woman but also fashions the imposing characterization of the chief celebrant of the *misa de amores*. In short, Moner's *Sepultura* marks the climactic point of the parodic trend in *cancionero* poetry.

Traces of De-ritualized Textuality

A clear sign of desacralization is the loss of the ritualistic nature of the liturgical text. Mancilla herself provides some telltale markers of Moner's de-ritualized *misa*. An excellent illustration of this process of de-ritualization is Mancilla's own version of the sections of the Mass. Let us take, for instance the following passage (stanza 17), which exemplifies her special rendition of the Requiem:

---

[22] Quoted in Archer, "The Workings of Allegory in Ausiàs March," 170. In his study of Ausiàs March's allegory, Archer sheds light on the quintessential aspects of that author's esthetic.

La confessión acabada,
luego por réquiem Manzilla
   començó:
—O Verdad, nuestra abogada,
no le falte honrrada silla,
   pues bivió
en tu fe santa alabada;
tu lumbre alumbre su fama,
y tu bondad favorezca
   su querella;
a quyen tal brasa derrama,
haz, Señora, que padesca
   dentro en ella
y, d'allý, venga en la llama.—
(Vv. 192–205; *2 OC,* 138) (For the translation, see p. 200 below.)

At first reading, the passage impresses us for the absence of any self-evident link with the wording of the original prayer: "requiem aeternam dona ei(s), Domine" (eternal rest grant unto them/him/her, o Lord). Typical of this passage as, for that matter, of Moner's entire *misa,* is the omission of direct quotations from the Latin text. A faint reminiscence of "lux perpetua luceat ei(s)" (and may perpetual light shine unto them/him/her) is perceivable in "tu lumbre alumbre su fama." But the difference between "su fama," the object of Mancilla's invocation, and its counterpart, "requiem aeternam," in the Latin Mass is substantial. The considerable distance between Moner's requiem and its Latin model needs no special commentary. One detail, however, should not pass unnoticed. Mancilla adds a dreadful spin to the crucial image of *lumbre. Lumbre,* faithful translation of *lux,* mutates into the ominous *brasa* (burning coal), as the priestess alludes to some generic evildoer who revels in turning the coal poignantly mentioned into a wild fire spreading far and wide. Moner challenges the reader to conjure an appropriate interpretation for the cluster of metaphors (*lumbre, brasa, llama*) that Mancilla leaves unspecified. To be sure, no challenge is posed by the curse leveled by the priestess at that nondescript evildoer, for whom she wishes nothing better than a horrid death in the midst of the raging flame: "y, d'allý, venga en la llama."[23]

---

[23] There are other passages in which the author achieves a clear effect of distancing from the Latin source. At some points in the unfolding of the *misa,* one of the three celebrants indulges a perverse inclination toward admonition, menace, and downright condemnation. Thus, the animosity that, as we have just seen, Mancilla vents off against those who would fan the fires of destruction ("quyen tal brasa derrama" [v. 202]) is matched by the resentment Costumbre voices in her warning addressed to women in general:
   —Las que presumen çevar
   guárdense bien dell anzuelo,

Needless to say, the curse runs counter to the salvific intention governing the organic makeup of the Mass. From its original conception, the Mass is definitely not designed for the condemnation of anyone. A condemnatory Mass: here is an oxymoron and a paradox combined! With good reason, then, one may be surprised by the dubious integration of deviant phrases into a coherent composition that attempts to reproduce in their proper sequence the essential sections of the sacred ceremony. What saves the day in Moner's case is the aplomb with which the author allows his Mass to assimilate his daring distortions. Judging from the textual evidence just analyzed, we may safely hypothesize that Moner honed his

> que, si no,
> podráse alguno vengar;
> ca no deven ser soffridas
> que sin causa desconbidan
> por antojo.
> Algunas serán medidas
> de la medida que myden
> y, de enojo,
> tan bien tarde, arrepentidas.
> (Vv. 237–47; *2 OC*, 140) (For the translation, see p. 200 below.)

Notably, Costumbre enhances the distancing effect mentioned above by piously entoning the warning into a complete statement of an *epístola* of her own making: "La Costumbre fue a cantar / la epístola, boz al cielo. / Entonó . . ." (vv. 234–36; *2 OC*, 139–40). Another conspicuous invective against false lovers is disguised as an integral component of a pious invocation, and delivered in unison by the three celebrants at the beginning of the Mass:

> —Al que s'arma de mentira,
> tu justicia le condene
> de manera
> que ayan temor de tu ira.
> (Vv. 189–91; *2 OC*, 138) (See the translation on p. 200 below.)

The priestesses apply a curious slant to the sacrosanct sections of the Mass. This slant and the attendant harsh language are foreshadowed by the skewed dedication the poetic persona sees fit to attach as the conclusion of his preliminary address to the lady:

> —Mas, porqu'es mucha razón
> que se suene de la vida
> bien gastada,
> embío's missa, y sermón,
> y sepultura complida,
> celebrada
> en vuestra condenación.
> (Vv. 71–77; *2 OC*, 134) (See the translation on p. 198 below.)

Ostensibly, there are discordant notes in Moner's *misa*. Witness the following expressions, similar to one just cited (v. 77): "que ayan temor de tu ira" (v. 191), "haz, Señora, que padesca, / dentro en ella" (vv. 202–3), "guárdense bien dell anzuelo" (v. 238).

technique of not only avoiding adverse criticism but also forestalling charges of mishandling or violating the Church's most venerable canons of worship.[24]

There is no doubt that Moner sets his *misa* apart from the protocol of the original Mass. In so doing, the author delves into the dramatics of what may be labeled "denatured ritual." With this terminology, I propose an esthetic analogue for the physical or chemical phenomenon denoted by the process of denaturing.[25] An explanation for the analogy I envisage is not hard to imagine. Overall formalism and specific formulaic textuality constitute the natural attributes of the Mass. Moner, as we have seen, casts off most of these attributes and retains only the skeletal infrastructure of the Eucharistic liturgy. Thus, his artistic enterprise becomes impervious to the criticism and charges mentioned above simply because in his "denatured *misa*" there is little ritual left to criticize. The innovation signaled by Moner's inventive dramatics cannot be overestimated.

Distancing: A New Perspective

Moner's experimentation with the parody of the Mass raises the possibility of a new perspective on the origins of Spanish theater of the fifteenth century. Such a perspective involves an innovative approach to the manner in which the necessary esthetic distance between spectators and performers comes into being. A word is in order here on the classic essay, in which Charlotte Stern charts the transition evinced "from medieval ritual to Renaissance art." Stern gauges the progression along the route of that transition by the degree of spectator participation, noting the following:

> The effort by medieval composers to achieve total immediacy and thus assure maximum emotional involvement by the audience is strikingly apparent in *La Sibila de la Noche de Navidad* (The Sybil of Christmas Eve). ("The Early Spanish Drama," 182)

Stern goes on to explain that the *Sibila* "was performed as part of the midnight Christmas mass in the cathedral of Toledo, perhaps as early as the thirteenth century" ("The Early Spanish Drama," 182). What may come as a surprise is the evidence that the "immediacy" and "emotional involvement by the audience," underscored by Stern as trademarks of medieval liturgical drama typified by *La Sibila de la Noche de Navidad*, persists centuries later in some nonreligious works

---

[24] Somehow, Moner manages to keep under the radar, so to speak, the details of the type that, in circumstances pertaining to writers like Dueñas, Ribera, and Núñez, would have met the strident repudiation of offended readers of many stripes.

[25] In *Webster's New World Dictionary* we find the following definition of "denature:" "to change the nature of; take natural qualities away from."

by such prominent playwrights as Juan del Encina, Lucas Fernández, Gil Vicente, and Bartolomé Torres Naharro. Stern points out that it was not until 1516 that the aforementioned transition took full effect to become an actual transformation. According to this scholar, in that same year the *mise en scène* in Italy of Torres Naharro's *Comedia Himenea* marks the mutation of the ritual drama into a full-fledged theatrical performance in the modern sense of the term ("The Early Spanish Drama," 194). In the following passage, Stern summarizes her vision of the birth of Spanish theater at the dawn of the Renaissance:

> In this cursory survey, I have attempted to trace the rediscovery of aesthetic distance in Spain and with it the rebirth of dramatic art during the transitional period between the Middle Ages and the Renaissance. The reawakening process extends over several decades. First, there is the gradual widening of distance, physical and psychical, between audience and actors in the plays preceding the *Himenea*, but it is Torres Naharro who takes the tremendous leap forward and treats us to a full-fledged example of dramatic illusion. ("The Early Spanish Drama," 198)

Stern further explains that her theory of the evolution of Spanish theater is based on the criterion of audience participation and response. In order to identify and define the radical mutation she analyzes, Stern relies on two main sources: Susanne K. Langer's notion of "illusion" as distinguished from "delusion," and the concept of "psychical distance" explored by the British psychologist, Edward Bullough. Langer and Bullough respectively provide an all-important insight into the gestation of theatricality and, to quote directly from Stern, "the aesthetic detachment necessary for the appreciation of a work of art" ("The Early Spanish Drama," 179–80).

The criterion elaborated by Stern comes in handy in situating Moner's *misa* in the trajectory of transition that she sketches out. We discover that the very innovative achievements that Stern underscores in Torres Naharro's *Comedia Himenea* may be evidenced in Moner's obvious interest in what we may call the "play factor." We need not go into the profound implications that Huizinga discusses at length in his classical *Homo Ludens*. Instead, for pragmatic reasons, we will adhere to the narrow purview attendant upon the guidelines proposed by Stern. In the light of Stern's argument, the very notions of "psychical distance" and "illusion" may be readily found in the playacting of the three priestesses: Mancilla, Costumbre, and Experiencia. Moner's *misa*, composed in the mid-1480s, anticipates by three decades the momentous significance Sterns ascribes to the performance of *Comedia Himenea*.

Sacramentality in a New Key

Thus far we have seen the effects that the parodic modes—especially those Hutcheon identifies as "transcontextualization" or "recontextualization"—instill in the ritual of the Mass. Specific manifestations of these modalities may include, as we have seen, the reconstitution of the Christian ritual by the interpolation of pagan elements or by the substantial change in the formulas or language of the sacred ceremony. Hutcheon's theory charts a pattern of desacralization or denaturing, one that betokens a particular type of mutation: as the sacred quality of the ritual is diminished, what remains is an efficacy of a secular rather than religious nature. In other words, the denatured ritual is no less efficacious in a setting appropriate to its nature (specifically a theatrical setting) than is the original ritual within the precincts of a church.

In summation: what Moner elaborates is a kind of sacramentality of his own. His ersatz sacramentality is evident in two differences inherent in the novelty harbingered by his *misa*. First, there is an irrevocable break from the age-old tradition linking the Mass to the allegorical interpretation, to which Amalarius, the German bishop of the Carolingian era, gave wide currency in his influential commentaries.[26] Hardison (*Christian Rite and Christian Drama in the Middle Ages*, 35–79) and Surtz (*The Birth of a Theater*, 35–66) demonstrate that the Amalarian allegorization involves not only the stylized officiation of the celebrants (priests, deacons, acolytes) but also the lockstep participation of the members of the congregation in the sacred ceremony. Concerning this interaction between congregation and celebrants, Surtz states:

> Amalarius views the Mass in terms of sacred drama and role playing, the events of the liturgy being considered as re-enactments of Old Testament practices or as rememorative allegory of the life of Christ. Celebrant and congregation play rapidly changing and often simultaneous roles. (*The Birth of a Theater*, 36)

It is clear, then, that Amalarius posits a type of allegory as a function of a spectacle that does not change the nature per se of a ritualistic observance in keep-

---

[26] Hardison provides the following sketch of the career of Amalarius, bishop of Metz (780?-850):

> A prominent figure at the courts of Charlemagne and Louis the Pious, an ambassador to Constantinople, and a lifelong student of the liturgy, Amalarius wrote two, and perhaps three, interpretations of the Mass. The first is the *Eclogae de ordine Romano* (814), and the most influential is the *Liber officialis*, which Amalarius saw through three editions between 821 and 835. (*Christian Rite and Christian Drama in the Middle Ages*, 37)

ing with the mystery of transubstantiation.[27] In diametric contrast to the strict observance of the Eucharistic liturgy espoused by the Amalarian tradition, Moner proposes a substantial transformation in both the praxis and the doctrine implicit in that liturgy.

The second difference mentioned above is the absence of playacting of the type that characterized the numerous "sacramental plays" and "miracle-of-the-sacrament plays" described under such labels by Lynette R. Muir.[28] What Moner fashions, then, is not a religious but a literary ritual, one that stems from a special notion of surrogate sacramentality. "Surrogate" here refers to a special field of operation, divested of the theological connotations of the original Mass. Though of tenuous theological potency, the overall surrogate tenor in question is fully operative within its appertaining field. Consistent with Moner's vision of the Mass as a literary artifact is a paradigm of a foundational analogy at play between the original ritual and its parodic counterpart. The analogy is multiform. The iconic *canción* (¡"Ay del byen que mal me haze. . .!"), already analyzed in some detail (see pp. 36–37 above), becomes the analogue of the bread and wine: the species, that is, of the awesome sacrament at the heart of the Mass. Thus, as a "transcontextualization" of the primary sacrament, Moner's select *canción* is transubstantiated into a text displayed as the ultimate existential epiphany of the lover. That *canción* epitomizes what we may call the "life-text"—"L'ystoria de quyen muryó" (the story of this man, who has just died) (*Sepultura*, v. 639), to use Moner's own wording—pertaining to the lover portrayed as the devotee of

---

[27] Well aware of the importance duly accorded to the canon of the Mass in Amalarius's allegorization, Hardison proffers the following explanation:

In the medieval mind the idea of commemoration fused with the doctrine of the Real Presence: if the bread and wine are truly changed at the moment of Consecration into the flesh and blood of the Savior, then Christ must be literally present at every Mass. Allegorical interpretation moved outward from this insight to find dramatic significance in each of the major prayers and ceremonies. Ultimately, every detail of the service was considered symbolic. (*Christian Rite and Christian Drama in the Middle Ages*, 43)

[28] Typically, the playacted Mass is featured in a mystery play, such as the *Mystère de Saint Martin*, the *Geu Saint Denis*, or a *sacra rappresentazione* (for example: *Come Cristo fa celebrare le messe*) (Muir, "The Mass on the Medieval Stage," 223–25). Muir describes various specimens of the theatricalized Mass in vogue throughout Europe in religious pageants, especially during the feast of the Corpus Christi. Of special interest is the following observation:

Floats with tableaux and minimal dialogue were a common feature of the Spanish Corpus Christi processions during the fourteenth and fifteenth centuries, but it is in the sixteenth, under the threat of the Reform, that *autos* and *farsas* were specially composed for the occasion, many of them presenting groups of allegorical or historical figures discussing, preaching about, and praising the sacrament of the Mass. (227)

God-the-Truth. By virtue of the parodic principles posited by Hutcheon, such a "life-text" asserts itself as an alternate Gospel. The auctorial persona, the protagonist of Moner's *misa*, in exemplary *imitatio-Christi* form, achieves his crowning distinction as *mártir de amor* (martyr of love) duly canonized.

We see, then, how the parodic intention and its concomitant practices condition a veritable mutation of the liturgical service (especially the service of the Mass) and come to bear on a process of transition from religious ritual to secular theater. Now we are ready to investigate how, by his deft use of the mode of parody, Moner operates in the middle ground he has discovered between theology and esthetics. In the intermediate field of his poetics, Moner works out a remarkable conflation of the religious and the secular and, thus, brings into effect the unlikely notion of a marriage of sacramentality and theater.

Full Circle

From the foregoing discussion we gather a wide variety of issues: the ones that come to bear on the extensive body of criticism focused on the *misa de amores* and kindred compositions. As I have indicated, this love-centered literature is well represented mostly in the *cancionero* poetry and, sporadically, in some passages of the *novela sentimental*. Whinnom and Gernert stake out two fundamental contrasting positions that help us synthesize those issues and see them in a clear light. Whinnom states the premise of his lucid argumentation in a succinct and straightforward manner:

> No cabe duda de que los escritores medievales eran menos sensibles que nosotros al decoro en los asuntos religiosos (*La poesía amatoria,* 22; There can be little doubt that medieval writers were less sensitive than we are regarding the decorum befitting matters of religion).

This critic does not spare examples to validate the point expressed in the following statement:

> Nuestros poetas, bien familiarizados con los conceptos religiosos, no se sentían cohibidos al apercibirse de algún paralelo picante (*La poesía amatoria,* 22; Well familiarized with religious subjects, the poets in question felt no compunction when they became conscious of some prurient allusion).

The nonchalant attitude of these authors may be appropriately epitomized in the famous French saying: *Honi soit qui mal y pense.* The "paralelo picante" is quite evident in the numerous examples adduced by Whinnom (*La poesía amatoria,* 23–33).

Gernert on her part expands considerably on the issues analyzed by Whinnom and describes them in such terms as "fenómeno de tránsito entre la esfera religiosa y la no-religiosa" (a process of transfer between the religious and non-religious sphere), "intercambio entre la esfera religiosa y aquella profana" (an interchange between the religious and secular sphere), "imitación de modelos sagrados en la iconografía profana de tema amoroso" (an imitation of sacred models within the non-sacred iconography dealing with the subject of love) (*Parodia y «contrafacta»*, 22, 23 n. 1).

While Gernert and Whinnom deal with many of the same aspects of the subject matter under consideration, Gernert's own minute and persistent meditation leads her to disagree radically with Whinnom's interpretation. Her main objection is that the erotic hints brought to light by Whinnom do not apply to the entire vast body of literature that throughout the Middle Ages featured the adaptation of a religious model to a secular modality. According to Gernert, latent eroticism has nothing to do with the *misas* and the other specimens of paraliturgical or parareligious literature that pique our interest.

What Gernert finds problematic in the parlance of many critics is the widespread, indiscriminate use of the term "parody."[29] She instinctively associates the term with the burlesque slant, off-color humor and satirical intention, represented by the *vagi clerici*: the goliards of the twelfth and thirteenth century. She wastes no time in pointing out that the goliardic tendencies are definitely out of synch in respect of "las composiciones amorosas tardomedievales" (love-related works of the late Middle Ages) that fall within the purview of her research. Not surprisingly, she voices her disapproval of what she regards "el empleo sumamente incorrecto del término 'parodia' para designar estos textos" (the egregiously incorrect use of the term "parody" to designate these texts) (*Parodia y «contrafacta»*, 1: 21). Consequentially, Gernert proffers a reading quite different from the one that others would consider pertinent to a parodic presentation:

> [E]l estudio del corpus textual tanto desde la perspectiva de las prácticas literarias cuanto de las sociales y teológicas, permite leer estos textos no ya como parodias de cuestiones de fe, sino como expresiones de una espiritualidad laica muy sentida y sinceramente vivida. (*Parodia y «contrafacta»*, 1: 21; The study of this body of writings from not only a literary but also a social and theological perspective allows us to read these texts [*las composiciones amorosas tardomedievales*: 'late-medieval compositions about love'] no longer as parodies of matters of faith but, rather, as expressions deeply felt and sincerely lived on the part of the laity).)

In short, Gernert considers the term "parody" inadequate for the purpose of her study. As one might expect, the upshot of her argument entails an all-important substitution, which she efficiently carries out: she replaces "parody" with "*con-*

---

[29] For various examples of this use of the term, see Gernert, (*Parodia y «contrafacta»*, 1: 21, n. 2).

trafactum," a term borrowed from a field other than literary criticism. She fully justifies her choice with a resolute, clear statement:

> [E]l término *contrafactum*, procedente de la musicología, tiene la ventaja de referirse por un lado a un fenómeno de tránsito entre la esfera religiosa y la no-religiosa, y de remitir, por una partre, a un procedimiento de referencia intertextual a *hipotextos* bíblicos y litúrgicos, sin que se especifique la intencinalidad de este recurso (*Parodia y «contrafacta»*, 1: 22; The term *contrafactum*, borrowed from musicology, has the advantage of referring to, on the one hand, a case of transition from a religious to a non-religious sphere and, on the other, a process of intertextual referencing to biblical or liturgical hypotexts, without specifying the intention of such a procedure).

By the substitution Gernert seeks to obviate coming face-to-face with a forbidding conundrum: the determination as to an author's innocuous or perverse intention.

When brought to bear upon our broad critique of Moner's *Sepultura* in the light of the principles set forth in Hutcheon's theory, Gernert's insights open up the prospect of a recontextualization of the entire discourse on the so-called *religio amoris* (religion of love). In my own efforts at defining this new context, I have found it useful to make reference to Gerli's essay ("La religion del amor") on the manifestations of parody or *contrafactum* as the case may be. Gerli speaks poignantly of the "amalgama de lo sagrado y lo profano" (the amalgamation of the sacred and the profane) (67), the "sincretismo del amor cortés" (the syncretism of courtly love) (67), "la amalgama del amor humano y la religion" (the amalgamation of human love and religion) (67). In addition, he underscores the function of the Christian theological system in "crear orden y prestar la coherencia de algo familiar, el cristianismo, al confuso laberinto de los sentimientos eróticos" (creating order and lend coherence of something familiar, Christianity, to the confused labyrinth of the erotic passions) (70). In the final analysis, he envisions in the religion of love an overarching balance between the sacred and the profane. That balance betokens the interplay of ambivalence.[30] What Gerli calls 'the deification of profane love' ("la divinización del amor profano") or 'the tempation of deifying what is human' ("la tentación de divinizar lo humano") (78) implies the reverse process: the deification of profane love has, as the obverse side, the profanation of divine love.

There is a good measure of ambiguity in the lofty ambivalence intuited by Gerli. Is God's love brought down to the level of the profane or is profane love raised up to the sphere of the divine? The answer to these questions resides, I suggest, in the cycle operative in Moner's esthetic. The process of desacraliza-

---

[30] This effect of ambivalence is not any different from the one produced by Aleixandre's poem discussed above (see pp. 81–82).

tion allows us to witness the cycle in its complete evolution. Moner does, indeed, accommodate the scope of divine love to a human level. It is important, however, to bear in mind that, in that scaling down process, he discovers the dynamic of a theater that points the way back up in a journey toward the communion with the Summum Bonum.

The study of Moner's *Sepultura* may be seen as contribution toward the validation of Hutcheon's position: it draws a sharp distinction between the conventional and nonconventional view of parody. By virtue of its essential adherence to authentic Christian devotional practice, Moner's poem neutralizes the distancing effect inherent in the conventional interpretation of parody. The literary compositions inspired by sacred motifs become, as a rule, distanced from the liturgy by the very artistic elaboration they carry out on the liturgical model. That notwithstanding, Moner's masterpiece closes the circuit of parody and returns to the starting point: the model that in the first place served as inspiration for the artistic elaboration. Through the conventionalism of parody, Moner's creativiy recaptures, paradoxically enough, the spirit of true Christian worship. By successfully achieving the delicate equilibrium between the profane and divine realms, Moner has found the formula to spiritualize the human without disparaging the divine. In other words, that formula plays out in a round trip of sorts: a journey departing from and returning to the salvific efficacy of the liturgy.

VII.
DRAMATIZATION ON THE WAY
TO PERFORMANCE

Dramatics Awaiting Performance

So far we have traced some indices of potential theatricality in the *cancioneros*. Now we can take a look at the evidence that comes to light regarding varying degrees of spectacular display.[1] There are, in fact, some *cancionero* poems that may serve as a springboard for a full-fledged theatrical rendition. In this respect, Andrée Crabbé Rocha has something noteworthy to say about some special compositions of the *Cancioneiro geral*, the Portuguese counterpart of the Castilian *Cancionero general*. Crabbé Rocha muses over those crucial passages that, doubtless, would pose a challenge for the most gifted actor:

> Mais n'importe quel soliloque sentimental et circonstanciel, qui s'accommode d'être mimé, gagne beaucoup à la magie des planches et au talent de l'interprète. . ... Le *C[ancioneiro] G[eral]* compte quantité d'exemples de cette potentialité dramatique (117; whether sentimental or circumstantial, the soliloquy that lends itself to being acted out in mime has much to gain from stage magic and the interpreter's talent. . ... [T]he *Cancioneiro Geral* offers abundant examples of this dramatic potential).

This critic opens our eyes to a wide perspective, which, by its very nature, begs to be complemented by a study of a narrow scope. Within such a scope, Josep Lluís Sirera takes up issues precisely of the kind confronted by Moner in his journey toward an eventual staging of a sizeable piece, such as *Sepultura d'amor*. In one of his studies, Sirera draws a sharp distinction between two trends in current

---

[1] In order to avoid digressions that would take us far afield, I will forgo, for the time being, a discussion of the theatricality of the allegorical castle, a topic I have taken up on other occasions ("The Theatrics of the *Auto de amores* in the *Tragicomedia* called *Celestina*," 86–91, and "Ausiàs March's Text of Subjectivity and Francesc Moner's *Auto de Amores* of the Early Spanish Renaissance," 35–39). I will focus on the theatrics concomitant with Moner's handling of the *sepultura/misa* symbiosis.

criticism on medieval theater: one deals with spectacle and pageantry or, as he puts it, "cuantas formas complejas de espectacularidad sea dable aislar (entradas reales, fastos cortesanos, fiestas rurales, urbanas y aristocráticas, ceremonias vinculadas a rituales religiosos, etc.)" (as many complex kinds of spectacle as it is possible to identify—such spectacles as royal visits, courtly celebrations, rural, urban, aristocratic festivities, ceremonies linked to religious rituals, and so forth) ("Diálogo de cancionero y teatralidad," 352); the other trend has to do with textual analysis, that is, "el estudio de los textos literarios, en tanto en cuanto dotados de una determinada carga—mayor o menor—de teatralidad" (the study of literary texts, insofar as they are endowed—some more, some less—with theatricality ("Diálogo de cancionero y teatralidad," 352). In keeping with the latter trend, Sirera brings to light the hitherto neglected dramatic properties inherent in three remarkable *cancionero* pieces: namely, Fernand Sánchez de Calavera's "Ffuy a ver este otro día" [ID 1663], Costana's "Al tiempo que se levanta" [ID 0732], and Pedro de Cartagena's "Si algún dios de Amor havía" [ID 0903].

Here we need not retrace the course of Sirera's analysis. Instead, we will follow in Sirera's footsteps by applying his approach to Moner's fashioning of his own stage-worthy textuality. After all, the conspicuous aspects we are about to discover in Moner's experimentation with the representational mode readily find easily recognizable analogues in the aforementioned compositions reviewed by Sirera.

Well represented in the *cancioneros* (especially in the *Cancionero general*) is a type of courtly-love entertainment that consists of a multifarious display of a so-called *invención*. This theatrical form, doubtless familiar to Moner, involves the integration of an epigrammatic, versified statement—the *invención* in question—usually accompanied by a music-and-dance routine. For a review of this type of spectacle, to which, as we shall see presently, Moner himself made a substantial contribution, we may recur to Macpherson, from whom we borrow the following description:

> The game of Courtly Love became the ideal vehicle for the literary after-dinner soirées and the post-tournament festivities: occasional poems, riddles, *motes, letras, invenciones, preguntas,* and *respuestas* became the staple diet of such reunions, because they particularly lent themselves to group activity, required no great depth of erudition or scholarship, and depended rather on native intelligence and quickness of wit in all its senses ("The Game of Courtly Love," 101).[2]

----

[2] Macpherson provides, also, the precise definition of the essential terminology: The *invención* of one, two, or three octosyllables, occasionally supplemented by a line of *pie quebrado* (half line), aspired at its best to be a harmonious combination of *divisa* and *letra* and grew naturally from the tournaments of the fifteenth century. In Spain the participants would ride into the lists with an elaborate crest (*cimera*), painted upon or affixed to their helms, or a striking emblem (*divisa*) embroidered

Of course, even though conceived within the context of a joust or tournament, Macpherson's definition may be readily adapted to the ambiance of a banquet or similar festive occasion.

A sizeable collection of *invenciones* and *letras* is found in the *Cancionero general* (see ff. 140–43v of the first edition, dated 1511).[3] The interested reader may peruse these pieces in the edition by Joaquín González Cuenca, who delineates an up-to-date biographical sketch for each of the contributing poets.[4] One of the most distinguished among these is Pedro de Cartagena, to whom the rubric attributes the prestigious role of arbiter of many of the *invenciones*.[5] Moner was

---

on their clothing, the scabbard of their sword, or the trappings of their horse. This image was designed to be interpreted in conjunction with the *letra* in verse composed to accompany it. ("The Game of Courtly Love," 104)

González Cuenca adds some details worthy to be taken into account:

La *invención* consta de dos partes, el cuerpo y el alma, es decir, una parte plástica o icónica (una reja, un pelicano, una noria, unas plumas. . .), bien en forma de objeto, que solía llevarse sobre el yelmo como cimera. . , bien en pintura o bordado, y otra literaria, de *letra* o *mote*, es decir, una copla o lema alusivos al icono (González Cuenca, 2: 575; The *invención* consists of two parts, the body and the soul, so to speak: the palpable or iconic part [a grille, say, or a pelican, a waterwheel, some feathers], was shaped as an object that could be worn at the top of a helmet as a crest or conceived as a painting or a piece of embroidery; the literary part was made up of a *letra* or *mote*, that is a stanza or emblematic saying that alluded to the aforementioned icon).

[3] This homogeneous section of the *Cancionero general* is headed by the following rubric: "Aquí comiençan las invenciones y letras de justadores y tanbién lo que Cartagena dixo a algunas de ellas, declarando su parescer" (here begin the *invenciones* and the *letras* of the jousters and, also, what Cartagena said about some of the *invenciones* and *letras*, and the judgment he passed on them) (2: 575). Macpherson goes into a thorough analysis of each set of *invención* and *letra* in Castillo's entire collection, which totals 116 pieces, counting those that appear in both early editions (respectively, of 1511 and 1514) of the *Cancionero General* (*The* Invenciones y Letras *of the* Cancionero General, 15). Following is Macpherson's precise description of these pieces:

The 'invenciones y letras de justadores' collected over a period of twenty years by Hernando del Castillo. . .reflect one of the most characteristic and colourful facets of court life under the Catholic Monarchs. These compositions grew naturally and spontaneously from the pageantry of the late Middle Ages in Spain: the tournaments, jousts, *pasos de armas* and *fiestas* in which the nobility and their entourage temporarily put aside the cares and responsibilities of military commitments and attendance at court, and indulged, as comrades and rivals, in the luxury of playing war games and word games. (*The* Invenciones y Letras *of the* Cancionero General, 7)

[4] See *Cancionero general*, 2: 575–625.

[5] Cartagena is entrusted with the role of responder to the first seven *invenciones* included in the *Cancionero General* (Macpherson, *The* Invenciones y Letras *of the* Can-

on familiar terms with both Pedro and his brother, known as Antonio Franco, "señor de Villafuerte" (Cocozzella, *1 Introducción*, 12–13).[6] Although Pedro is well represented in the *Cancionero* and Antonio rates but a short *letra* corresponding to the *invención* of "una campana" (a bell) (*Cancionero general*, no. 463; 2: 579), Moner does not discriminate and dedicates to each a tailor-made composition.[7] Quite significant in relation to Moner's embryonic dramaturgy is the tournament held in Barcelona on 22 April 1486. The event, which Moner had every opportunity to witness personally, is recorded, complete with its twelve sets of *invenciones* and *letras*, in the *Jardinet d'orats*, a renowned *cançoner* comprised in Biblioteca Universitària de Barcelona, ms. 151.[8]

From this abundant documentation it is reasonable to deduce that Moner exploited to the fullest the potential of the *invenciones*, which González Cuenca defines as "juegos literarios o parateatrales cargados de simbolismo y alegoría, relacionados con los *momos*" (literary or para-theatrical wordplay, charged with symbolism and allegory in the manner of the mummeries) (2: 575, n. 1). There is every reason to believe Moner was well aware of the dramatic possibilities inherent especially in those *invenciones* that González Cuenca, in expanding his definition, calls "'dinámicas' por su carácter de representación" (*dynamic* for their representational nature) (2: 575, n. 1). In fact, González Cuenca points to an actual "escenficación" (staging) that, according to the testimony of Garcia de Resende, took place in Évora, Portugal, on December 29, 1490 (González Cuenca, 2: 575–76, n. 1).

---

cionero General, 16). Macpherson links these seven pieces to a specific event: "the strong probability is that the series derives from the tournament which formed part of the spectacular celebrations staged in Valladolid on 3 April 1475" (16). The critic duly acknowledges that "[t]his opening series strongly suggests that at the age of twenty-one Pedro de Cartagena was already recognized in Castile as a poet of some stature. . ." (16).

[6] There was another brother, known as Alfonso de Sarabia. For additional biographical data on Pedro de Cartagena and his family (including his two brothers), see Macpherson, *The* invenciones y letras *of the* Cancionero General, 43–44, 47–48.

[7] See "Coplas hechas a ruegos de Cartagena" (Stanzas written on Cartagena's request) (*1 OC*, 240–43), and "Respuesta a Villafuerte" (Response to Villafuerte) (*1 OC*, 239–40). For a commentary, see Cocozzella, *1 Introducción*, respectively 139–42, 239–40. We have already made reference to Cartagena's distinction as a poet and his special relationship with Moner (see above, pp. xxvii). For additional data on the identity of Antonio Franco, see Perea Rodríguez, *Estudio biográfico*, 173, n. 43. As to Antonio Franco's contribution to the *Cancionero general*, see no. 7 in Macpherson, *The* invenciones y letras *of the* Cancionero General, 47–48.

[8] The text that interests us here appears in ff. 125–126R under the following rubric: "Esto fué unes justes, o torneig, en Barchinona, a 22 d'abril any 1486 y son estos los motivos y ximeres" (Following are the jousts or tournaments held in Barcelona on April 22, 1486, and these are the motifs and the headgear). See Riquer's transcription in *Juan Boscán y su cancionero barcelonés*, 32–34.

Among the *invenciones* collected in the *Cancionero general*, some, in all probability, hold in store special implications in terms of Moner's own handling of the "paratheatrical" genre. Eye-catching, indeed, is entry no. 507 (*Cancionero general* 2: 600), which documents the unusual participation of a lady—namely, Doña Leonor de Centelles, Marquesa de Crotone (see above, pp. xix–xx).[9] Given that Moner dedicated to the very Marquesa a treatise on "paciencia," we may justifiably assume that the author was well acquainted with the noblewoman.[10] Proof positive of the Marquesa's talent is the manner by which she advertises the exemplary valor of two warriors—her husband and her son—who chose to die in Constantinople rather than renege on their faith (González Cuenca, 2: 600, n. 2).

Another case that piques our curiosity is that of entry no. 467, in which young King Ferdinand is portrayed wearing a crest in the shape of an anvil. The epigraph reads as follows: "Sacó el Rey Nuestro Señor en otras justas un yunque por cimera" (In other tournaments our lord, the King, came out wearing a crest in the shape of an anvil) (*Cancionero genera,l* 2: 582).[11] González Cuenca informs us that Alonso de Palencia, in his *Crónica de Enrique IV*, describes said *cimera* and dates the *justas* in question to the spring of 1475. According to Palencia, there was a political intention behind Ferdinand's intervention in the tournament. The anvil signaled royal displeasure with the festivities, which the king considered disrespectful to the memory of the recently deceased Enrique IV. The ironic twist is not lost on the chronicler: the *yunque* (anvil) turns out to be a portent of the punitive measures the king intends to enact against the organizers of the offensive festivities that he himself does not hesitate to take part in.[12]

Yet another telltale sign of a possible connection with the *Cancionero general* consists of the terms "vestido de negro" (attired in black) contained in one of

---

[9] The entry consists of a device referring to the fire by which Mucius Scaevola, the warrior of Roman antiquity, tested his heroic mettle ("La marquesa de Cotrón traía bordados en el braço unos fuegos en forma como los de Cévola" (The Marquesa de Cotrón wore embroidered on her sleeve an image in the form of Scaevola's fire) [*Cancionero general* 2: 600]). (See no. 55 in Macpherson, *The* invenciones y letras *of the* Cancionero General, 73–74.) Perea Rodríguez dates the Marquesa's invención in the period after Moner's death: in the one or two years the noble woman spent in Italy prior to her own death (1502). Obviously, Moner could not have known the Marquesa's ingenious embroidery concerning Scaevola's deed (Perea Rodríguez, 105–6).

[10] In the *editio princeps*, the rubric corresponding to the treatise reads: "Moner. / A la marqueza de Cotro sobre Paciencia" (Moner: To the Marquise of Cotró, about *patience*) (fol. B5ᵛ). For the text of the treatise, accompanied by an English translation, see Cocozzella, *Fra Francesc Moner's Bilingual Poetics of Love and Reason*, 179–84. See, also, p. xix above.

[11] See no. 15 in Macpherson, *The* invenciones y letras *of the* Cancionero General, 52.

[12] For full bibliographical references to Palencia's account, see González Cuenca, 2: 282–83, n. 3.

the *invenciones* sported by the poet Luis de Torres (no. 509; *Cancionero general,* 2: 601).[13] Torres's apparel is just as lugubrious as that of the lovers paraded in Moner's *Momería*, a composition we are about to consider for close analysis.[14] On the basis of data adduced by Gonzalo Fernández de Oviedo, González Cuenca deduces that Luis de Torres, dressed in black, participated in the spectacle in Barcelona "por la tarde, antes de la cena, entre la Lonja y el mar" (in the evening, before supper, in the area between the Lonja and the sea), shortly before or after December 7, 1492, the date of the attempt against King Ferdinand's life (González Cuenca, 2: 601, n. 3).

What's in a Mummery?

It is apparent that Moner cherished his own notion of a superspectacle with *invención* and *letra*. There is abundant evidence about the circumstances fostering Moner's knowledgeability of the type of theater in vogue in his community. There are also signs of Moner's abiding interest in the theater. Such interest entails a substantial investment of artistic talent and bespeaks a know-how born of firsthand experience of the exigencies of the *mise en scène*.[15] A case in

---

[13] For a full description see no. 57 in Macpherson, *The* Invenciones y Letras *of the* Cancionero General, 75.

[14] For the color symbolism in the *cancioneros* see Lama de la Cruz. This scholar adduces various examples of black as symbol of death, mourning, sadness, and constancy in love (272–74).

[15] Highly pertinent to Moner's fashioning of his own contribution to the theatrical mode are some prominent issues that beg to be addressed. We may begin with two —namely, patronage and venue—that readily come to mind. We may take into consideration the prominent members of the nobility that, as Sirera points out, provided generous sponsorship and, with their palatial dwellings, suitable venue for a representation that required a gigantic staging. Sirera recognizes worthy patrons at the highest ranks of the aristocracy not only in Valencia (the likes of the Condes de Oliva, the Duques de Gandía, the Duques de Calabria) but also in Rome (the Borja papacy) and Naples (the Aragonese dynasty) ("Una quexa ante el Dios de Amor. . .del Comendador Escrivá como ejemplo posible de los autos de amores," 268). There is every reason to deduce that Moner in Barcelona, his hometown, would take full advantage of the resources inherent in an urban layout as splendid and in a cultural milieu just as vibrant as that of the cities accounted for by Sirera. Besides, not to be underestimated is the support that Moner received from his Maecenas, the Count, Joan Ramon III, with whom he maintained close ties for many years. As we know, Moner lived in the Cardona household during the most prolific years of his career (around 1485–1491). This is not to exclude the possibility or even probability of Moner's beneficial relationship with other prominent members of the Catalan upper crust: especially those he may have come into contact with during his residence as a page at the court of John II of Aragon.

point is one of Moner's shortest compositions that appears in both of the extant basic texts—the aforementioned *editio princeps* and the all-important Vatican manuscript.[16] In the manuscript the composition bears the title "Momaria," that is, "Momería" (literally Mummery). The epigraph, which functions as a veritable stage direction, affords a rare, if not unique glimpse into an actual staging and performance.[17] The staging consists of a huge structure (probably made of wood), shaped as a swan. Through an opening in the middle of its frame, the gigantic bird disgorges a group of six courtiers in somber attire, who immediately take to the floor and begin to dance to the slow rhythm of a sad melody. The melody matches their gloomy expression ("los gestos cubiertos de velos negros") (their faces covered with black veils). Each man carries a torch and wears a cap (described in their totality as "sombraretes franceses" [caps in the French style]), surmounted by a black feather, on which a motto of two or three verses, different in every case, is attached. Besides the customary epigrammatic stanzas of the six mottoes, the verbal component of the otherwise musical program includes three stanzas (*coblas*), each comprising twelve octosyllabic verses. The verses feature the following rhyme scheme: *a b c a b c / e f g e f g*. Apropos of the three stanzas, the stage direction clearly states they are carried, without indicating exactly how, in the beak of the swan ("Traýa el sisne en el pico las siguentes coblas" [the swan

---

As may be surmised, the issue of patronage goes hand in hand with that of a venue fit for royal and aristocratic entertainment. So, whenever we hypothesize on a suitable staging for *La noche*, we envisage a type of space that Ferrer Valls describes in the following terms:

> En el ámbito restringido de los palacios el espacio real transformado en espacio teatral es la sala o el patio, que entoldado e iluminado queda convertido en un gran salón palaciego, apto para acoger un elevado número de espectadores (311; Within the confines of a palace, the common space transformed into theatrical space consists of a hall or a courtyard. Outfitted with a tarpaulin and appropriate lighting, the courtyard becomes a palatial auditorium, sufficiently large to accommodate a high number of spectators).

Needless to say, Barcelona's most monumental edifices—the seats of civil and religious governments (the *Consell*, the *Principat*, the bishopric), not to mention the royal palace, the Cathedral, and the *Lonja*, the medieval equivalent of the stock exchange—provided, in conjunction with their surrounding areas, the halls, patios, cloisters, and plazas (the *Plaça del Rei*, for example), suited to be transformed into the "espacio teatral" envisaged by Ferrer Valls.

[16] For a complete description of these texts, see Cocozzella, *1 Introducción*, 65–88. For the Vatican manuscript, see, also, the article by Vicent Martines Peres (see the bibliography).

[17] For the inscription as it appears in the 1528 edition see p. 209 below; for the corresponding translation, see p. 211 below. For a complete description of this composition see Cocozzella, *1 Introducción*, 65–88, and Surtz, Estudio preliminar, 46–47. See, also, the discussion on pp. 110–11, 117, 120–21, 153, and 166 below.

carried in its beak the following stanzas]). Also, there are explicit indications that, in the course of the program, the three *coblas* will be read to the ladies in the audience ("dressadas a las damas y leýdas" [read in front of the ladies to whom they were addressed]). We can only guess whether this is a reference to the respective *amada* of the six lovers that have just come out of the swan's belly.

Beyond question is the kinship of Moner's *Momería* with the *entremés* and those other "entretenimientos" that, in Ferrer Valls's words, "tienen lugar en otros momentos de la fiesta, generalmente después del banquete, vinculándose a bailes y danzas" (take place at various intervals during the feast, generally after the banquet, and are accompanied by dances and formal balls) ("El espectáculo profano en la edad media: espacio escénico y escenografía," 311). That kinship has been well established in previous discussions on Moner's playlet (Cocozzella, *1 Introducción*, 93–99; Surtz, Estudio preliminar, 46–47).[18] To recap those discussions, we may quote the following concise statement by Surtz:

> La *Momería* de Moner se representaría en un salón de la corte de algún noble y serviría de marco para un baile con las damas a quienes iban dirigidas las coplas. Es buen ejemplo del modo en que los entretenimientos áulicos servían para dramatizar los ideales cortesanos de la época. Desde luego, todos los participantes son nobles disfrazados, pues la aristocracia era la única clase considerada capaz de experimentar sentimientos sublimes (Estudio preliminar, 47; Presumably Moner's *Momería* would be presented in a hall of a palace of some member of the nobility and might serve as a background for a dance with the ladies to whom the stanzas were addressed. It is a good example of the way upper-class entertainment was used to dramatize the courtly ideals of that epoch. Needless to say, all the participants

---

[18] It is appropriate to call attention here to the background provided in the study by Milà y Fontanals, who traces the evolution of the *entremés* during the fourteenth and fifteenth centuries in the Catalan domain (*Obras completes*, 232–56). Useful data may be found, also, in Olivar Bertrand (*Bodas reales entre Francia y la Corona de Aragón*, 29–64) and Alvarez Pellitero (Introducción general 44–49). Scholberg points to chaps. 3 and 5 of the *Crónica del halconero de Juan II* (by Pedro Carrillo de Huete) for some interesting details concerning the *entremés* and kindred forms of pastime in the Castilian court during the first half of the fifteenth century (Scholberg, *Spanish Life in the Late Middle Ages*, 116). In his history of secular drama of the fourteenth and fifteenth century in the Iberian Peninsula (in the domains of Castilian, Catalan, and Portuguese), Shergold presents an abundantly documented overview of the type of entertainment in vogue at the court and in the aristocratic circles during Moner's lifetime. Shergold describes various manifestations of spectacular events that are known by a variety of names, such as, besides the *entremés, misterio, invención, momería, empresa, representação* (*A History of the Spanish Stage from Medieval Times until the End of the Seventeenth Century*, 113–42).

are noblemen in disguise because the aristocracy was the only social class considered capable of experiencing sublime sentiments).[19]

Our attempt at a fair assessment of Moner's contribution is facilitated by using as a backdrop N. D. Shergold's well-documented account of the Spanish secular drama of the fourteenth and fifteenth centuries (*A History of the Spanish Stage from Medieval Times until the End of the Seventeenth Century*, 113–42). In light of Shergold's overview, it is clear that Moner's *Momería* is a far cry from the dazzling pageantry of the aforementioned royal celebrations held at the Aljafería in Zaragoza in 1399 and in 1414.[20] Much closer to the theatricality illustrated by Moner's piece are two shows put on in 1461 in Jaén in the household of Miguel Lucas de Iranzo, the *condestable* of Castile. In one, to quote directly from Shergold's account,

> the dancers, who were members of the Condestable's household, appeared in the hall or ballroom in the guise of strangers, with vizards, and elegantly dressed in cloth of light green (Shergold, 124).

In the other, we witness a truly startling act involving a dragon and a group of young pages:

> the head of the serpent, said to have been very big and made of painted wood, was thrust into the hall from an antechamber, and by some sort of mechanism it propelled the pages one by one from its mouth, shooting out great tongues of flame (Shergold, 125).

---

[19] Eugenio Asensio observes that the *momo* era a un tiempo una enmascarada y el enmascarado que en ella iba. Los enmascarados eran la flor de la corte, desde el rey hasta el paje, y desplegaban un lujo asiático en vestidos y joyas. La tramoya y montaje requería artistas inventivos, casi ingenieros teatrales. . .. Los momos tomaban sus argumentos ordinariamente del mundo caballeresco. . .. De la maravillosa abertura imaginativa del comienzo saltaban con desenfado a la crónica mundana, a los galanteos de damas y galanes allí presentes. Parecía que la raza de los caballeros andantes y de los grandes enamorados encarnaba en los asistentes al serão. (Quoted in Rico, *Textos y contextos*, 227, n. 66; A *momo* is a masquerade and the masked person that took part in it. The masked persons were the cream of the courtly society from the king to the page. They showed off extreme luxury in clothes and jewelry. The machinery and stagecraft required artists of great skill, who had to be practically theatrical engineers. . .. The *momos* took their plots from the world of chivalry. . .. From the spellbinding overture at the opening of the spectacle, they would switch, nonchalantly, right into the chronicle of current events or into the flowery flattery of the ladies and gallants gathered for the occasion. It would appear that the entire breed of knights-errant and great lovers was embodied in the participants at the soiree).

[20] Shergold goes into a detailed description of these festivities. See pp. 115–22.

We detect a noteworthy coincidence in two details: 1) the "sombraretes franceses y penas negras" worn by the dancers presented by Moner ("sallíen los momos con un contrapás nuevo") are remarkably similar to the "sombreros de Bretaña, [y] en ellos penas negras," sported by the men that took part in Iranzo's *ballo in maschera*; 2) the gigantic swan that, through an opening in the middle of its frame ("abierto el sisne por el medio"), dislodges a group of six courtiers invites comparison with the huge serpent that, as the quote shows, spits out a number of young men.[21]

What we learn from a comparison with pertinent dramatic and paradramatic performances diligently reviewed by Shergold is that Moner fashions a genuine show of *momos*. Specifically, he comes up with the type of song-and-dance routine that Shergold classifies as one of the four variants of the same genre.[22] Shergold complements his generic definition with the following observation:

> From the literary point of view, the importance of these festivities is that they establish certain themes as characteristic of court drama, in particular those taken for the literature of chivalry (*A History of the Spanish Stage*, 141).

Precisely this "literature of chivalry" and, to quote Shergold again, the "fondness for a world of romance" (141) inspired the curious attire (especially the headgear) of those personages that took part in the splendid tournaments so fashionable in Moner's lifetime.

The cultural context for Moner's *Momería* brings to mind "la fastuosa representación" (the dazzling spectacle) and "los ingeniosos montajes" (the ingenious stagecraft) that, as I pointed out on another occasion, "debían de caracterizar los numerosos espectáculos, profanos y religiosos, tanto públicos como particulares, que se sucedieron a lo largo del siglo XV" (must have characterized the numerous spectacles, secular and religious, both public and private, performed in succeeding periods throughout the fifteenth century) (*1 Introducción*, 95). In short, these are the "decorative and theatrical aspects" underscored by Macpherson in his essay on the festivities in vogue at the court of Ferdinand and Isabella. While referring to the "[b]anquets, dances, poetry readings, *invenciones*, and *entremeses* [that] filled the evenings," Macpherson marvels at the "[e]xtravagant blazons and emblems [that] adorned the pavilions, the standards, banners, clothing and armor of the knights, the tabards of the heralds and the trappings of the horses"

---

[21] The similarity is not lost on Francisco Rico, who comments on both Moner's text and the one excerpted from the chronicle pertaining to Iranzo's *fiestas*. (Rico, *Texto y contextos*, 216, 226–27.

[22] For his classification Shergold abides by the following criteria:
'Momos were of four kinds: those that play dice; those that dance; those that bring gifts, perhaps with some association with the Christmas play; and those that introduce a tournament. (141)

("The Game of Courtly Love," 101). Macpherson calls attention to the close equivalents to the Catalan *castells* and *roques*:

> Scaffolding (*cadalsos*) was brought in at great expense to construct mock castles and towers richly decorated with drapes and cloth of gold; they provided a secure vantage point from which the ladies of the court could better see and be seen (101).

Evidently, even when intended for the spectators (the ladies) rather than the performers (knights and courtiers), the *cadalsos* in the courtly circles of Castile were no less conspicuously theatrical than were the contemporaneous *castells* and *roques* in Barcelona, Valencia, and Zaragoza.[23]

The Mainstream and Other Traditions

Demonstrably, the type of dramatic representation that Sirera discerns in the *cancionero* pieces he analyzes shares with Moner's *Momería* characteristics radically different from the ones long recognized in the Spanish theater of the early Renaissance. Juan del Encina (1468—late 1529 or early 1530), whom Henry W. Sullivan hails as "one of Renaissance Spain's most talented and representative sons" (Sullivan, *Juan del Encina,* 19), enjoys the well-deserved acclaim as not only chief exponent but also veritable "father" of that theater.[24] Without disparaging in any way the recognition due to Encina's first-rate contribution as a dramatist, it is fair to acknowledge the existence of what Surtz calls "a rival fifteenth-century dramatic tradition" (Surtz, *The Birth of a Theater,* 20).[25] Pointing to signs of the development of other types of theater besides the one so worthily championed by Encina, Surtz observes:

---

[23] As I have indicated, I will defer to a study of the allegorical castle any further discussion of a staging of such a large scale as the one described by Macpherson, Ferrer Valls, and others.

[24] See Sullivan for a comprehensive account of this playwright's life and works.

[25] Pertinent to this issue is Stern's observation:

The picture emerges. . .of a court theater in Castile in the early sixteenth century that was far more extensive than the extant record suggests. In fact, one is left with the distinct impression that theatrical activity was booming and that Encina was hardly alone in writing for the stage. Yet significant numbers of these early plays may be irretrievably lost. Moreover, information on socioeconomic conditions of the early court theater and the nature of the performances hardly compares with the wealth of material for the seventeenth-century drama. (*The Medieval Theater in Castile,* 18)

The convention of seeing Juan del Encina as the "father" of Castilian drama is useful because it is his plays that establish a school whose influence can still be felt at the end of the sixteenth century. But we must not forget that we can find in the fifteenth century evidence for other theaters that might have given rise to a dramatic tradition independent of that initiated by Encina or that might have influenced Encina and his school (*The Birth of a Theater,* 19).[26]

After witnessing Moner's *Momería*, it is not farfetched to surmise that in Moner's production we may well find the "fifteenth century evidence for other theaters" that Surtz refers to. There is a tenable hypothesis to be advanced regarding the sharp differentiation between, on the one hand, the theater of the mainstream, headed by Encina, and, on the other, the inconspicuous but no less significant counterpart in the undercurrent represented by the likes of Moner, the poets adduced by Sirera, and other authors that remain to be discovered. I propose, then, a hypothesis, which may be formulated as follows: the distinction between the type of theater "fathered" by Encina and the kind conceived by Moner and a number of *cancionero* poets resides in two counterposed dynamics. The straightforward thrust of the dialogue in the former contrasts with the meandering flow of the monologue in the latter.

We may envisage in *Momería* an embryonic phase of the dramatic monologue. As I have attempted to show elsewhere, that same monologue, with its ebb and flow, protean nature, and overall elasticity of form, comes into operation in full swing in the theatricality of the so-called "auto de amores" (a play about love), documented in two of Moner's compositions: namely, *La noche* and *Bendir de dones* (Cocozzella: "Ausiàs March's Text of Subjectivity and Francesc Moner's

---

[26] Surtz's viewpoint is, doubtless, relevant to a study of the early Spanish religious theater. He points out three plays, which constitute signal exemplars of Franciscan spirituality. As Surtz demonstrates, these pieces exemplify a theatrical strain distinct from the one championed by Encina and fellow members of the "Salamanca school." Focusing on the signs of that distinction with specific reference to the dramatics of a Nativity play, he observes:

> Encina controls meaning by incorporating into the text of the play the proper interpretation of the event it treats. The Franciscan plays, on the other hand, suggest an interpretation through the juxtaposition of themes and motifs, leaving it to the spectator to participate in the performance by deriving that interpretation for himself. ("The 'Franciscan Connection' in the Early Castilian Theater," 149)

Fully consequential is the following deduction, which, needless to say, corroborates the statement just quoted above, in the body of this monograph:

> It is. . .clear that theater in late medieval Castile is not represented by a single dramatic tradition but rather by a constellation of possibilities for theater that coexisted with one another. ("The 'Franciscan Connection' in the Early Castilian Theater," 149)

Auto de Amores of the Early Spanish Renaissance;" "Fray Francisco Moner's *Auto de Amores*: Toward a Reassessment of Spanish Para-Mystical Literature of the Fifteenth Century;" "Fra Francesc Moner y el auto de amores en el dominio del catalán y del castellano a finales del siglo XV;" "The Theatrics of the *Auto de amores* in the *Tragicomedia* called *Celestina*," 74–75). We will soon have occasion to explore how the nature of the *auto*—especially as manifested in the compendium, the subjectivistic focus, and the overall dramatic intention—becomes adapted to the special theatrics of *Sepultura d'amor*.

The two types of theater, represented, respectively, by Encina and Moner, share an unquestionable legacy from the *cancioneros*. One eloquent aspect of that legacy consists in the dramatization of "so que veritatz autreia" (see pp. 41–43 above) through the presentation of the prototypical *mártir de amor* (martyr of love). We may compare Moner's presentation of the *mártir* with the one embodied in the shepherd Fileno, the protagonist of Juan del Encina's *Egloga II (Egloga en la qual se introduzen tres pastores: Fileno, Zambardo y Cardonio)*.[27] What makes the comparison appealing is apparent in the following excerpt from Sullivan's commentary:

> Thematically speaking, Fileno's literary suicide brings to its logical climax that phenomenon in Encina characterized by van Beysterveldt as the flight from love—the stricken swain is actually driven by the conventionalized "death of love" to a natural death at his own hand. The pat rhetoric of courtly love abounds throughout the work: even the opening prose rubric describes Fileno as a "prisoner of love." The lovelorn shepherd himself talks of Cupid's "first law of silence"—a fifteenth-century cliché—and displays symptoms of jaundiced anemia, lethargy, melancholy, and of "being beside himself." The rhetoric has thus been hypostasized into a theater of real suffering (*Juan del Encina*, 90).

One may argue that the theory of "the flight from love," espoused by van Beysterveldt apropos of Fileno's disastrous case, would not be applicable to Moner's portrayal of the lover. Rather than envision, let alone advocate, a radical departure from the code of courtly love, Moner, following in Ausiàs March's footsteps, endeavors to integrate the ideals and principles of courtly love into the religious model par excellence: the model of the *imitatio Christi*.[28] Despite the undeniable contrast, some underlying parallelism remains. It resides in Moner's and Encina's similar engagement in the very process that Sullivan, in the passage quoted above, describes in terms of the de-conventionalization of the "death of

---

[27] See Encina, 249–95. The piece is known, also, as Égloga de los tres pastores. For a concise analysis, see Sullivan, *Juan del Encina*, 87–90.

[28] For the religious paradigm implicit in Ausiàs March's treatment of courtly love, see: Cocozzella, "Ausiàs March's *Imitatio Christi*: The Metaphysics of the Lover's Passion," and "Ausiàs March's Sainted Eros: A Model of Christian Syncretism."

love." In both writers this *Liebestod* stresses the exemplarity of a life, which Sulli-
van, paraphrasing Fileno's epitaph, highlights as "a life dedicated to the service of
woman that was rewarded by disdain, pain, tears, and finally harsh death" (88).[29]
In both *Sepultura* and the aforementioned *Egloga II*, the leitmotif brings out the
naturalness—that is, the impression of an actual experience of suicide—pain-
fully obvious in Fileno's demise and not so obviously displayed, though persis-
tently alluded to, in Moner's obsessive *memento mori*.[30] We may conclude, then,
that Moner employs no less effectively than does Encina those deictic, theatrical
strategies that culminate in what Sullivan calls "a theater of real suffering" (90).

Voilà the sense of the real, the immanence so wondrously captured by Moner
and Encina and infused by the two authors with a stirring stage presence. And
we are reminded of the haunting obiter dictum, the extraordinary understate-
ment, wryly proffered by that proverbial bullfighter, whose nebulous voice reso-
nates in some nook and cranny of our minds: "¡Aquí se muere de verdad!" (Here
we die for real!).

Foreshadowing the Theatrics of Parody and Intertextuality

Hutcheon's theory takes into full account the process by which sacred ritual
incorporates and assimilates secular and even pagan components. There are two
observations that need to be advanced in light of Hutcheon's rough-and-ready
definition of parody (see p. 75 above). First, the notion of a parody devoid of
comic slant is not a contradiction in terms. Second, the field of modern art such
as envisioned in Hutcheon's study, may be broadened to include works such as

---

[29] In Encina's Égloga XII the epitaph reads as follows:

O, tú que passas por la sepultura
del triste Fileno espera si quieres
y leyendo verás quien sirve a mugeres
cuál es el fin que a su vida procura.
Verás como un premio de fiel servidor,
Amor y Zefira, por mi mala suerte,
me dieron trabajos, desdeños, dolor,
lloros, sospiros y, al fin, cruda muerte.

(Encina, 295; O wayfarer, as you walk by the tomb of wretched Fileno,
pause, if you please, and, as you read, behold the end that a man devoted to the ser-
vice of women prepares for his own life. Lo and behold: in reward for my faithful
service both Love and Zefira granted me, to my dire misfortune, travails, disdain,
grief, tears, sighs, and, in the end, violent death.)

[30] For the sake of brevity we cannot adduce here some poignant instances, especially
in *La noche*, of a tormented meditation of the authorial persona on the option of suicide.

Moner's *misa*, to which, as will become clear upon close investigation, Hutcheon's theory is well suited.

One would find of interest the two items—namely, "the modalities of self-reflexivity" and "intertextuality (or transtextuality)" (*A Theory of Parody*, 20) —that Hutcheon considers prominent in modern art (20). One specific example, among the many Hutcheon provides, may well strike us as particularly relevant. It is a musical composition by Peter Maxwell Davies, entitled *Missa super L'Homme Armé*, a tour de force featuring an intricate interaction of heterogeneous ingredients, ranging from the incomplete text of an anonymous fifteenth-century Mass to references to Joyce's *Ulysses* (*A Theory of Parody*, 15). Davies's parody betokens, in the final analysis, a refurbishing operation that reveals, in Hutcheon's words, "unorthodox relationships between foregrounded and backgrounded material" (15). Despite all the appearances of anachronism, Davies's *Missa* and Moner's counterpart bear comparing precisely in terms of the "self-reflexivity" and "intertextuality," indicative of the expansive inclusiveness that Hutcheon detects in the complex phenomenology of parody. After reminding us that parody does not balk at the boundaries of genre and medium, Hutcheon has good reason to muse: "Literature is famous for parodying non-literary discourse" (*A Theory of Parody*, 18).

It is instructive, then, to juxtapose Davies's and Moner's parody of the Mass given the many centuries that separate the two. Even a quick comparison between the two compositions makes quite evident the principles of intertextuality they both share: the flexibility and amplification inherent in the workings of the parody as defined, analyzed, and illustrated by Hutcheon. Flexibility and amplification bespeak the elasticity of a plot viable for representation on stage.

How does Moner fashion such a plot? At the outset of our inquiry, we are confronted by the determinants of what I propose to call the "intrinsic theatricality" of Moner's text. For an insight into this intrinsic dimension, we may rely on Cátedra's exploration of the theatrical potential inherent in some liturgical and paraliturgical texts, intended for devotional consumption in Spanish religious and lay communities during the fifteenth century. Cátedra's book, *Liturgia, poesía y teatro en la edad media*, deserves special attention because it provides an illuminating background for the pivotal issues highlighted in the conception, gestation, and composition of Moner's *misa*. Cátedra focuses on two fifteenth-century texts. One, identified as "Estorias responsorias," constitutes a collection of laudatory hymns and kindred chants used in the various processionals that marked the festivities held in honor of Saint Thomas Aquinas.[31] The second is a

---

[31] The "Estorias" (a series of antiphonal versified sections both in Latin and in the corresponding translation into Spanish) take up ff. 101ʳ–173ʳ of a manuscript housed in the Convento de Santo Domingo el Real (Madrid). No specific rubric is adduced to identify this codex. For the "Estorias," Cátedra provides a general outline, a full description, complete with commentary and an edition: see *Liturgia*, 137, 137–67, 529–68.

miscellaneous collection of Castilian poems, which, according to Cátedra, were
set to music and were meant as integral components of processionals (*Liturgia*,
171–72). Throughout his study, Cátedra refers to the collection as *Cancionero
musical de Astudillo*.[32] He points out that all the pieces comprised in the *Can-
cionero* are related to the festivities scheduled during the week, usually referred to
as "mirabilis," that is, December 24–31 (176).[33]

It would be hardly feasible to expect to recapture in rapid review the breadth
and depth of Cátedra's heuristic enterprise. For the time being, we shall concen-
trate on those points that in Cátedra's discussion unveil for us the notion of a
Zeitgeist or, to put it in Ortegian terms, the *circunstancia* of the late Middle Ages.
In the domains of Castilian and Catalan, Cátedra allows us to detect the surge of
new sensibilities in religious piety. These, in turn, translate into innovative devo-
tional practices in a spirit of a revival. In the final analysis, Cátedra demonstrates
that, at the heart of this complex phenomenology of *vivencia* and *circunstancia*,
reside the symptoms of a dynamic interaction in the liturgy between the Latin
text, which enjoys a long-standing tradition, and a fresh, new, vernacular coun-
terpart of that text.[34]

In addressing the interaction in question, Cátedra delves, often in micro-
scopic detail, into multifarious issues that it is impossible to take into full account
here and now. For the purpose of our discussion, suffice it to highlight the essen-
tial points in his overall exploration. Regarding the broad dialectic between the

---

[32] The *cancionero* in question occupies ff. 1–8 of a manuscript in the archive of the
Real Monasterio de Santa Clara in the town of Astudillo, situated in the vicinities of
Palencia, north-east of Valladolid. This manuscript is not identified with a specific rubric
either. For a groundbreaking analysis of each of the poems included in the *Cancionero
musical de Astudillo*, see Cátedra, *Liturgia*, 245–351.

[33] Cátedra goes into a specific description of the content and the liturgical place-
ment ("enclave o cronología litúrgicos") (liturgical enclave or technology) of the Astudi-
llo collection (*Liturgia*, 245–46). Following is one of Cátedra's explanations of the litur-
gical function of said collection:

Como el oficio de santo Tomás [see "Estorias" above], como algunos manuscritos
que nos han preservado textos en lengua vulgar para los que se ha propuesto un
uso litúrgico, como las *carols* inglesas, consideradas por algunos como verdaderos
himnos procesionales, como los textos y músicas del mismo tenor incluidos en los
laudarios italianos, los poemas de Astudillo habrían de integrarse en un códice
que reuniera los textos y la música de las ceremonias acostumbradas (*Liturgia*, 177;
Like many other documents — for example: the office of Saint Thomas, the manu-
scripts that preserve texts in the vernacular (texts for which a liturgical use has been
proposed), the English carols, which some consider authentic processional hymns,
and the texts and music included in the collections of the Italian *laude*, kindred to
the carols — the Astudillo poems constituted, in all probability, an integral com-
ponent of a manuscript that contained the lyrics and music in vogue at that time).

[34] For a comprehensive definition of Ortega's terminology, see p. 30 n. 1 above.

vernacular and the liturgical or paraliturgical Latin, the Spanish philologist speaks in terms of displacement and adaptation ("verdadero acto de desplazamiento y adaptación" [veritable act of displacementand adaptation] [*Liturgia,* 161]) as in the case of the bilingual "Estorias responsorias" already referred to. Cátedra employs the analogous terminology of substitution and complementarity in order to designate in the *Cancionero de Astudillo* mechanisms analogous to those of the *Estorias*. It is highly instructive to ponder the manner in which he acknowledges the remarkable "mezcla de elementos oficiales y no oficiales de la liturgia" (admixture of official and non-official elements of the liturgy). In the *Estorias*, the shift from Latin to the vernacular ("verdadero desplazamiento hermenéutico" [a veritable hermeneutic displacement]) parallels "la asociación de textos y música tan distantes" (the association of texts and music so different from one another), documented in the Astudillo manuscript.[35]

The pertinence of Cátedra's commentaries vis-à-vis Moner's *misa* will become apparent if we bear in mind two pivotal issues. The first has to do with the phenomenon of substitution or complementarity just referred to. Cátedra, who is well aware of the complementarity of the vernacular with respect to Latin, probes into the circumstances in which the former, the language, after all, of the masses ("todos los creyentes" [all believers] [130]), gains entrance into the precincts of the latter.[36] In light of the bearings Cátedra sets for his own analysis, it is clear that in the case of Moner's *misa* the process of substitution or complementarity goes all the way. In his *misa*, the vernacular completely supplants Latin.

The phenomenology so thoroughly investigated by Cátedra comes into full swing in Moner. But that is not the entire picture. There is another predominant issue that begs attention. To identify it, Cátedra goes so far as to coin a colorful neologism: *performativo* as in "el sentido y las estructura 'performativas' [sic]" (the *performative* sense and structure) and "la *ordinatio* 'performativa' del texto por la mano del copista y del rubricador" (the performative *ordinatio* of the text at the hand of the scribe or the author of the rubrics) (*Liturgia,* 159). Cátedra never ceases to remind us that the mechanisms of substitution and complementarity he

---

[35] The parallelism becomes evident by a simple juxtaposition of the *cancionero* proper (fols. 1–8) and the Latin processionals (fols. 9–49). Both texts appear in the same codex. The details of Cátedra's exposition may be followed on pp. 176–77. We have already accounted for the text of the *cancionero* proper. For a full description of the Latin processional and an explanation of how it was carried out, see Cátedra, *Liturgia,* 176–96.

[36] Besides the Mass, such dramatized episodes as *Planctus Mariae, Visitatio sepulchri, Quem quaeritis, pastores,* among other kindred items—tropes, antiphons, *epístolas farcidas,* and the like—attest, according to Cátedra, to "las diferentes fiestas, en las que la lengua vulgar fue utilizada en forma complementaria, si se quiere como un elemento de apoyo festivo de la liturgia latina" (the various feasts in which the vernacular was employed, on occasion, as a festive ingredient in support of the Latin liturgy) (*Liturgia, poesía y teatro en la edad media,* 130).

unveils at every turn lend themselves to be seen as functions of a performance. In short, he recognizes a theatricalization or enactment of one kind or another. True to form, he does not fail to proffer concrete examples for his theory on *estructura performativa*. To that end, he calls attention to the example of components of miscellaneous vernacular texts that become integrated into communal ceremonies of the Christmas and Easter cycles (*Liturgia*, 176).[37]

Cátedra's dissection of that "estructura performativa" is very helpful in profiling the nature of Moner's own dramaturgy. Specifically, in Moner's *misa* those traits come to light in the very context in which Cátedra envisions the transition "de la poesía de uso litúrgico al teatro litúrgico" (from the poetry used in the liturgy to liturgical theater) (25). In addition, he comments on the momentous "despegue de un teatro específicamente religioso" (the launching of a specifically religious theater) (25). The purview of Cátedra's critique is epitomized by a pivotal statement, in which this scholar brings together the various techniques evidenced in the *teatro litúrgico* he refers to. In that statement, Cátedra mentions such compositional strategies as *interpolación* (interpolation), *yuxtaposición* (juxtaposition), *solapamiento* (concealment), *engarces* (stringing together), and *enclaves* (homogenous clusters) (25–26).

---

[37] Apropos of the Astudillo anthology, Cátedra explains:

Habrá que admitir también que nuestro cancionerillo ha sido elaborado para ser utilizado en el ámbito de costumbres litúrgicas que, no por extravagantes, dejan de estar documentadas en otros lugares. Costumbres litúrgicas que, como las de la Navidad o las de Semana Santa, se entremezclan con celebraciones piadosas de más amplia participación y en las que, entre otras cosas, se incorpora la lengua vulgar y la organización *teatral*, cualquiera que sea su rango, su nivel, su complicación y su formalización verdaderamente dramática (*Liturgia*, 176; It is fair to say that our *cancionero* [Astudillo] has been compiled to be utilized in the realm of liturgical practices that, despite their extravagance, are documented in various other places. Like their counterparts in the Christmas and Easter season, these liturgical practices become assimilated into religious celebrations of massive proportions. Among the various aspects of these celebrations is the interfacing of the vernacular with a theatrical arrangement, no matter what quality, level, complexity, and genuinely dramatic form this arrangement may assume).

VIII.
Embryonic and Full-Fledged Theatricality

Moner's *Momería*: The Complexity of the Monologue

At play in Moner's *Momería* are the main phases in a trajectory that Jean-Claude Aubailly discovers in the gestation of the "monologue dramatique" (dramatic monologue) in French literature of the late Middle Ages. Aubailly's analysis brings to light two aspects for which we may perceive an equivalency in Moner's construction of a stage-worthy representation: first, the fashioning of a text charged with what Crabbé Rocha considers "potentialité dramatique" (dramatic potential) (see p. 90 above); and second, the sense of challenge that the text conveys to the prospective performer. In fundamental agreement with Crabbé Rocha, Aubailly addresses the two aspects concurrently. He alludes to the touch-stone or criteria a critic may employ in assessing the *vis dramatica* inherent in a literary composition:

> En fait, il semble que les critères les plus sérieux soient des critères internes reposant sur le texte lui-même. En effet le théâtre doit donner l'illusion de la vie ; ce sont des personnages doués d'une existence vraisemblable ayant une présence tangible qu'il doit présenter au public (*Le monologue, le dialogue et la sottie*, 6; In fact, it turns out that the most convincing criteria are the internal ones residing in the text itself. Indeed, theater should provide the illusion of life itself. What theater must present to the spectators is a group of personages endowed with a verisimilar existence, that is, a tangible presence.)

Before discussing the dramaturgy of the monologue, Aubailly affords us a glimpse of the process by which the reciter of a narrative becomes a veritable actor. The process is evinced by contrasting two specimens of "l'histoire lue" (read narrative) —namely, the *Sermon des repeuz franches* (The Sermon of Free Meals) and the *Discours du trépas de Vert Janet* (Speech of the Hanging of Green Janet)—both dated at the beginning of the sixteenth century.[1] Aubailly underscores the much more powerful impression that the latter composition produces. This is especially true by virtue of shortening or eliminating altogether the psychic distance between the reader, in the role of reciter, and the character, whom the reader/reciter strives to impersonate (*Le monologue, le dialogue et la sottie*, 14–15).[2]

---

[1] The two works are entered in the bibliography below under the heading of "Anonymous." For a discussion of this type of narrative, see Aubailly, *Le monologue, le dialogue et la sottie*, 9–15. For the dating of the two compositions, see p. 492, n. 3. Jelle Koopmans and Paul Verhuyck, recent editors of the *Sermon des repeuz franches*, date it around 1480, some seventeen years after Villon's death (1463). Obviously, they dispute Villon's authorship of the piece: "l'auteur est anonyme; parisien d'origine ou d'adoption, il appartient à la mouvance de Villon" (the author is anonymous; he is Parisian by birth or by adoption; he belongs to Villon's entourage) (quoted in Vielliard, 709). As for the second example of "histoire lue" adduced by Aubailly, Brunet mentions the undated edition of the *Discurs* by the printer, Loys Coste (*Manuel du libraire et de l'amateur de livres* ,749–50). We find the following entry in Viollet-Leduc and Méray's *Bibliographie*:

> Le discurs du trépas de Vert-Janet est un mauvais titre. C'est le discours que tient Vert-Janet en allant au trépas, c'est-à-dire à la potence. Vert-Janet est un voleur; ses regrets mêlés de ris et de pleure, ses recommandations au bourreau Patéchaud, sont d'un burlesque à la fois comique et touchant (137; *The Speech of the Hanging of Vert-Janet* is not an appropriate title. It is the speech that Vert-Janet delivers on the way to his *passing*, that is, to the gallows. Vert-Janet is a thief. His expressions of repentance, a mixture of laughter and crying, together with her admonitions to the executioner, Patéchaud, are a farce, comical and pathetic all in one").

Of interest is, also, the following description we find in the *Catalogue raisonné de la Bibliothèque Elzévirienne*:

> Piece rouennaise postérieure à 1544, et qui peut être un monologue dramatique recite à quelque fête des Conards, sur la pendaison d'un voleur (18; A work about the hanging of a thief, written in Rouen later than 1544; it may be considered a dramatic monologue, recited during one of the feasts of the Conards).

For a history of the Confraternity of the Conards, see Carré de Busserolle.

[2] To appreciate Moner's crowning achievement, it is useful to bear in mind Aubailly's notion of "les limites de la mémoire scénique." This notion encompasses the space of the authentic monologue, the definition of which may be inferred from yet another of Aubailly's statements:

> On peut considérer qu'il y a monologue dramatique à partir du moment où l'identification de l'acteur à un personnage qu'il met en scène n'est plus un simple artifice de présentation, mais l'objet même du comique. Des lors cette identification ne se traduit plus par une simple imitation de ton et d'attitude, mais par une véritable re-création psychologique d'un type donné (*Le monologue, le dialogue et la sottie*, 108; Let us bear in mind that the dramatic monologue happens the moment the identification of an actor with the character he impersonates on stage is not simply a representational technique but, rather, the very crux of the comedy. From that moment on, the identification in question is carried out not simply as an imitation of voice and gesture but, rather, as a genuine re-creation of a particular stereotype.)

It is clear that the ideal manifestation of a literary mode that an author of a composition like Moner's *Momería* has in mind is what Aubailly calls "monologue-état d'âme" (monologue of a state of mind) a subgenre of "le monologue d'amoureux" (a lover's monologue).[3] Aubailly makes it quite evident that the markedly introspective "monologue-état d'âme" is not very common among the vast body of poetry that falls under his scrutiny. In fact, Aubailly adduces no more than three specimens—namely: *Monologue d'une dame fort amoureuse d'un sien amy* (Monologue of a lady very much in love with one of her suitors),[4] *Femme mocqueresse mocquée* (A woman who mocks and is mocked in return),[5] and *Fille esgarée* (A young woman gone astray). To be specific, Aubailly explains that only *Fille esgarée* exemplifies, in the critic's words, "un véritable débat dramatique que cherche à traduire les cheminements qui conduisent une âme de la douleur à la paix" (a thoroughly dramatic debate designed to display the paths that lead the human spirit from sorrow to peace) (192).[6] We may well deduce, then, that the introspection involved in a genuine "monologue-état d'âme" commands not so much intense audience participation as, rather, an engrossing phenomenology of a radical assimilation and identification. Such phenomenology includes the actor's assimilation of the role performed and identification with the personage portrayed.

The excursion into the field of Aubailly's analysis helps us identify and contextualize Moner's noteworthy contribution to theatrical literature. There are, needless to say, differences to be reckoned with. For instance, in contrast to the only three pieces that, as we have seen, Aubailly can adduce as exemplars of the "monologue-état d'âme," there are numerous counterpart specimens to be found in the *cancionero* poems and kindred compositions. Even a select account of these specimens lies beyond the scope of the present study. Suffice it to recall here the three monologues—Garci Sánchez's "Sueño," Escrivá's *Querella*, Corella's *Tragèdia*—we are about to consider for the special interest they hold in relation to Moner's production (see, below, pp. 122–27).

Even in our rapid review, we cannot fail to acknowledge that, outside the vast realm of the *cancionero* repertoire, there is a handful of monologues couched in the form of a ballad. The *romances* (to use the Spanish term for "ballads") are

---

[3] For an extensive list of poems that fit within this category, see Aubailly, *Le monologue, le dialogue et la sottie*, 161. A full discussion follows on 162–94.

[4] The author of this piece is Roger de Collerye, nicknamed "Roger Bontemps" (1468–1536). For the Collerye's biography see Héricault. The reference to the text of Collerey's *Monologue* is found in the bibliography below.

[5] A poem by Guillaume Alexis (born around 1425; died probably in 1486 during a pilgrimage to Jerusalem: see Piaget and Picot, vi, xiv). For the text of this composition see "Guillaume Alexis" in the bibliography.

[6] The essential information concerning this text is found under "Anonymous" in the bibliography.

accessible to the reader of our day through the collections appropriately called *romanceros*, no less numerous and widespread than are the *cancioneros*.[7] To be sure, the ballad, by its very constitution belonging to the narrative oral tradition, does not lend itself to a protagonist's protracted musings on his or her own tormented psyche. There are, however, three fascinating *romances* that readily come to mind precisely because of those very somber and pathetic musings. These exceptional poems may be identified, respectively, by the titles "El prisionero" (The Prisoner), "Moraima," and "El enamorado y la Muerte" (The Lover and Death).[8] Moner may well have been familiar with the haunting lyrics, in which the prisoner bemoans the sorrows of his loneliness, relieved only by the song of the nightingale; the young Moorish woman (Moraima) hints at her erotic encounter with a "cristiano," who leaves her duped, embarrassed, and disgraced; a young man ("el enamorado"), who dreams of a blissful embrace with his lady-love and ends up being unceremoniously abducted by none other than the Grim Reaper, "la Muerte" of the title. Due consideration must be given to these rare romances in reference to the theatricality of such works as Moner's *Sepultura* and *Momería*. Indeed, the deep pathos that permeates them harmonizes so well with the "sentido" blended into the "letras matizadas" we have already commented upon (see pp. xxii–xxiii above).

Taking into account not only the analogies with the French "monologue d'amoureux-état d'âme" but also the affinities evident in the prevailing mournful strains of the *cancioneros* and the reflective mood of a few exceptional *romances*, we are ready to examine Moner's dramatic monologue in its primary phase. For a start, we may ponder an astute observation proffered by Émile Picot: "le monologue dramatique met en scène la personne même qui le récite" (a dramatic monologue represents on stage the very person that recites the monologue) (*Le monologue dramatique dans l'ancien théâtre français*, 3). In most cases Moner, distinguished *cancionero* author that he is, unburdens the full charge of his poetic expression, laden with lovesickness, onto the lover represented in the guise of the auctorial persona. Thus the referent of the "personne" mentioned by Picot is none other than Moner's artistic alter ego.

The case of *Momería* is, however, unusual. Here Moner devises not an individual but a collective persona. Besides its multifarious symbolism, Moner's "swan" attains the status of an allegorical figure. Such a birdlike structure may

---

[7] Useful and manageable is the vast *Romancero general* compiled by Durán (see bibliography below). Worthy of mention is, also, Wright's collection (*Spanish Ballads*), which showcases the Spanish text with facing English translation (see bibliography below). For a survey of the copious vein of early Spanish balladry, see Deyermond, *The Middle Ages*, 124–29; Alborg, *Edad Media y Renacimiento*, 1: 219–43; and Foster, *The Early Spanish Ballad*. For its comprehensive scope, thorough analysis, and readability, Menéndez Pidal's *Romancero hispánico* remains the indispensable classic study on the subject.

[8] For the corresponding texts, see the bibliography.

be regarded as a comprehensive embodiment of the six men who come out of its innards. The allegorical figuration is manifest in the swan's self-appointed role as guardian and leader in the metaphorical journey of the six lovers. While virtually appropriating the grief of these dispirited personages, the big bird so states: "Sentí'l dolor de su lloro / y quise serles abrigo, / endressa de su camino" (*1 OC*, 155) (see translation on p. 211 below). Not surprisingly, in a crucial first-person statement, the complaints (*querellas*) of the gallants are equated with the wailings of the proverbial swan: "Sus querellas son los gritos / que yo doy quando la muerte / me requiere como a ellos" (*1 OC*, 156) (see translation on p. 211 below). In light of this declaration, there can hardly be any doubt as to the destination of the aforementioned journey. Figuratively or allegorically, the six lovers are death-bound.

In sum, Moner's *Momería* is a superb example of the lover's monologue. By ways of the personified and allegorized swan, Moner's theatrical sketch expresses in a dramatically audible manner the complaints of lovers one and all. Although unusual, the clearly drawn role of the swan defines the playacting of the six lovers by a counterpoint arrangement. Consequently, in the overall field of enactment there is a contrast profiled in stark terms: on the one side, the gigantic bird, remaining motionless, is the agent of an eerie voice-over; on the other, the "players," swaying in choreographed steps, sport the paradoxical eloquence of their silence. In the final analysis, a play of mutual complementarity is established between a single stentorian declamation and a multiple voiceless expression of the compressed speech encapsulated in each dancer's *invención* and *letra*.

We may well deduce that in *Momería* Moner showcases the full spectrum of the monologue of lamentation. He devises the stirring epiphany of the lover's expression—that is, the voiced, explicit theatricalization of the drama latent in a few epigrammatic, often enigmatic verses. And these turn out to be the aforementioned *invención*, the quintessential écriture, emblematic text of *cancionero* lyricism.

There is, last but not least, another issue that begs for due consideration apropos of Moner's characterization of the swan. The issue has to do with what we may call a "living or performing stage." The swan is, obviously, an integral component of the stage setting. Concurrently, as speaker of the monologue and mouthpiece of the collective cast of characters, that same component takes an active participation in the performance and assumes a significant function in the evolution of the plot. This hybrid nature and the latent kinetic properties of the living stage may well be Moner's ultimate answer to the notion of the "topophilia" (see pp. 29–31 above). *Momería*'s "topophilia" marks Moner's first momentous step toward the development of his own allegorical theater.

The Monologue as *Sueño, Querella,* and *Tragèdia*

At this stage of our discussion one point needs to be clarified: the monologue we have just discovered in the subsurface of the history of Spanish theater proves to be the ultimate epiphany of the text of solitude, usually identified in the *cancioneros* by such rubrics as *infierno, purgatorio, sepultura, batalla.* So far, we have been able to distinguish the state of immanence, the ambiance of gloom, the woebegone expressionism, the inner spatiality, the hall of the mirror of passions, among other signs of the monologue of solitude. In our effort to formulate a precise definition we are struck by the flexibility, complexity, and malleability of the monologue in question, which, in fact, comprises various renditions of three main literary modalities: the lament, the dialogue, and the narrative.

Take, for instance, the aforementioned "Sueño," authored by the renowned *cancionerista,* Garci Sánchez de Badajoz.[9] Beneath Gallagher's concise commentary already discussed (see pp. 12–13 above), we detect the rather complex structure of the overarching monologue, announced as an *écriture* ("en la forma en que aquí escriuo" [in the manner in which I am writing here]) in the very first stanza of Sánchez's poem. The auctorial voice, lodged in the customary tone of lamentation in a direct address to the ladylove ("la mucha tristeza mía que causó vuestro deseo" [this great sadness of mine caused by your whims] [vv. 1–2]) shifts into a first-person narrative ("Yo soñava que me iva / desesperado de Amor" [I dreamt I was wandering in despair because of Love] [vv. 11–12]). The narrative incorporates the intervention of the God of Love (Amor) and his dialogue with a canorous bird: "Dime, lindo ruiseñor" (Tell me, beautiful nightingale) (v. 21). There is a smooth transition from the dialogue to the nightingale's protracted account of the death of the poet's persona and the reaction of the winged fauna to that sorrowful event:

De allí nos quedó costumbre,
las aues enamoradas,
de cantar sobre su cumbre
las tardes, las aluoradas,
cantares de dulcedumbre.
(Vv. 61–65; From then on, from those of us who are in love the custom originated of singing, in the evening and at at dawn, sweet songs on his tomb.)

Thus, the nightingale's sentimental speech produces the effect of not only a narrative (that of the nightingale himself) within a narrative (the overarching frame of the poetic account) but also a dialogue (the quick question-and-

---

[9] For the text of this composition, known, also, as *Sepultura de amor,* see, besides the entry included in the bibliography below, Gallagher, *The Life and Works of Garci Sánchez de Badajoz,* 116–18.

answer between the bird and the protagonist [vv. 41–45]) within a dialogue (the exchange between the bird and Amor [vv. 21–70]). The overall effect of the poem qua monologue is masterfully rounded out in the last stanza, which reverts to the protagonist's original mood of profound melancholy. The stanza reads as follows:

> Vime alegre, vime ufano
> de estar con tan dulce gente,
> vime con bien soberano
> enterrado honradamente
> y muerto de vuestra mano.
> Assí, estando en tal concierto,
> creyendo que era muy cierto
> que veía lo que escrivo,
> recordé y halléme bivo,
> de la qual causa soy muerto.
> (Vv. 71–80; I saw myself happy, I saw myself self-assured for being among such pleasant people; I saw myself in a supreme state of bliss, having been buried with full honors, my death having been dealt by your hand. Then, while I was at peace in the belief that what I saw in the dream just described really happened, I woke up and found myself alive, but the awakening is the cause of my death).

We may consider, also, the *Querella ante el Dios de Amor* (The Complaint Brought to the God of Love) by another distinguished *cancionero* poet, the Valencian author that goes by the title Comendador Escrivá.[10] In the *Querella*, which inter-

---

[10] As for the problematic identity of this gifted poet, see *Cancionero general [de Hernando del Castillo]*, ed. Joaquín González Cuenca, 2: 472, n. 2. Through an extensive research of numerous documents, Perea Rodríguez specifies three possibilities as to the identity of El Comendador Escrivá: (1) Joan Ram Escrivá (father), Maestre Racional of Valencia, an outstanding personality, who distinguished himself as an economist, diplomat, and high-ranking member of the military at the service of both John II of Aragon and his son, Ferdinand the Catholic, in the kingdoms of Valencia and Naples from the late 1470s to the time of his death around 1502 (*Estudio biográfico*, 185–91); (2) Joan Ram Escrivá (son), who, in 1501, succeeded his father as Maestre Racional and, at that post, throughout his distinguished career spanning from 1501 to 1548 (the year of his death), rendered invaluable services to King Ferdinand the Catholic, Queen Juana of Naples, and the emperor, Charles V (*Estudio biográfico*, 192–94); (3) Pirro (or Pedro) Luis Escrivá, "caballero de la Order del Hospital de San Juan" (ca. 1494–1571), who wrote a treatise on the construction of castles—he actually built two of them in Italy—and, as the exemplary courtier that he was, authored his own specimen of the *novela sentimental*, the special genre of Spanish prose narrative that deals with the suffering and the melancholic strains of passionate love (*Estudio biográfico*, 197–200). In view of the chronology pertinent to the compilation of the *Cancionero general*, Perea Rodríguez argues in favor of the candidacy of Joan Ram Escrivá (son) for the authorship of the poems attributed to

mingles some passages in prose with others in verse, the paradigm of the mono-logue typified by Garci Sánchez's "Sueño" is amplified considerably. In a pio-neering essay on Escrivá's work, Sirera demonstrates that it consists of four parts:

(1) the introduction which voices the protagonist's laments about his wretched condition, born of unrequited love;

(2) the encounter between the afflicted lover and Love himself (Amor), who strives to no avail to lift his interlocutor's spirits by distracting him from his dejection;

(3) the *querella* proper, during which the protagonist has a chance to vent his grievances to his heart's content in front of none other than the *belle dame sans merci* herself; while the lady, in return, does not mince words in her brusque reply: "¿Y quién a vos os forçaba / a quererme sin quereros?" (And who forced you to love me without my loving you?) (*Teatro medieval*, edited by Lázaro Carreter, 220);

(4) the anticlimactic epilogue, which, in a dramatic demonstration of Amor's ineffectual intervention, depicts the protagonist in exactly the same condition that prompted his lamentations at the onset. (Sirera, "Una quexa ante el Dios de Amor. . .," 262)

Our preliminary analysis reveals that Garci Sánchez's "Sueño" and Escrivá's *Querella* epitomize the love-centered esthetic of the *cancioneros* precisely by the way the works prove to be a deft assimilation of multifarious ingredients into an organic whole. Those ingredients include episodic and descriptive narrative, regular dialogue and formal debate, and, above all, an ample dose of diffuse lam-entations and specific complaints. Most importantly, the organic whole we have just referred to remains within the bounds of the monologue.

With the perspective gained from our analysis, we may point to the com-manding presence of the first-person narrator and the concomitant foreground-ing of the auctorial voice. We may deduce that these features of such emblematic compositions as the "Sueño" and the *Querella* are prevalent, as well, in other exemplary specimens of the *cancionero* monologue. There are, also, some discrete

---

El Comendador Escrivá in that prestigious anthology. Of interest is, also, the following definition provided by Perea Rodríguez:

> El oficio de Maestre Racional, institución propia de la Corona de Aragón, era como una especie de delegado del rey para asuntos económicos en cada entidad de la Corona, por lo que solía haber uno en Aragón y otro en Valencia (183; The office of Maestre Racional, a distinctive institution of the Crown of Aragon, was that of a special delegate of the king, put in charge of the economic affairs in each of the Crown's domains. For that reason there was one *maestre* in Aragon and another in Valencia).

factors, on the basis of which we may profile various classes of that monologue. The nomenclature that readily comes to mind includes the "elegiac tone," "the complaint," "the split or splintered self," "the self-authenticating textuality" as labels attributable to, respectively, Garci Sánchez's "Sueño," Escrivá's *Querella*, Moner's *La noche* and *Bendir de dones*.

A self-evident proposition is born from taking stock of our argumentation: the dramatic monologue we have been discussing generates the thrust of a genuine theatrical dynamism. A close look at the typical text of the *cancionero* monologue unveils the theatrical qualities connatural to that text. These qualities are not, as Luis García Montero sustains, the figment of the imagination of misguided scholars. Rather, they are reliable indices of a natural evolution from lyricism to drama and, eventually, from ritual to theater.[11]

Escrivá's *Querella* leaves no doubt as to the stage-worthiness of a monologue that reflects the quintessential poetics of the *cancioneros*. To Escrivá and cohorts we are indebted in our efforts to fill the enormous gap that we cannot but acknowledge in the history of Spanish theater of the Middle Ages. The gap is evident, indeed, in the bleak panorama, the landscape of utter desolation, depicted in the histories of the early theater performed in the Castilian language. Here is how one critic summarizes what he perceives as the "inexistencia" of Spanish medieval theater:

[E]l número de textos no puede ser más reducido. Es un panorama desalentador para los que insisten en el desarrollo paralelo de este tipo de representación en toda la Europa cristiana. (García Montero, *El teatro medieval*, 43; The number of texts could not be scantier. This is a disheartening sight for all those who

---

[11] Typical is the following assertion by García Montero:
Unas veces se forzaron los textos, hasta el punto de hacer aparecer como obras teatrales poemas sin ningún sentido dramático. La crítica positivista, necesitada de datos para seguir manteniendo ininterrumpido el hilo de la evolución teatral, puso muchas veces como único requisito el hecho de que apareciera un mínimo diálogo. Así, el teatro medieval castellano se convirtió en un saco sin fondo donde todo cabía, porque nunca se ha tenido menos conciencia de los límites que conforman la realidad ideológica de un género (*El teatro medieval*, 19; At times the texts were manipulated to the extent of making poems look like theatrical pieces even though they did not exhibit any dramatic sense whatsoever. Lacking any evidence that would sustain the hypothesis of an uninterrupted line in the evolution of a theater, positivistic critics on many occasions have posited as the only requisite the mere appearance of a minimum of dialogue. Consequently, medieval theater in the Castilian domain turned out to be a bottomless sack, into which one could make anything fit simply because those critics could not have been less mindful of the boundaries that determine the definition of an actual genre.)
For an extensive discussion of the evolutionary process I mention here, see my "From Lyricism to Drama: The Evolution of Fernando de Rojas's Egocentric Subtext."

insist on a parallel development of this type of theatrical performance throughout Christian Europe.)

As the statement suggests, the disheartening effect is aggravated by the comparison between the early history of Spanish and, to pick a compelling example, French theater.[12] To this day the conventional view has been that there is no substantial evidence, no extant stage-worthy texts that would attest to a continuous theatrical tradition from the *Auto de los reyes magos* ("The Play of the Three Kings), dated in the late twelfth century, to the *Representación del nacimiento de Nuestro Señor* (The Play of the Birth of Our Lord) composed by the poet Gómez Manrique toward the middle of the fifteenth century (Deyermond, *The Middle Ages*, 208–14).[13]

Now we may take a look at another specific case that may well be considered fresh evidence of a theater of monologue within the geographic domain and cultural ambiance of the *cancioneros* of the fifteenth century. The case is that of a short composition, entitled *Tragèdia de Caldesa* (Tragedy of Caldesa), which, as has been established, was written in 1458 by the Valencian humanist Joan Roís de Corella (1435–1497).[14] Although written in the Valencian brand of the Cata-

---

[12] Very useful is Oscar Mandel's succinct survey of French medieval theater within its wide European context (*Five Comedies of Medieval France*). For purposes of comparison, one may bear in mind such classical specimens mentioned by Mandel as *Le Garçon et l'Aveugle, Le jeu de Saint Nicholas, Le jeu de la Feuillée, Robin et Marion, Le Cuvier*. These plays, of course, find no equivalents in the history of Spanish theater for the period in which they were written (from the thirteenth to the fifteenth century).

[13] In her survey of Spanish theater in the Middle Ages (*The Medieval Theater in Castile*), Charlotte D. Stern points to numerous activities of a theatrical nature, evidenced in the domains of both Castilian and Catalan. There is no denying, however, that even her thorough research does not yield a significant number of concrete texts suitable for an actual representation on stage.

[14] For an updated overview of Corella's career, see the chapter ("Joan Roís de Corella") that Martos contributes to the recently published *Història de la literatura catalana*. In that chapter Martos provides a brilliant critique of Corella's signal accomplishments. The precise dates of Corella's birth (September 28, 1435) and death (October 6, 1497) are provided by Cantavella ("On the Sources of the Plot of Corella's *Tragèdia de Caldesa*," 75) and Martos ("La revaluació crítica de Joan Roís de Corella. Notes," 1). See, also, Chiner, "Aportació a la biografia de Joan Roís de Corella." A general account of Corella's life and works may be found in Riquer, *Història*, 3: 254–320. For the latest scholarly research on Corella, see Martines, "Comentaris a la bibliografia sobre Joan Roís de Corella," and Martos, "La revaluació crítica de Joan Roís de Corella". For an overview of the intellectual life in the Valencia of the 1400s, see Fuster, "Poetes, moriscos i capellans." A useful summary of the medieval history of Valencia in particular and the Catalan-speaking world in general is found in Delgado-Librero, The Mirror *of Jaume Roig*, 7–13. This scholar complements her succinct, lucid account with extensive, up-to-date bibliographic references. For the dating of *Tragèdia*, see Riquer, 3: 292 and Cantavella, 75, n. 1. Cantavella's note deals with the essential bibliographical data and kin-

lan language, Corella's *Tragèdia* reflects the mood of the *cancioneros*, especially because Corella himself is a leading representative of the Catalan *cançoner* par excellence — the so-called *Jardinet d'orats*, preserved in a unique codex (MS. 151 in the library of Universitat Central de Barcelona).[15]

Corella devises a plot that could not be more simple in structure but, at the same time, more complex in its implications. The protagonist, an unmistakable artistic portrait of the auctorial persona, presents himself in a strange predicament. His ladylove has locked him up and left him to languish for an entire afternoon in one of her house's darkest rooms. To make matters worse, the protagonist, in an understandable effort to relieve the endless moments of his tension, looks out through a tiny window (poca finestra), which affords him a limited view of the courtyard. Right then, to his horror, he catches a glimpse of his lady engaged in a torrid embrace with another man — the "other man," the primordial rival.

The plot of Corella's *Tragèdia* stems fully and exclusively from the auctorial monologue — a jeremiad rife with laments, admonitions, imprecations. Despite the straightforward dramatization of the central character's morbid passion and raw emotions — jealousy, resentment, rage — Corella's *Tragèdia* has puzzled generations of scholars who cannot come up with a satisfactory explanation for the categorical designation that makes up its very title. The Italian Catalanist, Annamaria Annicchiarico, confronts the troublesome issue head on when she entitles her essay on Corella's intriguing piece with the direct question, "Perché 'tragedia'?" (Why Tragedy?). Annicchiarico cannot answer the question basically because she does not accept the full-fledged theatricality of Corella's *Tragèdia*. We may add that Corella's masterpiece provides a memorable exemplar of the monologue of narcissism mentioned above (p. 59–60).[16]

---

dred details. Cingolani situates Corella's composition between two periods in the history of the author's output. Each is made up a different type of prose work: mythological subjects in one, sentimental narratives or treatises on love in the other (Joan Roís de Corella, 78–82).

[15] See the edition by Sergi Gascon and the essay by Jaume Torró in the bibliography below.

[16] For the topic of the protagonist's myopic purview in Corella's *Tragèdia*, see Cocozzella, "From the Perspective of a Narcissistic Lover." For a general study on Corella's masterpiece, see Cocozzella, *Text, Translation, and Critical Interpretation of Joan Roís de Corella's* Tragèdia de Caldesa. In the latter book, a full discussion of the topic at issue here is found on pp. 65-82.

IX.
STAGE-WORTHY ACTION:
EXTRINSIC AND INTRINSIC DIMENSIONS

The *Extra Ecclesiam* Realm

At first blush, we experience in Moner's *Sepultura* a sense of immersion into the *extra ecclesiam* realm, which constitutes the allegorical field of the protagonist's psyche. The relatively simple process of immersion runs parallel to the full-fledged theatricalization of the dramatic monologue. At the outset, we witness the auctorial persona deliver his plaintive reproach leveled squarely at the ladylove (vv. 1–42). This is accomplished with calculated histrionic effect. The speaker's impassioned tone and intense directness prompts us to imagine the actual presence of that *belle dame sans merci*, who, while listening in silence, reveals a deep involvement in her response by gesture, facial expression, and overall demeanor. The soliloquist goes so far as to make reference to a snippet of the lady's speech. Her harsh wake-up call ("¡Ea, Moner, despertad!" [v. 36]) is followed by kindred unceremonious injunctions (vv. 37–42). Though quite direct from the looks of it, the quotation proves to be less than verbatim, as it is couched in the speaker's own "forma cetrina" (v. 35). So the auctorial persona confesses.

A surprising change occurs in stanza 4 (vv. 43–56), where the direct address to the lady abruptly shifts into a firsthand report of a dialogue in two sections, respectively introduced by "Respondíle" (I replied to her) (vv. 42–50), and "Respondió" (She retorted) (vv. 51–56). The unexpected insertion of an aside (vv. 46–50) in the reported dialogue raises the level of complexity by an unexpected twist of the self-centered meditation. After this short and strange digression of an aside within a dialogue within a narrative within a monologue, the face-to-face confrontation with the ladylove resumes with a resentful resolution to break off the love relationship (vv. 64–70). The resolution culminates in the startling utterance of a dreadful curse:

> embío's missa, y sermón,
> y sepultura complida,
> celebrada
> en vuestra condenación. (Vv. 74–77.) (For he translation see p. 198 below.)

When the narrative proper begins—"En un campo de crueza / mi cuerpo muerto ha caýdo / de través. / Vino por él Gentileza, / púsolo encima estendido / d'un pavés / que l'enprestó la Simpleza." (vv. 78–84)—the first-person speaker absents himself from the visual field. The narrator's voice, evidently, becomes a voice-over. At this moment, we are struck by a spate of activities, which create the eyeful of a spectacle. In the section of the stage representing the aforementioned "campo," Gentileza stretches out the "cuerpo muerto" on a shield of sizable length.[1] In the meanwhile, Mancilla, at the head of a funeral cortege, comes out of some unspecified area inside the church ("Salió de dentro" [v. 88]). As the latter group proceeds to meet Gentileza and her charge, Mancilla intones a chant by which she welcomes "the body" to the sacred precinct: "Ven, cuerpo que no bivías" (v. 92). "¡Ven, cuerpo sin alma vivo" (v. 99). While weeping profusely, she decries not only the lover's untimely death and lifelong suffering but also the ladylove's cruelty. The voice-over account does not fail to set in relief, by a special audio technique, the stagey effect of the episodes already referred to: the burial of the protagonist, the construction of the monumental tomb, and the discovery of the epigram concealed in the dead man's mouth.

Strictly from the purview of dramaturgy, we have so far been able to identify a cluster of activities as a discrete unit related to the transition from the nondescript "campo" into the sacred structure represented by the "capilla" (v. 85) in particular and the church ("La yglesia llena de lumbre") (v. 164) in general. In this unit of transition we see unfold before our eyes the semiosis of an all-inclusive flexibility. This is the most reliable indication of the multifarious intertext, inherent in the mode of parody. Doubtless, such intertext poses a significant challenge to the stage director, commissioned to arrive at a proper balance between the various acoustic and visual effects that make for an engaging spectacle.

Engaging, indeed, is the type of spectacle that may be fashioned out of the diverse material provided by the ceremonial of the transition mentioned above. The moment the protagonist's monologue directed to the ladylove draws to a close, and we begin to listen to the voice-over account, we watch Gentileza and Mancilla join in a twofold procession, cadenced in solemnity. Mancilla's chant ("cantava a boz altilla" v. 91) broaches a musical strain, which will be continued in the *misa* proper.[2] Worth mentioning is the factor of musicality, which opens Moner's intertext to a wide gamut of parodic references or allusions.

The allusion or reference that most readily comes to mind is the traditional Gregorian chant. This could well provide the natural pattern for not only Man-

---

[1] Gentileza, we presume with the help of her entourage, attends to the task of transporting the body over to one of the church's chapels.

[2] See the following passages: "La Costumbre fue a cantar / la epístola, boz al cielo. / Entonó" (vv. 234–36); "Ell evangelio fue tal / de la Speriencia entonado / por solfá (vv. 248–50); "Tras l'offerta que he cantado" (v. 317).

cilla's *a-voz-altilla* aria but also kindred acts by the other personages who, at particularly significat moments in Moner's *Sepultura*, present respective parodies of important sections of the Mass. The elasticity of the parodic mode allows for one piece or another within the vast repertoire of the Gregorian chant to be incorporated, with or without adaptation, into the actual performance of Moner's *misa*. A case in point is that of the famous hymn usually identified by its opening verse, "In Paradisum deducant te angeli." In fact, even though Moner makes no specific mention of the hymn, there can be little doubt that "In Paradisum" would make an ideal accompaniment for Gentileza's procession.

It goes without saying that the undisputed prominence and availability of the Gregorian chant would not preclude in any way the opportunity for the *meneur* to borrow, as well, from sources other than the Gregorian corpus. Not to be overlooked in this respect is the wondrous blossoming of highly talented composers of religious music—the likes of Josquin des Prez, Guillaume Dufay, Johannes Ockeghem—in a period that coincides with Moner's lifetime. The list of these famous personages should be complemented by the less renowned, though no less talented Pedro de Escobar, born in Portugal and active in Spain, specifically at the court of Isabel la Católica.[3] In view of the numerous musical scores they authored for the Mass, these chief exponents of the music of the Renaissance contribute suitable material toward the fulfillment of the potential inherent in a composition such as Moner's, patterned after the sacred ritual and suited for the stage.[4]

The *Misa* Proper

What we have analyzed so far may be considered the first phase of the performance of Moner's *Sepultura*. The second phase begins at the onset of the *misa* proper (v. 164) and extends to the completion of the Offertory ritual (v. 316). Whether derived from the traditional chant or from the latest symphonic arrangements by the leading contemporary composers, there is no change in the high level of musicality attendant upon the solemnity of the spectacle. A radical change is evidenced, however, in the verbal components of the parodied ritual. The "Church Latin" is replaced by Castilian Spanish, and that is not all. There are no quotations from the Holy Writ—the Epistles, for instance, the Gospels, or the Psalms—or from the prescribed liturgical formulas such as "Kyrie

---

[3] Useful information on these composers may be obtained from the Internet at this site: https://en.wikipedia.org/wiki/. In each case, add the respective name after the final /: Josquin_des_Prez, Pedro_de_Escobar, Guillaume_Du_Fay, Johannes_Ockeghem.

[4] It is not hard to imagine how determinate components or motifs from the Mass of a Dufay or an Escobar could perform pretty much the same function in the theatricalization of Moner's *Sepultura* as does a musical score in the running of a modern movie.

eleison," or "Requiem aeternam." Instead, for each of those components, Moner works out a complete substitute beyond the bounds of the remake or *rifacimento*.

Worth mentioning in the context of Moner's *contrafactum* is yet another theatrical rendition. In accordance with time-honored custom, the ceremonial of the Offertory bears close resemblance to the performance of a dance. In referring to the ceremonial, especially in terms of "[t]he deployment of the celebrant, the deacons, and the subdeacons around the altar," Hardison observes: "one might almost speak of the choreography of the Mass" (*Christian Rite and Christian Drama in the Middle Ages*, 59). Small wonder, then, that Moner should have in mind a choreography of his own for Firmeza, Baldón, and Mancilla, clearly assigned to the Offertory, and for those personages like Gentileza, Costumbre, and Experiencia, whose presence is implied.[5]

In addition to the choreographic detail, the Offertory dramatized by Moner holds in store the potential for a rather complex representation. As I have attempted to show, the plot Moner devises for the *misa* proper evolves out of the core motif, which we may call the life-text of the auctorial persona. The full existential dimension of the life-text in question is an outgrowth of the shift from *canción* to "historia prosecutiva" (v. 344) or "[l]'ystoria de quyen muryó" (v. 639), the emblem of Moner's refurbished "Gospel." Key to Moner's representation, then, is not only the conceptualization of the life-text but also its concretization in theatrical form. What stands out in Moner's rendition of the Offertory is the disclosing of a wide-ranging transformation unfolding in three theatrical operations.

First, there is the procession, duly organized for the exhibition of the *canción*. It provides the raison d'être for the entire ceremony. We would expect the director to arrange to parade the literary text to best visual effect, after magnifying it onto a large canvas, encased within an eye-catching frame.

The second operation of the spectacle based on the Offertory is acoustic rather than visual. The circumstances of a full-fledged dramatization necessitate the vigorous recitation of the text that has taken pride of place in the procession. For the sake of convenient implementation, the occasion may well require the foregrounding of the voice-over. Now "el muerto" (v. 301), epiphany of a former lover, one who managed to crystallize his lifelong suffering into an iconic *canción* (vv. 301–3), is the narrator par excellence. Not surprisingly, it is up to him to deliver the poem in an awe-inspiring manner. One would expect as much from a ghostly denizen of the otherworld. Of course, there is nothing to prevent the resourceful director from harmonizing the eerie recitative with a tune or two derived from popular hits like the ones collected in the famous *Cancionero musical de Palacio*.

---

[5] Moner's interest in choreographed performance is well attested by the aforementioned "Momería" (see pp. 104–9 above).

The dramatic operation, the third completing the series of integral components of the Offertory, stretches beyond the parameters of that all-important ceremony. In fact, it coincides with the third general phase in the theatricalization of Moner's *misa*. As it reaches that third phase, the action of the plot has shifted from the space of the procession to the two locations: the altar and the pulpit. They constitute the setting for Mancilla's and Experiencia's officiation in respective order. It must be said that the details of Mancilla's discharge of her priestly function are not spelled out in Moner's text. They are left to be evoked and put into effect by the ingenuity of the stage director.

All the same, the director must take into consideration the two foremost functions of the celebrant-in-chief: first, what Mancilla does is a carry-over of the Offertory; second, Mancilla's intervention is actualized on stage strictly as a parody reflecting the traditional structure of the Mass and the tripartite plan of Experiencia's presentation. Central to Mancilla's enactment is the parody of the rite of transubstantiation. One may easily imagine how Mancilla carries out her ritual. The text of the *canción*, enlarged and framed as described above, would make a useful prop to be exhibited on the altar right in front of Mancilla. At the crucial moment, Mancilla, in the midst of her hieratic movements and recitations, bows down and utters some formulaic counterpart of "Hoc est enim corpus meum" and "Hic est enim calyx sanguinis mei." With this, Mancilla's parasacramental role is duly fulfilled.

Intrinsic Dimensions

We have already seen that Mancilla's enactment of the parody of transubstantiation pertains to the third phase in the overall theatrical structure of Moner's *Sepultura*. In fact, this "para-sacramental" episode occurs at a climactic moment of that phase. It constitutes the ultimate implementation of the leitmotif of "dead man talking." A reflection on that implementation holds in store a rewarding insight into the praxis of what I propose to call "intrinsic theatricality." I apply this label to the type of spectacle that may be fashioned by tapping into the subtextual implications of a reading or recitation of the *Sepultura* of interest here. What is at play is the conversion of the written text (*écriture*) into spectacle. The spectacle is realized when the written text is invested with visual and acoustic representation. We have already seen how the spectacle unfolds in phases 1 and 2 described above. Also, we have witnessed some manifestations of this show of sight and sound in not only the double procession headed by Mancilla and Gentileza but also in the solemn presentation of the *canción*, a ceremony that preludes the Offertory proper. What remains to be reviewed is the manner in which the grand spectacle continues in phase 3, ushered by the Offertory.

After Firmeza and Baldón take the *canción* to the altar, and Mancilla receives the offering, the stage becomes filled with the captivating cooperation between

Experiencia and Mancilla, each operating within her own space: the former on the pulpit, the latter at the altar. The dynamic of parallelism, simultaneity, and mutual complementation, inherent in the performance of the two personages, evokes once again the reciprocity between conciseness and expansion. The short/ long dialectic may be taken as an illustration of a natural blossoming—the flowering, that is, of the type of theater that remains intrinsic in Experiencia's sermon. Experiencia controls the oratorical potential of the text; Mancilla, for her part, takes charge of expanding the outreach of that text by translating it into a happening of considerable stage presence and heightened visual appeal. Consequently, the ritualistic action of Mancilla and her cohorts, Costumbre, Gentileza, Firmeza, Baldón, around the altar may be envisioned in strict correspondence with the three sections of Experiencia's sermon.

In the alternation between the group near the altar and the individual on the pulpit we may distinguish three cycles, which, by a slight adaptation of Experiencia's own nomenclature, we may label "declarative," "expositive," and "prosecutive." Experiencia, we may recall, employs the terms in describing the layout of her sermon in three sections. As a close study of these reveals, each deals with a particular text or a homogenous textual compound. It goes without saying that the sections of the sermon delivered by Experiencia evolve in unison with the cycles of the performance controlled by Mancilla.

Since we have already discussed Experiencia's sermon, it is convenient now to concentrate on Mancilla's role in her interaction with her co-celebrant, who has taken to the pulpit. Clearly, the first of the three cycles mentioned above has to do with the theme the lady preacher enunciates with lapidary incisiveness.[6] Now it is up to Mancilla to bolster the sermonizer's "declarative" intention by applying to the text of the "tema" the same magnifying and framing techniques put to use to best advantage in order to broadcast the full signification of the *canción*. Thus, while Experiencia delivers the "declarative" part of her sermon (vv. 345–442), Mancilla leads the other celebrants and some members of the congregation in a circular dance in front of the altar. In the middle of the circle stands an individual holding a pennant inscribed in bold lettering with the text of the sermon's theme as it appears in vv. 324–30 of the *Sepultura*.[7] The dancers move

---

[6] For the commentary on the theme of Experiencia's sermon, see above, pp. 61–64.

[7] García de la Concha adduces evidence of the use of pennants in some religious plays by Juan del Encina and Lucas Fernández. This usage reflects the dramatic presence of the pennant, which provides an attractive visual complementation for the hymns (the "Vexilla Regis," for example) sung in the course of processions and similar liturgical and paraliturgical ceremonies. García de la Concha underscores the role of the pennant and a variety of other objects in enhancing the overall aura of symbolism pertaining to the religious ceremony or theatrical performance:

Un elemento, en este caso el Pendón, por fuerza de su función sistemática, cobra un valor adicional, emblemático, que construye discurso por sí mismo dentro de la

in a slow rhythm, in well-measured steps. The orderly sway and emblematic circularity of the group bring to mind the ensemble of the *carole*, especially the one so pictorially presented in minute detail in the *Roman de la rose* (vv. 794–1276).[8]

The *carole* nicely complements the first part of Experiencia's sermon. The circularity of the dance as well as the sedate demeanor of the dancers may well be taken as outward signs of the control of the intellect over passionate love. Demonstrably, Mancilla strives to put in evidence Experiencia's initial efforts at what on another occasion I have called "the rhetoric of reasoning" (*Fra Francesc Moner's Bilingual Poetics of Love and Reason*, 27–82). But, as we have seen, Experiencia's reasoning proves to be flawed, and the preacher's emotions eventually gain the upper hand. At the point when Experiencia goes into her antifeminist tirade, thereby commencing the second part of the sermon, reason gives way to non-reason. Meanwhile, Mancilla, ready to do her part in accentuating the startling surge of emotionalism, instructs the group in front of the altar to break loose. Immediately, the *carole* turns into a *charivari*.[9]

Not at all unusual in Moner's production is the unexpected outburst of a tempestuous scene. Witness the incident recorded at the beginning of *Bendir de dones*, the longest of Moner's Catalan poems. The protagonist recounts how, during one of his pensive walks in Barcelona's central quarter, the midnight silence is shattered by the hubbub emanating from the nearby Plaça del Rei: "Una remor y gran crida / avalotada sentí. / Temoritsà, molt, sens mida (I heard a welter of noise and shouts. It frightened me a great deal, beyond measure) (vv. 21–23). Similarly, in the prose work entitled *La noche*, Moner's longest composition, the protagonist meets with a rowdy brawl involving various malicious characters (178–79). These, as the protagonist confesses, "[t]rahían tan gran barahunda que yo me espanté de velles" (they raised such a row that, upon seeing them, I became frightened) (178).[10] Doubtless, the boisterous histrionics of the *charivari* is alive and well in the horrifying episode of *Bendir* and in that of *La noche*.

---

pieza donde aparece, relacionándola al tiempo con otras piezas del sistema. ("Teatro litúrgico medieval en Castilla" 136; By virtue of its systematic function, a prop like, in this case, the pennant attains an added value, an emblematic one. This value constitutes in itself a kind of discourse within the piece in which it appears, while it interrelates such a piece with the others integrated into that same system.)

[8] For a thorough summary of the famous passage (the *carole* in the Garden of Delight), see Félix Lecoy, "Introduction [Analyse]," in Guillaume de Lorris and Jean de Meun, *Le roman de la rose*, ed. Félix Lecoy. Vol. 1. (Paris: Honoré Champion, 1965), xlv–lxiii.

[9] For a description of the *charivari* as illustrated in some eye-catching miniatures added to the text of the famous *Roman de Fauvel*, see Mühlerthaler, *Fauvel au pouvoir*, 427–30. The miniatures are found on ff. 34ʳ to 36ᵛ of Manuscript Paris, BN Fr. 146.

[10] For a commentary on this episode, see Cocozzella, *Fra Francesc Moner's Bilingual Poetics of Love and Reason*, 106–7.

It is not untoward, then, to envision, for Moner's *Sepultura* a *carole* followed by a *charivari* in a type of performance, with which, evidently, the author was quite familiar. Consequently, we may readily imagine the revelry of Mancilla and company in front of the altar. The Brueghelesque scene would be complete with the hoisting and brandishing of pennants or posters bearing the inscription of the most inflammatory statements, culled from Experiencia's wholesale condemnation of women: "Quyen las quiere las enoja" (v. 471), "Ángeles son y raposas / en leones enxeridas" (vv. 488–89), "Son estrago de las vidas (v. 499), "Son crueles enemigas / de quyen s'esfuerça a querellas" (vv. 516–17), "Engañan con lazo çyego" (v. 562).[11]

Now, let us reflect on the lively spectacle we have just visualized and would propose as an essential complementary component to Experiencia's sermon. The projection of parts 1 and 2 of that sermon onto the stage constitutes, in itself, a powerful and lasting statement that contributes to making explicit what remains implicit in the written text. What is being boldly dramatized is Experiencia's oratorical strategy of charting a moralistic journey toward a cathartic therapy. The therapy is implemented as a way of purging off the toxic affections attendant upon the animosity toward women.

Notably, the *charivari* factor perceptible in Experiencia's antifeminist tirade holds in store beneficial effects (e.g., those of the aforementioned catharsis or purge) similar to the ones that a number of scholars have brought to light apropos of the carnivalesque strain in medieval literature. James Burke, for instance, observes that "[o]fficial culture in the Middle Ages. . .not only tolerated the carnivalesque but doubtless also understood it as beneficial in many ways" (*Desire against the Law*, 33). He refers to Glending Olson's suggestive theories concerning "[t]he rowdy doings of carnival and charivari" and points out that for Olson "the medieval stress on the benefits of these doings results from a desire to provide a recreational or hygienic rationale for the carnivalesque" (*Desire against the Law*, 29). In summation, I would argue that the blending of the *carole* and the *charivari* into the texture of Moner's *Sepultura* reflects the respective correlation between the "declarative" and "expositive" function in part 1 and 2 of Experiencia's sermon. It may be argued, also, that the blending and correlation in question parallel the progression from the "via illuminativa" to the "via purgativa,"

---

[11] Ryan D. Giles ("Hanging Bells on the Cat") detects resonances of the charivari in such masterpieces of Spanish medieval literature as Juan Ruiz's *Libro de buen amor* (fourteenth century) and Alfonso Martínez de Toledo's *Arcipreste de Talavera*, also known as *Corbacho* (dated 1438). Giles's discussion centers on the various manifestations of the charivaresque motifs as indices of theatricality. For the theatricality inherent in the *Libro de buen amor*, see, also, Gerli, "El silencio en el *Libro de buen amor*: ¿Lagunas textuales o lectura dramática?"

as expounded in the ascetic and mystical literature that exercised considerable influence on Moner's own writing.[12]

Not to be overlooked is the third way, the *via unitiva*, also represented both in Experiencia's sermon and in Mancilla's complementary performance. We have already dealt with Experiencia's and Mancilla's specific roles, deftly interrelated by Moner to implement the dramatics of his *via unitiva*: that is, the ultimate communion between Moner's persona and the Divine Lover.

To round out our commentary, we may hark back to Mancilla engaged in the process of carrying out the most important ritual in Moner's parody: the ritual of a reinvented transubstantiation. Let us fix our eyes on that all-important prop: the magnified text of Moner's *canción*. Mancilla bows down in front of that icon, recites her performative formula, and ushers in two epiphanies: (1) the apotheosis of the lover, incarnated in the auctorial persona; and (2) the glorification of the Divinity, regarded in the supreme attribute of Verdad. We will leave it to the resourceful imagination of the stage director to figure out a way of representing theatrically the emblematic manifestations of the sublime. The stage director would thus fulfill the ultimate aspiration of Moner's artistry.

---

[12] For an overview of this influence on what I propose to call Moner's "wisdom text," see Cocozzella, *Fra Francesc Moner's Bilingual Poetics of Love and Reason*, 131–73. It may be noted that, in positioning the *via illuminativa* before the *via purgativa*, Moner inverts the traditional order, which, nevertheless, he follows on other occasions (see the aforementioned *Fra Francesc Moner's Bilingual Poetics of Love and Reason*, 152).

X.
Visualizing the Stage

Words and Pictures

Judging from the foregoing discussion, it would appear that the notion of a stage in Moner is tied exclusively to a vague, nondescript setting, in which the theater of "innerness" is represented in the manner of a dramatic monologue. We may be thinking of the "campo de crueza" (*Sepultura*, v. 78) commented upon already, or, to adduce another example, the "hondo barranco lleno de abrojos" (the deep ravine full of thorny bushes) (*TMPW*, 79) the protagonist describes in the exordium of *La noche*. This notwithstanding, an indistinct *mise en scène*, although inherent in some isolated aspects of Moner's *oeuvre*, is hardly characteristic of Moner's most representative pieces. We need only take a quick look at three compositions—*Bendir de dones*, *La noche*, and *Sepultura d'amor*—to appreciate how Moner fashions a precise framework to deliver the experience of a genuine spectacular happening. In *Bendir*, *La noche*, and *Sepultura*, the spectacle unfolds within the confines of the plaza, the castle, and the church, in respective order. A thoughtful reflection on these prominent exemplars of a closed-in, well-defined space reveals in them a collective showcase of the essential semiotics of Moner's theatrics.

Each of the three aforementioned literary masterpieces may be regarded as a cluster of motifs, orchestrated for an eventual performance on stage. For a fruitful approach to the semiotics, motifs, and orchestration in question, Mary Carruthers analyzes the relationship between words and pictures and links the inventiveness of the intellect and imagination to corresponding visual (especially architectural) representation.[1] For the purposes of the present discussion, we may follow in the footsteps of Miguel-Prendes, who employs Carruthers's principles

---

[1] Mary Carruthers and Jan M. Ziolkowski "General Introduction," in *The Medieval Craft of Memory: An Anthology of Texts and Pictures*, ed. Mary Carruthers and Jan M. Ziolkowski (Philadelphia: University of Pennsylania Press, 2002), 1–31. In the collaborative introduction to the anthology they put together, Carruthers and Ziolkowski bring to light, in the invaluable documents comprised in the anthology, the radical interaction of the two primordial factors under consideration here:

for an approach to *Cárcel de amor*, the aforementioned *novela sentimental* by Diego de San Pedro. The following passage epitomizes Miguel-Prendes's suggestive scrutiny of San Pedro's tour de force:

> The description of the prison of love is an old rhetorical ornament called ekphrasis, which describes a work of art or architecture, imagined or real, in order to "paint ideas" in the public's mind. It possesses the quality of *brevitas* that holds within itself an abundance, or *copia*; that is, the possibility to be expanded into multiple interpretations. Carruthers explains how ekphrasis was used in Scriptural exegesis to paint in one's mind the Heavenly City and how this activity was commonly associated with the creative act of making a temple of the heart ("Reimagining Diego de San Pedro's Readers at Work: *Cárcel de amor*," 20–21).

To help us understand how the structural principles—ekphrasis, *brevitas*, *copia*—underscored by Miguel-Prendes come to bear upon the construction of a stage, such as may be envisaged for Moner's *Sepultura* and, for that matter, for *La noche* and *Bendir* as well, we may take into account the issues raised by Stephen Nichols in a fundamental essay on ekphrasis. Nichols demonstrates that ekphrasis, which he succinctly defines as "the description of a visual art work" ("Ekphrasis, Iconoclasm, and Desire," 134), encompasses a wide range of implications. These have to do for the most part with the faculty of looking, manifested in the act of either glancing or gazing. As borne out by his analysis, ekphrasis discloses an important parallelism between the two operations of looking and the techniques of *brevitas* and *copia* pointed out by Miguel-Prendes. Glance is to *brevitas* as gaze is to *copia*.[2]

Now, let us see how ekphrasis comes into play in *Sepultura*. A quotable passage, pertinent for its visual appeal and iconic function, consists of the description of lover's sepulcher in the following verses:

La Manzilla, enmudescida
   de pesar,

---

both words and pictures, intimately and collaboratively related as devices for composing thoughts and memories. (2)

No less captivating than this summary statement is the following commentary that accompanies it:

In the words can be found many pictures—in the pictures many words. Moreover, it is not so apparent where one medium leaves off and the other begins, for many of the pictures are visual puns and pictures of words and many of the words are verbal paintings and drawings. In medieval learned cultures...such a thorough mixing of media, especially the visual and the verbal, was commonplace. (2)

[2] An extensive discussion of the various facets of glance and gaze, *brevitas* and *copia*, may be found in Cocozzella, *Text, Translation, and Critical Interpretation*, 111–33.

con ambas manos asidas,
hizo una tumba a medida,
   byen labrar,
d'estas letras esculpidas:
"Quyen hizo trist'el morir
   d'este hombre
no se acuerda de su nombre."
La tumba puesta a dos passos
do l'Amistad se enterró
   mucho ha,
el cuerpo tomó en los braços
y de dentro l'enterró,
   dond'está
libre de más embaraços.
En la cubyerta, al un lado,
puso esculpyda la cruz
   que confyesso;
en el otro, está labrado
una muy grande avestruz,
   do el pescueço
va de estas letras sembrado:
"Pyedras y ponçoñas trago,
   y a las vezes
me matan muy pocas nuezes."
(Vv. 137–63; *2 OC*, 136–37. Translation on p. 199 below.)

These verses unfold in full ekphrastic mode. Here the *brevitas* of the spectator's look is engaged in the sculptural incisiveness of the description. The instantaneous blink of the eye, that is, the act of glance or *conspectus*, to borrow the technical term employed by Carruthers, recaptures the image of the tomb in two details: the cross and the gigantic ostrich, both presented, we may assume, in bas-relief.[3] At the same time, the attention the spectator pays to the enigmatic inscription

---

[3] We would be well served to allow Carruthers and Ziolkowski to explain in their own words the role of instant vision in the rather complex marriage of memory and creativity:
A fourth-century grammarian, Julius Victor, whose work was especially influential in the earlier Middle Ages (and who, in turn, was most indebted to the first-century author Quintilian), wrote that *memoria* is "the firm mental grasp of things and words for the purpose of invention." To ensure this security, material is first cut up into *divisiones* or *distinciones*, and then these segments are mentally marked and memorized in readily recoverable order such as numerically or alphabetically. In this way, error is avoided: for if the pieces are securely bound together in a sequential order (such as one, two three, etc.), none can be overlooked or forgotten. Each segment should be "short" (*brevis*) no larger than what your mental eye can encompass in a single glance or *conspectuss*. (4)

(the *letras* quite visible on the ostrich's neck) attests to the second principle we are dealing with: that of *copia*. Concomitant to *copia* is the act of gazing with its natural proclivity to protracted, contemplative, and meditative vision. The riddle that defies solution warrants a repetitive, perhaps obsessive, confrontation with the text: What does it mean? By its very nature, the elusive answer does not obviate a persistent asking of the question. Indeed, it guarantees it.[4]

A View from the Miniature

Upon close analysis, we begin to see that the *copia-brevitas* paradigm proves to be fruitful in Moner's creative enterprise. As I will attempt to demonstrate, the paradigm inspires the author's most ambitious efforts. Demonstrably, in *Bendir*, *La noche*, and *Sepultura*, Moner attains remarkable success in an esthetic formula that articulates the *copia* of a wide scope with the *brevitas* of a compact spatiality. To put it succinctly, the formula illustrates Moner's ingenious rendition of the principle of *maximum in minimo*. For an effective illustration of this paradoxical duality of *multum/parvum*, *maximum/minimum*, we may tap the reliable source consisting of the numerous manuscript illuminations readily accessible to a writer of Moner's cultural background and social standing.[5] High among these codices rank those examples that, to this day, attest to the enduring sphere of

---

[4] It bears observing that by the use of the emblematic inscription of an enigmatic nature, notable examples of which may be found in *Sepultura* and, more abundantly in *La noche*, Moner integrates into his allegorical stage a type of device, usually referred to as *invención*. As one of those common "decorative and theatrical aspects" identified by Macpherson ("The Game of Courtly Love," 101), the device figures prominently in the forms of lavish entertainment evidenced in the aristocratic circles and at court throughout the Spanish realm during the fifteenth century (see pp. 102–4 above).

[5] Truly instructive in terms of the paradigm described above is the analogy to be derived from the Prologue of Shakespeare's *Henry V*. Here the personage identified as Chorus exhorts the spectators to indulge in flights of unrestrained imagination in order to conjure up visions of clashing armies and panoramas of vast expanse. By so doing they can compensate for the obvious deficiencies of a humble stage, which Chorus variously describes as "unworthy scaffold," "little place," "cockpit," "girdle of these walls," and, unforgettably, "this wooden O" (William Shakespeare, *The Life of Henry the Fifth. Twenty-Three Plays and the Sonnets*, ed. Thomas Marc Parrot, Edward Hubler, and Robert Stockdale Telfer. Rev. ed. [New York: Scribner's, 1953], 438). This discussion calls to mind the felicitous pictorial metaphor formulated by Whinnom: "La poesía amatoria cancioneril es el arte de la miniatura" (the love-centered poetry of the *cancioneros* is the art of the miniature) (*La poesía amatoria*, 50–51). In my judgment, the scope of Whinnom's image may be broadened considerably. It may be argued that Moner intuits a macrocosmic proportion in the miniature-like aspects of that poetry. By virtue of this blowup of sorts, the art of the miniature reflected in the *canción* and kindred genres becomes the

readership and influences of the *Roman de la rose*.[6] In all likelihood, that sphere encompasses an author like Moner, who spent two years of his adolescence in France and, while there, learned the French language.[7] In France, perhaps the young Moner enjoyed ample opportunity to peruse some manuscript of the *Roman* and compare its text with its illustrations. In any circumstance, the comparison would be instructive as to not only the function of the glance as definer or localizer, but also the metaphysical dialectic between *brevitas* and *copia*.

We do not have the data to identify the actual manuscript or manuscripts Moner may have had a chance to examine. All the same, we can readily find appropriate samples of such codices that attest to the function and dialectic in question. Take, for instance, the upper portion of fol. 1 of British Museum MS. Egerton 1069 (15th c.),[8] and the entire fol. 142 of University of Valencia MS.

---

pictorial source for the configuration of an actual stage suited to the inner theater of the psyche or the soul.

[6] F. B. Luquiens, "The *Roman de la Rose* and Medieval Castilian Literature," *Romanische Forschungen* 20 (1907): 284–320. Luquiens provides concrete evidence of the influence of the renowned French poem on Spanish literature of the late Middle Ages. In addition, Marta Marfany ("La influència de la poesia francesa des d'Andreu Febrer a Ausiàs March," *Estudis Romànics* 34 (2012): 259–87) illustrates with abundant documentation the influence of French poetry on Catalan literature of the first six decades of the fifteenth century. We may take into account Marfany's following statement:

A mitjan segle xv els poetes catalans llegien poesia francesa. No era una novetat ni una moda efímera, sinó un hàbit cultural adquirit per tradició, l'origen del qual es remunta a la segona meitat del segle xiv, sobretot a partir del matrimoni el 1380 de Joan d'Aragó (1350–1396) amb Violant de Bar (c. 1365–1431), directament emparentada amb la Corona francesa.. . . Tots dos monarques tingueren. . .un paper decisiu en la circulació de textos poètics francesos, per exemple del *Roman de la Rose* (259; In the mid-fifteenth century, the Catalan poets read French poetry. This was not a novelty nor was it an ephemeral fashion. It was a cultural habit acquired by a tradition that harks back to the second half of the fourteenth century, specifically to the year 1380 with the marriage of Joan d'Aragó [1350–1396] to Violant de Bar [c. 1365–1431], who was closely related to the French Crown.. . . Both monarchs played a decisive role in the diffusion of French poetry, for example the *Roman de la rose)*.

[7] In the biographical sketch provided by Barutell and printed in *editio princeps*, we learn that [Moner] "[f]uese luego. . .a França, y sirvió allí dos años un gran señor de aquel reyno, a donde aprendió la lengua françesa" (afterwards, moved to France, where he served a nobleman of high rank of that realm for two years. There he learned the French language) (Barutell, 230).

[8] Panoramic View of the Garden of Déduit. See the caption of the illustration no. 3 in John V. Fleming, *The Roman de la Rose: A Study in Allegory and Iconography* (Princeton, NJ: Princeton University Press, 1969). The illustration is found, also, in Cocozzella, *Text, Translation, and Critical Interpretation of Joan Roís de Corella's* Tragèdia de Caldesa, 213.

387 (ca. 1420).[9] In both cases, the whole depiction apprehended in one glance eloquently spells out the nature of *brevitas*. At the same time, it is evident that the *brevitas* is endowed with a concomitant *copia*—that is, with the potential for creative expansion. What is at play in both samples is a pictorial version of a complex nucleus, which can be amplified ekphrastically in considerable detail by turning back to the suggestive text of the *Roman*. The ekphrastic potential of the glance-generated nucleus encapsulated in the miniature of Egerton 1069 may be appreciated by reviewing a modernized version of that same nucleus encompassing the setting of the *Hortus Deliciarum* and the action within it.[10]

Commenting on the Egerton 1069 folio, Fleming recognizes in this obvious representation of the Jardin de Déduit (*Roman de la rose*, vv. 45–1276) the artist's plan to highlight the essential motifs of the original text. He points out "in the cluttered composition. . .the attempt of a fifteenth-century artist of no mean skill to do partial justice to the richness of its detail" (*The Roman de la Rose: A Study in Allegory and Iconography*, 24). Fleming underscores the miniaturist's self-imposed concentration on what that artist considers the most significant details:

> The visual scene is quite complete in the poem. It requires of the illustrator not imaginative detail, but selective and coherent organization. (24)

The same condensed representation of setting and action is found in the aforementioned Valencian manuscript, which highlights, as Fleming puts it, "the history of Pygmalion's passion" (*Roman de la rose,* vv. 20817–21214).[11]

The utmost degree of comprehensiveness is shown in a fourteenth-century manuscript, on fol. 1 of Bibliothèque Nationale, MS. Fr. 1576.[12] Here the min-

---

[9] Synoptic Illustration of the Story of Pygmalion and Galatea. See the caption of the illustration no. 22 in Fleming, *The Roman de la Rose.* The illustration is also found in Cocozzella, *Text, Translation, and Critical Interpretation of Joan Roís de Corella's* Tragèdia de Caldesa, 215.

[10] See the illustration facing p. 34 in René Louis, *Le Roman de la Rose: Essai d'interprétation de l'allégorisme érotique* (Paris: Champion, 1974).

[11] Fleming makes a convincing case for not only the affinity between Jean de Meun's poem and its visual counterpart but also the primary function of exemplarity stemming from both renditions of the myth. He aptly observes that "[t]he literary techniques which Jean de Meun employs in the *exemplum* of Pygmalion, no less than the pictorial techniques of the artists who illustrated it, can properly be called 'iconographic'" (236). For a comparable eyeful "visual gloss" of the Pygmalion myth, see f. 62ᵛ of Paris, Bibliothèque Nationale MS. Fr. 12592 (see Plate 10, Synoptic Illustration of the Story of Pygmalion and Galatea in Sylvia Huot, *The* Romance of the Rose *and Its Medieval Readers: Interpretation, Reception, Manuscript Transmission* [Cambridge: Cambridge University Press, 1993], 281.

[12] See the illustration listed as no. 4 in Fleming, *The Roman de la Rose: A Study in Allegory and Iconography.*

iaturist strives to contain the entire *Roman* in one picture. In sharp contrast to the other artists in the previous examples just discussed, this master does not focus on one crucial passage of the *Roman*, complex though that passage may be. Instead, as Fleming explains,

> [h]e. . .has made a kind of summary painting, a summary of what he thinks the *Roman* is about. To do this he has introduced into his little painting a number of emblematic elements which would have been transparent to any sophisticated fourteenth-century reader, however arcane they may initially seem to us. (24)[13]

The illustrations just reviewed are directly related to Moner's handling of both the ekphrasis and the allegory. To put that direct relationship in evidence, we need only focus on the all-encompassing picture, which Fleming describes as "summary painting," and compare it with a woodcut engraving (figure 4), which appears in the aforementioned handsome book printed in 1528 in Barcelona by the enterprising Carlos Amorós.[14] As we have indicated (see above, pp. xxxiv–xxxvi), the book, the frontispiece of which is shown in figure 3, turns out to be the *editio princeps* of Moner's bilingual production. The point to be stressed is that both "the summary painting" and the *grabado* respond to the same compositional principle. They both display a design, which is, all in one, wide-ranging and compact to such an extent as to fit within a circumscribed setting. Turning our attention specifically to the aspects of Moner's creativity, we notice that the woodcut captures the *conspectus* or *brevitas* of an entire, easily-recognizable structure, that of the castle. On the *copia* side of the equation, that same engraving highlights the quintessential areas where the action of *La noche* takes place: that is to say, the sections demarcated for the conversation between the man and the woman, the man's climbing of the staircase, and the man's confrontation of the swooping eagle. Besides these areas, the *grabado* also includes a space for the figure of the shining sun (figure 4).

The fundamental semiotics of the *grabado* as an abstract of a stage and a plot becomes applicable to *Sepultura d'amor*, *La noche*'s sister composition. In other words, by the way the engraver visualizes the structural principles of *La noche*, we can figure out the spatial layout and eventual plot development of *Sepultura*. From the perspective of the *conspectus*, we envisage at first glance in *Sepultura* two main loci of dramatic action. These are discernible, respectively, outside and inside the church building: *extra* and *intra ecclesiam*. The former locus designates psychic space; the latter pertains to spiritual or soulful place. *Extra ecclesiam* is

---

[13] For a full explanation of this comprehensive miniature, see Fleming, *The Roman de la Rose: A Study in Allegory and Iconography*, 22–27.

[14] For a detailed description of Amorós's book, listed in the bibliography below under "*A*," see Cocozzella, *Introducció*, 86–90, and *1 Introducción*, 65–69.

the aforementioned "campo de crueza" (vv. 78–80), which the protagonist revisits through nightmarish flashbacks to the lurid scenes of his violent death and the sight of his abandoned, inert body (vv. 43–70, 78–79, 654–80).[15] In contrast with the amorphous "campo de crueza," the field of dramatic display located *intra ecclesiam* is clearly configured and notably expanded to encompass three main venues: 1) the chapel-sepulcher compound, 2) the main altar, 3) the pulpit (figure 5). What remains to be investigated is how this threefold stage corresponds to respective nuclei of performance integrated into a complex plot.

The Book of Hours, also, may have provided Moner with the pictorial medium, which would help him visualize the stage for his theatrical presentation. We should bear in mind, however, that, pending additional research, the evidence of the effects of this medium on Moner's dramatics is, at present, less than substantial. All in all, it is not hard to figure out how the visual factor inherent in the silent reading that characterizes the so-called *prière de coeur* (prayer of the heart) may find its repercussion on a staging effect.[16] Saenger notes that:

> References to the eyes and vision become frequent in the rubrics of fifteenth-century prayers. As the primary organ of reading, the eyes were regarded as channels by which external impressions passed directly to the heart. ("Books of Hours and the Reading Habits of the Later Middle Ages," 147)

Then he points to a memorable exemplum: an episode in the life of Saint Augustine, related by Denis the Carthusian (1402–1471). The bishop of Hippo, near death, "had the Penitential Psalms painted on the walls so that he could rest his eyes upon them and thereby contemplate them" (147). In those highly suggestive paintings, which reflect and inspire all in one the vivid imagination of a reader absorbed in contemplative prayer, one may well discover the primal impulse that comes to a head in the fashioning of a full-fledged performance on a stage.

---

   [15] Moner's handling of this spatial dialectic is analyzed in Cocozzella, "Fra Francesc Moner's Psychic Space / Soulful Place."
   [16] Saenger proffers the following definition for the *prière*: "for writers of the fifteenth century, prayer of the heart meant that the act of praying transpired within the mind of the person praying" ("Books of Hours and the Reading Habits of the Later Middle Ages," 145).

XI.
Configuring the Actual Stage:
The Pragmatics of the *Mise en Scène*

Monologue in the Dark, Playacting in the Light

Let us take another look at Escrivá's *Querella* and Corella's *Tragèdia*, the literary monologues already mentioned. Since the identity of Escrivá is quite problematic, we cannot ascertain whether he and Corella, both fifteenth-century authors from Valencia, belonged to the same generation.[1] What I intend to demonstrate is that the two masterpieces, no matter what the relationship between their authors turns out to be, constitute a faithful illustration of the way a theatrical performance was conceptualized throughout the Middle Ages and the early Renaissance. Henry Ansgar Kelly, in his book-length study, *Ideas and Forms of Tragedy from Aristotle to the Middle Ages*, helps us considerably with the configuration of an actual stage for that theater. Kelly underscores the pivotal role that some extraordinary passages in Isidore of Seville's famous *Etymologies* play in the history of the medieval *mise en scène*. In his minute analysis of those passages in books 8 and 18 of Isidore's magnum opus, Kelly indicates that Isidore rightfully uses the term *scena* "to refer primarily to the large roofed building at the rear of the open air Roman theater" (41). We will soon return to the symbolism implicit in Isidore's definition of *scena* in particular and the dark place in general. Worthy of special attention are Kelly's comments on Isidore's notion of performance. Take, for instance, the following observation:

---

[1] Perea Rodríguez points out that Joan Ram Escrivá and his homonymous son belonged to quite different literary circles: the father, in close association with such authors as Luis de Castellví, Bernat Fenollar, Miquel Pérez, and Joan Roís de Corella, attended with them the renowned sessions (*tertulias*) in the house of the well-to-do Valencian merchant, Berenguer Mercader (*Estudio biográfico,* 195); by contrast, the son established close ties with poets like Francesc Gilabert de Fenollet, and Juan Fernández de Heredia, fellow members of his own generation, which encompassed the last decade of the fifteenth century and the first half of the sixteenth (*Estudio biográfico,* 196–97). See, also, the biographic sketch on Comendador Escrivá (above, p. 123, n. 10).

According to Isidore, the poet sang the whole piece while others gesticulated, with much the effect perhaps of a puppetmaster supplying voices for his puppets, or an "actor" like Mel Blanc for animated cartoons. Or we may think of the Japanese silent movies of the 1920s, when a narrator (*benshi*) supplied commentary, or speakers pronounced dialogue from behind the screen. (44)[2]

As one would expect, the paradigm that may be extrapolated from Isidore's definitions was subjected to diverse interpretations and underwent changes and adaptations throughout the centuries that followed Isidore's lifetime.[3] This is

---

[2] For an illustration of the "Isidorian theater" we may adduce the images contained, respectively, in two manuscripts: Bibliothèque de l'Arsenal, Paris, MS. 664, fol. 1ᵛ, and Vatican, MS. Urbinas Latinus 355, fol. 1ᵛ. The Arsenal manuscript is known as *Térence des Ducs*, ca. 1400. It gives a medieval vision of ancient Roman theater. We see Calliopius reading the text of a play by Terence, while some jesters wearing masks translate that text into dramatic gesticulations. A renowned commentator on Terence's works, Calliopius is a contemporary of that famous playwright (second century BC). Illustration available on the Internet: http://www.theatrales.uqam.ca/chronologie/TerenceDesDucs.html. For a reproduction of the entire miniature in full color, see Hartnoll, *The Theater: A Concise History*, 34. See the discussion of this illustration in Massip, *Història del teatre català*, 60–61, and Kelly, *Chaucerian Tragedy*, 159. MS. Urbinas Latinus 355 contains Nicholas Trevet's commentary on Seneca's tragedies. The illuminated frontispiece illustrates an imagined performance of *Hercules furens*. Kelly provides a detailed description of the miniature and adds that it is "reproduced in color in the edition of Trevet's *Expositio Senece* on *Hercules furens*, facing p. 1" (*Chaucerian Tragedy*, 18, 18 n. 41).

[3] By piecing together and carefully assessing details derived from the *Etymologies*, Joseph R. Jones ("Isidore and the Theater") arrives at a description of the type of dramatics and concomitant staging that make up Isidore's idea of a theater. In the words of Mary H. Marshall, Isidore's notions were "endlessly repeated throughout the Middles Ages" (quoted in Jones, 16). Jones points to Isidore's widespread influence evidenced "in the dictionaries and glossaries at every scholar's disposal" and in "the illustrators' conceptions which appear in considerable numbers after the fourteenth century and which often add elements derived ultimately from Isidore" (16). Jones segues with a noteworthy observation:

Isidore's work was so fundamental to Western scholarship by the eleventh century that it is frequently impossible to distinguish what is first-hand acquaintance with Isidore. . .from what had become clichés of erudition. (18)

In a recent essay Pietrini does not mince words in adding her testimony regarding Isidore's role in the configuration of a theater of the Middle Ages and the early Renaissance. Referring to Isidore's notion of *scaena* as "una estructura edificada a la manera de una caseta con un *pulpitum*" (a structure built in the manner of a cubicle with a pulpit) ("La invención del teatro y de la escena en la Media Edad," 102), she states: "lo que está claro es que la descripción tuvo mucho éxito en los siglos posteriores y en la época humanística se tradujo en figuraciones que interpretan las palabras a la luz del imaginario teatral que empieza a circular" (103; what is clear is that [Isidore's] description attained great success

quite evident in the numerous treatises, commentaries, and actual dramatic texts, whether written in Latin or in the vernacular, meticulously analyzed by Kelly. All changes and adaptations notwithstanding, the essentials of Isidore's paradigm persisted at least until the end of the fifteenth century; and, interestingly enough, they persisted in the type of monologue we have discovered in the *cancioneros* and kindred literary texts. In this vast body of love-centered literature we may readily trace some vestiges of Isidorian dramatics. Also, we may recognize especially in the *cancioneros* the rich potential for the adaptation of the typical lovelorn expressionism to the principles of that Isidorian idea of a theater. These principles include the tone of lamentation and the contrast between a dark interior space (usually the lover's chamber) and an exterior area (usually the surroundings of that chamber) drenched in light. Above all, the Isidorian principles prompt us to envisage a type of theater that involves a monologue complemented by a spectacle of mimes: a kind of spectacle that Kelly defines, somewhat laconically, as a "dumbshow with voice-over" (219).

Kelly has blazed a trail of research toward a plausible answer to Annicchiarico's query (see p. 127 above).[4] The answer lies in the peculiar aspects of the "Isidorian paradigm:" the dark/light contrast, which Corella translates into coordinating and counterpoising the plaintive monologue delivered by the protagonist in the dimly lit chamber and a close equivalent of the Isidorian pantomime: the plot conceived and enacted by Caldesa, the protagonist's ladylove. The plot involves, also, Caldesa's cohorts, who operate stealthily and silently in broad daylight.

For the sake of clarity and specificity, a word is in order about the configuration of an actual stage to be proposed for Corella's masterpiece. The data provided in the narrative coexisting with the protagonist's monologue are more than sufficient to bring to the fore some especially significant issues of spatiality. If we look at the corresponding drawing (figure 2), we distinguish, at a glance from left to right, the sketch corresponding to the aforementioned chamber and courtyard. We discern, of course, nothing unusual or unexpected in the layout of the left side of the drawing. Apparently, there is nothing unusual or unexpected on the right side either. But, upon closer study, we discover a surprising detail that to this day has passed unnoticed. If we look at the position of the small window, we cannot but come to the realization that the range of vision it affords to the distraught onlooker is very limited. And here is, then, the unavoidable conclusion and astonishing revelation the spatial factor entails: Caldesa herself, for reasons

---

in subsequent centuries and in the age of humanism was translated into configurations that interpret Isidore's words in accord with imaginary forms of a theater that was beginning to come into vogue in that epoch).

[4] Stemming from Kelly's study is my own extensive discussion of the applicability of the "Isidorian stage" to Corella's *Tragèdia*: see Cocozzella, *Text, Translation, and Critical Interpretation of Joan Roís de Corella's* Tragèdia de Caldesa, 151–81.

of her own, must have made the necessary arrangements and precise calculations of time and place in order to make sure that the shocking scene will be fully visible to the eye of her captive and captivated lover.

Now we can say that we have come to an understanding of the meaning of Corella's title. The *Tragèdia* proves to be an ingenious adaptation of the Isidorian principles to which Kelly devotes a landmark study. Corella transforms the Isidorain dramatics into a Shakespearean exploration of the motives of the silenced, resentful woman, who considers herself abused. She unveils, as the crux of the tragic condition, the paradoxical interaction between the two protagonists: 1) the male character who monopolizes speech—he delivers the uninterrupted monologue—but remains, throughout, pathetically and pathologically incapable of action; 2) the female nemesis, who is in absolute control of the action—she hatches out the plot of retribution—but is relegated to a secondary role even though she is the primary motivator of a "dumb show."

The Isidorian Paradigm

The issue of theatricality is highly pertinent to Moner's *Sepultura* and, specifically, to his *misa*. We have analyzed such intrinsic indices of that theatricality as the mode of immanence, the affirmation and celebration of true love, and the commanding stage presence of the ego-centered voice of the protagonist. Also, we have acknowledged the "forma cetrina," the "letras matizadas del sentido," the "estil dur" à la Ausiàs March, the "tono menor," among other stylistic modes. All betoken the characteristic rhetorical tenor of that voice. Now it is time to follow up on the discussion initiated above (see pp. 123–27) concerning Escrivá's *Querella* and Roís de Corella's *Tragèdia*. Not unlike Escrivá and Corella, Moner is indebted to the description and theories put forth by Isidore of Seville. What we are about to highlight is the role the Isidorian paradigm, outlined, as I have just indicated, in Kelly's landmark publications, specifically plays in Moner's *Sepultura*.

We may start with the incisive passage in which none other than Giovanni Boccaccio faithfully recaptures not only the configuration of the Isidorian stage but also its concomitant mode of performance. In Boccaccio's last work, entitled *Esposizioni sopra la Comedia di Dante*, we read:

> Chiamano. . .i comedi le parti intra sè distinte delle loro comedie «scene»; per ciò che, recitando li comedi quelle nel luogo detto scena, nel mezzo del teatro, quante volte introduceano varie persone a ragionare, tante della scena uscivano i mimi trasformati da quegli che prima avevano parlato et fatto alcuno atto, e, in forma de quegli che parlar doveano, venivano davanti dal popolo reguardante e ascoltante il comedo che racontava (Boccaccio 4–6; quoted in Kelly, *Chaucerian Tragedy*, 16 n. 26; Comedians [that is,

poets who composed comedies] call the separate sections of their comedies "scenes," because, when they recited them in the place called the scene in the middle of the theater, each time that they introduced various personages to speak, mimes would come forth from the scene. The mimes would have transformed themselves from the characters whose words and actions the *comedi* had spoken and performed before, and would appear as those who were now supposed to speak; they would come before the people, who were looking on and listening to the comedians speaking the lines.) (Translation Kelly, 16)[5]

Characteristic of Boccaccio's description are the graphic details, derived, no doubt, from some leading glossator of Isidore's text. Kelly points to the eloquent example of Nicholas Trevet, whose *Expositio super tragedias Senece*, written between 1314 and 1317 (*Chaucerian Tragedy*, 17 n. 37), may well be the source of

---

[5] I have made some slight changes in Kelly's translation. Worth bearing in mind is, also, the following excerpt from the *Esposizioni*, in which Boccaccio clarifies what he means by "scena," and proffers further observations concerning the histrionics of the *mimi*:

E queste cotali comedie poi recitavano nella scena, cioè in una piccola casetta, la quale era constituita nel mezzo del teatro, stando d'intorno alla detta scena tutto il popolo, e gli uomini e le femine, della città ad udire. E non gli traeva tanto il disiderio di udire quanto di vedere i giuochi che dalla recitazione del comedo procedevano: li quali erano in questa forma: che una spezie di buffoni, chiamati «mimi», l'uficio de' quali è sapere contrafare gli atti degli uomini, uscivano di quella scena, informati dal comedo, in quegli abiti ch'erano convenienti a quelle persone gli atti delle quali dovevano contrafare, e questi cotali atti, onesti o disonesti che fossero, secondo che il comedo diceva facevano (Boccaccio, *Esposizioni*, 37–38; Quoted in Kelly, *Chaucerian Tragedy*, 16 n. 29; Then they recited these comedies in the scene, that is, in a little house set up in the middle of the theater, around which all the people of the city, both men and women, stood to listen. These people were drawn by the desire not so much to hear as to see the acting that proceeded from the recitation of the author of the comedy. This is the way the play was acted out: some jesters of the type called "mummers," whose task is to know how to mimic human actions, would come out of that scene. These actors were instructed by the author as to what specific actions were appropriate and who the characters were, whose actions they were supposed to imitate. The actors performed said actions, whether decent or indecent, according to the instructions of the author). (Translation mine)
In yet another noteworthy comment, Kelly points out Isidore's influence on Boccaccio's idea of a theater:

In his later works, namely, the *Genealogia* and the commentary on the *Inferno*, Boccaccio gives a basically Isidorian picture of the ancient theater, according to which the role of the poet was not to act but to sing (Boccacio says recite) his poetry while mimes pantomimed the action: "Scelestis compositis fabulis, eas mimis introductis recitabant in scenis" (Having composed wicked fables, they recited them in the scenes, while mimes were brought on). (Translation Kelly, *Chaucerian Tragedy*, 15)

the aforementioned vivid illumination of Urbinas Latinus 355, the fourteenth-century Vatican manuscript.[6] Reflecting on not only Boccaccio's depiction but also the manuscript illustrations allows us to ponder the fulfillment of Isidore's long-lasting contribution.

There are two aspects of Isidore's influence that call for special attention. First, there is the quintessential counterbalance between the authors of the dramatic texts and the *mimi*. Boccaccio and, for that matter, the extant illustrations as well make it quite clear that the *comedi* express their recitation within the precincts of the "piccola casetta," whereas the *mimi*, to paraphrase the bard, "strut and fret their hour" upon the larger area of the stage. The second aspect we are referring to consists of the representation of the "scena" as a locus of darkness. The attribution of gloom harks back to Nicholas Trevet, who in his commentary on Boethius's *De consolatione* states:

> Dicitur a scena greco vocabulo, "umbra"; unde dicebatur scena quasi obumbratio, quia ibi abscondebantur persone cantantes carmina tragica et comica (quoted in Kelly, *Ideas and Forms of Tragedy*, 127; Scene is a Greek word for shade; hence it meant a shadowing, because in it were hidden persons who sang tragic and comic poems). (Kelly's translation)[7]

---

[6] For a precise description of the illumination, see Kelly, *Chaucerian Tragedy*, 18. Giorgio Padoan, in his annotation to the *Esposizioni*, observes that the same notion of the "scena" is found, also, in Trevet's commentary on Seneca's *Thyestes* (see Boccaccio's *Esposizioni*, ed. Padoan, 782 n. 85). Here we may add the *Térence des Ducs* discussed above (p. 148, n. 2).

[7] In order to clarify Trevet's terminology, Kelly takes into account the affinity with the wording of a crucial passage excerpted from William of Conches's own commentary on *De consolatione* (book I, prose I). Conches (ca. 1090–ca. 1155) notes that

> scena enim dicebatur quedam pars theatri qua abscondebantur persone et exibant; unde dicebatur scena, quasi obumbratio. Scena enim est umbra (Quoted in Kelly, *Ideas and Forms of Tragedy*, 71 n. 11; The *scena*, so called, was that section of the theater in which the actors hid and from which they came out. For this reason it was called *scena*, a term suggesting a shadowed area. Indeed, *scena* means shadow). (Translation mine)

Kelly provides the following gloss on the all-important term "persone," at issue in the context of the Isidorian paradigm:

> Unlike Huguccio [da Bologna, mid twelfth century] (one of Trevet's favorite authorities), who has the hiding persons come out and make gestures to the words of a reciter, Trevet identifies the hiding persons with Isidore's singers of tragedy and comedy. And since Isidore clearly identifies these with the poets themselves, perhaps this is Trevet's understanding as well. (Kelly, *Ideas and Forms of Tragedy*, 127)

For a discussion of the dark ambiance in connection with Joan Roís de Corella's *Tragèdia de Caldesa*, see Cocozzella, *Text, Translation, and Critical Interpretation*, 162–66.

If we ponder the interaction inherent in Boccaccio's vision of the *comedi/mimi* equation, we discover a notable coincidence with the dramatic structuring of Moner's *Momería*, a work I have already interpreted (see pp. 110, 120–21). The massive "swan," which, as we have indicated, takes center stage in Moner's mummery, may be seen as Moner's counterpart to the Isidorian dark "scena." By the same token, the six lovers, who come out of the belly of the bird-like structure and then go about their dance routine without uttering a word, remind us of the "persone" evoked by the illustrious Florentine writer: "della scena uscivano i mimi," "venivano davanti dal popolo," "secondo che il comedo diceva facevano." There can be little doubt, then, as to the fundamental design of the theatrical stage and theatricalized action inherent in Isidore's signal texts and in the works of Isidore's interpreters: Huguccio da Bologna, William of Conches, Nicholas Trevet, Giovanni Boccaccio — to name just a few of the literary figures studied by Kelly. It is safe to deduce that in Moner's *Momería* we find unmistakable signs of a primary assimilation of the Isidorian model. Close analysis reveals that, beyond this primary level, Moner's sense of the dramatic holds in store a high degree of elaboration that turns its model into a matrix of superior inventiveness.[8]

As we probe the makeup of *Momería*, we gain an insight into Moner's creativity. It is commensurate to the various adaptations the author manages to bring to bear upon the interaction between the reciter standing within the "scena" or in close proximity to it and the silent performers moving or motioning outside that dark, cheerless place. First and foremost among Moner's adaptations is the transformation of the "scena" into the matrix of a complex dramatics of the dark chamber. The unfolding of the dramatics parallels, in strict correspondence, the evolving of a highly effective dramatic monologue.

---

[8] Cátedra ("Teatro fuera del teatro: tres géneros cortesanos") underscores the significance of Moner's *Momería* within the mainstream of the literary tradition that finds a prominent exponent in Enrique de Villena (1384–1434), distinguished scholar of the Spanish Renaissance. In light of the evidence adduced by Cátedra, it is clear that book 18 of Isidore's *Etymologies* had considerable bearing on the theatricality championed by Villena and, eventually, by Moner. For an overview of Villena's life and works see Gascón Vera, "Enrique de Villena: ¿Castellano o catalán?" and Torres-Alcalá, *Don Enrique de Villena: un mago al dintel del renacimiento.*

XII.
A Religious Theater Newly Fashioned:
Semiotic Functions

The Dramatics of the Soulful Place

A critical moment in the analysis of Moner's *Sepultura d'amor* is the discovery of the multifarious operation by which the author exploits to a full extent the dramatic potential inherent in the Isidorian master plan. To hark back to some basic concepts already discussed, the primordial phenomenon in that operation may be envisaged as a movement of transition from the realm of "psychic space" to that of "soulful place" (see, above, pp. 145–46).[1] Not surprisingly, the phenomenon reminds us of the familiar Isidorian trajectory from the "scena" or the dark chamber to the open stage.

The trajectory may be represented as the straight vertical line in the format of a diagram (see figure 5). The simplicity of the projection, which leads directly to the "soulful place," accrues in complexity as it branches out in three different directions. These are symbolized by the lines A, B, C. A, which assumes a central position, advances to a general, nondescript area. By contrast, the collateral B and C points, respectively, lead to the well-defined perimeters of the pulpit and the altar. As it gradually gains in complexity, that primordial journey of transition is enhanced by a metaphysical dramatization through the functions of the leading allegorical personages: Costumbre represents an unspecified comprehensive spatiality, Experiencia displays the transformative powers of the pulpit, Mancilla puts into action the sanctifying ministry connatural to the altar.

Before delving into the metaphysical allegory adumbrated here, a few words are in order concerning the extent of the change Moner brings about in the Isidorian prototype. What remains unchanged is the role of the protagonist, the auctorial persona, who delivers the monologue mostly as the voice-over emanating from the dark chamber. We are struck, however, by a considerable transformation evidenced in the behavior of Costumbre, Experiencia, and Mancilla

---

[1] For a discussion of these spatial designations, see Cocozzella, "Fra Francesc Moner's Psychic Space / Soulful Place."

—the characters who correspond to the Isidorian mummers (*mimi*). While the *mimi*, as we have pointed out, remain silent, the former—that is, the priestesses of Moner's *Sepultura*—do not. For the sake of specificity, we must not fail to observe that Mancilla's and Costumbre's speeches are kept to a bare minimum. The personage who relies heavily on oratory as a display of virtuosity in verbal expression is, of course, Experiencia.

After this initial observation, we may probe into the metaphysical dynamic that promotes the evolution of the sacramental plot of Moner's *Sepultura*. To come to grips with metaphysical and sacramental functions, we may delve into the interaction of the three priestesses with one another. We realize that each priestess is invested with her own function that comes to bear not only on said interaction but also, more significantly, on the existential bonding of the three foundational texts: namely, the "Epistle," the "Gospel," and the emblematic *canción*. It is the *canción*, we may recall, that figures prominently as the object of the Offertory. It bears reminding ourselves that Moner customizes these texts specifically for the plot of his *Sepultura*.

How, then, does each priestess contribute to the advancement of the plot? Let us begin with Costumbre, who appears center stage as shown in our diagram (figure 5). Costumbre is the archetypal denizen of an uncharted territory of unspecified boundaries. In her privileged purview as the main inhabitant of the soulful place, she may be perceived as the custodian of the aforementioned three basic texts. It is worth noting that, as the embodiment of the most abstract representational level of the allegory, Costumbre is not commissioned with any specific function of her own. Her mere presence serves, nonetheless, as a catalyst with respect to the action of the two significant others. Indeed, by the simple fact that she occupies the crucial locus of centrality, Costumbre coordinates and, thus, facilitates the operation of her two cohorts, each of whom resides in a well-circumscribed field within the allegorical domain.

For purposes of illustration we may imagine a twofold process of relinquishment and appropriation. Costumbre relinquishes two indispensable texts: the "Epistle" and the "Gospel;" Experiencia appropriates them and then elaborates upon them by the homiletic and cathartic operations already discussed (see pp. 61–72). In other words, Experiencia devises her own rough-and-ready method of putting into practice the *via illuminativa* and the *via purgativa* in that order and, by way of that method, she processes the substitute scriptural passages: the Epistle and Gospel readings Moner has made ready for the occasion. What lies ahead as a consequence of the process brought into effect by Experiencia is a chain of transformations and mutations, which may be envisaged in accordance with the following steps:

(1) By virtue of her sermonizing, Experiencia actualizes to a very high degree the dramatic potential inherent in the passages in question. These

are taken as intellective and emotive signifiers in strict adherence to the all-important principles of "letras matizadas del sentido."

(2) Costumbre reappropriates the "Epistle" and the "Gospel," now fully enhanced by Experienicia's intervention, and brings to bear their refurbished textuality upon the *canción* by calling into play the mechanics of superimposition (see, above, pp. 79–83).

(3) Once the superimposition takes effect in the conversion of the *canción* into a life-text, Costumbre transfers to Mancilla that *canción*, which by now has become an icon of an individual's, that is the lover's existence.

(4) Bringing to a climax the *via unitiva* started in part 3 of Experiencia's sermon, Mancilla carries out the ultimate phase of mutation by subjecting the life-text to the ritual of desacralized transubstantiation.

The metaphysical functions just reviewed afford us a new perspective on the Spanish theater of the late Middle Ages. From that perspective, we are able to discern the embryonic strains of an unusual genre of religious drama. Let us turn our attention to this dramatic form, one that beckons close investigation.

Early Traces of Sacramental Theatricality

The collective function of the three foremost allegorical personages and the interaction that prevails among them define the theatricality of Moner's *Sepultura d'amor*. Let us summarize what each personage contributes to the collaborative effort. In her central locus, as shown in the diagram of figure 5, Costumbre stands for the power of integration. Costumbre represents the semiotic field illustrated by the conflation of the human text (*canción*) and its scriptural surrogate (the invented "Epistle" and "Gospel"). Costumbre, in other words, embodies the consciousness of the integral self. Experiencia, by contrast, adopts an analytic approach, one that transforms Costumbre's icon of compact textuality into a kaleidoscopic blossoming of subtextual signifiers. These constitute the inquiry into the nature of love. How can we reconcile the coarseness of the erotic drive with the subliming virtues of *fin'amors*? Do these virtues, in fact, immunize the sincere, if somewhat naïve lover from any flaw or culpability? In the twists and turns of her ratiocination Experiencia strives, but with little success, to come to grips with thorny issues. She does not draw clear and direct answers to the questions we have just posed. Nevertheless, she does draw a sharp distinction between true and false lovers and inveighs against the collusion of the latter with the whimsical and reckless women that respond to their lustful and indecent advances. Experiencia revels in reaping the harvest of the crop she has her way of cultivating: those blossoming signifiers referred to. She loses no time in allowing her righteous indignaticn to ventilate and winnow out slander on the rampage, abuses perpetrated, reputations destroyed. Thus, the misconduct of the wicked is exposed and duly protested. What Experiencia takes to the storehouse is the gathered fruits of the vindication she strenuously endeavors to exact. Consequently, she exalts the suffering of the honorable lover and renders homage to God-the-Truth. Ultimately, what she has left to treasure is "l'ystoria de quyen muryó," the crowning achievement of her laborious efforts. As we have indicated, the "ystoria" (read 'historia) is distilled in that all-important *canción* of the Offertory.

Experiencia's assertion of such moral values as truthfulness, honesty, and loyalty, in both the service of love and the worship of God, gives way to the officiation of a higher order: the order of the super-priest Mancilla. Mancilla's transposition of what is human (Experiencia's full contextualization of Moner's *canción*) into what is divine (the conversion of the processed *canción* into a living testimonial of sanctifying suffering) is patterned after the ritual of the Eucharist, the sacrament par excellence.

We see, then, that by the general allegorical tenor of *Sepultura d'amor* as well as by the plot dynamic that springs forth from the individual roles and collective interaction of the three celebrants, Moner profiles a notion of sacramentality we can readily latch on to. The notion may be described in terms of the salvific powers of the Eucharistic ritual, which stems from the devotional practice (Costumbre) and, desacralized though it is, takes effect through the collaboration between the preacher (Experiencia) and the primary priest (Mancilla). In the final analysis, what Moner profiles is one of the earliest, if not the earliest, manifestations of the sacramental theater in Spanish literature.

What remains to be investigated is to what extent Moner's dramaturgy sheds light on the origins of the *auto sacramental*, that uniquely Spanish literary genre that reached the peak of its development in the creations of Pedro Calderón de la Barca (1600–1681).[2] There is one incontrovertible fact to be taken into account: the action that constitutes the plot of Moner's *Sepultura* takes place inside the church. This fact comes to bear squarely on the issue that lies at the heart of a crucial controversy. On the one side, scholars like Parker and Wardropper maintain that the *auto sacramental* was born as an integral component of the liturgical

---

[2] For the early history of the *auto*, see such studies as those by John J. Allen and Domingo Ynduráin, "Prólogo," in Pedro Calderón de la Barca, *El gran teatro del mundo*, ed. John J. Allen and Domingo Ynduráin (Barcelona: Crítica, 1997), xxlll–lxiv; Ignacio Arellano and J. Enrique Duarte, *El auto sacramental* (Madrid: Ediciones del Laberinto, 2003); Ricardo Arias, *The Spanish Sacramental Plays*. Twayne's World Authors Series 572. (Boston: Twayne Publishers), 1980; Louise Fothergill-Payne, *La alegoría en los autos y farsas anteriores a Calderón* (London: Tamesis, 1977); and Bruce W. Wardropper, *Introducción al teatro religioso del siglo de oro: Evolución del Auto Sacramental antes de Calderón* (Salamanca: Anaya, 1967).

service, carried out, in Parker's words, "en el Santuario como parte del culto y no al aire libre" (not in the open but inside the sanctuary, as a component of the worship ceremony) (quoted in Wardropper, *Introducción al teatro religioso del siglo de oro,* 57).[3] On the opposite side, Flecniakoska and Lázaro Carreter, among others, argue that the *auto* in question evolved from a discrete tradition, independent from the liturgy and kindred ceremonies, conducted either inside or outside the temple.[4]

Evidently, Moner's idea of a religious theater may be cited in support of the position espoused by Parker, Wardropper, and company. There are, however, some noteworthy discrepancies with respect to some specific points adduced by Wardropper. From this critic's argumentation we gather that in the eastern sector of the Peninsula (the *Levante*), especially in cities like Valencia and Barcelona, urban centers famous especially for the nonpareil pageantry of their Corpus Christi processions, the environment could hardly be propitious for the birth of the liturgical auto.[5] It is fair to say that the theatricality of Moner's *Sepultura*

---

[3] In the gestation of the *auto sacramental,* Wardropper perceives a radical difference from the way religious theater developed in the rest of Europe. Taking as exemplary the case of the religious representations in the Cathedral of Seville, Wardropper observes:
El drama litúrgico, pues, salió de la catedral en el siglo XVI, y si se hubiera conformado al modelo europeo, habría producido un ciclo de misterios. Al contrario, produjo autos sacramentales. Tenemos, por lo tanto, que considerar el género sacramental como una forma del drama litúrgico que no conoció las etapas intermedias: a saber, los *cuadros al vivo* y los misterios (*Introducción al teatro religioso del siglo de oro,* 58; [T]he liturgical drama, then, moved out of the cathedral in the sixteenth century and, had it followed the European model, would have produced a cycle of mystery plays. Instead, it produced sacramental plays. Therefore, we must consider the sacramental genre as a form of liturgical drama that did not go through any intermediate phase: namely, the *tableaux vivants* and the mystery plays).

[4] Various theories regarding the origins of the *auto* are discussed in Arias, *The Spanish Sacramental Plays,* 51–55.

[5] Wardropper calls attention to the *tableaux vivants* (*cuadros al vivo,* as he calls them) (58), that were paraded in said processions. It is well to bear in mind the four points that Wardropper brings into focus in the following summary of his presentation:
(1) había, tanto en España como en otros países europeos, una tradición dramática relacionada con la fiesta del Corpus; (2) en el Levante de España la tradición—aliada a la procesión del Corpus—seguía más de cerca la europea que en el resto de España; (3) en Castilla y Andalucía esta tradición no se desarrolló en la procesión, sino en la catedral, de la cual fue expulsada a las plazas; (4) su evolución empezó por ser semejante a la de los tropos medievales, pero se detuvo antes de llegar a la formación de los misterios. De esta situación histórico-cultural brotaron los autos sacramentales, dotados de un fondo litúrgico de que carecían, naturalmente, los dramas del Corpus al norte de los Pirineos (*Introducción al teatro religioso del siglo de oro,* 59; (1) in Spain, as well as in some other European countries, there was a theatrical tradition related to the feast of Corpus Christi; (2) in

would be a star witness in agreement, but only partially, with Wardropper's case. Moner's composition confirms Wardropper's hypothesis concerning the liturgical origins of the *auto* but runs contrary to that critic's deduction that the liturgical *auto* could not have been conceived in Barcelona or any other cultural center in the *Levante*. It takes but a look at Moner's *Sepultura*, produced, after all, in Barcelona, to make us realize that, with all the dazzling pageantry of its processions, that vibrant cultural center of Catalonia could indeed be the birthplace of the *auto sacramental*, just as it was for Moner's prototypical experiment.

All the while, we should be aware that our discussion would not be complete without paying due attention to the sui generis nature of Moner's dramatics. Moner's *misa* is radically different from the *auto sacramental*, which as a genre, shows forth a distinctive doctrinal tenor. Representative of the consensus among the most authoritative critics is Arias's recognition of this feature in Fernán López de Yanguas's *Farsa Sacramental*, in all probability written before 1521, generally regarded as the first documentation of the *auto sacramental*.[6] According to Arias, it is precisely the symptomatic doctrinal tenor, taken as a distinguishing mark of Yanguas's *Farsa*, that attests to "a certain moment [when] the Eucharist became the main subject of the [sacramental] plays" (*The Spanish Sacramental Plays*, 54). In Arias's judgment, there can be little doubt that Yanguas heralds

---

eastern Spain, that tradition—linked to the Corpus Christi procession—followed its European counterpart more closely than it did in the rest of the country; (3) in Castile and Andalusia the tradition in question originated not in the procession but in the cathedral, from which it was evicted to the town square; (4) at its inception, said tradition developed in a way similar to that of any medieval trope but, then, came to a halt right before reaching the period of gestation of the mystery plays. This is the historical-cultural tradition from which the *auto sacramentales* were born. The *autos* were endowed with a liturgical background, which, of course, went missing in the dramatic pieces pertaining to the celebrations of Corpus Christi north of the Pyrenees).

[6] The approximate date is proposed by González Ollé (Arias, *The Spanish Sacramental Plays*, 60), who cogently explains why Yanguas's piece deserves to be considered a genuine *auto sacramental*. Especially instructive in this respect is Arias's following paragraph:

Cotarelo called this piece the first sacramental play. A. A. Parker strongly opposed him on this. Wardropper agrees with Parker giving as a reason the lack of allegory, though "we can find in it, in embryonic form, some of the elements which characterize the Calderonian *auto*." In addition, there is no question that "the symbolism of the [shepherds'] names opens the door to the allegory to come." More recently, González Ollé considers the play a genuine *auto*, not only because it has a eucharistic theme, but because there is in the play a certain type of allegory, for "the central theme is dealt with in a way which is technically very close to allegory." (61)

a new theater, in which "[t]he decisive factor is the presence of the Eucharistic theme in the text of the play as the essential element" (54).[7]

Arias's sharp profile of the nascent *auto sacramental* makes the contrast with Moner's religious drama self-evident. Let us concentrate on the main motif Arias describes in the following passage:

> The structure of the play [Yanguas's *Farsa Sacramental*] is very similar to that of the Nativity plays. The great novelty is the theme and the way it is presented. The Eucharist becomes a synthesis of the history of salvation. (61)

In light of our discussion it is clear that Moner is not interested in the dramatization of an ideological construct per se: the doctrine, that is, of the Eucharist, envisaged as the climax of the history of salvation from the global perspective of the Old and New Testaments combined.[8] Strictly speaking, Moner's dramatization is functional rather than theoretical. It reflects a pragmatic approach to the salutary intervention of the priest vis-à-vis the plight of the individual. It capitalizes, in other words, on the miraculous way the Eucharistic ritual brings about the redemption of the individual who is the auctorial persona. That individual not only has found true love but also has become an exemplary sufferer (a veritable *mártir de amor*) in his wholehearted devotion to God-the-Truth.

In an attempt to classify Moner's theatrical piece, we are well advised to be guided by Arias's assessment of the controversy that surrounded Yanguas's innovative *Farsa*. Arias states:

> The controversy clarifies the fact that the play is a borderline case which naturally presents certain difficulties of classification common to most early manifestations of a new literary genre. (61)

In view of this sensible observation, we will not be surprised, let alone disappointed, that Moner, who lived one or two generations before Yanguas, should not conform to a well-established, clearly defined literary mode. Moner did fully engage his creative imagination to create an *auto sacramental*, composed in his own way, simply because there were no models to follow. He naturally invented a unique, new dramatic form. It follows that Moner's could not be but an embryonic *auto*, endowed as it was with sacramentality. This does not mean, however, that the entire composition into which Moner integrates such an *auto* represents

---

[7] Arias corroborates this comment with the following observation: "The Eucharistic theme has to be an essential part of the play" (54).

[8] Arias provides a useful explanation of how the Eucharist epitomizes nothing less than a Christological fulfillment of all Sacred Scripture. For a concise statement on the significance of the Eucharist according to the Liturgical Office of Corpus, which had profound repercussions on the very essence of the *auto sacramental*, see Arias, 16–20.

a primitive or rudimentary phase of invention and accomplishment. As our study shows, Moner's *Sepultura d'amor*, taken as an organic whole, happens to be a fully-developed, highly-sophisticated play. Accordingly, we would not hesitate to grant Moner due credit for a lasting legacy. In his feat of ingenious creativity we recognize the following points: (1) tracing the transition from ritual to theater; (2) establishing the *cancionero* as a source of dramatic literature; (3) deft handling of the esthetic of parody and desacralization in order to develop a parareligious genre that secularizes the sacred service without doing away with the essential miraculous powers of the liturgy.

CONCLUSION

Retrospective Observations

Our journey of exploration has come to an end. We have traveled through the gloomy ambiance that envelops the Spanish *canción* of the fifteenth century and kindred love-centered Castilian or Catalan composition in prose or in verse. Now it is time to reflect on the outcome of our exploration. There are three areas of investigation that command our attention for the potential of discovery they hold in store. The areas may be identified as (1) dramatics, (2) theatricality, and (3) sacramentality. The dramatics is that of the monologue, the typical, if not exclusive, expression of the immense literary corpus we have referred to. The *cancionero* itself may be considered, on the whole, an expanded monologue. What we have discovered is the multifarious function of the monologue as the instrument of introspection par excellence. Deeply absorbed in that introspection is the afflicted lover, the woebegone sufferer or veritable *mártir de amor* we have found incarnated, more often than not, in the auctorial persona. It is well, now, to ponder the various psychic modes that a monologue's introspection allows us to probe: the spatiality of innerness, the "hall of mirrors of passions," the effect of the "split or splintered self," the realm of immanence, the overall ambiance of darkness, the compulsive claim to sincerity and truthfulness, the esthetics of the unesthetic *forma cetrina*. The list is far from complete.

From dramatics we proceed to theatricality. In this second phase of our study, we have focused on a literary mode that deviates radically from the conventional notion of a theatrical representation. In effect, we have come upon a kind of stage-worthy composition that stems not, as convention would have it, from a dialogue but from a monologue: precisely the kind of monologue that has become the cynosure of our analytic quest. It bears pointing out that works like Corella's *Tragèdia* and Moner's *Momería* document, the former in Valencian-Catalan, the latter in Castilian, a very early manifestation of the lover's mournful monologue projected onto an actual *mise en scène*. From Jones, Kelly, and Marshall we have learned that the spectacle is the outcome of an age-old tradition that harks back to some seminal definitions proffered by none other than Isidore of Seville, the renowned seventh-century prelate and etymologist.

Sacramentality, the third area in our list, showcases the thorny issues of religious parody. In the wake of Hutcheon's innovative theories, we have pursued a fresh interpretation of a few enigmatic poems, by which representative *cancionero* authors work out ingenious and bold versions of devotional literature, scriptural passages, and, most intriguing of all, the Eucharistic liturgy pertaining to the Mass. Hutcheon's suggestive ideas have proven to be particularly revealing especially when brought to focus upon a close study of Francesc Moner's *misa de amores*, one of the most complex specimens of its kind.

It is useful to review the insights yielded by what may be considered a novel approach to Moner's masterpiece and to the type of religious parody it eminently represents. In light of our research, evidence may be adduced as to the general orientation of those *cancionero* poets that would allow their creative spirit to mirror the pattern of devotional practices and liturgical ceremonies. What we have discovered is that, in this mirroring process, the pattern is profoundly transmuted but not violated in any shape or form. In other words, the parodists put into effect a categorical departure from the realm of the sacred with the intent to demarcate a clear distance between the ritual proper and the artistic modality involved in playacting in the best sense of the term. In the end, these fine authors direct their efforts toward replacing the ritual with its theatrical counterpart.

We now realize that not all these authors should be expected to be equally successful, if successful at all, in attaining the proper distancing they aim at. It is safe to say that most, if not all of them, are not particularly adept at "playing around" with extremely sensitive issues: those that have to do with the doctrinal tenets and theological verities that mold the beliefs to which the community of the faithful at large staunchly adheres. In fact, as pointed out, practically all these parodists meet with the wrath of many generations of scandalized readers.

To our knowledge, Moner is the only parodist among the *cancionero* poets who with consummate skill manages to theatricalize to a full extent the issues crystallized in the core notion of sacramentality. He wins the day by sagaciously choosing the path of what we propose to call "desacralization." Ultimately, that path leads to a theatrical effect of a sui generis mutation that preserves the formalism but changes the substance of the ritual. The formalism is evident in the function with which Moner invests the passages that correspond to the Epistle, the Gospel, and the Offertory in his *misa*. Of course, we need to remind ourselves all along that the three passages constitute, not an actual performance of the ritual, but an analogous rendition of it. Thus the very operation of the analogy betokens the radical change we have been referring to. We observe, then, that for the recitation or chanting of two of those three passages—the Epistle and the Gospel—Moner invents his own text for the occasion. By the same token, for the Offertory the author produces an object (the emblematic *canción*) to replace the "species" (the bread and wine), a sine qua non for the celebration of the traditional Mass.

Our discussion has brought us full circle to the definition of sacramental theater, the unusual type of representation born of Moner's ingenious handling of the parody of the Mass. Now we can see that Moner's ingenious creativity stems from the conflation of two main factors: on the one hand, the Isidorian paradigm consisting of the recitation of a monologue, complemented by a panto-mime cast for multiple personages; on the other, the performance of a desacral-ized ritual displayed in a full-blown allegorical spectacle.

In conclusion, we may declare confidently that there is new light to be shed on the embryonic phase in the development of Castilian and Catalan theater. In his often quoted book referred to already, López Morales skeptically observes, though in all sincerity and goodwill, "[e]l lector se preguntará con razón qué tiene que ver con el drama esta especie de *bal masqué* cortesano que fue el momo, donde a lo sumo algún galán recitaba unas coplas a su dama" (71; in a show of mummers—the courtly masked ball of sorts that it was—one courtier or another would recite, at best, a few verses to his lady. Readers will ask themselves with good reason: What does this show have to do with dramatic performance?). Armed with some fresh information and enlightened by insights gained through a protracted reflection of our own, we trust we have provided an appropriate response to López Morales's query.

Toward Further Research on the Performable Monologue

An extensive meditation on Moner's production in general and *misa* in particu-lar opens up new perspectives on the Spanish theater of the late Middle Ages (especially of the fifteenth century). By shedding considerable light on Moner's own perspective on theatricality, the present monograph posits the possibility of a merger of two traditions hitherto deemed irreconcilable: one, transmitted through the mediacy of Isidore of Seville, stemming from classical Roman comedy (Ter-ence, Plautus) or tragedy (Seneca) and exhibiting throughout the Middle Ages var-ious mutations, analyzed by scholars like Grismer, Jones, Kelly, Marshall, Stern, Webber; the other, born of the liturgy as illustrated in its full development in stud-ies by Cátedra, Hardison, Harris, Surtz. Worthy of special attention is Enders's delving into the origins of medieval theater. This critic takes as the starting point of her cogent argumentation the well-established practice of the legal disputation or, to use her own terms, "the disputational conflict of forensic rhetoric" (*Rhetoric and the Origins of Medieval Drama*, 8). She then posits the theory of an interac-tion between two kinds of theatrical evolution: one parallels the rhetorical tradi-tion stemming from the pseudo-Ciceronian *Ad Herennium* and the Ciceronian *De inventione*; the other originates from the Christian liturgy and develops within the parameters of the ritual. She focuses on a process, which she calls "*letteraturizza-zione*" or "aestheticization" (5).[1]

As we have indicated, Moner's *Momería* evinces the "Isidorian paradigm," the origins of which, as Stern demonstrates (*The Medieval Theater in Castile*, 53–70), may be traced back to classical, that is, Roman, theater.[2] The signs of the aforementioned merger begin to come to light at the point at which such factors of Isidorian vintage as the dark chamber and the interaction between the reciter and the mimes become adapted to the ritualistic infrastructure of the *misa de amores*. That adaptation, in turn, makes for the hybrid nature of Moner's stage-worthy esthetic, which plays out through the workings of parody translated into a theatrical mode.

The commentary on the genetic link perceptible between March's Poem 105 and Moner's *Obra en metro* (see above, pp. xxxii–xxxiii, 47–54) broaches the discussion on the projection of both March's and Moner's dramatic monologue onto the realm of modernity. Purificación Ribes Traver illustrates this projection in the trajectory she is able to trace between March's poem and "Holy Sonnet 14"[3] by the English "metaphysical poet," John Donne (1572–1631). Ribes Traver

---

[1] Jody Enders (*Rhetoric and the Origins of Medieval Drama* [Ithaca, NY: Cornell University Press, 1992]) summarizes her theory as follows:

> A revised perception of the performance of conflictual discourse suggests a single performance continuum encompassing both law and drama. Such a recasting is intended neither to be all-inclusive nor to challenge the notion that medieval drama "originated" in the pantomime tradition or in the Christian liturgy. Rather it expands those theories to suggest that the delivery of agonistic, forensic discourse was also the site of noteworthy fusion of law, play, rhetoric, ritual, and poetics in early Occidental culture. (8)

[2] Enders focuses on book 18 of the *Etymologies* and provides an illuminating account of Isidore's insights into the primordial conflict (*agon*) that attests to the permanence of the Graeco-Roman legacy: the commingling of the various constituents—"combat, law, disputation, spectacle, sport, and play" (84)—that came to bear on the emergence of the medieval theater. Of particular interest is Enders's precise summary of that all-important Isidorian source:

> There Isidore conflates historically (and, of course, etymologically) warfare, law, judgment, drama, sport, and spectacle, articulating a complex relationship shared by sixty-nine fields as seemingly diverse as wars and ball playing. As his attention shifts almost imperceptibly from warfare (1–14) to forensic rhetoric (15) to spectacle (16) to sport (17–26) to the circus (27–41) to the theater (42–51) to the amphitheater (52–69), his exposition is rendered coherent by a focus on the theatrical space in which each combat ritual is played out. (78)

[3] *Holy Sonnets, 10* in Robbins's recent edition (see the bibliography below).

delves into the coincidence she detects in the works of the two authors in terms of the esthetics of subjectivity that has been analyzed in my monograph.[4]

In deference to March's modernity, it would not be farfetched to expand the range of affinities that Poem 105 exhibits with Donne's sonnet to encompass, as well, such icons of unsettling dissonance and alienation as the poem "No worst, there is none" by Gerard Manley Hopkins (1844–89). To be sure, despite the esthetic of gloom and despondency the two poets share, the March-Hopkins connection, though certainly valid for a comparative study, does not rest on any historical documentation. Strictly on the basis of circumstantial evidence, well-warranted is, on the other hand, the supposition of a link between Ausiàs March and Salvador Espriu (1913–1985), doubtless one of the principal Catalan writers of the twentieth century. Espriu, who showed a predilection for the classics in his native language, read March with special care and derived from March the essential outlook on the tragic vision (Cocozzella, "Aspectes de la persona tràgica en Salvador Espriu," especially 87–88). Espriu vies with March in internalizing the tragic vision in a monologue ("monòleg interior")[5] incarnated in the auctorial persona, an individual of flesh and blood, called Salom de Sinera (Shalom of Sinera). The modernity of Ausiàs March's monologue reaches a high point in the enhancement of Salom's tragic vision as anatomized in Josep Maria Castellet's landmark study on Esprius's production (*Iniciación a la poesía de Salvador Espriu*). In Salom's primordial existential monologue, ultimately inspired by Ausiàs March, we contemplate, as Castellet demonstrates, the integration of the reminiscences from miscellaneous sources, such as the *Book of Job*, the exponents of Jewish mysticism, and the "negative" theologies of Meister Eckehart and Nicholas Cusanus (*Iniciación a la poesía de Salvador Espriu*, 143–84).[6]

---

[4] Tucker Brooke ("The Renaissance," in *A Literary History of England*, ed. Albert C. Baugh (New York: Appleton, 1948] 313–696) underscores in Donne's entire collection of sonnets the traits for which Ribes Traver finds unmistakable affinities in March's magnificent verses. Donne's sonnets, Brooke notes, "show little piety and are remarkably egocentric, dealing mainly with Donne's two phobias: his sense of personal unworthiness and the terrors of Judgment Day" (635). This goes to show that March can foreshadow, across cultural and temporal boundaries, the poetics conceived in strife-ridden religion and hammered out in turbulent language by a kindred spirit.

[5] Espriu himself applies the term to one of his earliest works (*El Dr. Rip* [1931]), which is, in fact, a dramatic monologue (Cocozzella, "Aspectes de la persona tràgica en Salvador Espriu," 75–77).

[6] Harris and Sirera propose suggestive perspectives on the modernity of Spanish theater of the late Middle Ages and early Renaissance. Harris stresses the highly innovative use of the expository narrator in the *Farsa del juego de cañas espirituales* by Diego Sánchez de Badajoz (died in 1549). Especially instructive are his concluding remarks:

> The comparison, drawn by some scholars, between Sánchez's inventive use of the shepherd narrator and Brecht's deliberate cultivation of the *Verfremdungseffekt* in the mid-twentieth century also helps modern readers to avoid the mistake of

In sum, the study of Moner's *Sepultura* and *Momería* brings to our attention a number of issues. Prominent among these are: the foreshadowing of modernity, the conflation of religious and secular love, the phenomenology of desacralization, the full circle of parody. Such issues go hand in hand with the gestation of an unconventional type of theater in Barcelona and Valencia at the dawn of the Renaissance. I view my monograph as a contribution to laying the groundwork for the exploration of the various aspects of this unconventionality.

The aspect that immediately strikes our interest is the variable form of the overall dramatic composition. This reflects the protean nature of the monologue, flexible in structure and broad enough in scope to integrate a wide range of components. A sense of modular adaptability governs the design of a multifarious assemblage. In dealing with works like Roís de Corella's *Tragèdia de Caldesa*, Escrivá's *Querella*, Moner's *Momería, Sepultura d'amor*, and *La noche*, we have been already familiarized with the components that perform the function of structural modules. A representative sample of these may be found in the following list: diffuse lamentations and specific complaints, regular dialogue and formal debate, the descriptive narrative, choreographic interpolations (*carole* or charivari), the sermon or philosophical disquisition, sections of the Mass or portions of the books of hours, processional chants or hymns, scriptural readings, the misogynistic tirade, emblematic descriptions (*letras, invenciones, motes*, and the like).

It takes the imagination of the author to mold the modules into an original artistic creation. In Corella's *Tragèdia*, for instance, the solipsistic plaintive speech of the lover is pitted against the speechless behavior of the transgressive ladylove. In Escrivá's *Querella*, the blend of lamentations, dialogue, and debate produces a sense of enhanced awareness of the lover's chronic state of melancholy. Of course, similar techniques are operative in Moner's literary production. In *Momería*, we witness the interaction between the collective and individ-

---

regarding the expository narrator as necessarily 'primitive' theatrical role.. . . [T]he more recent theatrical experiments of directors as different as Brecht and Peter Brook.. .have radically expanded ideas of what is both permissible and possible in the theatre. ("Puppets, Minstrels, Kings, and Shepherds: Expositor Narrators in the Early Spanish Theatre," 160)

Sirera, on his part, refers to the "planteamientos escénicos que hoy nos parecen plenamente actuales pero que hunden sus raíces en los siglos anteriores" (techniques of a mise en scène that to us appears one hundred per cent of our day and age, although its origins hark back many centuries ago) ("El *Cancionero General*, entre nosotros," 629). To illustrate his point, he adduces the exemplary *Angels in America* by Tony Kushner: "auténtica *danza de la muerte* sobre los efectos devastadores del sida en los años ochenta y en la que no falta, como final, la aparición de una *nube medieval* con el ángel anunciador del nuevo apocalipsis" (a veritable *dance of death*, dramatizing the devastating effects of AIDS in the 1980s —a spectacle complete with a "medieval cloud" in the final scene, in which an angel appears and announces a new Apocalypse) ("El *Cancionero General*, entre nosotros," 629).

ual impersonation of the afflicted lover. In *Sepultura d'amor*, the amalgamation reaches a high level of complexity as it illustrates a distinctive transubstantiation: the transmutation of the lover into a Christ-like figure. The ingenious intertwining of various components into a well-structured plot characterizes not only the *Sepultura* but also *La noche*. In the latter, such stock-in-trade building blocks as the narrative and the sermon, debates and laments, depictions of iconic *invenciones* (that is, *letras* and *divisas*), the staging of allegorical representations, and even a firsthand involvement with a disturbing charivari are adapted to a paradoxical coordination of movements: the progress (rise) or regress (fall) in a human being's primordial drive toward communion with the Creator.

In respect of the mise en scène, each of the compositions I have just mentioned, authored, respectively, by Corella, Escrivá, and Moner, is suited to the type of spectacle described by Sirera in his excellent review of present-day adaptations of medieval texts (narratives, poems, sermons, treatises) to a representation on stage ("El *Cancionero General*, entre nosotros"). Sirera focuses on some memorable montages that Ana Zamora fashioned out of Christological motifs borrowed from medieval texts[7] and he himself undertook by culling passages representative of various genres in Castilian and Catalan-Valencian literature of the fifteenth and sixteenth century.[8] In his study Sirera is concerned mainly with theatrical representations created out of a collection of miscellaneous texts. Among the "principios constructivos" (constructive principles) he identifies, there is one that generates a type of montage he describes as follows:

> Dramaturgia entendida como un *proceso de montage* de materiales diversos y heterogéneos (con caracteres literarios o no), enlazados bien con analogías temáticas o de otro tipo ("El *Cancionero General*, entre nosotros" 628; A dramaturgy understood as a process of integrating into a montage various heterogeneous ingredients. Whether or not they are of a literary nature, these ingredients are intertwined by virtue of an analogy of motifs or of any other kind).

At the same time, he does not dispute the convenience of applying said "principios" to "la teatralidad inherente a una parte de la poesía del *Cancionero General*" (the theatricality inherent in a good portion of the poetry of the *Cancionero General*) ("El *Cancionero General*, entre nosotros," 628). In the final analysis, he does not overlook the feasibility of transforming said principles into strategies to

---

[7] Specifically mentioned and commented upon are Ana Zamora's *El auto de los Reyes Magos* and *Misterio del Cristo de los gascones* (Sirera, "El *Cancionero General*, entre nosotros," 626–27).

[8] The description pertains to the play entitled *Per Sant Lluc* (premiered in 2007). Sirera makes reference to his notable contribution not only as a playwright but also as a director and scholar deeply committed to the promotion of medieval theater ("El *Cancionero General*, entre nosotros," 628 n. 26).

be applied to Escrivá's masterpiece. He asks, "¿Es posible plantear estas estrate-gias en una obra tan compleja como la *Quexa* del Comendador Escrivá?" (Is it possible to deploy these strategies in the case of a work as complex as Escrivá's *Quexa*?) And the immediate answer is a resounding "Por supuesto" (of course) ("El *Cancionero General*, entre nosotros," 629). The query followed by such an unhesitating reply constitutes a firm endorsement of not only the montages staged by Zamora and cohorts but also that emblematic "obra tan compleja." Of course, the unmistakable reference to Escrivá's *Quexa* applies, as well, to kindred pieces that have been identified (Moner's *Momería*, *Sepultura*, and *La noche*, for example), and to those still to be discovered.[9]

The upshot of my study is to enhance our awareness of the distinction already drawn by Sirera between two theatrical modes: one illustrated by the spectacle aptly described as a complex montage of heterogeneous components; the other, just as complex, inspired by, rather than derived from, miscellaneous sources and ultimately conceived as an independent entity, born of the creativity of a single author. My intention is to make accessible to the reader—especially the English-speaking reader—a number of specific theatrical pieces, the genre of which happens to be nonspecific. I have in mind plays of a fully-developed plot and well-rounded structure. Though precisely defined as compositional units, these masterworks have been overlooked or neglected largely because they do not conform to the profile of any of the well-established dramatic genres. I am grati-fied that, in the wake of my 1991 edition of Moner's *Obras castellana*, *Momería* has gained due recognition as a legitimate specimen of the Spanish theater of the fifteenth century. It appears in *Teatro castellano de la edad media*, edited by Ron-ald E. Surtz (pp. 145–49) and in *Teatro medieval*, edited by Miguel Ángel Pérez Priego (pp. 265–69) and receives honorable mention in two of Stern's landmark publications ("The Medieval Theater: Between *Scriptura* and *Theatrica*," 125; and *The Medieval Theater in Castile*, 177).[10] In the hope that this beginning would augur some happy returns, I have devoted a recent publication (*Text, Translation,*

---

[9] As Severin points out, the aforementioned *Sepultura de Macías* (see p. 12, n. 22 above) adduces three entities (the poet, the tomb, and the dead Macías), treated as verita-ble dramatis personae engaged in a dialogue with one another. After comparing the San Pedro poem with Guevara's homonymous composition (see my description on p. 13, n. 23 above), Severin underscores the theatricality of the former piece: "*Sepultura de Macías* rep-resents an advance over the two-person debate, and another step toward the early theatre. Both of these poems could have been given as court recitation. Such a recitation of San Pedro's . . . poem invites either a multiplicity of actors or a multiplicity of voices spoken by one person (as recommended by Alonso de Proaza in his prefatory verses to *Celestina*)." Severin, "The *Sepultura de Macías* by San Pedro—But Which San Pedro?" in *Medieval and Renaissance Spain and Portugal*, ed. Martha E. Schaffer and Antonio Cortijo Ocaña (Woodbridge, UK: Tamesis, 2006), 307.

[10] Previous to my edition of 1991, Álvarez Pellitero had already included Moner's *Momería* in her anthology (see *Teatro medieval*, pp. 245–49). For the pertinent commen-

and Critical Interpretation of Joan Roís de Corella's Tragèdia de Caldesa) to a full-fledged study of a notable case in point: Corella's *Tragèdia de Caldesa*, hitherto unrecognized as a theatrical piece. I have argued in favor of a timely appreciation of Corella's careful elaboration of an embryonic (hence, unconventional and unclassifiable) rendition of the tragic mode, so prominently advertised in the very title of Corella's tour de force. In much the same vein I now advocate considering Moner's *Sepultura* as concrete evidence of a genre in the making: that of the *auto sacramental*. Also, in a study in progress I propose Moner's *La noche* as a thoroughly scripted theatrical plot with nondescript generic form.

My research, then, leads me to the conclusion that a scouring of such a vast body of literature as that of the *cancioneros* may well lead to the discovery of compositions that are fully theatrical even though there is no ready-made classification for them. With the prospect of this discovery in mind, we should not forget that a theatricality analogous to that of the *cancioneros* is operative in other literary monuments, such as Juan Ruiz's *Libro de buen amor* and Alfonso Martínez de Toledo's *Arcipreste de Talavera* (Gerli, "El silencio en el *Libro de buen amor*"; Giles, "Hanging Bells on the Cat: Charivari and the Theatrics of the *Arcipreste de Talavera o Corbacho*"). We have come to realize that the "unconventional theater" that all along has appeared generically amorphous to us, betokens, after all, its own morphology: that of the flexible and expansive monologue. As I have indicated, in our approach to this new kind of theater, we may rely on the principle of the "modular assemblage," which brings to mind, metaphorically speaking, the layout of an ingenious collage. This novel approach may well change the panorama of the history of the Spanish theater of the fifteenth century.

---

taries, see Álvarez Pellitero, Introducción general, pp. 49–51; Pérez Priego, Introducción, pp. 31–38; Surtz, Estudio preliminar, pp. 47–48.

Appendices

Sepultura d'amor[1]

[PREAMBULO][2]

1   —Señora, por que sepáys
vuestras palabras pesadas
    qué han podido,
es menester que leáys
estas letras matizadas[3]   5
    del sentido;
que con ellas acabáys.
Y pues la cosa va ansí,
que ya m'avéys consumido
    sin porqué,   10
sól'os demando este sí:
que a los otros que an servido,
    por mercé
no los tratéys como a mí.

2   De los otros haved cura,   15
que de mí ya es todo hecho,
    pues hezistes.
Un mal con otro mesura,
pero darlo en tal derecho
    como distes,   20
¡sobr'el negro no ay tintura!

---

[1] For the basic information regarding the text and translation of *Sepultura* and *Momería*, see pp. xliv–xlvi above.

[2] The subtitles included here between brackets are my own addition. For the English version of these items, see my translation on pp. 197–208 below.

[3] For an explication of "letras matizadas" and "forma cetrina" (v. 36), the other all-important iconic phrase in Moner's discourse, see pp. xxii–xxvi, 37–41 above.

Por ende, quered mirar:
no tiréys a desconcierto
   vuestra espada,
que pensaréys no toquar,   25
quando avréys un hombre muerto,
   por nonada,
qual no podréys reparar.

3   Palabras, todas metzina,[4]
trahen de vos, por mensaje   30
   d'enemigo,
   una nueva repentina.
Dizen en vuestro lenguage
   lo que digo
en esta forma cetrina: 35
"¡Ea, Moner, despertad!
¡Otra vela es ja venida!
   ¿Qué hazéys?,
que la ley de humanidad
por mí hos demanda la vida.   40
   Le devéys,
assí que presto pagad."—

4   Respondíle sin dudar:
—Visto de vuestro esgremir
   me venía   45
(Pues que le plaze matar,
a mí me plaze morir.
   Todavía,
no devyera assí passar
el ruydo con las nuezes.)—   50
Respondió de tal quilate
   que he provado:
—Dan los xaques tantas vezes,
qu'a la postre vyene'l mate.
   De qu'es dado,   55
por otro iuego te avezes.—

5   —Vuestra plática y manera
me hyryó con poco tyento
   d'una injuria:

---

[4] *Metzina* is the common Catalan word for "poison."

tan atendida vandera,   60
que, sin más alargamyento,
 de gran furia,
me dio muerte lastimera.
Assí que no speréys más
desconcyerto ny servicio 65
 de mi parte.
Vuestra guerra me dio paz
por merced y beneficio,
 de tal arte,
que n'os iré más detrás.   70

[EL ENTIERRO]

6 Mas, porqu'es mucha razón
que se suene de la vida
 bien gastada,
embío's missa, y sermón,
y sepultura complida,   75
 celebrada
en vuestra condenación. —
En un campo de crueza
mi cuerpo muerto ha caýdo
 de través.   80
Vino por él Gentileza,
púsolo encima estendido
 d'un pavés
que l'enprestó la Simpleza.

7 Levólo en una capilla 85
que con fuego es consagrada
 d'afición.
Salió de dentro Manzilla
tras su muy byen ordenada
 processión   90
y cantava a boz altilla:
— Ven, cuerpo, que no bivías,
ny poder morir devyeras
 por exemplo.
Ven entra[5] querellas mías, 95

---

[5] Read "entre." The confusion "entra" / "entre" is caused by the influence of Catalan phonetics.

que pues amaste a de veras,
   este templo
con dolor haz alegrías.

8   ¡Ven, cuerpo sin alma bivo!
     Tu vida fueme sin pausa   100
        muy plañida.
     ¡Quánto el dolor es esquivo
     de ver tu muerte sin causa
        padecida
     por tan amargo motivo!—   105
     Estonces la Gentileza,
     traýdo el cuerpo pesado,
        descargóle.
     La Manzilla, de cortesa,
     descubrió el gesto finado,   110
        y besóle
     sin espanto ny fereza.

9   Manzilla llorava quanto
     quyen le dyo muerte s'alegra,
        si lo sabe,   115
     diziendo con gran quebranto:
     —O hermosura tan negra,
        ¿dónde cabe
     crueza que dure tanto?—
     Mientra qu'el cuerpo llorava   120
     viole en la boca un papel
        poco sano.
     Tomólo por ver qué hablava.
     Lo que havía scrito en él,
        de su mano,   125
     en esta forma sonava:

10   "Con todo, muerte, me pesas,
     que si tal vida durara,
     major culpa me matara."[6]

---

[6] The lover (Moner's persona) expresses regret that his death has not come sooner. His statement suggests that a longer life would have exposed him to more reprehensible culpability and, eventually, to a more painful and lamentable death. The term *culpa* here is full of irony: it reflects the ladylove's jaundiced appraisal of the unimpeachable conduct of her faithful suitor.

11   Gentileza no esperó   130
cerimonias, visto el uso
    que decoro,[7]
sino qu'el cuerpo tomó
y en la yglesia lo puso
    entr'el coro   135
y el altar, do lo dexó.
Las letras fueron leýdas;
la Manzilla, enmudescida
    de pesar,
con ambas manos asidas,   140
hizo una tumba a medida,
    byen labrar,
d'estas letras esculpidas:

12   "Quyen hizo trist'el morir
    d'este hombre   145
no se acuerda de su nombre."

13   La tumba puesta a dos passos
do l'Amistad se enterró
    mucho ha,
el cuerpo tomó en los braços   150

---

[7] The hermetic passage, "visto l'uso / que decoro," defies interpretation. That notwithstanding, it is helpful to bear in mind some significant hints. The semantic field of *uso* is related to that of *costumbre* (allegorized as one of the main characters in Moner's *misa*): the reference would be to the customary or ritualistic actions as featured in the ordinary of the Mass. *Decoro*, the second pivotal term, betokens the voice of the first-person speaker, here in the usual role of narrator or expositor. Pertinent to this context is the meaning of "recitar de memoria" (to recite by heart), which González Cuenca registers for *decorar* in the *Cancionero General* (see *Glosario*, 187). It is fair to say that Moner's *agudeza* (ingeniousness) stretches beyond the confines of the dictionary definition. Arguably, Moner's *decoro* is reminiscent of the French *de coeur* as in *prière de coeur* (prayer of the heart) in the parlance of fifteenth-century devotional literature (Saenger, 145). For all intents and purposes, Moner converts the French phrase into a verb: "I *de-coeur*." Saenger specifies that "for writers of the fifteenth century, prayer of the heart meant that the act of praying transpired within the mind of the person praying" ("Books of Hours and the Reading Habits of the Later Middle Ages," 145). We would hasten to add, however, that Moner's adherence to the "letras matizadas del sentido" implies, true to form, not only mental meditation but also emotive display in order to do justice to the presence of *de coeur* in *decoro*. According to Saenger, open to discussion is the issue of whether the *prière de coeur* entails oral delivery either aloud or *sotto voce* (145). Needless to say, Moner's assertion in the narrator's voice ("decoro") leaves no doubt as to the orality of the performance.

y de dentro l'enterró,
   dond'está
libre de más embaraços.
En la cubyerta, al un lado,
puso esculpyda la cruz   155
   que confyesso;
en el otro, está labrado
una muy grande avestruz,
   do el pescueço
va de estas letras sembrado:[8]   160

14   "Pyedras y ponçoñas trago,
       y a las vezes
    me matan muy pocas nuezes."[9]

---

[8] The ostrich may be taken as a symbol of the fortitude of the exemplary lover personified in Moner. In Juan de Borja's *Empresas morales* (Prague: Nigrim, 1581), we find the following explication for the emblem of the ostrich:

Los hombres esforçados y valerosos no solamente se saben aprouechar de su virtud en los buenos y prosperos succesos, pero aun de los muy grandes trabajos y aduersidades sacan muy grande vtilidad y prouecho.... Lo que se significa en esta empresa del Auestruz con el hierro en la boca, y la letra, SIC NVTRIVNTVR FORTES, que quiere decir, ASSI SE SVSTENTAN LOS FVERTES. (See: Henkel and Schöne, col. 806; Daring and brave men not only rely on their virtue in good and propitious circumstances but also derive advantage and benefit from arduous deeds in times of adversity.... All this is symbolized by this image of the ostrich with a piece of iron in its mouth and by the inscription *Sic nutriuntur fortes*, which means *Thus the strong get their nourishment*.' [Translation mine]).

[9] In addition to its ordinary meaning, this term may refer to the "nuez de ballesta, donde prende la cuerda y se encaja el virote, por la semejanza de la nuez" (the *nut* of the crossbow, where the cord is hitched and the dart is engaged: due to the similarity with a nut) (Covarrubias, "Tesoro de la lengua castellana o española según la impresión de 1611...," 832). Covarrubias's definition allows us to discern a twofold metaphor at the heart of Moner's enigmatic *letra*: one concrete object (the "nut" of the crossbow) implies the symbolic correlative (the dart itself) that brings about the deadly outcome of the *batalla de amor*.

[COMIENZA LA MISA: ORACIONES PRELIMINARES]

15 La yglesia llena de lumbre,
las campanas a gran pryssa,   165
  son salidas
Esperiencia y la Costumbre
y Manzilla, por la missa
  ya vestidas,
con gestos de manssedumbre. 170
Y todas tres a la par
en ell altar de Verdad
  pobrezico,
escomiençan confessar
a la Verdad l'amistad,   175
  y baxico,
en esta forma rezar:

16 —A ti, Verdad, nuestro dýa,
conorte de nuestro daño,
  confessamos   180
qu'eres nuestra buena guýa;
renegamos del engaño
  que tomamos
de quyen tus vías desvýa.
Al que sin fingir sospira, 185
no suffras que tanto pene
  su hoguera.
Al que s'arma de mentira,
tu justicia le condene
  de manera   190
que ayan temor de tu ira.—

17 La confessión acabada,
luego por réquiem Manzilla
  començó:
—O Verdad, nuestra abogada, 195
no le falte honrrada silla,
  pues bivió
en tu fe santa alabada;
tu lumbre alumbre su fama,
y tu bondad favorezca 200
  su querella;

a quyen tal brasa derrama,
haz, Señora, que padesca
        dentro en ella
y, d'allý, venga en la llama. —   205

18   Por kyryeleysón, tras esto,
        dixo Manzilla este verso
                lastimero:
        —D'amor es muerto más presto
        quyen tuvo maior esfuerço   210
                de primero
        que quantos salen del puesto.
        La muerte d'éste repara
        la querella verdadera
                del qu'es fiel;   215
        pero, si no le matara,
        su vida mejor no fuera
                ca por él
        nuestra secta s'ensanchara. —

19   D'esta triste missa seca   220
        fue, tras esto, la oratión
                d'este modo:
        —Verdad, aquel que te pecca
        tú le das por punición,
                sobre todo,   225
        el purgatorio d'Erbequa.[10]
        Mas a quyen anduvo claro,
        donde saben conosçer
                tal semblante,
        ya l'a costado por caro,   230
        pues la vida fue a perder;
                el restante,
        Señora, tenga reparo. —

---

[10] The name "Arbeca" (the exact equivalent of "Erbequa" in Catalan phonetics) is that of a small municipality in the province of Lleida. The Catalan "Arbeca," and the Castilian "Babia" are signal words in popular idioms derisive of someone's absentmindedness. Compare "Vens d'Arbeca!" (see *DCVB*) and "Estás en Babia!" with the English "You must be dreaming!" Moner's phrase has all the makings of a tongue-in-cheek designation of a place in fantasy land: a utopian Purgatory.

[LA EPISTOLA, EL EVANGELIO Y EL OFERTORIO]

20   La Costumbre fue a cantar
         la epístola, boz al cielo.   235
            Entonó:
        —Las que presumen çevar[11]
         guárdense bien dell anzuelo,
            que, si no,
         podráse alguno vengar;   240
         ca no deven ser soffridas
         que sin causa desconbidan
            por antojo.
         Algunas serán medidas
         de la medida que myden   245
            y de enojo,
         tan bien tarde, arrepentidas.—

21   Ell evangelio fue tal
         de la Speriencia entonado
            por solfá: 250
        —Quyen ama d'amor leal
         a mujer que no ha provado
            bivyrá
         toda su vida con mal.
         Y la qu'es más singular,   255

---

[11] Here and on numerous other occasions Moner uses çevar ('to catch with bait') in reference to those ill-intentioned women bent on employing their charms in order to seduce their naïve and misguided suitors. For the list of specific documentation of this acceptation of çevar, see note on v. 237 of *Sepultura d'amor* in *2 OC*, 167–68. For further discussion on the eroticized "cevar," see Cocozzella, *1 Introducción* 126–27. González Cuenca registers "cevarse" as the only occurrence of that verb in the entire *Cancionero general* (See González Cuenca, "Glosario" 159). He refers to the verse "del que del aire se ceva" ('of the one that feeds on air') included in Pedro de Cartagena's incisive response to an "invención" contributed by Don Juan Enríquez to the special section dedicated precisely to "invenciones y letras de justadores" within that famous anthology (See *Cancionero general* 2: 575, 580). "Cevar" appears in various conjugated forms eight times in Moner's Castilian poems (See Cocozzella, "Glosario" 207). Cartagena's aforementioned verse finds a close analogue in "sevas d'eyuno" (read "cevas de ayuno" ['you find sustenance in fasting']) integrated into Moner's *villancico* entitled "La aguililla" (see v. 45; *1 OC* 213). Worth mentioning are the three adaptations of the Catalan expression "péixer de vent" ('to feed on the wind') found in *Cobles de les tisores*, vv. 120, 156, and *Bendir de dones*, v. 290.

donde se mira querer
  sin ficción,
rebuelve por ensayar
su poder con su saber,
  a ssazón   260
que haze pyedras tirar.

22   —Los que tyenen calentura
        no syenten el pulso d'ellas,
          a[u]nque[12] tyenten.
        Los sanos levan mesura   265
        con que bastan a entendellas,
          que sy myenten,
        según cuesta, pro les dura.
        No es posible conçertar
        dos voluntades en una: 270
          apuradas,
        syempre ell una va engañar.
        Oy es Amor la Fortuna,
          que en sus gradas
        no pueden sino rodar.   275

23   Todavía, nunqua fue
        ningún amor acabado
          sin emyenda,
        porque más vale la fe
        del coraçón açendrado   280
          que la prenda
        que se da por l'alquilé.[13]
        Y en nuestro culto sagrado
        tal sacrificio s'offrece
          de contino   285
        que l'engaño es condenado;

---

[12] *DCECH* (1: 413) registers *anque* as a substandard variant ("forma vulgar") of *aunque.* I emend the text following the reading of MS. Vaticanus Latinus 4802, designated as "B," one of the two basic texts in my critical edition of Moner's *Obras castellanas.* For a full description, see Cocozzella, Introducció, 91–92 and *1 Introducción,* 69–75.

[13] In describing the various aspects of the vicious conduct, which she unsparingly attributes to women, Experiencia insinuates suspicion of some dubious transaction of one form or another. Here, because of the rhyme or for other unspecified reasons, Moner makes use of the Catalan term for 'rental fee:' "l'alquilé" instead of the Castilian "el alquiler."

y quyen Verdad favorece
    será dyno
de llamars'el más honrrado. —

24   Acabó Esperiencia   290
    su sentencia, cosa çierta,
        según sé;
    bolvió su dulce presentia
    la Manzilla por la offerta,
        do la fe   295
    offrecyó con reverencia.
    Luego Firmeza y Baldón
    vinieron de compañía
        a offrecer;
    han traído esta canción   300
    qu'el muerto, quando bivía
        sin plazer,
    la hizo de su passión:

25   "¡Ay del byen que mal me haze,
    mi grave dulce tristeza!   305
    Quanto la pena me plaze,
    el desconcyerto me pesa.
    ¡Amor, dolor comportar,
    haver por byen vuestro no,
    jamás nadye como yo … !   310
    ¡Mas nunca vos suppe amar,[14]
    ny vos sabéys ultrajar!
    Vuestro tratar me deshaze
    porque passa de crueza:
    ser vos la causa me plaze,   315
    mas la manera me pesa."

[EL SERMON: EXORDIO Y PARTE I]

26   Tras l'offerta que he cantado
    Esperiencia se subió,
        sossegada,
    para'l sermón decorado.   320

---

[14] In keeping with the criteria pertaining to my critical edition of Moner's *Obras castellanas* (see the bibliography below), I retain the spelling of *suppe* (v. 311), *ffin* (v. 345), *affana* (v. 368), *balestero* (v. 668) in place of the familiar *supe*, *fin*, *afana*, *ballestero*.

Manzilla la santiguó.
   Santiguada,
por tal tema ha començado:
—"Humanal inclinatión,
por la discreta acordança   325
   de Natura
en el gentil coraçón,
o yrá Amor, con esperança
   de folgura,
tras el byen de su intentión".   330

27   Y por ser agradesçido
mi sermón por los leales,
   como deve,
havrá de ser dividido
en tres partes principales,   335
   lo más breve
que podré con mi sentido.
Del tema declarativa,
será muy buena materia
   la primera;   340
la segunda, expositiva
del vangelio de la feria;
   la tercera,
historia prosecutiva.

28   Natura, a ffin que recrezca   345
las obras de quyen es syerva
   natural,
no dexa el hombre peresca:
en el fijo le conserva;
   por lo qual   350
pedernal quyere la yesca.
Encyende por el cañón
del sentymyento al sensible,
   razonable,
y dales inclinatión   355
necessaria y convenible,
   deleytable,
para su generación.

29   Por esta causa se liga
        entr'ell ombre y la mujer   360
            ell amor;
        y por esso es tan amiga
        la beldad d'este querer
            so color
        de byen, que byen nos fatiga.   365
        La fermosura açendrada
        por este fin la dessea
            quyen la affana
        y tanbyén el que s'agrada
        d'alguna cosa muy fea,   370
            tan de gana,
        como si fuesse esmerada.

30   D'esta sola causa vyenen
        los amores positivos
            y civiles,   375
        porque los unos los tyenen
        muertos, los otros muy bivos,
            tan sotiles
        que del ayre se mantyenen.
        Sólo el coraçón gentil[15]   380
        puede alcançar de amor gloria,
            por tal ley,
        qu'el rudo, grossero, çivil,
        quando vence, es su victoria
            la del buey   385
        que pisa la liebre al cobil.[16]

---

[15] "Al See, also, "el gentil coraçón" (v. 327 above). "Al cor gentil rempaira sempre amore," we read in Guido Guinizelli's famous poem. Experiencia would agree whole-heartedly: from her point of view, true love in a well-ordered universe is a token of blissful relationship with the beloved and a matter of sophistication, that is, elegance of manners, refinement of taste, sublimation of passion, control of emotion, purification of heart and mind. For the essential data pertaining to this poem, see Contini's introductory note in his edition of *Poeti del duecento*, vol. 2, pp. 460–61.

[16] The wording in this passage calls to mind v. 5 ("no es la liebre en el cobil") of Moner's shortest composition (eight octosyllables), entitled "La manzana quemada." For the text of this poem and the accompanying commentary, see *1 OC*, respectively, 153 and 91–93. The prototype of the intriguing imagery in the two passages is documented in two *cansos* of the troubadour Arnaut Daniel: X, vv. 43–44 ("Ieu sui Arnautz qu'amas l'aura, / e chatz la lebre ab lo bou" ['I am Arnaut who hoards the air and hunts the hare with the ox']) (Arnaut Daniel, 274); and XIV, vv. 3–4 ("can cassava·l lebr' ab lo bou"

31   Con esperança se crýa
        el bivo amor d'este son
            aplazible,
        que juzga la fantasía,   390
        por las leyes d'afición,
            ser possible
        la cosa según querrýa;
        que assí como se delyte[17]
        en amor franco, ganoso   395
            de más dar,
        no puede ser se limite
        en lo que es difficultoso
            d'alcançar,
        sino por dicha d'embite.[18]   400

32   Es tanbyén amor causado
        de folgura, se m'entyende.
            Por tal fuero,
        quien en al está occupado
        muy pocas vezes se prende: 405
            l'ombre entero
        ha menester tal cuydado;
        y si alguno es prendido,
        en otros males rebuelto

['When I used to chase the hare with the ox']) (Arnaut Daniel, 327). Introducing some significant variations of his own, Petrarch imitates Arnaut's motif of the hunt with the ox: Rima 212, vv. 7–8 ("et una cerva errante e fugitiva / caccio con un bue zoppo, e 'nfermo, e lento" [I hunt a wandering, runaway doe with a lame, sickly, and slow ox]) (Petrarca, 376); and Rima 239, v. 36 ("e col bue zoppo andrem cacciando l'aura" [we will be chasing the air with the lame ox]) (Petrarca, 404). Remarkable, also, is the reminiscence of Arnaut's passage in March's Poem 64, which reads: "Llir entre cards, ab milans caç la ganta / y ab lo branxet la lebre corredora" (Lilly among thorns, I hunt the stork with a hawk and, with a lap dog, a hare on the run' [translation mine]) (vv. 25–26) (March, 258). According to Ernst Curtius, the various versions of the absurd hunt in question constitute sundry examples of the topic of "the world upside down" (94–98). As attested by the age-old tradition of the so-called *adynata* or *impossibilia*, the topic is symptomatic of the general, arguably cosmic, upheaval caused by vitiated love (Curtius, 97 n. 27). In light of Curtius's commentary, we may come to understand how in Moner's *Sepultura*, Experiencia uses the *adynaton* of the ox and the hare in support of a proposition she holds as unshakable principle of her doctrine.

[17] This word is a hybrid between the Castilian *deleite* and the Catalan *delit*. Moner takes poetic license in order to preserve the rhyme with *limite* and *embite*.

[18] Read "envite."

       d'esta mena,   410
o conosce que es querido,
o de presto torna suelto:
       una pena
y un solo altar es servido.

33   De no ser a ser tan dyno,   415
       l'umana naturaleza
          traspassada,
es peso, estorva'l camino
de la ánima, da franquesa
          inclinada   420
a dos hytos por un tino.
La bondad y la maldad
son los dos hytos en quyen
          ell'atina,
mas la noble voluntad,   425
syempre so color de byen,
          determina
qu'es un tino de bondad.

34   Assí que aquel qu'enamora,
       la razón por la qual ama   430
          le dispensa;
y haunqu'es cyerto qu'enpeora,
dexando el fruto por rama,
          él se pyensa
que en escoger la mejora.   435
Tras el byen de su intentión
quyere ell ombre, según esto,
          byen mirando;
y es dada declaración
del tema por mí propuesto,   440
          abreviando
por proseguir mi sermón.

[SERMON: PARTE SEGUNDA]

35   Ell evangelio nos cuenta
       muchas y breves verdades
          en su texto.   445
La primera me destyenta
vyendo las desigualdades

     que en aquesto
     descubre quyen se scarmyenta.
     Mujeres en tyempo passado,   450
     en esta casa, des que hera,
          eran polo;
     oy es el mundo mudado,
     que no hay mujer que byen quyera,
          sino sólo   455
     por trasquilar su ganado.

36   El hombre moço que vyene
     a querellas y servillas
          sin cautela
     pyensa que, pues hojos tyene,   460
     qu'es possible descobrillas
          con su vela;
     mas l'engaño sobrevyene;
     y de que cahe una vez
     en sus lazos y azechanças   465
          peligrosas,
     caherá tanbién las diez,
     que las nuestras speranças
          mentirosas
     hazen xavón en los piez.   470

37   Quyen las quiere las enoja,
     según que por deshazellos
          se derraman.
     Su desconcierto s'arroja
     no según culpa d'aquellos   475
          que las aman,
     mas como se les antoja.
     Toda una vida se guasta[19]
     en sallir de sus prizions
          verdaderas: 480
     rescate no les abasta.
     ¡Quán terribles condiciones
          y maneras
     en tan escogida casta!

---

[19] *Guasta* is the equivalent of *gasta* in medieval Catalan (*DCECH*, 3:121).

38   En saber que son hermosas   485
      luego tyenen amanidas
            mil celadas.
      Angeles son y raposas
      en leones enxeridas,
            tan iradas   490
      quanto en al son temorosas.
      Descargan su poderío
      para ver con su licencia
            qué podrán.
      Con l'estómago vazío   495
      d'enamorada consciencia,
            siempre dan,
      do más las aman, desvío.

39   Son estrago de las vidas
      que por ellas syn mercedes   500
            se despyenden.
      Do no temen ser vencidas,
      por offender con sus redes
            se destyenden,
      pues saben que son queridas.   505
      A quyen el mal sobresana
      no l'aprovecha destresa
            la más alta.
      Danlos cesto por mansana,
      y si no dexan la empresa,   510
            nunca falta
      en fin la muerte temprana.

40   En cómo darán fatigas
      es todo el studio d'ellas
            ha mil años.   515
      Son crueles enemigas
      de quyen s'esfuerça a querellas,
            con engaños,
      conjurationes y ligas.
      ¡El major plazer que syenten,   520
      en que l'ombre, por sus obras,
            torna loco!
      ¿De que pensáys s'arrepyenten?
      Estonces doblan las sobras:

con lo poco   525
no hay seso que no destyenten.

41   Syendo las más d'esta suerte,
        quyen ha con ellas pendencia,
            a mi ver,
        todo su seso convyerte   530
        en esforçar la paciencia
            por poder
        ser flaco contra lo fuerte.
        Con l'affición que s'esmera
        crýa el temor d'enojallas   535
            y el dudar.
        No descubren la fuslera:[20]
        miran jugar las agallas[21]
            sin mirar
        el porqué ni la manera.   540

---

[20] *Fuslera* is also documented in *Obra en metro*—"que el menester es pyedra de toque / por quien se descubre mejor la fuslera" (vv. 384–85; *2 OC* 89; the person in need is surely the touchstone: through him all the riffraff is duly exposed). Here the term refers metaphorically to the inferiority that Experiencia imputes to women in general. *Fruslera*, which Corominas lists as a variant of *fuslera* (*DCECH* 2: 585) is equivalent to *fruslería*, defined as "cosa de poco valor o importancia" (a thing of little value or importance *DEA*).

[21] *Agallas* are pieces of gall, the excrescence that dries in the shape of little balls especially on the trunk of oaks and kindred trees (see *DEA*). For the game of galls that Moner is referring to, see the following description by Bartolomé de las Casas: "Juegan al juego que se dice pasa pasa, que tan sotilmente pasan de una mano a otra unas agallas o avellanas" (*DHLE*; they play the game called 'pass on,' as they deftly shift some galls or hazelnuts from one hand to the other). There can be little doubt as to the sinister connotations that Moner associates with the game of galls. In *La noche* the protagonist is struck by the spectacle of a woman — the allegorical personage named *Esperanza* (Hope) —engaged in a *pasa pasa* of her own: "Stonçes sacó, no sé de dónde, unas agallas, y puestas ensima la mesa con todo su aparejo, empessó a jugallas muy más sotilmente que nunca vi" (*TMPW* 130; she, then, pulled out of nowhere some pieces of gall, placed them on the table with all her props, and began playing with them with such skill as I had never seen before). The bewildered spectator wastes no time in rebuking that personage for her much too clever and therefore suspicious sleight of hand: "Falso juego es el tuyo y tu sotileza dañosa, especialmente a los hombres mossos que han visto pocas cosas, porque les das entender que tocas donde no llegas y llegas donde no tocas" (*TMPW* 131–32; yours is a treacherous game, and your nimbleness, dangerous, especially to young men that have not seen much of the world. You would make them believe that you touch where you cannot reach and reach where you cannot touch).

42 ¡Qué desventura y sinyestro
   por este templo bendito,
        consagrado,
   qu'el fingido sea dyestro
   de dar mejor en el hito   545
        de su lado,
   qu'el verdadero qu'es nuestro!
   Y es cyerto que son tornadas
   de condición tan estraña
        que han plazer   550
   de ser vistas e ensayadas
   d'alguno que las engaña
        por perder
   quyen adoran sus pisadas.

43 Nuestros devotos amables   555
   son desechados a çagua,
        de rendón,
   y los fingidos, mudables,
   se precian de mejor paga,
        en que son   560
   a la Verdad muy culpables.
   Engañan con lazo çyego
   por no sentir estrechura.
        ¡Que les sobre!
   Do gozan, descubren luego   565
   l'engaño poco les dura
        porqu'el cobre
   no tyene a prueva del fuego.

44 Como quyer dure la venda,
   engañan sin poder ser   570
        engañados,
   que sy ellas çierran la tyenda,
   no pueden ellos perder,
        pues los dados
   les han dexado por prenda.   575
   Estos nos vengan a osadas,
   según la epístola canta
        sin mentyr;
   ellas quedan byen pagadas,
   mas lo que a mí me quebranta   580

es soffrir
ser nuestras leyes quebradas.

45   Ya en nuestras fyestas no hay
plazer qu'ell alma le tome
      sin mixturas.   585
¡Ay, ayes y más ay ay!
¡Llaga qu'el seso se come,
      desventuras,
querellas, agravyos assay!
A quyen las ha byen seguido,   590
acatadas y adoradas
      nunqua quyeren,
y de quyen ha mal querido,
las más d'ellas agradadas;
      de que mueren   595
los que las han byen servido.

46   Este açidente repuna,
que en amor no hay más amores
      con hervor.
Mujeres hazen fortuna   600
en esta casa de flores,
      cuyo olor
ya no lo syente nynguna.
D'este studio engañoso
en que pyensan más ganar,   605
      sólo queda
que nuestro Dios es quexoso
y dexa con furia rodar,
      en su rueda,
la silla de nuestro reposo.   610

47   Todavía es muy mejor,
queryendo, ser engañado
      que engañar,
porqu'el affán y dolor
ya vyene gualardonado   615
      en pensar
que tyenen servido Amor;
y más vale un pensamyento
en esta casa sellado
      de my emprenta   620

qu'el común contentamyento
del engaño conçertado,
    ca de tryenta
los veynte y nueve son vyento.

48 Despúes aquí donde stamos,   625
    officios baxos y altos
        que offrecemos
    por los fyeles los pagamos;
    y si de vida son faltos,
        no podemos   630
    honrar más que los honrramos.
    Aquella Verdad que es vado
    por passar al byen eterno,
        assistente,
    quyera escusar su peccado   635
    Y es l'evangelio hodierno,
        moralmente,
    en esta parte acabado.

    [SERMON: PARTE TERCERA]

49 L'ystoria de quyen muryó,
    para dever sermonaros   640
        de su vida,
    es tan dyna que si no
    que yo temo d'enojaros,
        sin medida
    diría quánto sirvió;   645
    mas, en suma, vos aviso
    que tuvo amor y firmeza
        y fe tanta,
    que, si davan paraýso
    por esta nuestra riqueza,   650
        fuera santa
    su alma según que hizo.

50 Con todo, es cosa devida
    que diga quyén concertó
        que muriese: 655
    una tal, una escogida
    que nunqua hombre hirió
        que no fuesse

    peligrosa la herida.
    La d'éste no tuvo par,   660
    que la ballesta era gruesa
        y de passa
    el braço; quyero callar
    porque no tengo cabeça,
        sino escasa,   665
    para poderl'alabar.

51   Con la herida mostrada,
    fue dond'era el balestero
        que le dyo.
    Luego por él fue tentada   670
    con una prueva d'azero
        que tocó
    all alma temorizada.
    Quiso tornar do venía
    por no despertar la ira   675
        más sañuda;
    y al despedir que hazía,
    tiróle con una vira
        tan aguda
    que le mató en aquel dýa.   680

52   La muerte Moner nos priva;
    la dama nos a quedado
        por reffrán:
    ella hermosa y esquiva,
    él de firme y transportado,   685
        no ternán
    ygual ninguno que biva.
    All alma del cuerpo den
    nuestras rogarias l'abrigo
        qu'él dexó;   690
    a ella que quyera byen,
    tanto que sepa el que digo
        como yo.
    Ad quem nos perducat. ¡Amen!—

[TERMINA LA MISA]

53   Luego en haver sermonado   695
     L'Esperiencia como supo,
          por su espacio,
     según ya estava ordenado,
     a la Manzilla le cupo
          el prefacio,   700
     d'estas palabras formado:
     —Verdad, nuestra medianera,
     clarifica nuestros votos,
          te rogamos.
     Bendito quyen en ty espera,   705
     porque a tus fyeles devotos,
          donde stamos,
     tu gran bondad les prospera.—

54   Por *preceptis*, en su ton,
     dixo del modo siguyente   710
          tal cantar:
     —Tus reglas, Señora, son:
     firmeza, ausente y presente;
          conçertar
     servicios con gualardón.   715
     Quyen murió no fue de dos.
     Su querella, qué tal es,
          ja sabéys.
     Assí que, con nuestro Dyos,
     acabad, Señora, pues   720
          que podéys,
     que le conoscan por vos.—

55   Por *Agnus* dijo: —Verdad,
     all alma, si le soys buena,
          le aiudara,   725
     que paresçe crueldad,
     en ambos mundos gran pena,
          no hallara
     en ningún cabo piedad.
     Las honrras que yo le hago   730
     al cuerpo sin sentymyento
          poco vale:
     si no le dan otro pago,

no cumple meresçymyento,
   ny me cale   735
encarescervos su trago.—

56   Bolvióse estonçes Manzilla
por qu'el officio acabasse,
   ya prolixo,
congoxada a maravilla.   740
Por el *Requiescat in pace*
   assí dixo
con la boz algo flaquilla:
—¡Dios absuelva tus peccados!
Quanto yo soy lastimada   745
   que moriste,
si son assí perdonados,
yo seré más alegrada,
   que fue triste
por todos nuestros finados.—   750

[CONCLUSION]

57   Con esta missa acabada
son accabadas las bodas
   de my vida.
De muchos fue pïedada,
mas Manzilla sobre todas   755
   la ha plañida.
Si os paresçe qu'es pagada …
no me doy que no's deys nada!
Y, en fin, d'aquý enmudesco
   para syempre.   760
Mi muerte es bien empleada:
yo tengo lo que meresco.
   Vuestro tempre[22]
puede tirar do hos agrada.

---

[22] *Tempre* is a Catalan word, which Moner employs on a number of occasions, in both his Castilian and Catalan works, in the prominent acceptations registered in *DCVB* (10: 478). In *Sepultura* the term finds a close equivalent in "temper," its English cognate, in the sense of "frame of mind; disposition; mood" (*Webster's New World Dictionary*) or "particular state of mind or feeling; habit of mind" (*Webster's New Universal Unabridged Dictionary*). Elsewhere, Moner uses *tempre* in the sense of 'moderation,' 'relief,' 'respite:' "ny trahe consigo sosyego ni tempre" (it doesn't bring calm or moderation) (*Obra en metro*,

The Burial of Love
(Translation)

[PREAMBLE]

1. My Lady, if you want to know what your words, so burdensome, have accomplished, you only have to read these verses nuanced with feeling… and, having read them, you've done your job. So, this is the way things have turned out: you've ruined my life for no reason at all. This time, I beg of you, say yes to my request: do not treat those others that have courted you as harshly as you have treated me.

2. Please be considerate with others, now that you are through with me. Through, indeed! You render evil for evil, but to render it with such audacity as you can, no color will wipe out a black stain! So, be careful! Do not brandish your sword so recklessly. You may think, "I didn't even touch him" but end up killing a man, and for what? This is a wrong you cannot undo!

---

v. 257, *2 OC*, 84); "Qu'el mal, que tan mal nos strata, / que no los consiente quexa, / ni ablar, do busquen tempre" (the illness that afflicts us in such an ill manner / does not allow them [the lovers] to complain, / nor talk, by which they could find some relief' (*Momería*, *1 OC*, 156; see below, p. 322). A similar meaning is found in March's Poem 92, v. 117: "pensar no puch ma dolor haja tempre" (I cannot imagine my suffering will find any moderation) (*Obra completa*, 379). There is, also, an enigmatic expression, which Moner uses in his short treatise, entitled "Resposta a Jaume de Ribes" (*Oc*, 127–35). Referring to the abuses ("mals tractes de nova sort" ['ill treatment of a new kind']) he avowedly receives from his lady, the author observes: "Mes negú no pot tenir a les puntes del tempre" (*Oc*, 128). In all probability, he alludes to the breaking point or the limit of endurance, beyond which no one is able to tolerate ("negún no pot tenir") said abusive behavior. *Temple*, which appears in two of Moner's Castilian works (*Quejas al alma* and the aforementioned *Obra en metro*) encompasses the same semantic field as does *tempre*. The acceptation "Fermesa adquirida pel caràcter, per la intelligència o per l'exercici" (*DCVB*, 10: 478) is illustrated in the following passages: "qu'el temple no's da por al / salvo por más affligiros" (stamina is not given you for anything other than to endure more and more afflictions) (*Quejas al alma*, vv. 151–52, *1 OC*, 237); "allí el que es osado con temple resista" (there, let the man of daring resist firmly, *Obra en metro*, v. 508, *2 OC* 93). In yet another passage of *Obra en metro* (vv. 521–22), *temple* refers to the Stoic virtue of equanimity and sound judgment: "Mas yo que, sin seso, en medio del fuego, / d'amor encendido, sin temple, tan loco… (While I, senseless, immersed in fire, / inflamed with love, bereft of judgment, completely insane) (*2 OC*, 94).

3. Your words dripping with poison bear your message; they're a startling bit of news, the message of a foe. In your language, they say what I say in this sour style of mine: "Moner, hello, wake up! It's time for another wake! What are you doing? Through me the law of humankind demands you give up your life. You know what you owe. So, pay up at once!

4. I answered without hesitation: "I came within the range of your fencing skills." (Well, she likes to kill, and I like to die. Still, she shouldn't foist what is noise for what is music.) She retorted in the manner I have become used to: "So many times you've heard the word 'check!' Sooner or later, you'll hear 'check mate.' Now that you've heard it, try your hand at a new game!"

5. Your words and way of talking wounded me, causing me injury in short order. Then, as your banner was very much in favor, your vehemence brought me a piteous death without much ado. Needless to say, from now on you don't have to expect much trouble or wooing on my part. The war you've waged has given me peace. As it turns out, this is a good thing and a big favor: I'll not hang around you any longer.

[THE BURIAL CEREMONY]

6. It is truly right and just that we should boast of a life lived so well. Thus, I will dedicate this Mass, together with the sermon and proper funeral, in celebration of your condemnation. My fallen body lay lifeless, flat on a field of cruelty. Gentility came to the rescue and laid it outstretched on a shield that Simplicity had lent her.

7. She took him to a chapel consecrated with the fire of affection. Lady Compassion came out of the church in good order at the tail end of a procession. She sang in a high-pitched voice: "Come, o body that was never alive! You did not deserve to die just to set an example! Come in the midst of my laments. Your love was for real; so, this temple makes joy out of grief.

8. Come, o body without soul, and yet alive! I have been weeping over your life relentlessly. Oh, how reluctant my sorrow is to see you suffer a senseless death as a result of such a bitter affront!" At this point, Gentility put down the heavy body she was carrying. Lady Compassion courteously unveiled the dead man's face and kissed it without a hint of fear or repulsion.

9. The lady who caused this man's death is quite happy, nonchalant, much though Compassion cried, saying in a disconsolate voice: "O wretched beauty! How can you be so cruel and for such a long time?" As she was crying over the body, she noticed in the dead man's mouth a piece of paper, all crumpled up. She pried it out to see what it said. What the dead man had written on that paper in his own hand sounded like this:

10. "Even so, O Death, you burden me with regret. Should such a life as mine endure, an even greater fault would kill me."

11. In observance of the ritual, which I recite by heart, Gentility did not stand on ceremony. She picked up the body, carried it further into the church, and deposited it between the choir stalls and the altar. There she left it. The verses were read. Compassion, distraught with grief, kept wringing her hands, while constructing a well-proportioned sepulcher, a splendid structure, inscribed with the following words:

12. "The woman that caused this man's miserable death doesn't even remember his name."

13. Compassion took the body in her arms and laid it in the tomb situated a couple of steps away from the very spot where Lady Friendship had been buried a long time ago. There the body now lies, free from further trouble. On the lid, she sculpted on one side the cross, in which I believe, and, on the other, fashioned the very large image of an ostrich, showing the following words around its neck:

14. "I swallow stones and poisonous herbs; but the time may come when just a few nuts will do me in."

[THE MASS BEGINS: PRELIMINARY PRAYERS]

15. The church is filled with light, the bells are ringing swiftly. Here, with meek countenance, Mesdames Experience, Custom, and Compassion have just come out, fully vested for the celebration of the Mass. All three stand in a row, in front of the humble altar of God-the-Truth and begin professing their devotion to Truth, while reciting the following prayer sotto voce:

16. "To you, o Truth, light of our day, solace of our affliction, we confess you are our trusty guide. We deplore the deceitful treatment we receive from those lovers that have strayed from your ways. As for those whose

sighs are not a sham, do not allow their fire to hurt them so much. May your justice bring condemnation upon those who arm themselves with lies: such a condemnation that they will live in fear of your wrath."

17. After the profession of faith, Compassion recited the following prayer for the Requiem: "O Truth, our advocate, this man's life was spent, faithfully, in praise of your holy name. Grant that he be not deprived of a place of honor. Let your light be the light of his fame. May your goodness favor his grievances. As for the one who scatters the embers, may that person perish in them, and be scorched in the ensuing flames!"

18. Soon afterwards, Compassion recited these mournful verses for the Kyrie: "The man who shows bravery from the start dies of love sooner than do all those who desert their posts. The death of this man comes to validate the righteous complaint of one who is truly faithful, although he would not have fared any better, had he not been killed. Because of him our ranks would have swollen."

19. In the course of this sorrowful dry Mass, the collect followed in this manner: "O Truth, to those who sin against you grant, we pray, in punishment, above all, the Purgatory of Podunk; but a man who walks clear of sin among those who honor his righteousness, he has already paid dearly by losing his life. The only thing left to do, my Lady, is to demand reparation."

[THE EPISTLE, GOSPEL, AND OFFERTORY]

20. Lady Custom, facing skywards, came forth to sing the Epistle. She intoned: "You, ladies, bent on setting the bait, watch out for the hook. Someone may take vengeance! Indeed, women should not be allowed to rebuff a lover for no reason at all, not even on a whim. Some ladies will be judged by the way they judge others and, much too late, shall regret the resentment they have provoked."

21. This is the Gospel that Experience intoned by solfa: "The man who faithfully loves a woman he has not put to the test shall live a life full of miseries. Once she realizes that she is being loved without deceit, even the most special of women will go to any length, resorting to her energies and wits, in an effort to make her lover want to tear his hair out.

22. The people who suffer from high fever do not feel the pulse of their illness, try as they may. Men in good health have enough common sense

to deal with women's ways. If they tell lies, they'll pay a high price: much too high for them to endure. It is impossible to harmonize two wills into one. When the chips are down, invariably one is going to deceive the other. Nowadays, Love has become Lady Fortune: lovers cannot but roll their chances on Fortune's wheel.

23. There is, to be sure, no sublimation in love without self-discipline. Worthier is the purified faithful heart than the keepsake pawned for the purpose of a trade-off. In our sacred worship we offer, unceasingly, the kind of sacrifice by which deception is condemned so that the devotee of Truth may be worthy of being called most honorable among men."

24. Experience delivered her recitative: certitude is her byword, I know that for sure. Compassion turned around — her countenance was sweet — and, ready for the Offertory, proffered then and there her faithfulness reverently. Then, Constancy and Injury came forth to make their joint offering. They brought the following *canción* that the deceased fashioned out of his passion during his joyless life:

25. "Alas, the good that makes me ill, sadness so sweet and grievous. As much as pain pleases me, so is my distress hard to bear! Oh Love to be borne in suffering! The acceptance of 'No!' as a favor! Has a man ever loved as I love? But you say I don't know how to love you! You say you can do me no harm, but the way you mistreat me destroys me — a way crueler than cruel. You're the cause of my grief? What a pleasure! You abuse me no end? That is real torture!"

[THE SERMON: EXORDIUM AND PART I]

26. After the Offertory you've just heard me chant, Experience calmly stepped up to the pulpit to deliver her extemporized sermon. Compassion imparted the blessing. After the blessing, Experience proceeded to state the following theme: "[Either] human instinct, by the judicious agreement of Nature in the sensible heart, or love, moved by the hope of attaining pleasure, will seek the good of its intention."

27. To be duly appreciated by loyal lovers, my sermon will have to be divided into three main sections. I will try to be as concise as possible in providing my explication. The first section, declarative of the theme, is quite appropriate in laying out the subject matter. The second is expositive: it recounts the Gospel of the day. The third is a "prosecutive story."

28. In order to foment the survival of her creatures, Mother Nature, who herself is their innate handmaid, does not allow humankind to go extinct but preserves the species through its offspring. That is why the fuse requires the flint stone. By means of the cannon of emotion, [Nature] fires up the sensual and intellectual appetites and instills in them the necessary, convenient, and pleasurable predisposition toward procreation.

29. This is what causes love to create a bond between man and woman. This is why beauty is such a good friend of the kind of desire that appears under the guise of goodness and a good deal of trouble stirs within us. For the sake of goodness a man pursues beauty in earnest and so does anyone who takes pleasure, so eagerly, in things that are quite ugly as if they were refined.

30. From the single aforementioned cause both the vile and the positive kind of love originate — that is to say: some espouse a love that is deadly; others nurture a love that is alive and so ethereal as to be sustained by thin air. Only the "gentle heart" can attain bliss through love. Consequently, should the love of the coarse, gross, vile kind prevail, its victory would be that of "the ox that steps over the hare in the lair."[23]

31. 'Living love' is nurtured by hope in this pleasurable mode because of the lover's imagination, which, swayed by the natural drives of affection, considers anything possible that it wishes to be possible. Thus, those who take delight in generous love, that is, a love always ready to give more and more, cannot restrain themselves in the face of whatever proves to be enticing even though arduous to attain and acquired by luck of the draw.

32. Let me be clear: sensuality is, also, a cause of love. Accordingly, rarely does a man, not completely absorbed in the passion of love, become overpowered by it. The cares of love take over a man's entire life. A man, enslaved by love, should he become afflicted by extraneous but just-as-vicious ills, either will become aware his love is being requited or will immediately regain his freedom. Only one ailment is suffered, only one god adored.

33. Whether love is worthy or not, human nature is bypassed because it is a burden, as it hinders the course of action of the soul, which is moved by generosity to aim at two targets with only one shot. Good and evil

---

[23] See p. 185–86, n. 16 above.

are the two targets which love aims at. Noble will, however, prompted always by what appears to be good, decides it is an option for goodness.

34. Thus, the man who falls in love is excused by the reason for which he loves. Although he doubtless becomes a worse person opting for the branch rather than the fruit, he thinks that in choosing he makes the object of his choice better than it is. This means a man loves in pursuit of the good of his intention—that is, his quest for the good. At this point I am through with the declaration of the theme I proposed. I'll be brief so that I may proceed quickly to the next section of my sermon.

[THE SERMON: PART II]

35. The Gospel concisely teaches us many lessons in its text. Foremost is the lesson that perturbs me a great deal in view of the injustices that are quite apparent to one who has amended his ways in matters of love. In the past, women have been the cynosure in this temple for as long as the temple has been standing. Today the world has changed: there are no longer women of good will; there are only women hellbent on drawing water to their own mills.

36. The young man who falls in love and woos women assumes that, thanks to his vigilance, sharp-eyed as he is, he will be able to expose them for what they are. Their deceitfulness, however, gets the best of the young fellow. If they catch him but once in their parlous trapping and bushwhacking, they will surely catch him ten times over. Our own hopes, full of illusions, are nothing but ice beneath our feet.

37. Whoever loves them infuriates them, as is shown by the way they go out of their way to utterly destroy their lovers. They vent off their frustrations simply on a whim—not because of any fault of the men that love them. A fellow may waste his entire life trying to break loose from a woman's shackles, which are much too real. No ransom is good enough for these ladies. What a terrible state of affairs! What a way to treat such a select coterie of lovers!

38. Presuming to be beautiful, they have all kinds of tricks up their sleeves. They are angels and a crossbreed of foxes and lions. They get extremely irate if anything arouses their fears. They exercise their power just to test to what extreme they can carry out their abuses. Utterly void as they are of a lover's mentality, they invariably lead astray the men that love them most.

39. They are the bane of the lives of those who endure unrequited sacrifice for women's sake. When they do not fear defeat, they outdo themselves by inflicting injury with their snares, as long as they are well aware of being loved. As for the men that have the false impression of having been cured of his lovesickness, not even the greatest skill can be of any avail. These men are sold a pig in a poke, and, if they persist in the service of love, a premature death will befall them without fail.

40. Since time immemorial women's cunning has been devoted entirely to how they can stir up trouble. With their deceits, treacherous plans, and cliques, they prove to be cruel enemies of the men that spare no

effort in serving them. This is the way they get most pleasure! Let a man go mad because of their handiwork! Do you think they feel sorry for what they do? They had rather redouble their abuses, and, in no time at all, there is no sane mind they cannot stress to the limit.

41. Here is what I think: considering that most women are of such a perverse nature, whoever is at odds with them is at wits' end bolstering his patience to be able to confront their strength with his weakness. While striving to do better and better, such a man lives in trepidation and in fear of their anger. These ladies do not reveal their base intentions. They seek the opportunity to play their tricks and could not care less about the why and the how of their actions.

42. Oh, what a calamity! Oh, what a misfortune, for this blessed and consecrated temple, that not a true lover, one of our fellowship, but a fraud should be quite skillful at scoring bull's-eye for his own benefit! The fact is that women have become of such a strange condition that they take pleasure in being seen and wooed by someone who deceives them while they wreck the life of the man that worships the very ground they tread on.

43. Our devout followers, worthy of being loved, are abruptly shoved to the end of the line, while fake lovers, fickle as they are, boast of earning top wages. In this they commit a grave sin against God-the-Truth. These cheats play tricks and hide their noose. They do not feel the tight squeeze. How I wish it would choke them! They have their fun but, sooner or later, discover that their cheating doesn't do them much good. Copper they are that will not resist the test of fire.

44. Let the bargain sale go on and on. The deceivers shall go on cheating without being cheated; and, if the ladies shut up shop, these fellows have nothing to lose, for said ladies have left their suitors, just for keepsake, the wares they have squandered on them. Indeed, these men will avenge us as the chanted Epistle has just stated so verily. The ladies have it coming. But what really perturbs me is that we allow our laws to be violated.

45. During our feast days no longer is there any sheer joy to take hold of our souls. Alas, alas, woe to us all! Ours is a wound that gnaws at our brains, ours the misadventures, lamentations, affronts galore! Women never show any affection toward the men that court them in a proper manner: attentively, adoringly. Most women look with favor on the men

that fancy them in an evil way. That is why death truly befalls the men that serve women truly.

46. This state of affairs is quite disgusting. No longer do we find in love the virtues of fervent love. Women make their fortunes in this house of flowers but not one of them is capable of smelling the fragrance. The upshot of their deceitful scheming, from which they plan to profit ever more, is that our God will voice His displeasure, and the place in which we find peace our God will cause to spin away, in wild rotation, in God's own wheel.

47. This notwithstanding, much better is it for a man in love to suffer rather than to commit deception because sweat and tears are well rewarded by the awareness that they come in the service of love. Even a single thought stamped in this house by my seal of approval earns more merit than the usual gratification, which, after being finagled in deceitful ways, in most instances blows away with the wind.

48. In short, this is where we stand: the sacred offices we offer, be they solemn or otherwise, are dedicated as suffrage of our worshipers; and, if these are no longer alive, ours is the best way of honoring them. By the intercession of Truth, who is the passageway that leads us to the everlasting Good, may this worshiper's sins be remitted. In its moral aspect, today's Gospel comes to an end in this section.

[THE SERMON: PART III]

49. The story of this man who has just died—I must go on with my sermon and tell you about his life—is of such merit that, if I were not afraid to bore you beyond measure, I would speak of the extent of his devotion in the service of love. But, to be brief, I want you to know that his love, constancy, faithfulness were of such caliber that, if Paradise is awarded for the riches of our virtues, his soul is holy in accordance with the worthiness of his deeds.

50. At any rate, it is only fair for me to reveal who brought about this man's death. What a woman! A lady of a select breed! Never did she strike a man without inflicting a perilous wound. This man's wound is unparalleled, when we consider that the crossbow was sturdy and the bolt pierced right through his arm. I had rather not talk about it, considering I am not fit for the task. I lack the talent to speak worthily of such a wound.

51. With the wound in plain sight, our man walked over to the spot where the archer who had targeted him was standing. In response, the archer subjected the wounded man to a trial of steel and, with that, shook his soul with terror. Afraid of stirring up even more vehement anger, the man tried to return to the place from which he had come; but, just as he was getting ready to leave, the archer launched another shaft at him. So sharp an arrow killed him that very day.

52. Death has taken Moner away from us. His ladylove has become proverbial among us: she, beautiful and aloof; he, perseverant and ecstatic, will find no equal among the living. May our prayers grant his soul protection—never mind of the body he has left behind. May she learn to love truly and be as cognizant as I am of what I am talking about. *Ad quem nos perducat. Amen!*

[THE ENDING OF THE MASS]

53. No sooner had Experience delivered her sermon to the best of her ability than Compassion, who had been standing at her own place, took her turn with the preface in accordance with the ordinals. These were her words: "O Truth, our intercessor, honor our requests, we beseech you. Blessed are those who place their hopes in You. Your supreme goodness redounds to the benefit of the believers in our midst that remain faithful to You."

54. For the *Preceptis*, Compassion offered, in the appropriate intonation, the following chant: "O Truth, your rules are: be steadfast, whether in presence or absence, and make the reward commensurate with the services rendered. The man, who has just died, never shared his love with two women. You are aware of the merits of his complaint. May it please you, then, my Lady, as powerful as you are, that he, with the assent of our God, be known as one of yours."

55. For *Agnus Dei* she said: "Oh, Truth, be good to this man and it will be most beneficial to his soul. Clearly, it would be cruel for him to have to endure much suffering in this and in the other world, and not find sympathy anywhere. Whatever honor I may render him will be of little avail, now that his body has lost all sensation. If he is not given a just reward, all his merits will come to naught, and I need not make you marvel at the hardships he lived through."

56. Grieved beyond belief, Compassion turned around to conclude the ceremony, which had lasted long enough. For the *Requiescat in Pace*, she

spoke as follows in a rather feeble voice: "May God absolve your sins! Tormented as I am because of your death, I will feel somewhat relieved once your sins are forgiven. Your death was sad news, indeed, for all our faithful departed."

[CONCLUSION]

57. With the completion of this Mass, all the festive celebrations have come to an end in my life—a life that has been pitied by many. Lady Compassion, more than anyone else, has mourned over it. Do you think my life has been well rewarded? Well, I don't care if you don't care at all! At long last, from this moment on I shall remain silent forever. There is a good reason for my death. I got what I deserve. So, let your fancy lead you wherever you like.

Momeria[24]

I

Momería consertada de seys: yvan dentro de un sisne, vestidos con iubones de razo negro y mantos de lluto, forrados de terciopelo negro, cortos y hendidos al lado drexo; y todo lo al, negro: sombraretes franceses y penas negras; y el cabello hexo negro; los gestos cubiertos de velos negros. Traýa el sisne en el pico las siguentes coblas, dressadas a las damas y leýdas. Abierto el sisne por el medio, sallíen los momos con un contrapás nuevo, cada qual con su letra, y todos sobre las penas, con sus achas también negras.

1   Señoras, por cuyos nombres
       cada qual d'estos, por fe,
       perdería cyent mil vidas,
       embiáys plañyr los hombres
       sin causa, quitto porque   5
       soys todas desgradescidas.
       En la soledad demoro
       con vida triste que sigo,
       enmudescido, cetrino.
       Sentí'l dolor de su lloro   10
       y quise serles abrigo,
       endressa de su camino.

2   Tráygoles, como vedes,
       por falta de beneficio
       en conforme companýa   15
       Vuestras Mercedes, ¡mercedes!
       Ellos que aviven servicios,
       y yo que sirvo de guía;
       que, según el mal es grave,
       y cierta es la perdicyón,   20
       si no mesuran cruesas,
       yo lastimo que soy ave;

---

[24] This work lends itself to a detailed analysis of the symbiosis between *letra* and *divisa* (text and icon) as discussed in such seminal studies as Deyermond's "La micropoética de las invenciones" and Macpherson's classical monograph (*The* Invenciones y letras *of the* Cancionero general). Of great interest for the study of not only Moner's *Momería* but also his *La noche* are the various items included in the bibliography that complements Deyermond's essay.

    quedando ço la rasón
    todas Vuestras Gentilesas.

3   Qu'el mal, que tan mal nos trata,   25
    que no los consiente quexa,
    ni ablar, do busquen tempre,
    cruel será si les mata,
    mas mucho más si les dexa
    la vida que dura siempre;   30
    cuyos males van scritos
    con letras de negra suerte
    quales son en padescellos.
    Sus querellas son los gritos
    que yo doy quando la muerte   35
    me requiere como a ellos.

II

Son las propriadades del signe que guía; y en los amores muchos le han tomado
en tal sentimento. Después es muy callado, mui mal ensañoso, cetrino, y nunca
apenas grita asta que prenustica su muerte por stinto natural. Y stonses bosea y
grita fasta que muere, como en las palabras y caso ya se dize. Los motes ho letras
fueron éstas que se siguen sobre las penas:

1   No me da pena la pena,
    mas pensar quién me condena.

2   La mía, por ser publica,
    ya s'estima,
    mas lo secreto lastima.   5

3   Es mi pena tan crescida,
    tan grave, biva y fuerte,
    que su vida me da muerte.

4   Entre las penas, la pena
    que más me pena y aquexa   10
    es porque bivir me dexa.

5   Que si d'ella se sirvyera,
    aunque por ella muriera,
    no me diera.

6   Si del bien de su servycio   15
     mi vida no se templara,
     con éstas no me ygualara.

Mummery
(Translation)

I

A mummery choreographed for a cast of six men. These were mummers riding inside a structure shaped like a swan. The swan carried in its beak the stanzas shown below, addressed to the ladies and read to them. Through an opening in the middle of the swan the mummers filed out swaying to the rhythm of a new dance. Each dancer displayed his own verses dealing with the pains of love. All the mummers wore loose-fitting shirts made of black satin and, as a sign of mourning, matching capes lined with black velvet. Their capes were short with a slit on the left side. The men were dressed entirely in black: black were their French hats and the feathers stuck on top, black the dye of their hair, black the veils that covered their faces. The torches in their hands were also black.[25]

1. My Ladies, in your name, each of these men, out of his faithful love, would sacrifice his life a thousand times. You oblige these men to mourn for no reason other than that all of you are so ungrateful. I dwell in solitude in the sad life I lead, silenced and embittered. I feel the sorrow of these men in their crying and wish to be their protector and beacon along their journey.

2. As a suitable companion for them, I present them to you because, as you can see, they and I are all without reward. My Ladies, grant them your favors! Let them be revived in your service, while I serve as their guide. Consider their grave malady and their lives, inevitably wrecked, if they do not find a way to mollify your cruelty. I grieve, even though I am only a bird; but all of you, gentle Ladies, are beneath the bounds of reason.

3. The illness that treats us in such an ill manner and does not allow them to complain or speak up in order to seek relief, will be cruel if it kills them, but even more cruel if it grants them a life that goes on

---

[25] For the sake of clarity this translation includes some changes in the order of the sentences of the original text.

endlessly. Their ills are written in black, as black as is their lot to endure them. Their laments are the wails I blare out when death beckons me and them all together.

II

The properties of the swan are those of one who serves as a guide: in matters of love, many have interpreted his role in that sense. In addition, the swan is very quiet, ill-natured to the extreme, sullen, and hardly ever cries out until the time when, by instinct, he foretells his own death. Then, he hollers and shouts, just as it is stated in the inscription of his emblem. Following are the inscriptions or verses that deal with the suffering of these lovers:

1. My pain does not pain me except when I consider who it is that pains me.

2. Being open to the public, my pain is appreciated. What hurts me is secrecy.

3. My pain is full-grown, so grievous, lively, and strong that its life makes me die.

4. Amidst all pains, the pain that pains and afflicts me the most is the one that keeps me alive.

5. If my lady acknowledged it as a token of my service, even though I should die of my pain, I wouldn't mind.

6. Even if my life would not be more at peace because of the benefits I enjoy thanks to the service to my lady, I would not compare my pain with that of all these other men.

Illustrations

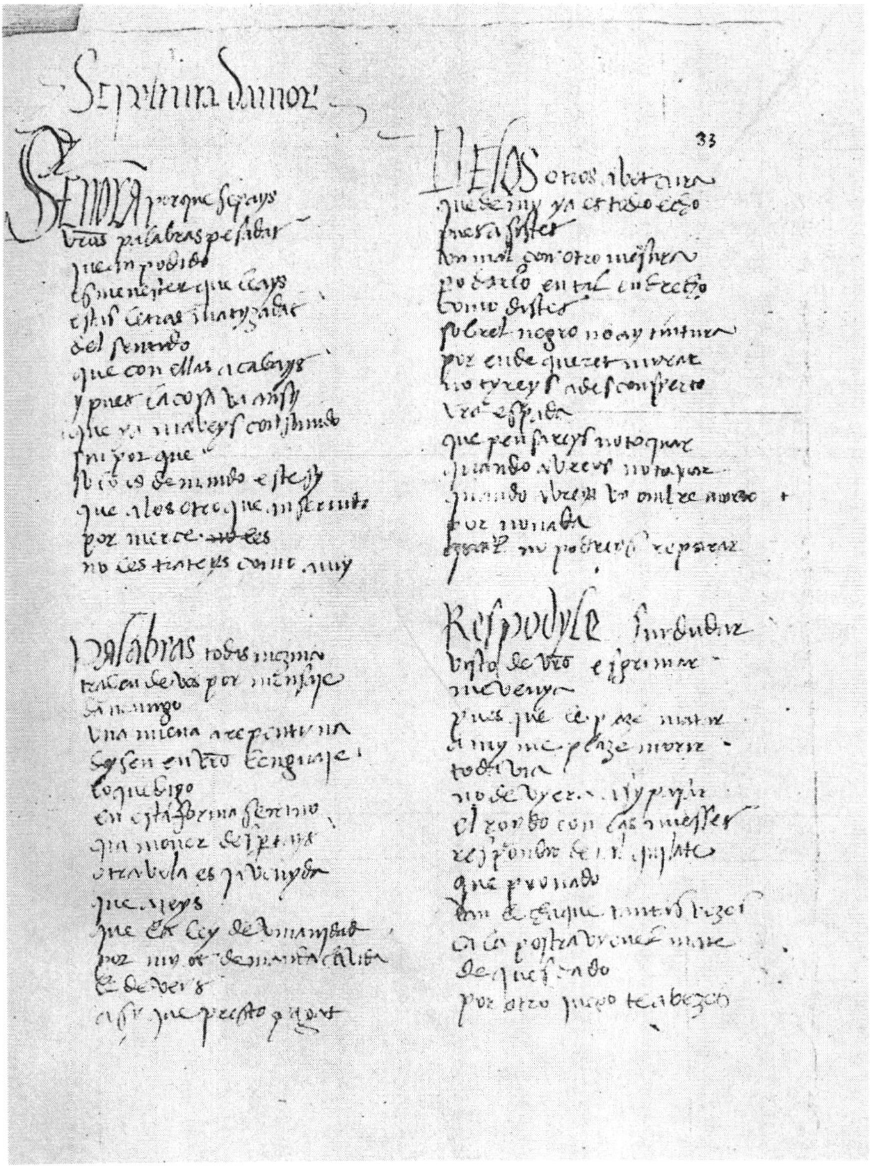

Figure 1. Title page of Moner's *Sepultura d'amor*, in MS. Vaticanus Latinus 4802, f. 33 (late fifteenth century).

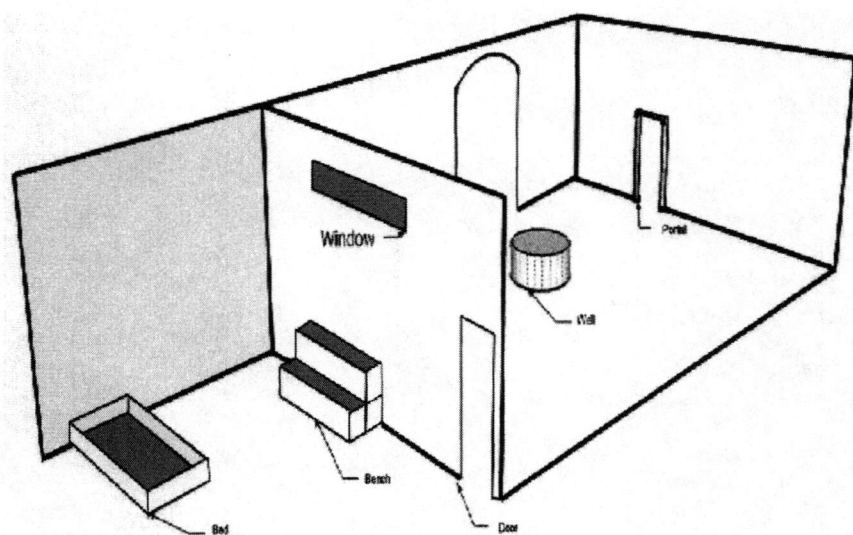

Figure 2. A view of the stage for Roís de Corella's *Tragèdia de Caldesa*: The dark chamber and adjoining sunlit courtyard.

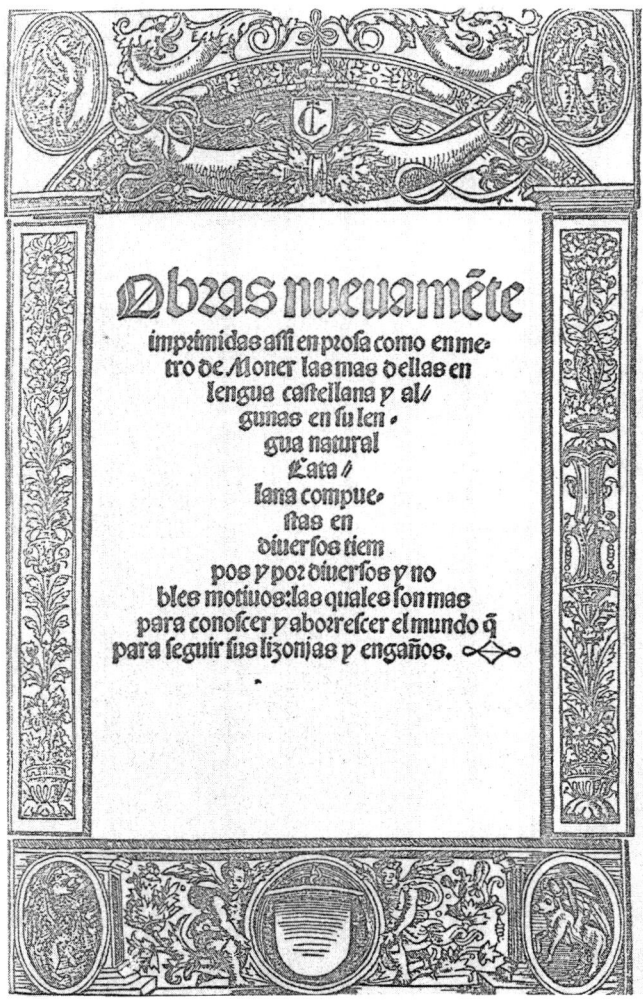

Figure 3. Frontispiece of the *editio princeps* of Moner's works (1528).

Figure 4. The castle of Moner's *La noche*: The woodcut that occupies f. A2ᵛ of the *editio princeps*.

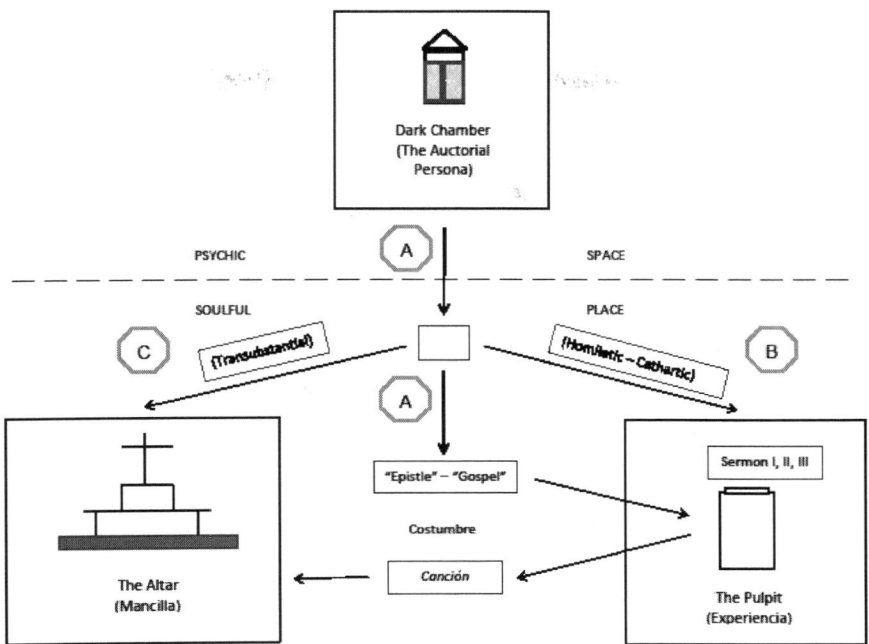

Figure 5. Moner's *misa de amores*: Allegorical functions, configuration of plot and stage.

EXTRA ECCLESIAM

I. Preamble (vv. 1–70)

II. Conclusion (vv. 751–64)

INTRA ECCLESIAM

I. The Chapel and the Sepulcher (vv. 71–163)
(a) End of the speech of complaint and reproach addressed to the lady-love; transition to the narrative proper (vv. 71–84)
(b) The preliminary ceremony of the funeral: intervention of Gentileza, Simpleza, Mancilla, and the group of the procession (vv. 85–137)
(c) The burial proper and the description of the tomb (vv. 138–63)

II. The Altar (vv. 164–316; 695–750)
(a) Presentation of the three celebrants: Experiencia, Costumbre, Mancilla (vv. 164–77)
(b) The three celebrants in unison: "Confesión" (profession of faith to God-the-Truth) (vv. 178–91)
(c) Mancilla: Requiem (vv. 192–205)
(d) Mancilla: Kyrie eleison (vv. 206–19)
(e) [Mancilla]: "Oración" (vv. 220–33)
(f) Costumbre: The Intoned Epistle (234–47)
(g) Experiencia: The Intoned Gospel (248–89)
(h) Firmeza and Baldón: The Offertory
i. Preliminary ritual (vv. 290–303)
ii. The *canción* as offering (vv. 304–16)
(i) Mancilla: Prefacio (vv. 695–708)
(j) Mancilla: *Preceptis* (vv. 709–22)
(k) Mancilla: *Agnus* (vv. 723–36)
(l) Mancilla: *Requiescat in pace* (737–50)

III. The Pulpit (vv. 317–694)
(a) Sermon, Part I (vv. 317–442)
(b) Sermon, Part II (vv. 443–638)
(c) Sermon, Part III (vv. 639–94)

Figure 6. The layout of Moner's allegorical Mass

BIBLIOGRAPHY

Abreviations [The Works of Fra Francesc Moner: Basic Texts and Editions]

A: *Obras nueuamete imprimidas assi en prosa como en metro.* Barcelona: Car-
        los Amorós, 1528. (Cf. the facsimile by Antonio Pérez y Gómez. Valen-
        cia: Tipografía Moderna, 1951. This is the *editio princeps* of Francesc
        Moner's Works; see Cocozzella, Introducció, 86–90; *1 Introducción,*
        65–69).

B: Vaticanus Latinus 4802 (manuscript of the end of the fifteenth century
        or the beginning of the sixteenth; see Cocozzella, Introducció, 91–92; *1
        Introducción,* 69–75).

Oc: Moner, Francesc. *Obres catalanes.* Edited by Peter Cocozzella. Els Nos-
        tres Clàssics 100. Barcelona: Barcino, 1970.

1 OC: Moner, Francesc. *Poemas menores.* Vol. 1 of *Obras castellanas.* Edited by
        Peter Cocozzella. Lewiston, NY: Edwin Mellen Press, 1991.

2 OC: Moner, Francesc. *Poemas mayores.* Vol. 2 of *Obras castellanas.* Edited by
        Peter Cocozzella. Lewiston, NY: Edwin Mellen Press, 1991.

TMPW: Moner, Francesc, in Peter Cocozzella, "The Two Major Prose Works
        of Francisco de Moner: A Critical Edition and Translation." PhD diss.,
        Saint Louis University, 1966.

Alatorre, Antonio. "Algunas notas sobre la Misa de amores." *Nueva Revista de
    Filología Hispánica* 14 (1960): 325–28.
Alberni, Anna, Lola Badia, and Lluís Cabré, eds. *Translatar i Transferir: La
    transmissió dels textos i el saber (1200–1500).* Santa Coloma de Queralt: Uni-
    versitat Rovira i Virgili, 2010.
Alborg, Juan Luis. *Edad Media y Renacimiento.* Vol. 1, *Historia de la literatura
    española.* Madrid: Gredos, 1966.
Alegre, Francesc. "Sermó de amor, scrit per manament del Rey Don Juan, de
    inmortal memoria per Francesch Alegre." [Apéndice 4]. In *Amor y pedeagogía
    en la edad media (estudios de doctrina amorosa y práctica literaria),* by Pedro
    Manuel Cátedra, 205–11. Salamanca: Universidad de Salamanca, 1989.
———. *Somni de Francesc Alegre recitant lo procés d'una qüestió enamorada.* In
    Novel·les amoroses i morals, edited by Arseni Pacheco and August Bover i
    Font. Les Millors Obres de la Literatura Catalana 73. Barcelona: Edicions
    62, 1982. Pp. 121–38.

Alemany Ferrer, Rafael, ed. *Ausiàs March i el món cultural del segle XV*. Alacant: Universitat d'Alacant, 1999.

———, Josep Lluís Martos, and Josep Miquel Manzanaro, eds. *Actes del X Congrés de l'Associació Hispànica de Literatura Medieval*. 3 vols. Alacant: Institut Interuniversitari de Filologia Valenciana, 2005.

Allen, John J., and Domingo Ynduráin. Prólogo to *El gran teatro del mundo*, by Pedro Calderón de la Barca, xxiii–lxiv. Edited by John J. Allen and Domingo Ynduráin. Barcelona: Crítica, 1997.

Alonso, Dámaso. *Góngora y el "Polifemo."* 3 vols. Madrid: Gredos, 1967.

Álvarez Pellitero, Ana Mª. Introducción general. *Teatro medieval*, edited by Ana Mª Álvarez Pellitero. Colección Austral A157. Madrid: Espasa-Calpe, 1990. 9–81.

Amador de los Ríos, José. *Historia crítica de la literatura española*. 7 tomos. Madrid: Imprenta a cargo de José Fernández y Cancela, 1861–65.

Annicchiarico, Annamaria. "Perché 'tragedia'?: il gioco delle 'ambiguità' nella *Tragèdia de Caldesa* di Joan Roís de Corella." *Boletín de la Real Academia de Buenas Letras* 43 (1991–1992): 59–79.

Anonymous. *Le discurs du trépas de Vert-Janet*. Rouen: Loys Coste, n.d.

———. *Le recueil des repues franches de maistre François Villon et de ses compagnons*. Edited by Jelle Koopmans and Paul Verhuyck. Geneva: Droz, 1995.

———. *Sermon joyeux de la fille esgarée*. In *Recueil de farces, moralités et sermons joyeux*. 3 vols., edited by Adrien Jean Victor Leroux de Lincy and Francisque Michel. Paris: Techener, Libraire, 1837. 3:59–64.

Aquinas. *The Summa Theologica of Saint Thomas Aquinas*. Translated by Fathers of the English Dominican Province. Revised by Daniel J. Sullivan. 2 vols. Chicago: Encyclopaedia Britannica, Inc., 1952. Great Books of the Western World, 19–20.

Aragone, Elisa. Introduction to *Diálogo entre el Amor y un Viejo*, by Rodrigo Cota, 9–63. Edited by Elisa Aragone. Firenze: Felice Le Monnier, 1961.

Archer, Robert. *Aproximació a Ausiàs March: estructura, tradició, metàfora*. Barcelona: Empúries, 1996.

———. "L'obra poética de Pere Joan de Masdovelles." *Els Marges* 49 (1994): 63–78.

———. *The Pervasive Image: The Role of Analogy in the Poetry of Ausiàs March*. Purdue University Monographs in Romance Languages 17. Philadelphia: John Benjamins Publishing Co., 1985.

———. *The Problem of Woman in Late-Medieval Hispanic Literature*. Woodbridge, UK: Tamesis-Boydell & Brewer, 2005.

———. "The Workings of Allegory in Ausiàs March." *Modern Language Notes* 98, no. 2 (1983): 169–88.

Arcipreste de Hita. *Libro de buen amor*. Edited by G. B. Gybbon-Monypenny. Clásicos Castalia 161. Madrid: Castalia, 1988.

Arellano, Ignacio, and J. Enrique Duarte. *El auto sacramental.* Madrid: Ediciones del Laberinto, 2003.

Arias, Ricardo. *The Spanish Sacramental Plays.* Twayne's World Authors Series 572. Boston: Twayne Publishers, 1980.

Arnaut Daniel, *Canzoni.* Edited by Gianluigi Toja. Firenze: Sansoni, 1960.

Aubailly, Jean-Claude. *Le monologue, le dialogue et la sottie: Essai sur quelques genres dramatiques de la fin du moyen âge et du début de XVe siècle.* Paris: Honoré Champion, 1976.

Aubrun, Charles V. Introduction. *Le chansonnier espagnol d'Herberay des Essarts (XVe siècle).* Bibliothèque de l'École des Hautes Études. Bordeaux: Feret et Fils, 1951.

Avalle-Arce, Juan Bautista. "Cartagena, poeta del Cancionero General." *Boletín de la Real Academia Española* 47 (1967): 287–310.

Azáceta, José María, ed. *Poesía cancioneril.* Barcelona: Plaza y Janés, 1984.

Bach y Rita, Pedro. Introduction to *The Works of Pere Torroella, a Catalan Writer of the Fifteenth Century,* by Pedro Torroella, 1–87. Edited by Pedro Bach y Rita. New York: Instituto de las Españas en los Estados Unidos, 1930.

Bachelard, Gaston. *The Poetics of Space.* Translated by Maria Jolas. Boston: Beacon Press, 1969.

Badia, Lola, ed. *Literatura medieval.* Vols, 1–3 of *Història de la literatura catalana.* Barcelona: Enciclopèdia Catalana, Editorial Barcino, Ajuntament de Barcelona, 2013–2015.

Badia, Lola, Carlos Alvar, Pedro M. Cátedra, and Jaume Vallcorba Plana, eds. *Studia in Honorem Prof. M. de Riquer.* 3 vols. Barcelona: Quaderns Crema, 1986–1991.

Baker, Armand F. "Antonio Machado y las galerías del alma." *Cuadernos Hispanoamericanos* 306–7 (1975–1976): 647–78.

Baldissera, Andrea, and Giuseppe Mazzocchi, eds. *I canzonieri di Lucrezia. Los cancioneros de Lucrecia. Atti del convegno internazionale sulle raccolte poetiche iberiche dei secoli XV–XVII.* Padua: Unipress, 2005.

Baroja, Pío. *Juventud, egolatría (1917).* In *Obras completas.* Vol. 5. Madrid: Biblioteca Nueva, 1948. 153–226. 8 vols. 1946–51.

Barutell, Miguel Berenguer de. Dedicatòria-Prefaci. *Oc,* 229–32.

Beer, Jeanette, Ben Lawton, and Patricia Hart, eds. *Romance Languages Annual 1994.* West Lafayette, IN: Purdue Research Foundation, 1995.

Beltrán, R., J. L. Canet, and J. L. Sirera, eds. *Historias y ficciones: coloquio sobre la literatura del siglo XV (Actas del Coloquio Internacional organizado por el Departamento de Filologia Espanyola de la Universitat de València, celebrado en València los días 29, 30 y 31 de octubre de 1990).* València: Universitat de València —Departament de Filologia Espanyola, 1992.

Beltran, Vicenç. *La canción de amor en el otoño de la Edad Media.* Barcelona: PPU, 1988.

————. *El cançoner de Joan Berenguer de Masdovelles*. Barcelona: Publicacions de l'Abadia de Montserrat, 2006.

————. "Guevara." In *Acta del IX Congreso de la Asociación Hispánica de Literatura Medieval*, edited by Carmen Parrilla and Mercedes Pampín, 1: 43–81. A Coruña: Universidade/Editorial Toxosoutos, 2005.

————. *Poesía, escriptura i societat: els camins de March*. Castelló–Barcelona: Publicacions de l'Abadia de Montserrat, 2006.

————, ed. *Poesía española. 2. – Edad Media: Lírica y cancioneros*. Barcelona: Crítica, 2002.

Beresford, Andrew M., Louise M. Haywood, and Julian Weiss, eds. *Medieval Hispanic Studies in Memory of Alan Deyermond*. Woodbridge, UK: Tamesis, 2013.

Beysterveldt, Antonie Adrianus van. *La poesía amatoria del siglo XV y el teatro profano de Juan del Encina*. Madrid: Insula, 1972.

Boase, Roger. *The Troubadour Revival: A Study of Social Change and Traditionalism in Late Medieval Spain*. London: Routledge & Kegan Paul, 1978.

Boccaccio, Giovanni. *Esposizioni sopra la Comedia di Dante*. Edited by Giorgio Padoan. Vol. 6 of *Tutte le opere di Giovanni Boccaccio*. Edited by Vittore Branca. Milano: Arnoldo Mondadori, 1965.

Borel, Jean-Paul. *Raison et vie chez Ortega y Gasset*. Neuchatel: A la Baconnière, 1959.

Boudet, Jean-Patrice, and Hélène Millet, eds. *Eustache Deschamps en son temps*. Paris: Publications de la Sorbonne, 1997.

Bousoño, Carlos. *Teoría de la expresión poética*. 6th ed. 2 vols. Madrid: Gredos, 1976.

Brooke, Tucker. *The Renaissance*. In *A Literary History of England*, edited by Albert C. Baugh, 313–696. New York: Appleton, 1948.

Brunet, Jacques-Charles. *Manuel du libraire et de l'amateur de livres*. Vol. 4. Bruxelles: Meline, Cans et Comp, 1839.

Burke, James F. *Desire against the Law: The Juxtaposition of Contraries in Early Medieval Spanish Literature*. Stanford, CA: Stanford University Press, 1998.

Burke, Kenneth. *The Rhetoric of Religion. Studies in Logology*. Berkeley: University of California Press, 1970.

Butterworth, Philip, ed. *The Narrator, the Expositor, and the Prompter in European Medieval Theatre*. Turnhout: Brepols, 2007.

Cabré, Lluís. "From Ausiàs March to Petrarch: Torroella, Urrea, and Other Ausimarchides." In *The Medieval Mind: Hispanic Studies in Honour of Alan Deyermond*, edited by Ian Macpherson and Ralph Penny, 57–73. Woodbridge, UK: Tamesis, 1997.

Campo Tejedor, Alberto del. "Diversiones clericales burlescas en los siglos xiii a xvi: Las misas nuevas." *La corónica* 38, no. 1 (Fall 2009): 55–95.

Cancioneiro geral de Garcia de Resende. Edited by A. J. Gonçálvez Guimarãis. 5 vols. Coimbra: Imprensa da Universidade, 1910.

El cancionero catalán de la Universidad de Zaragoza. Edited by Mariano Baselga. Zaragoza: Cecilio Gasca, 1896.

Cancionero de Estúñiga. Edited by Nicasio Salvador Miguel. Madrid: Editorial Alhambra, 1987.

Cancionero de Juan Alfonso de Baena. Edited by J. M. Azáceta. 3 vols. Madrid: Consejo Superior de Investigaciones Científicas, 1966.

El cancionero del siglo XV: c. 1380–1520. Edited by Brian Dutton. 7 vols. Salamanca: Universidad de Salamanca, 1990–91.

Cancionero general [de Hernando del Castillo]. Edited by Joaquín González Cuenca. 5 vols. Madrid: Castalia, 2004.

Cancionero musical de palacio. 2 tomos. Edited by José Romeu Figueras. Barcelona: Consejo Superior de Investigaciones Científicas, 1965.

Cançoner dels Masdovelles (Manuscrit n. 11 de la Biblioteca de Catalunya). Edited by Ramon Aramon i Serra. Barcelona: Institut d'Estudis Catalans, 1938.

Cantavella, Rosanna. "On the Sources of the Plot of Corella's *Tragèdia de Caldesa.*" In *The Medieval Mind: Hispanic Studies in Honour of Alan Deyermond,* edited by Ian Macpherson and Ralph Penny, 75–90. London: Tamesis, 1997.

Capellanus, Andreas. *Andreas Capellanus on Love.* Edited and translated by P. G. Walsh. London: Gerald Duckworth & Co., 1982.

Caravaggi, Giovanni, Monika von Wunster, and Giuseppe Mazzocchi, eds. *Poeti cancioneriles del secolo XV.* L'Aquila-Roma: Japadre, 1986.

Carré de Busserolle, Jacques-Xavier. *Notice sur l'abbaye des Conards, confrérie célèbre qui a existé a Rouen du quatorzième au dix-septième siècle, a Evreux, de 1345 à 1420.* Rouen: Librairie Nouvelle, 1895.

Carrós Pardo de la Casta, Francesc. *Consuelo de amor. Las obras de Francesch Carroç Pardo de la Casta.* Edited by José Enrique Reyes-Tudela. Valencia: Albatros-Hispanófila, 1987.

———. *Regoneixença i moral consideració contra les persuasions, vicis i forces d'amor.* In *Novel·les amoroses i morals,* edited by Arseni Pacheco and August Bover i Font. Les Millors Obres de la Literatura Catalana 73. Barcelona: Edicions 62, 1982. Pp. 155–86.

Carruthers, Mary, and Jan M. Ziolkowski. "General Introduction." In *The Medieval Craft of Memory: An Anthology of Texts and Pictures,* edited by Mary Carruthers and Jan M. Ziolkowski, 1–31. Philadelphia: University of Pennsylvania Press, 2002.

Cartagena, Pedro de. "Otra suya, en que introduze interlocutores: el dios de Amor y un enamorado" ("Si algún dios de Amor havía" [ID 0903]). *Cancionero general,* 2: 125–42.

Casas Rigall, J., and E. Ma Díaz Martínez, eds. *Iberia cantat. Estudios sobre poesía hispánica medieval.* Santiago de Compostela, 2002.

Castellet, Josep Maria. *Iniciación a la poesía de Salvador Espriu.* Madrid: Taurus, 1971.

Catálogo-índice de la poesía cancioneril del siglo XV. Edited by Brian Dutton, et al. 2 vols. Madison, WI: Hispanic Seminary of Medieval Studies, 1982.

Catalogue raisonné de la Bibliothèque Elzévirienne, 1853–1865. Paris: Librairie A. Franck, 1866.

Cátedra, Pedro Manuel. *Amor y pedagogía en la Edad Media: estudios de doctrina amorosa y práctica literaria.* Acta Salmaticensia, Estudios Filológicos 212. Salamanca: Universidad de Salamanca, Secretariado de Publicaciones, 1989.

———. *Liturgia, poesía y teatro en la edad media: estudios sobre prácticas culturales y literarias.* Madrid: Gredos, 2005.

———. "Teatro fuera del teatro: tres géneros cortesanos." In Quirante Santacruz, *Teatro y espectáculo en la edad media: Actas del Festival d'Elx 1990,* 31–46.

Chartier, Alain. "La belle dame sans mercy." In *Alain Chartier: The Quarrel of the Belle dame sans mercy,* 43–95. Edited and translated by Joan E. McRae. New York: Routledge, 2004.

Chartier, Roger, ed. *The Culture of Print: Power and the Uses of Print in Early Modern Europe.* Translated by Lydia G. Cochrane. Cambridge: Polity Press, 1989.

Chiner Gimeno, Jaume J. "Aportació a la biografia de Joan Roís de Corella: noves dades sobre el seu naixement i la seua mort." *Caplletra* 15 (tardor 1993): 49–62.

———. *Ausiàs March i la València del segle XV (1400–1459).* València: Generalitat Valenciana. Consell Valencià de Cultura, 1997.

———. "1997, any March? Noves dades sobre el naixement d'Ausiàs." In *Ausiàs March i el món cultural del segle XV,* edited by Rafael Alemany Ferrer, 13–43. Alacant: Universitat d'Alacant, 1999.

Cingolani, Stefano Maria. *Joan Roís de Corella: la importància de dir-se honest.* València: Edicions 3 i 4, 1998.

Cocozzella, Peter. "Aspectes de la persona tràgica en Salvador Espriu." *Zeitschrift für Katalanistik* 8 (1995): 74–103.

———. "Ausiàs March and the 'Truth' of the Troubadours." In *Studia in Honorem Prof. M. de Riquer.* 3 vols. Edited by Lola Badia, Carlos Alvar, Pedro M. Cátedra, and Jaume Vallcorba Plana. Barcelona: Quaderns Crema, 1986–1991. 1: 111–32.

———. "Ausiàs March's *Imitatio Christi*: The Metaphysics of the Lover's Passion." In *Romance Languages Annual 1994,* edited by Jeanette Beer, Ben Lawton, and Patricia Hart. West Lafayette, IN: Purdue Research Foundation, 1995. Pp. 428–33.

———. "Ausiàs March's Sainted Eros: A Model of Christian Syncretism." *Catalan Review* 5, no. 1 (1991): 79–93.

———. "Ausiàs March's Text of Subjectivity and Francesc Moner's *Auto de Amores* of the Early Spanish Renaissance." In *Renaissance du théâtre médiéval: XIIe Colloque de la Société Internationale du Théâtre Médiéval. Lille, 2–7 juillet*

2007, edited by Véronique Dominguez, 19–41. Louvain-la-Neuve: Université Catolique de Louvain / Presses Universitaires de Louvain, 2010.

———. "The Dramatics of the *Misa de Amores*: Parody and Desacralized Ritual in the Gestation of Spanish Religious Theater of the Early Renaissance." *Anuario de Estudios Medievales* 46.2 (2016): 689–723.

———. "El Comendador Escrivá's Legacy: The Valencian *Auto de Amores* of the Fifteenth Century." *Cincinnati Romance Review* 11 (1992): 10–25.

———. "Fra Francesc Moner y el auto de amores en el dominio del catalán y del castellano a finales del siglo XV." *Estudios sobre teatro medieval.* Edited by Josep Lluís Sirera Turó. València: Publicacions de la Universitat de València, 2008. 57–80.

———. *Fra Francesc Moner's Bilingual Poetics of Love and Reason: The "Wisdom Text" by a Catalan Writer of the Early Renaissance.* Currents in Comparative Romance Languages and Literatures 173. New York: Peter Lang, 2010.

———. "Fra Francesc Moner's Psychic Space / Soulful Place." *Caplletra* 53 (Tardor 2012): 9–34.

———. "Fray Francisco Moner: Bilingualism, Love, and Experience in Spanish PreRenaissance Literature." In *Estudis de llengua, literatura i cultura catalanes. Actes del Primer Col·loqui d'Estudis Catalans a NordAmèrica (Urbana, 30 de març1 d'abril de 1978)*, edited by Albert PorquerasMayo, Spurgeon Baldwin, and Jaume MartíOlivella, 209–39. Montserrat: Publicacions de l'Abadia de Montserrat, 1979.

———. "Fray Francisco Moner's *Auto de Amores*: Toward a Reassessment of Spanish Para-Mystical Literature of the Fifteenth Century." *La mistica spagnola: Spagna, America Latina. [Proceedings of the "X Conferencia Mediterránea" (Rome, July 2–4, 1987).* Edited by Gaetano Massa. Oakdale, N.Y.: Dowling College, 1989, 47–71.

———. "Fray Francisco Moner's Dramatic Text: The Evolution of the Spanish *Auto de Amores* of the Fifteenth Century." *Revista de Estudios Hispánicos* 26 (1992): 21–36.

———. "From Lyricism to Drama: The Evolution of Fernando de Rojas's Egocentric Subtext." *Celestinesca* 19, no. 1–2 (1995): 71–92.

———. "From the Perspective of a Narcissistic Lover: Joan Roís de Corella's *Tragèdia de Caldesa.*" *Catalan Review* 22 (2008): 229–61.

———. "Glosario." *2 OC* 203–23.

———. Introducció. *Obres catalanes.* By Francesc Moner. Edited by Peter Cocozzella. Els Nostres Clàssics 100. Barcelona: Barcino, 1970. 7–97.

———. *1 Introducción*: Introducción. *Poemas menores.* Vol. 1 of *Obras castellanas.* By Francisco Moner. Edited by Peter Cocozzella. Hispanic Literature 2. Lewiston, NY: Edwin Mellen Press, 1991. 1–163.

———. *2 Introducción*: Introducción. *Poemas mayores.* Vol. 2 of *Obras castellanas.* By Francisco Moner. Edited by Peter Cocozzella. Hispanic Literature 2. Lewiston, NY: Edwin Mellen Press, 1991. 3–71.

————. "The Journey of Transcendence: A Boethian Leitmotif for Juan Ruiz's *Libro de buen amor.*" *Lemir* 13 (2009): 109–31.

————, ed. *Mediaevalia* 22 [*Mediaeval and Early-Renaissance Literature in Catalan*]. Binghamton, NY: State University of New York at Binghamton/The Center for Medieval and Early Renaissance Studies, 2000.

————. "Parody and Intrinsic Theatricality in a *Misa de Amores* by a Catalan Writer of the Fifteenth Century." *European Medieval Drama* 15 (2011): 199–232.

————. "Pere Torroella i Francesc Moner: aspectes del bilingüisme literari (catalano-castellà) a la segona meitat del segle XV." *Llengua & Literatura: Revista anual de la Societat Catalana de Llengua i Literatura* 2 (1987): 154–72.

————. "Pere Torroella: Pan-Hispanic Poet of the Catalan PreRenaissance." *Hispanófila* 86 (1986): 1–14.

————. "Salient Trends in Ausiàs March Criticism: Toward a Holistic Approach." *Proceedings of the First Catalan Symposium (Volume in Memory of Pauli Bellet)*. Edited by Josep M. Solà-Solé. New York, NY: Peter Lang, 1992. 29–56.

————. "Salvador Espriu's Idea of a Theater: The *Sotjador* vs. the Demiurge." *Modern Drama* 29 (1986): 472–89.

————. *Text, Translation, and Critical Interpretation of Joan Roís de Corella's* Tragèdia de Caldesa, *a Fifteenth-Century Spanish Tragedy of Gender Reversal: The Woman Dominates and Seduces Her Lover*. Lewiston, NY: Edwin Mellen Press, 2012.

————. "The Theatrics of the *Auto de amores* in the *Tragicomedia* called *Celestina.*" *Celestinesca* 29 (2005): 71–143.

————. "The Thematic Unity of Juan Rodríguez del Padrón's *Siervo libre de amor.*" *Hispania* 64 (1981): 188–98.

Coderch, Marion. *Ausiàs March, les dones i l'amor.* València: Institució Alfons el Magnànim—Diputació de València, 2009.

Collerye, Roger de. *Monologue d'une dame fort amoureuse d'ung sien amy.* In *Oeuvres de Roger de Collerye.* Edited by Charles d'Héricault. Paris: P. Jarnet Libraire, 1855. 73–79.

Condé, Baudouin de. "Li prisons d'amours." *Dits e contes de Baudoin de Condé et de son fils Jean de Condé.* 3 vols. Edited by Auguste Scheler. Bruxelles: Victor Devaux et Cie., 1866–1867. 1: 267–377.

Condé, Jean de. *La Messe des Oiseaux et le Dit des Jacobins et des Fremeneurs.* Edited by Jacques Ribard. Geneva: Droz, 1970.

Contini, Gianfranco, ed. *Poeti del duecento.* 2 vols. Milano-Napoli: Riccardo Ricciardi, 1960.

Cortijo Ocaña, Antonio. "The Complications of the Narrative Techniques in 15th Century Prose Literature on Love: The *Somni de Francesc Alegre recitant lo procés d'una qüestió enamorada.*" *Catalan Review* 11, no. 1–2 (1997): 49–64.

Costana. "Otras suyas, de cómo el Afición y el Esperança le vinieron a pedir estrenas en forma de ministriles, una noche" ("Al tiempo que se levanta" [ID 0732]). *Cancionero general*, 2: 52–59.

Covarrubias Orozco, Sebastián. *Tesoro de la lengua castellana o española según la impresión de 1611, con las adiciones de Benito Remigio Noydens publicadas en la de 1674.* Edited by Martín de Riquer. Barcelona: S. A. Horta, 1943.

Crabbé Rocha, Andrée. "Ebauches dramatiques dans le 'Cancioneiro Geral'." *Bulletin d'histoire du théâtre portugais* 2 (1951): 113–50.

Criado de Val, Manuel, ed. *Literatura hispánica: Reyes Católicos y Descubrimiento.* Barcelona: Promociones y Publicaciones Universitarias, 1989.

Curtius, Ernst Robert. *European Literature and the Latin Middle Ages.* Translated by Willard B. Trask. Bollingen Series 36. New York: Pantheon Books, 1953.

Daniel, Arnaut. *Canzoni.* Edited by Gianluigi Toja. Firenze: Sansoni, 1960.

Davidson, Clifford, and John H. Stroupe, eds. *Drama in the Middle Ages, Comparative and Critical Essays.* Second Series. AMS Studies in the Middle Ages 18. New York: AMS Press, 1991.

DCECH: Corominas, Joan, and José Antonio Pascual. *Diccionario crítico etimológico castellano e hispánico.* 6 vols. Madrid: Gredos, 1980–91.

DCVB: Alcover Sureda, Antonio María, and Francesc de B. Moll i Casanovas. *Diccionari catalá valenciá-balear.* 10 vols. Palma de Mallorca: Imprenta de Mn. Alcover, 1930–62.

DEA: Seco, Manuel, Olimpia Andrés, and Gabino Ramos. *Diccionario del español actual.* Madrid: Aguilar, 2005.

DECLC: Coromines, J. *Diccionari etimològic i complementari de la llengua catalana.* 10 vols. Barcelona: Curial, 1980–2001.

DHLE: Real Academia Española. *Diccionario histórico de la lengua española.* 11 fascículos. Madrid: S. Aguiree Torre, 1960–1974.

Delgado-Librero, María Celeste. Introduction. The Mirror *of Jaume Roig: An Edition and an English Translation of MS. Vat. Lat. 4806.* MRTS 350. Tempe, AZ: ACMRS, 2010. 1–59.

Deschamps, Eustache. *Eustache Deschamps: Selected Poems.* Edited by Ian S. Laurie and Deborah M. Sinnreich-Levi. Translated by David Curzon and Jeffrey Fiskin. New York: Routledge, 2003.

———. "Lay du desert d'amours." *Oeuvres complètes de Eustache Deschamps.* Edited by August Henri Edouard and Gaston Raynaud. 11 vols. Paris: Firmin-Didot, 1878–1903; repr. New York: Johnson Reprint Corp., 1966. 2: 182–92.

Deyermond, A. D. "Bilingualism in the *Cancioneros* and Its Implications." In *Poetry at Court in Trastamaran Spain: from the "Cancionero de Baena" to the "Cancionero General"*, edited by E. Michael Gerli and Julian Weiss, 137–70. Tempe, Arizona: Arizona State University, Medieval and Renaissance Texts and Studies, 1998.

———. *A Literary History of Spain: The Middle Ages*. New York: Barnes & Noble, 1971.

———. "La micropoética de las invenciones." In Casas Rigall and Díaz Martínez, *Iberia cantat*, 403–22.

———. "The Poetry of Nicolás Núñez." *The Age of the Catholic Monarchs, 1474–1516: Literary Studies in Memory of Keith Whinnom, BHS,* Special Issue. Edited by Alan Deyermond, and Ian Macpherson. Liverpool: Liverpool University Press, 1989. 25–36.

———. "Santillana's Love Allegories: Structure, Relation, and Message." In Fox, Sieber, and Ter Horst, *Studies in Honor of Bruce W. Wardropper,* 75–90.

———. *Tradiciones y puntos de vista en la ficción sentimental*. México: Universidad Nacional Autónoma de México, 1993.

Di Girolamo, Costanzo. "Ausiàs March and the Troubadour Poetic Code." In Gulsoy and Solà-Solé, *Catalan Studies: Volume in Memory of Josephine de Boer,* 223–37.

———. March, Ausiàs. Nota informativa / noticia biográfica. *Páginas del cancionero.* By Ausiàs March. Edited by Costanzo Di Girolamo. Trad. José Maria Micó. Madrid: Pre-textos, 2004. 61–67.

Díez Taboada, Juan María. "Vivencia y género literario en Espronceda y Bécquer." *Homenajes: Estudios de Filología Española.* Edited by Juan María Díez Taboada. Vol. 1. Madrid: Talleres Gráficos Romarga, 1964.

Domínguez, Frank A. "The Burlesque, the Parodic and the Satiric: A Brief Preface." *La corónica* 38, no. 1 (fall 2009): 43–53.

———. Carajicomedia: *Parody and Satire in Early Modern Spain.* With an edition and translation of the text. Woodbridge, UK: Tamesis Books, 2015.

Donne, John. *Holy Sonnets, 10:* ("Batter my heart, three-personed God, for you"). *The Complete Works of John Donne.* Edited by Robin Robbins. Harlow, UK: Longman-Pearson, 2010. 553–55. Poems Rev. Ed. 2010

Dueñas, Juan de. "Misa de amores de Juan de Dueñas" ("Beati de amores adsyd") ID 0369. See Piccus, 323–25.

Dutton, Brian, and Victoriano Roncero López, eds. *La poesía cancioneril del siglo xv. Antología y estudio.* Madrid-Frankfurt: Iberoamericana-Vervuert, 2004.

["El enamorado y la Muerte."] "La Muerte" ("Aquesta nit he somiat—somiava y no dormia"). Menéndez y Pelayo, *Antología de poetas líricos castellanos* 9: 361–62.

———. "Romance del Enamorado y la Muerte" ("Un sueño soñaba anoche"). Menéndez Pidal, ed. 62–64.

Encina, Juan del. *Teatro (segunda producción dramática).* Edited by Rosalie Gimeno. Madrid: Alhambra, 1977.

Enders, Jody. *Rhetoric and the Origins of Medieval Drama.* Ithaca, NY: Cornell University Press, 1992.

Escrivá, Comendador. *Querella ante el dios de Amor.* In Lázaro Carreter, *Teatro medieval,* 207–25.

Espriu, Salvador. *El doctor Rip: Potser només un relat.* In *Narrativa, 1.* Vol. 3 of *Obres completes: Anys d'aprenentatge.* Edited by Francesc Vallverdú. Barcelona: Edicions 62, 1986. 9–49.

Estúñiga, Tristán de. "Justa que hizo Tristán de Estúñiga a unas monjas porque no le quisieron por servidor ninguna de ellas. Y él tóvose por dicho que lo dexavan por ser él de hedad de treinta y cinco años. Y dízeles assí:" ("Soñava que vi justar" [ID 6752]). *Cancionero general [de Hernando del Castillo].* Edited by Joaquín González Cuenca 3: 483–89.

Fernández de Madrigal, Alfonso (el Tostado). *Breviloquio del amor y amiçiçia.* In *Del Tostado sobre el amor.* Edited by Pedro Manuel Cátedra. Barcelona: Stelle dell'Orsa, 1986. 69–135.

———. *Del Tostado sobre el amor.* Edited by Pedro Manuel Cátedra. Barcelona: Stelle dell'Orsa, 1986.

Ferrer, Francesc. *Obra completa.* Edited by Jaume Auferil. Els Nostres Clàssics. Barcelona: Barcino, 1989.

Ferrer Valls, Teresa. "El espectáculo profano en la edad media: espacio escénico y escenografía." In *Historias y ficciones: coloquio sobre la literatura del siglo XV (Actas del Coloquio Internacional organizado por el Departamento de Filologia Espanyola de la Universitat de València, celebrado en Valencia los días 29, 30 y 31 de octubre de 1990),* edited by R. Beltrán, J. L. Canet, and J. L. Sirera, 307–22. València: Universitat de València – Departament de Filologia Espanyola, 1992.

———. "El espectáculo profano en la Edad Media: espacio escénico y escenografía." http//www.uv.es/entresiglos/teresa/pdfs/espectprofano.PDF.

Flecniakoska, Jean-Louis. *La formation de l'"auto" religieux en Espagne avant Calderón (1550–1635).* Montpellier: Paul Déhan, 1961.

Fleming, John V. *The* Roman de la Rose: *A Study in Allegory and Iconography.* Princeton, NJ: Princeton University Press, 1969.

Forni, Kathleen. Introduction. *Literature of Courtly Love.* 1–6. TEAMS Middle English Texts Series. Originally Published in *The Chaucerian Apochrypha: A Selection.* Kalamazoo, MI: Medieval Institute Publications, 2005. http://www.lib.rochester.edu/camelot/teams/forcrtlvint.htm.

Foster, D. W. *The Early Spanish Ballad.* New York: Twayne, 1971.

Fothergill-Payne, Louise. *La alegoría en los autos y farsas anteriores a Calderón.* London: Tamesis, 1977.

Fox, Dian, Harry Sieber, and Robert Ter Horst, eds. *Studies in Honor of Bruce W. Wardropper.* Newark, DE: Juan de la Cuesta, 1988.

Fraker, Charles. Celestina: *Genre and Rhetoric.* London: Támesis, 1990.

———. *Studies on the Cancionero de Baena.* Chapel Hill: University of North Carolina Press, 1966.

Fuster, Joan. *Llengua, literatura, història.* Vol. 1 of *Obres completes.* Barcelona: Edicions 62, 1968.

———. "Poetes, moriscos i capellans." *Llengua, literatura, història.* 315–508.

Galé Casajús, Enrique. "La creación literaria en el seno de un clan familiar: la obra de Pedro Manuel de Urrea." In *El Condado de Aranda y la nobleza española en el Antiguo Régimen*, edited by José Casaus Ballester, 139–72. Zaragoza: Institucion «Fernando el Catolico» (C.S.I.C.), 2009. http://ifc.dpz.es/recursos/publicaciones/29/67/07gale.pdf.

Gallagher, Patrick. *The Life and Works of Garci Sánchez de Badajoz*. London: Tamesis, 1968.

Ganges Garriga, Montserrat. "Poetes bilingües català castellà del segle XV." *Boletín Bibliográfico de la Asociación Hispánica de Literatura Medieval* 6.1 (1992): 57–227.

García de la Concha, Víctor. "Teatro litúrgico medieval en Castilla: Quaestio metodológica." In Quirante Santacruz, *Teatro y espectáculo en la edad media*, 127–43.

García Montero, Luis. *El teatro medieval: polémica de una inexistencia*. Maracena (Granada): Editorial Don Quijote, 1984.

Garcia Oliver, Ferran. *En la vida d'Ausiàs March*. Barcelona: Edicions 62, 1998.

Gascón Vera, Elena. "Enrique de Villena: ¿Castellano o catalán?" http://cvc.cervantes.es/literatura/aih/pdf/10/aih_10_1_021.pdf.

Gerli, E. Michael. "El silencio en el *Libro de buen amor*: ¿Lagunas textuales o lectura dramática?" In Vilanova, *Actas del Décimo Congreso de la Asociación Internacional de Hispanistas*, 1: 207–14.

———. "*Fue la caza d'este día*: De unicornios y otras especies en peligro de extinción en la cultura cortesana del siglo XV." In Moore and Duque, *"Recuerde el alma dormida": Medieval and Early Modern Spanish Essays in Honor of Frank A. Domínguez*, 107–16.

———, ed. *Poesía cancioneril castellana*. Madrid: Ediciones Alkal, 1994. 3–34.

———. "Reading Cartagena: Blindness, Insight and Modernity in a *Cancionero* Poet." In Gerli and Weiss, *Poetry at Court in Trastamaran Spain*, 171–83.

———. "La 'religión del amor' y el antifeminismo en las letras castellanas del siglo XV." *Hispanic Review* 49, no. 1 (1981): 65–86.

———, and Julian Weiss, eds. *Poetry at Court in Trastamaran Spain: from the "Cancionero de Baena" to the "Cancionero General."* MRTS 181. Tempe, AZ: ACMRS, 1998.

Gernert, Folke. *Parodia y "contrafacta" en la literatura románica medieval y renacentista: historia, teoría y textos. I: Estudio. II: Textos*. 2 vols. San Millán de la Cogolla: Cilengua, 2009.

Gilderman, Martin. "La apoteosis del amante cortés. Hacia una interpretación del *Siervo libre de amor. Boletín de Filología Española* 12 (1972): 37–50.

Giles, Ryan D. "Hanging Bells on the Cat: Charivari and the Theatrics of the *Arcipreste de Talavera o Corbacho*. In Moore and Duque, *"Recuerde el alma dormida": Medieval and Early Modern Spanish Essays in Honor of Frank A. Domínguez*, 117–39.

————. *The Laughter of Saints: Parodies of Holiness in Late Medieval and Renaissance Spain.* Toronto: University of Toronto Press, 2009.

Gilman, Stephen. *The Art of* The Celestina. Madison: University of Wisconsin Press, 1956.

González Cuenca, Joaquín. "Glosario." *Cancionero general [de Hernando del Castillo].* 5: 115-411.

Grismer, Raymond Leonard. *The Influence of Plautus in Spain before Lope de Vega together with Chapters on the Dramatic Technique of Plautus and the Revival of Plautus in Italy.* New York: Hispanic Institute in the United States, 1944.

Guevara, [Nicolás]. "Otra suya, llamada *Infierno de amores*" ("*La boz*, amarga, llorosa" [ID 6171]). *Cancionero general [de Hernando del Castillo].* Edited by Joaquín González Cuenca. 2: 261–64.

————. *Sepultura de Amor.* ("Amor cruel, engañoso" [ID 0868]). See Rennert, "Der spanische Cancionero des British Museum (Mss. Add. 10431)," 64–79.

Guillaume Alexis. *Femme mocqueresse mocquée.* In *Recueil de poésie françoises de XVe et XVe siècle: morales, faciétieuses, historiques.* Vol. 10. Edited by Anatole de Montaiglon, and James Rohschild. Paris: Paul Daffis, 1875. 269–75.

Guinizelli, Guido. *Canzone IV* ("Al cor gentil rempaira sempre amore"). *Poeti del duecento.* Edited by Gianfranco Contini. 2: 460–64.

Gulsoy, Josep, and Josep M. Solà-Solé, eds. *Catalan Studies (Estudis sobre el català): Volume in Memory of Josephine de Boer (Volum en memòria de Josephine de Boer).* Col·lecció Lacetània 4. Barcelona: Hispam, 1977.

Hardison, O. B., Jr. *Christian Rite and Christian Drama in the Middle Ages: Essays in the Origin and Early History of Modern Drama.* Baltimore: Johns Hopkins Press, 1965.

Haro Cortés, Marta, Rafael Beltrán, José Luis Canet, and Héctor H. Gassó, eds. *Estudios sobre el* Cancionero General *(Valencia, 1511): Poesía, manuscrito e imprenta.* 2 vols. Universitat de València: Publicacions de la Universitat de València, 2012.

Harris, Max. "Puppets, Minstrels, Kings, and Shepherds: Expositor Narrators in the Early Spanish Theatre." In Butterworth, *The Narrator, the Expositor, and the Prompter in European Medieval Theatre,* 129–60.

————. *Sacred Folly: A New History of the Feast of Fools.* Ithaca, NY: Cornell University Press, 2011.

Hartnoll, Phyllis. *The Theater: A Concise History.* 3rd ed. updated by Enoch Brater. New York: Thames and Hudson, 1998.

Henkel, Arthur, and Albrecht Schöne. *Emblemata; Handbuch zur Sinnbildkunst des XVI. und XVII. Jahrhunderts.* Stuttgart: J. B. Metzler, 1967).

Héricault, Charles d'. [Introduction:] La vie et les ouvres de Roger de Collerye. *Oeuvres de Roger de Collerye.* Edited by Charles d'Héricault. Paris: P. Jarnet Libraire, 1855. viii–xxviii.

Hoepffner, Ernst. *Eustache Deschamps: Leben und Werke.* 1904; repr. Genève: Slatkine Reprints, 1974.

The Holy Bible. [Standard Text Edition]. Cambridge: Cambridge University Press, n.d.

Hopkins, Gerard Manley. "No Worst, there is none. Pitched past pitch of grief." *The Poems of Gerard Manley Hopkins.* Edited by W. H. Gardner, and N. H. MacKenzie. 4th ed. Oxford: Oxford University Press, 1970. 100.

Huizinga, Johan. *Homo Ludens: A Study of the Play-Element in Culture.* New York: Roy Publishers, 1950.

Huot, Sylvia. *The* Romance of the Rose *and Its Medieval Readers: Interpretation, Reception, Manuscript Transmission.* Cambridge: Cambridge University Press, 1993.

Hutcheon, Linda. *A Theory of Parody: The Teaching of Twentieth-Century Art Forms.* New York: Methuen, 1985.

Ilie, Paul. *Unamuno: An Existential View of Self and Society.* Madison: University of Wisconsin Press, 1967.

Isidore of Seville. *The* Etymologies *of Isidore of Seville.* Edited by Stephen A. Barney, W. J. Lewis, J. A. Beach, and Oliver Berghof. Cambridge: Cambridge University Press, 2006.

———. *Isidori Hispalensis Episcopi Etymologiarum sive Originum Libri XX.* 2 vols. Edited by W. Lindsay. Oxford: Clarendon, 1957.

Jardinet d'Orats: Barcelona, Biblioteca de la Universitat, ms. 151. Edited by Sergi Gascon. Bellaterra: Universitat Autònoma de Barcelona; Fundació "La Caixa," 1998.

Jones, Joseph R. "Isidore and the Theater." In Davidson and Stroupe, *Drama in the Middle Ages, Comparative and Critical Essays,* 1–23.

Jungmann, Joseph A. *The Mass of the Roman Rite: Its Origins and Development (Missarum Sollemnia).* Translated by Francis A. Brunner. 2 vols. New York: Benziger, 1951–55.

Kaplan, Gregory B. *"Tratado que fizo el obispo*: La contribución pre-renacentista de Alfonso Fernández de Madrigal a la evolución de la novela sentimental." *eHumanista* 4 (2004): 13–21.

Kelly, Henry Ansgar. *Chaucerian Tragedy.* Rochester, NY: D. S. Brewer-Boydell & Brewer, 1997.

———. *Ideas and Forms of Tragedy from Aristotle to the Middle Ages.* Cambridge: Cambridge University Press, 1993.

Kerkhof, M. P. A. M., and A. Gómez Moreno. Introducción. *Poesías completas.* By Marqués de Santillana. Edited by M. P. A. M. Kerkhof, and A. Gómez Moreno. Clásicos Castalia 270. Madrid: Castalia, 2003. 9–81.

Kurtz, Barbara E. "Diego de San Pedro's *Cárcel de amor* and the Tradition of the Allegorical Edifice." *Journal of Hispanic Philology* 8 (1984): 123–38.

Lama de la Cruz, Víctor de. "En torno al simbolismo de los colores en el *Cancionero general.*" In Haro Cortés, et al., *Estudios sobre el* Cancionero General *(Valencia, 1511),* 1: 265–83.

Langer, Susanne K. *Philosophy in a New Key: A Study in the Symbolism of Reason, Rite, and Art.* New York: Mentor-The New American Library, 1959.

Laurie, Ian S. "Eustache Deschamps: 1340(?)–1404." In Sinnreich-Levi, *Eustache Deschamps, French Courtier-Poet*, 1–72.

Lázaro Carreter, Fernando. Introducción. *Teatro medieval.* Edited by Fernando Lázaro Carreter. Madrid: Castalia, 1965. 9–94.

Lecoy, Félix. Introduction [Analyse]. *Le roman de la rose.* By Guillaume de Lorris, and Jean de Meun. Edited by Félix Lecoy. Vol. 1. Paris: Honoré Champion, 1965. xlv–lxiii.

———. *Recherches sur le "Libro de buen amor".* Paris: E. Droz, 1938.

Le Gentil, Pierre. *La poesie lyrique espagnole et portugaise a la fin du moyen age. Première partie: les thèmes et les genres. Deuxième partie: les formes.* 2 vols. Rennes: Plihon Editeur, 1949, 1952.

Lida de Malkiel, María Rosa. "La hipérbole sagrada en la poesía castellana del siglo XV." *Revista de Filología Hispánica* 8 (1946): 121–30.

———. *Juan de Mena, poeta del prerrenacimiento español.* México: Fondo de Cultura Económica, 1950.

———. *La originalidad artística de* La Celestina. Buenos Aires: Editorial Universitaria de Buenos Aires, 1970.

Llull, Romeu. *Obra completa.* Edited by Jaume Torró i Torrent. Els Nostres Clàssics, Col·lecció A 135. Barcelona: Barcino, 2009.

López de Yanguas, Hernán. *Obras dramáticas.* Edited by Fernando González Ollé. Clásicos Castellanos 162. Madrid: Espasa-Calpe, 1967.

López Morales, Humberto. "Problemas en el estudio del teatro medieval castellano: Hacia el examen de los testimonios." In Quirante Santacruz, *Teatro y espectáculo en la edad media*, 115–26.

———. *Tradición y creación en los orígenes del teatro castellano.* Madrid: Ediciones Alcalá, 1968.

Lorris, Guillaume de, and Jean de Meun. *Le roman de la rose.* Edited by Félix Lecoy. 3 vols. Paris: Campion, 1965.

———. *The Romance of the Rose by Guillaume de Lorris and Jean de Meun.* Translated by Harry W. Robbins. Edited by Charles W. Dunn. New York: Dutton, 1962.

Louis, René. *Le Roman de la Rose: Essai d'interprétation de l'allégorisme érotique.* Paris: Champion, 1974.

Lucena, Luis Ramírez de. *Repetición de amores.* Edited by Jacob Ornstein. Studies in the Romance Languages and Literaures 23. Chapel Hill: University of North Carolina Press, 1954.

Luquiens, F. B. "The *Roman de la Rose* and Medieval Castilian Literature." *Romanische Forschungen* 20 (1907): 284–320.

MacPherson, Ian. "The Game of Courtly Love: *Letra, Divisa,* and *Invención* at the Court of the Catholic Monarchs." In Gerli and Weiss, *Poetry at Court in Trastamaran Spain*, 95–110.

————. *The* Invenciones y Letras *of the* Cancionero General. Papers of the Medieval Hispanic Research Seminar 9. London: Department of Hispanic Studies, Queen Mary and Westfield College, 1998.

Mandel, Oscar. Introduction. *Five Comedies of Medieval France.* Translated by Oscar Mandel. New York: Dutton, 1970. 11–33.

Marcabru. Poem XXXVII ("Per savi·l tenc ses doptanssa"). https://trobadors.iec. cat/veure_d.asp?id_obra=924.

March, Ausiàs. *A Key Anthology.* Edited and translated by Robert Archer. The Anglo-Catalan Society Occasional Publications 8. Melksham, UK: Cromwell Press, 1992.

————. *Obra completa.* Edited by Robert Archer. Barcelona: Barcanova, 1997.

Marfany, Marta. "La influència de la poesia francesa des d'Andreu Febrer a Ausiàs March." *Estudis Romànics* 34 (2012): 259–87.

Marino, Nancy. "Un exilio político en el siglo XV. El caso del poeta Juan de Dueñas." *Cuadernos Hispanoamericanos* 416 (1985): 139–51.

Marshall, Mary Hatch. "*Theatre* in the Middle Ages: Evidence from Dictionaries and Glosses." *Symposium* 4 (1950): 1–30, 366–89.

Martin, Georges, and Marie-Claire Zimmermann, eds. *Ausiàs March (1400–1459): Premier poète en langue catalane.* Publication du Séminaire d'Études Médievales Hispaniques de l'Université Paris 13. Paris: Klincksieck, 2000.

Martin, June Hall. *Love's Fools: Aucassin, Troilus, Calisto and the Parody of the Courtly Lover.* London: Tamesis, 1972.

Martines Peres, Vicent. "El còdex *Vaticanus Latinus 4802*: Els textos literaris de Moner a cavall de diverses edicions." *Studi e Testi* 396 (2000): 215–41.

————. "Comentaris a la bibliografia sobre Joan Roís de Corella." *Estudis sobre Joan Roís de Corella.* Edited by Vicent Martines. Alcoi: Marfil, 1999. 5–39.

Martos Sánchez, Josep Lluís. *Fonts i seqüència cronològica de les proses mitològiques de Joan Roís de Corella.* Biblioteca de Filologia Catalana 10. Alacant: Universitat d'Alacant, Departament de Filologia Catalana, 2001.

————. "Joan Roís de Corella." *Literatura medieval: segle xv.* Ed. Lola Badia. Vol. 3 of *Història de la literatura catalana.* Barcelona: Enciclopèdia Catalana, Editorial Barcino, Ajuntament de Barcelona, 2015. 211–50.

————. "La restauración de las obras de Ausiàs March: Los cancioneros impresos del siglo XVI." In Baldissera, and Mazzocchi, *I canzonieri di Lucrezia,* 409–26.

————. "La revaluació crítica de Joan Roís de Corella." http://www.uoc.edu/ jocs/3/conferencia/ ang/martos2.html.

Mason, Michael. "Browning and the Dramatic Monologue." *Robert Browning.* Edited by Isobel Armstrong. Athens: Ohio University Press, 1975. 231–66.

Massip, Francesc. *Història del teatre català. I: Dels orígens a 1800.* Tarragona: Arola Editors, 2007.

————, ed. *Repensar el sombrío medioevo (Those Dark Ages Revisited): Nuevas perspectivas para el estudio de la cultura medieval y de la temprana Edad Moderna*

(New Perspectives for the Study of Medieval and Early Modern Culture. Kassel: Reichenberger, 2014.

Matulka, Barbara. *The Novels of Juan de Flores and Their European Diffusion*. New York: Institute of French Studies, 1931.

McNerney, Kathleen. *The Influence of Ausiàs March on Early Golden Age Castilian Poetry*. Amsterdam: Rodopi, 1982.

McRae, Joan E. Introduction. *Alain Chartier: The Quarrel of the Belle dame sans mercy*. Edited and translated by Joan E. McRae. New York: Routledge, 2004. 1–42.

Mena, Juan de. *El laberinto de Fortuna o Las Trescientas*. Edited by José Manuel Blecua. Clásicos Castellanos 119. Madrid: Espasa-Calpe, 1960.

Mendoza, Diego de. "Pues no mejora mi suerte." (ID 0119). *Cancionero general [de Hernando del Castillo]*. Edited by Joaquín González Cuenca. 2: 393, n. 1.

Mendoza, Fray Iñigo de. "Coplas que hizo Frey Iñigo de Mendoça, flaire menor, doze en vituperio de las malas hembras, que no pueden las tales dichas mugeres, e doze en loor de las buenas mugeres, que mucho triumpho de honor merecen." ("En este mundo disforme" [ID 0271]). *Cancionero*. Edited by J. Rodríguez-Puértolas. Clásicos Castellanos 163. Madrid: Espasa-Calpe, 1968. 223–32.

Mendoza Negrillo, Juan de Dios. *Fortuna y providencia en la literatura castellana del siglo XV*. Anejos del Boletín de la Real Academia Española 27. Madrid: Real Academia Española, 1973.

Menéndez Collera, Ana, and Victoriano Roncero López, eds. *Nunca fue pena mayor (Estudios de literatura española en homenaje a Brian Dutton)*. Cuenca: Ediciones de la Universidad de Castilla-La Mancha, 1996.

Menéndez Pidal, Ramón, ed. *Flor nueva de romances viejos*. 50a ed. Colección Austral 202. 1938. Madrid: Espasa Calpe, 2004.

———. *Romancero hispánico (hispano-portugués, americano y sefardí)*. 2 vols. Madrid: Espasa-Calpe, 1953.

Menéndez y Pelayo, Marcelino. *Antología de poetas líricos castellanos*. Edited by Enrique Sánchez Reyes. 10 vols. Edición Nacional de las Obras Completas de Menéndez Pelayo 17–26. Santander: Aldus, 1944–45.

———. *Orígenes de la novela*. Edited by Enrique Sánchez Reyes. 4 vols. Edición Nacional de las Obras Completas de Menéndez Pelayo 13–16. Santander: Aldus, 1943.

Miguel-Prendes, Sol. "Otra frontera de la ficción sentimental: la *Consolatio Philosophiae* de Boecio." *eHumanista* 28 (2014): 511–35.

———. "Reimagining Diego de San Pedro's Readers at Work: *Cárcel de amor*." *La corónica* 32.2 (2004): 7–44.

Milá y Fontanals, Manuel. *Obras completas*. Vol. 5. Barcelona: Librería de Alvaro Verdaguer, 1895.

Milton, John. *Paradise Lost. Complete Poems and Major Prose.* Edited by Merrit Y.
    Hughes. New York: Odyssey Press, 1957. 207–469.

———. Sonnet XIX: "When I consider how my light is spent." *Complete Poems
    and Major Prose.* Edited by Merrit Y. Hughes. New York: Odyssey Press,
    1957. 168.

Moner, Fra Francesc. *La aguililla. 1 OC* 211–17.

———. *L'ànima d'Oliver. Oc,* 137–65.

———. *Bendir de dones. Oc,* 179–211.

———. *Cobles de les tisores. Oc,* 167–78.

———. *Coplas hechas a ruegos de Cartagena. 1 OC,* 240–43.

———. *La manzana quemada. 1 OC* 153.

———. *Momería. 1 OC,* 153–63; *Teatro medieval,* edited by Ana Mª Álvarez Pel-
    litero, 245–49; *Teatro medieval,* edited by Miguel Ángel Pérez Priego, 267–
    69; *Teatro castellano de la edad media,* edited by Ronald E. Surtz, 145–49.

———. *La noche. TMPW,* 67–203.

———. *Obra en metro. 2 OC,* 75–100.

———. *Quejas al alma. 1 OC,* 232–39.

———. "Resposta a Jaume de Ribes." *Oc,* 127–35.

———. "Respuesta a Villafuerte." *1 OC,* 239–40.

———. *Sepultura d'amor. 2 OC,* 131–94.

———. ["Tratado sobre la paciencia."] *A* B5–B6; Cocozzella, *Fra Francesc Mon-
    er's Bilingual Poetics of Love and Reason,* 179–84.

["Moraima."] "Romance de una morilla del bel catar" ("Yo me era mora
    Moraima"). Menéndez Pidal, ed., *Flor nueva de romances viejos,* 232–33.

Moore, John K., and Adriano Duque, eds. *"Recuerde el alma dormida": Medieval
    and Early Modern Spanish Essays in Honor of Frank A. Domínguez.* Newark,
    DE: Juan de la Cuesta, 2009.

Mühlethaler, Jean-Claude. *Fauvel au pouvoir: Lire la satire médiéval.* Paris: Hon-
    oré Champion, 1994.

Muir, Lynette R. "The Mass on the Medieval Stage." In Davidson and Stroupe,
    Drama in the Middle Ages, Comparative and Critical Essays, 223–39.

Navarro Tomás, Tomás. *Métrica española: reseña histórica y descriptiva.* New York:
    Las Américas Publishing Company, 1966.

Nichols, Stephen G. "Ekphrasis, Iconoclasm, and Desire." *Rethinking the
    Romance of the Rose: Text, Image, Reception.* Edited by Kevin Brownlee,
    and Sylvia Huot. Philadelphia: University of Pennsylvania Press, 1992. 133–
    66.

———. Preface. In Sinnreich-Levi, *Eustache Deschamps, French Courtier-Poet,*
    xiii–xix.

Novel·les amorores i morals. Edited by Arseni Pacheco and August Bover i Font.
    Les Millors Obres de la Literatura Catalana 73. Barcelona: Edicions 62,
    1982.

Núñez, Nicolás. "Canción de Núñez, porque pidió a su amiga un limón" ("Si os pedí, dama, limón") ID 6208. *Cancionero general [de Hernando del Castillo]*. Edited by Joaquín González Cuenca. 2: 416–17.

———. [*Misa de amores*] "Aquí comiençan las obras de Nicolás Núñez y esa primera es una que hizo a una señora, en que le da forma cómo en estas coplas como en oras pueda rezar, porque una mujer de su casa lo había revuelto con ellas y dize." ("Estas Oras rezaréis") ID 6621. *Cancionero general [de Hernando del Castillo]*. Edited by Joaquín González Cuenca. 3: 150–60.

Núñez Rivera, Valentín. "Glosa y parodia de los *Salmos Penitenciales* en la poesía del cancionero." *EPOS* 17 (2001): 107–39.

Olivar Bertrand, Rafael. *Bodas reales entre Francia y la Corona de Aragón: Política matrimonial de los Príncipes de Aragón y Cataluña, con respecto a Francia, en el siglo XIV*. Barcelona: Editorial Alberto Martín, 1947.

Olson, Glending. *Literature as Recreation in the Later Middle Ages*. Ithaca, NY: Cornell University Press, 1982.

Parker, Alexander A. *La filosofía del amor en la literatura española 1480–1680*. Madrid: Cátedra, 1986.

———. "Notes on the Religious Drama in Medieval Spain and the Origins of the *Auto Sacramental*." *Modern Language Review* 30 (1935): 170–82.

Parrilla, Carmen, and Mercedes Pampín, eds. *Acta del IX Congreso de la Asociación Hispánica de Literatura Medieval*. A Coruña: Universidade/Editorial Toxosoutos, 2005.

Paterson, Linda M. *Trobadours and Eloquence*. Oxford: Clarendon Press, 1975.

Perea Rodríguez, Óscar. *Estudio biográfico sobre los poetas del* Cancionero general. Madrid: Consejo Superior de Investigaciones Científicas. Instituto de la Lengua Española. Anejos de la Revista de Filología Española. 2007.

Pérez-Bosch, Estela. "La religión del amor a través del *Cancionero general*: Jaume Gassull y su versión profana del salmo *De profundis*." In *Líneas actuales de investigación literaria: Estudios de literatura hispánica*, edited by Verònica Arenas Lozano, et al., 93–104. Valencia: Universitat de València, 2004.

Pérez Priego, Miguel Ángel. "Los infiernos de amor." In Casas Rigall and Díaz Martínez, *Iberia cantat*, 307–19.

———. Introducción. *Teatro medieval*, edited by Miguel Ángel Pérez Priego. Letras Hispánicas 646. Madrid: Castalia, 2009. 13–116.

Periñán, Blanca. Introducción. "Las poesías de Suero de Ribera. Estudio y edición crítica anotada de los textos." *Miscellanea di studi ispanici* 16 (1968): 13–44.

Perotti, Olga. "La poesía religiosa en el *Cancionero general* de 1511." In Baldissera and Mazzocchi, *I canzonieri di Lucrezia*, 247–62.

Petrarca, Francesco. *Canzoniere*. Edited by Michele Scherillo. 2a ed. Milano: Ulrico Hoepli, 1908.

Piaget, Arthur, and Émile Picot. [Introduction:] Notice sur Guillaume Alexis. *Oeuvres poétiques de Guillaume Alexis, prieur de Bucy.* Edited by Arthur Piaget, and Émile Picot. 3 vols. Paris: Librairie de Firmin Didot, 1908. 3: i–xv.

Piccus, Jules. "La *Misa de Amores* de Juan de Dueñas." *Nueva Revista de Filología Hispánica* 14.3/4 (1960): 322–25.

Picot, Émile. *Le monologue dramatique dans l'ancien théâtre français.* Geneva: Slatkine, 1970.

Pietrini, Sandra. "La invención del teatro y de la escena en la Media Edad: para una relectura de la iconografía terenciana." In Massip, ed., *Repensar el sombrío medioevo (Those Dark Ages Revisited): Nuevas perspectivas para el estudio de la cultura medieval y de la temprana Edad Moderna (New Perspectives for the Study of Medieval and Early Modern Culture).* Kassel: Reichenberger, 2014. Pp. 101–27.

Poeti del duecento. Edited by Gianfranco Contini. 2 vols. Milano/Napoli: Ricciardi, 1960.

Post, Chandler Rathfon. *Mediaeval Spanish Allegory.* Cambridge, MA: Harvard University Press, 1915.

Presotto, Marco. Introduzione. *La nao de amor. Misa de amores.* By Juan de Dueñas. Edited by Marco Presotto. Viareggio-Lucca: Mauro Baroni, 1997. 11–41.

["El prisionero."] "Romance del prisionero" (Que por mayo era, por mayo"). *Flor nueva de romances viejos.* Edited by Menéndez Pidal, pp. 212–13.

Quintilian. *Institutio oratoria.* Edited and translated by H. E. Butler. 4 vols. Loeb Classical Library. 1920; repr. Cambridge, MA: Harvard University Press, 1980.

Quirante Santacruz, Luis, ed. *Teatro y espectáculo en la edad media: Actas del Festival d'Elx 1990.* Elche (Elx): Instituto de Cultura 'Juan Gil Albert', Diputación de Alicante y Ajuntament d'Elx, 1992.

Recio, Roxana C. "Intertextuality in Carroç Pardo de la Casta." Cocozzella, ed., *Mediaevalia* 22: 157–81.

———. "Los *Triunfos* de Petrarca en los cancioneros: rastros de un género olvidado. In Haro Cortés, et al., *Estudios sobre el* Cancionero General *(Valencia, 1511),* 1: 341–69.

———. *Petrarca en la Península Ibérica.* Poetria Nova 4. Alcalá de Henares: Universidad de Alcalá de Henares-Madrid, 1996.

Rennert, Hugo A. "Der spanische Cancionero des British Museum (Mss. Add. 10431)." *Romanische Forschungen*, 10 (1899): 1–176.

Ribera, Suero de. "Missa de amor que fizo Suero de Ribera" ("Amor en nuestros trabajos") ID 0034. *Cancionero de Estúñiga.* Edited by Nicasio Salvador Miguel. Madrid: Alhambra, 1987. 667–71.

Ribes Traver, Purificación. "Religious Struggle in John Donne and Ausiàs March." *Sederi* 9 (1998): 135–48.

Rico, Francisco. *Texto y contextos: estudios sobre la poesía española del siglo XV.* Barcelona: Editorial Crítica, 1990.

Riquer, Martí de. *Història de la literatura catalana.* 3 vols. Barcelona: Ariel, 1964.

————. "Los escritores mossèn Joan Escrivà y el Comendador Escrivà." *Cultura Neolatina* 53 (1993): 85–113.

————. *Juan Boscán y su cancionero barcelonés.* Barcelona: Archivo Histórico —Casa del Arcediano, 1945.

Rocabertí, Bernat Hug de. *The Gloria d'Amor: A Catalan Vision-Poem of the 15th Century.* Edited by Harry Clifton Heaton. Columbia University Studies in Romance Philology. New York: Columbia University Press, 1916.

Rodríguez del Padrón, Juan. *Siervo libre de amor.* Edited by Antonio Prieto. Clásicos Castalia 66. Madrid: Castalia, 1976.

Rodríguez Risquete, Francisco J. "El cancionero de Lleonard de Sos." In *Actas del IX Congreso Internacional de la Asociación Hispánica de la Literatura Medieval (A Coruña, 18–22 de septiembre de 2001).* 3 vols., edited by Mercedes Pampín Barral and M. Carmen Parrilla García, 3: 455–63. A Coruña: Universidade da Coruña: Departamento de Filoloxia Española e Latina—Toxosoutos, 2005.

————. "El *Cançoner de l'Ateneu.*" In Alberni, Badia, and Cabré, *Translatar i Transferir,* 425–67.

————. Introducció. *Obra completa.* By Pere Torroella. Edited by Francisco Rodríguez Risquete. 2 vols. Barcelona: Editorial Barcino, 2011. 1: 1–165.

————. "El mestratge de Pere Torroella." Actes AILLC 13 (Girona 2003), Barcelona-Girona, PAM-ILCC, 2007, III, 337–362.

————. *Obra completa de Pere Torroella al cuidado de Francisco Rodríguez Risquete: Discurso de presentación pronunciado el 23 de noviembre de 2011 en la Universidad de Gerona.* http://www.narpan.net/bibliotecadigital/articles/doc download/191.

————. "La regoneixença de Francesc Carrós Pardo de la Casta." In Alemany, Martos, and Manzanaro, *Actes del X Congrés de l'Associació Hispànica de Literatura Medieval,* 3: 1379–89.

Rohland de Langbehn, Régula. "Problemas de texto y problemas constructivos en algunos poemas de Santillana: la *Visión,* el *Infierno* de los enamorados, el *Sueño.*" *Filología* 17–18 (1976–77): 414–31.

Roís de Corella, Joan. *Tragèdia de Caldesa.* In *Tragèdia de Caldesa i altres proses.* Edited by Marina Gustà. 2nd ed. Les Millores Obres de la Literatura Catalana 50. Barcelona: Edicions 62, 1985. 25–29.

————. *The Tragedy of Caldesa: Discussing a Momentous Event That Happened in the Company of a Lady.* Trans Peter Cocozzella. *Text, Translation, and Critical Interpretation of Joan Roís de Corella's* Tragèdia de Caldesa, *a Fifteenth-Century Spanish Tragedy of Gender Reversal: The Woman Dominates and Seduces Her Lover.* By Peter Cocozzella. Lewiston, NY: Edwin Mellen Press, 2012. 197–205.

Rojas, Fernando de. *La Celestina.* 9th ed. Edited by Dorothy S. Severin. Letras
 Hispanas 4. Madrid: Cátedra, 1995.
———. *Celestina: A Play in Twenty-one Acts.* Translated by Mack Hendricks Sin-
 gleton. Madison: University of Wisconsin Press, 1958.
Romancero general. Edited by Agustín Durán. Biblioteca de Autores Españoles
 10, 16. Madrid: Atlas, 1945.
Rubió Balaguer, Jordi. *Els Cardona i les lletres, discurso leído el día 7 de abril de 1957*
 en la recepción pública de D. Jorge Rubió y Balaguer en la Real Academia de Bue-
 nas Letres de Barcelona, contestación del académico numerario D. Agustín Durán
 Sanpere. Barcelona: Imp. Hispano-Americana, 1957.
———. "Literatura catalana." *Historia general de las literaturas hispánicas.* Edited
 by Guillermo Díaz-Plaja. Barcelona: Barna, 1953. 3: 729–930.
Ruiz-Gálvez Priego, Estrella. "La *Noche de Moner,* más propiamente llamada
 Vida humana." *Cahiers de linguistique hispanique medievale* 30 (2007): 167–82.
Saenger, Paul. "Books of Hours and the Reading Habits of the Later Middle
 Ages." In Chartier, R., *The Culture of Print: Power and the Uses of Print in*
 Early Modern Europe, 41–73.
Salinas, Pedro. *Jorge Manrique; o, tradición y originalidad.* Buenos Aires: Editorial
 Sudamericana, 1952.
Salvador Miguel, Nicasio. *La poesía cancioneril: El* Cancionero de Estúñiga.
 Madrid: Alhambra, 1977.
Sánchez de Badajoz, Garci. "Coplas del dicho Garci Sánchez a los galanes, fingi-
 endo que los vido presos en la casa de Amor, a los vivos y a los pasados, con
 las canciones que hizieron. Llámase *Infierno de Amor*" ("Caminando en las
 honduras" [ID 0662]). *Cancionero general [de Hernando del Castillo].* Edited
 by Joaquín González Cuenca. 2: 386–404.
———. [*Liciones de Job*]. "Comiençan las obras de Garci Sanches de Badajoz y
 esta primera es una que hizo de las *Liciones de Job,* apropiadas a sus pasiones
 de amor" ("Pues Amor quiere que muera") ID 1769. *Cancionero general [de*
 Hernando del Castillo]. Edited by Joaquín González Cuenca. 2: 366–82.
———. [*Sepultura de amor* or *Sueño*]. "Otra obra suya, recontando a su amiga un
 sueño que soñó" ("La mucha tristeza mía" [ID 0697]). *Cancionero general [de*
 Hernando del Castillo]. Edited by Joaquín González Cuenca. 2: 383–85.
Sánchez de Calavera, Fernán. "Este desir fiso e ordenó el dicho Fernand Sánchez
 de Talavera por contemplaçión de una su linda enamorada, en el qual desir
 va rrelatando él su entençión a ella e va ella rrespondiendo a él cada vna cosa
 de lo que le dise; e danse de los escudos el vno al otro como en gasajado de
 motes." ("Ffuy a ver este otro dia" [ID 1663]). *Cancionero de Juan Alfonso de*
 Baena 3: 1088–89.
Sánchez Rodríguez, Lourdes, and Enrique J. Nogueras Valdivieso, eds. *Aus-*
 iàs March y las literaturas de su época. Granada: Editorial Universidad de
 Granada, 2000.

San Pedro, Diego de. *Cárcel de amor.* Vol. 2 of *Obras completas.* Edited by Keith Whinnom. Clásicos Castalia 39. Madrid: Castalia, 1971.

———. *Poesías.* Vol. 3 of *Obras completas.* Edited by Dorothy S. Severin, and Keith Whinnom. Clásicos Castalia 98. Madrid: Castalia, 1979.

Santillana, Marqués de [Iñigo López de Mendoza.] *Poesías completas.* Edited by Manuel Durán. 2 vols. Clásicos Castalia 64, 94. Madrid: Castalia, 1975, 1980.

———. "Infierno de los enamorados." [ID 0028]. *Poesías completas.* Edited by Manuel Durán. 2 vols. Clásicos Castalia 64, 94. Madrid: Castalia, 1975, 1980. 1: 202–27.

Scholberg, Kenneth R. *Spanish Life in the Late Middle Ages.* University of North Carolina Studies in the Romance Languages and Literatures 57. Chapel Hill: University of North Carolina Press, 1965.

Segovia, Pedro Guillén de. "Los siete salmos penitenciales, trobados por Pero Guillén de Segovia" ("Señor, oye mis gemidos" [ID 1712]). *Cancionero general [de Hernando del Castillo].* Edited by Joaquín González Cuenca. 1: 315–48.

Severin, Dorothy Sherman. "*Cancionero:* un género mal nombrado. *Cultura Neolatina* 54 (1994): 95–105.

———. "The *Misa de amor* in the Spanish *Cancioneros* and the Sentimental Romance." In Beresford, Haywood, and Weiss, *Medieval Hispanic Studies in Memory of Alan Deyermond,* 174–88. Woodbridge, UK: Tamesis, 2013.

———. *Religious Parody and the Spanish Sentimental Romance.* Newark, DE: Juan de la Cuesta, 2005.

———. "The *Sepultura de Macías* by San Pedro — But Which San Pedro?" In *Medieval and Renaissance Spain and Portugal,* edited by Martha E. Schaffer and Antonio Cortijo Ocaña, 301–8. Woodbridge, UK: Tamesis, 2006.

Shakespeare, William. *The Life of Henry the Fifth. Twenty-Three Plays and the Sonnets.* Edited by Thomas Marc Parrot, Edward Hubler, and Robert Stockdale Telfer. Rev. ed. New York: Scribner's, 1953. 438–77.

Shergold, N. D. *A History of the Spanish Stage from Medieval Times until the End of the Seventeenth Century.* Oxford: Clarendon, 1967.

Sinnreich-Levi, Deborah, ed. *Eustache Deschamps, French Courtier-Poet: His Work and His World.* New York: AMS Press, 1998.

Sirera, Josep Lluís. "El *Cancionero General,* entre nosotros." In Haro Cortés, et al., *Estudios sobre el* Cancionero General *(Valencia, 1511),* 2: 615–30.

———. "Diálogo de cancionero y teatralidad." In Beltrán, Canet, and Sirera, *Historias y ficciones,* 351–63.

———. "Una quexa ante el Dios de Amor. . .del Comendador Escrivá como ejemplo posible de los autos de amores." Criado de Val, *Literatura hispánica: Reyes Católicos y descubrimiento,* 259–69.

Sobrer, Josep Miquel. "Ausias March, the Myth of Language, and the Troubadour Tradition." *Hispanic Review* 50 (1982): 327–36.

———. *La doble soledat d'Ausias March.* Barcelona: Quaderns Crema, 1987.

Spearing A. C. *Textual Subjectivity: The Encoding of Subjectivity in Medieval Narratives and Lyrics.* New York: Oxford University Press, 2005.

Stern, Charlotte D. "The Early Spanish Drama: From Medieval Ritual to Renaissance Art." *Renaissance Drama* 6 (1973): 177–201.

———. "Fray Iñigo de Mendoza and Medieval Dramatic Ritual." *Hispanic Review* 33, no. 3 (1965): 197–245.

———. "The Medieval Theater: Between *Scriptura* and *Theatrica.*" *The Cambridge History of Spanish Literature.* Edited by David T. Gies. Cambridge: Cambridge University Press, 2004. 115–34.

———. *The Medieval Theater in Castile.* Binghamton, NY: Medieval & Renaissance Texts and Studies, 1996.

Stilgoe, John R. Foreword ["Foreword to the 1994 Edition"]. *The Poetics of Space.* By Gaston Bachelard. Translated by Maria Jolas. Boston: Beacon Press, 1994. vi–x.

Suero de Ribera. *Las poesías de Suero de Ribera.* Edited by Blanca Periñán. In *Miscellanea di studi ispanici* 16 (1968): 5–138.

Sullivan, Henry W. *Juan del Encina.* Boston: Twayne, 1976.

Surtz, Ronald E. *The Birth of a Theater: Dramatic Convention in the Spanish Theater from Juan del Encina to Lope de Vega.* Princeton, NJ: Princeton University, Department of Romance Languages and Literatures, 1979. Madrid: Castalia, 1979.

———. Estudio preliminar. *Teatro castellano de la edad media.* Edited by Ronald E. Surtz. Clásicos Taurus 13. Madrid: Taurus, 1992. 11–61.

———. "The 'Franciscan Connection' in the Early Castilian Theater." *Bulletin of the Comediantes* 35 (1983): 141–52.

———. "Jaume Escrivà and the Perils of Female Writing in Late Medieval Valencia." *Catalan Review* 26 (2012): 201–14.

Tapia, Juan de. "Vna canción fecha por Johanne Tapia" ("Sanctus, sanctus, sanctus Deus" ID 0559. [Fragmento]. *Cancionero de Estúñiga.* Edited by Nicasio Salvador Miguel. 382.

Teatro castellano de la edad media. Edited by Ronald E. Surtz. Clásicos Taurus 13. Madrid: Taurus, 1992. 11–61.

Teatro medieval. Edited by Fernando Lázaro Carreter. Madrid: Castalia, 1965.

Teatro medieval. Edited by Ana Mª Álvarez Pellitero. Colección Austral A157. Madrid: Espasa-Calpe, 1990.

Teatro medieval. Edited by Miguel Ángel Pérez Priego. Letras Hispánicas 646. Madrid: Castalia, 2009.

Tillier, Jane Yvonne. "Misa de Amores." *Medieval Iberia: An Encyclopedia.* Edited by E. Michael Gerli. New York: Routledge, 2003. 569.

———. "Religious Elements in Fifteenth-Century 'Cancioneros'." PhD diss., University of Cambridge, 1985. http://ethos.bl.uk/OrderDetails.do?uin=uk. bl.ethos.355866.

Tocco, Valeria. "Gli inferni d'amore portoghesi e la tradizione allegorica europea." *Rendiconti dell'Istituto Lombardo. Accademia di Scienze e Lettere, Classe di Lettere e Scienze Morali e Storiche* 127 (1993): 297–359.

Toro Pascua, María Isabel. *El arte de la poesía: el Cancionero (Teoría e ideas sobre la poesía en los siglos XV y XVI).* Salamanca: SEMYR, 1999.

———. "La *Sepultura de amor* de Guevara. Edición Crítica." In Menéndez Collera and Roncero López, *Nunca fue pena mayor,* 663–89.

Torres-Alcalá, Antonio. *Don Enrique de Villena: un mago al dintel del renacimiento.* Madrid: Porrúa Turanzas, 1983.

Torró i Torrent, Jaume. "El *cançoner de Saragossa.*" In Alberni, Badia, and Cabré, *Translatar i Transferir,* 379–423.

———. "El mite de Caldesa: Corella al *Jardinet d'orats.*" *Atalaya: Revue Française d'Études Médiévales Hispaniques* 7 (1996): 103–16.

———. "El ms. 151 de la Biblioteca Universitària de Barcelona (*Jardinet de orats*): descripció i estudi codicològic." *Boletín bibliográfico de la Asociación Hispánica de Literatura Medieval* 6 (1992): 1–55.

Torroella, Pere. *Obra completa.* Edited by Francisco J. Rodríguez Risquete. 2 vols. Els Nostres Clàssics. Barcelona: Editorial Barcino, 2011.

Trudeau, Lawrence J., ed. "Ausiàs March." *Poetry Criticism: Criticism of the Works of the Most Significant and Widely Studied Poets of World Literature.* Vol. 179. Farmington Hills, Mich.: Gale Cengage Learning / Layman Poupard Publishing, 2016). 193–322.

Valera, Mosén Diego de. *Letanía de amores* ("¡O soberana señora!" [ID 0535]). *Boletín de la Real Academa de la Historia* 64, no. 3 (1914): 258–59.

———. *Salmos penitenciales dirigidos al amor* ("No te remiembres amor" [ID 1697]). *Boletín de la Real Academa de la Historia* 64, no. 3 (1914): 260–72.

Vega, Lope de. *Fuente Ovejuna.* Edited by Francisco López Estrada. 7th ed. Clásicos Castalia 225. Madrid: Castalia, 1996.

Vendrell de Millás, Francisca. "La corte literaria de Alfonso V de Aragón y tres poetas de la misma." *Boletín de la Real Academia Española* 19 (1932): 85–100, and 20 (1933): 69–91.

Via, Francesc de la. *Obres.* Edited by Arseni Pacheco. Barcelona: Quaderns Crema. 1997.

Vielliard, Françoise. Rev. of Le recueil des repues franches *de maistre François Villon et de ses compagnons.* Edited by Jelle Koopmans and Paul Verhuyck. *Bibliothèque de l'*École des Chartes 154.2 (1996): 708–9.

Vilanova, Antonio, ed. *Actas del Décimo Congreso de la Asociación Internacional de Hispanistas.* Barcelona: University Central de Barcelona, 1992.

Viollet-Leduc, Emmanuel Louis-Nicolas, and Antony Méray. *Bibliograpie des chansons, fabliaux, comtes en vers et en prose.* Paris: A. Claudin Libraire-Éditeur, 1859.

Wardropper, Bruce W. *Introducción al teatro religioso del siglo de oro: Evolución del Auto Sacramental antes de Calderón.* Salamanca: Anaya, 1967.

Webber, Edwin J. "The Literary Reputation of Terence and Plautus in Medieval and Pre-Renaissance Spain." *Hispanic Review* 24 (1956): 192–202.

———. "Manuscripts and Early Printed Editions of Terence and Plautus in Spain." *Romance Philology* 11 (1957–58): 29–39.

———. "Plautine and Terentian *Cantares* in Fourteenth-Century Spain." *Hispanic Review* 18 (1950): 93–107.

Webster's New Universal Unabridged Dictionary. New York: Barnes & Noble, 1996.

Webster's New World Dictionary of American English. 3rd ed. Cleveland and New York: Simon and Schuster, 1989.

Weiss, Julian. *The Poet's Art: Literary Theory in Castile c. 1400–60*. Medium Aevum Monographs 14. Oxford: Society for the Study of Mediaeval Languages and Literatures, 1990.

Whinnom, Keith. *Diego de San Pedro*. New York: Twayne Publishers, 1974.

———. [Introducción biográfica y crítica.] *Obras completas*. By Diego de San Pedro. Edited by Keith Whinnom. 2 vols. Clásicos Castalia, 39, 54. Madrid: Editorial Castalia, 1971–73. 1: 9–84.

———. [Introducción crítica]. *Cárcel de amor*. By Diego de San Pedro. Vol. 2 of *Obras completas*. Edited by Keith Whinnom. Clásicos Castalia 39. Madrid: Castalia, 1971. 7–72.

———. [Introducción crítica 1979]. *Poesías*. By Diego de San Pedro. Vol. 3 of *Obras completas*. Edited by Dorothy S. Severin, and Keith Whinnom. Clásicos Castalia 98. Madrid: Castalia, 1979. 9–98.

———. *La poesía amatoria de la época de los Reyes Católicos*. Durham, UK: University of Durham, 1981.

Wright, Roger, ed. and trans. *Spanish Ballads*. Warminster, England: Aris & Phillips, 1987.

Ximénez, Bachiller. "Otra suya, llamada *Purgatorio de amor*" ("De sentir mi mal sobrado" [ID 6745]). *Cancionero general [de Hernando del Castillo]*. Edited by Joaquín González Cuenca. 3: 436–50.

Ximénez de Urrea, Pedro Manuel. *Cancionero*. Edited by Martín Villar. Zaragoza: Imprenta del Hospiscio Provincial, 1878.

———. *Sepultura de amor compuesta por don Pedro de Urrea* ("El Delius, planeta que oras declara" [ID 4752]). In *Cancionero*. Edited by Martín Villar. Zaragoza: Imprenta del Hospiscio Provincial, 1878. 199–212.

Zimmermann, Marie-Claire. *Ausiàs March o l'emergència del jo*. València: Institut Interuniversitari de Filologia Valenciana / Barcelona: Publicacions de l'Abadia de Montserrat, 1998.

Zink, Michel. *The Invention of Literary Subjectivity*. Translated by David Sices. Baltimore: Johns Hopkins University Press, 1999.

INDEX

1 ?